The Crisis of Democratic Governance in Southeast Asia

Critical Studies of the Asia Pacific Series

Series Editor: **Mark Beeson**, Professor in the Department of Political Science and Interna-tional Studies at the University of Birmingham, UK.

Critical Studies of the Asia Pacific showcases new research and scholarship on what is ar-guably the most important region in the world in the twenty-first century. The rise of China and the continuing strategic importance of this dynamic economic area to the United States mean that the Asia Pacific will remain crucially important to poli-cymakers and scholars alike. The unifying theme of the series is a desire to publish the best theoretically-informed, original research on the region. Titles in the series cover the politics, economics and security of the region, as well as focussing on its institutional processes, individual countries, issues and leaders.

Titles include:

Stephen Aris
EURASIAN REGIONALISM
The Shanghai Cooperation Organisation

Toby Carroll
DELUSIONS OF DEVELOPMENT
The World Bank and the Post-Washington Consensus in Southeast Asia

Aurel Croissant and Marco Bünte (*editors*)
THE CRISIS OF DEMOCRATIC GOVERNANCE IN SOUTHEAST ASIA

Shahar Hameiri
REGULATING STATEHOOD
State Building and the Transformation of the Global Order

Hiro Katsumata
ASEAN'S COOPERATIVE SECURITY ENTERPRISE
Norms and Interests in a Regional Forum

Erik Paul
OBSTACLES TO DEMOCRATIZATION IN SOUTHEAST ASIA
A Study of the Nation-State, Regional and Global Order

Barry Wain
MALAYSIAN MAVERICK
Mahathir Mohamad in Turbulent Times

Robert G. Wirsing and Ehsan Ahrari (*editors*)
FIXING FRACTURED NATIONS
The Challenge of Ethnic Separatism in the Asia-Pacific

Critical Studies of the Asia Pacific Series
Series Standing Order ISBN 978–0–230–22896–2 (Hardback) 978–0–230–22897–9 (Paperback)
(outside North America only)

You can receive future titles in this series as they are published by placing a standing order. Please contact your bookseller or, in case of difficulty, write to us at the address below with your name and address, the title of the series and the ISBNs quoted above.

Customer Services Department, Macmillan Distribution Ltd, Houndmills, Basingstoke, Hampshire RG21 6XS, England

---

The Crisis of Democratic Governance in Southeast Asia

Edited by

Aurel Croissant
Professor, Institute of Political Science, Heidelberg University, Germany

and

Marco Bünte
Senior Research Fellow, Institute of Asian Studies,
German Institute of Global and Area Studies, Hamburg, Germany

First published 2011 by
PALGRAVE MACMILLAN

Palgrave Macmillan in the UK is an imprint of Macmillan Publishers Limited, registered in England, company number 785998, of Houndmills, Basingstoke, Hampshire RG21 6XS.

Palgrave Macmillan in the US is a division of St Martin's Press LLC, 175 Fifth Avenue, New York, NY 10010.

Palgrave Macmillan is the global academic imprint of the above companies and has companies and representatives throughout the world.

Palgrave® and Macmillan® are registered trademarks in the United States, the United Kingdom, Europe and other countries.

ISBN: 978–0–230–28235–3 hardback

This book is printed on paper suitable for recycling and made from fully managed and sustained forest sources. Logging, pulping and manufacturing processes are expected to conform to the environmental regulations of the country of origin.

A catalogue record for this book is available from the British Library.

Library of Congress Cataloging-in-Publication Data

Critical studies of the Asia-Pacific / [edited by] Aurel Croissant and Marco Bünte.
    p. cm.
    Includes index.
    ISBN 978–0–230–28235–3 (hardback)
    1. Democracy – Southeast Asia. 2. Democratization – Southeast Asia.
3. Southeast Asia – Politics and government – 1945– I. Croissant, Aurel, 1969–
II. Bünte, Marco, 1970–

JQ96.A91C75 2011
320.959—dc22   2011003943

10 9 8 7 6 5 4 3 2 1
20 19 18 17 16 15 14 13 12 11

Printed and bound in the United States of America

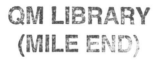

Contents

Illustrations

Tables

Figures

Acknowledgements

The editors of this volume are most grateful for generous financial support from the Fritz Thyssen Stiftung, Cologne, Germany. First drafts of some of the contributions in the volume have been presented at a workshop on Democratic Governance in Southeast Asia in January 2009, sponsored by the Fritz Thyssen Stiftung. The workshop was organized by the Institute of Political Science, Heidelberg University, and the Institute of Asian Studies, German Institute of Global and Area Studies (GIGA), Hamburg, and hosted by the Ruprecht-Karls-University, Heidelberg. We are grateful to Claudia Derichs, David Kühn, Stein Kuhnle, Subrata Mitra, Manfred Mols, Hans-Jürgen Puhle, Wolfgang Merkel, Philippe Regnier, and Patrick Ziegenhain for their comments, suggestions and criticisms during the workshop.

We would also like to thank Stephan Giersdorf, Sabine Mohammed, Arisa Ratanapinsiri, Teresa Schächter and Caja Schleich of Heidelberg University's Institute of Political Science for their assistance in the organization of the workshop. For their assistance in proofreading and formatting we are also grateful to Andrea Ficht, Deanna Stewart, Carl Carter and, especially, Christina Ecker. We thank the anonymous reviewers of the manuscript for their extremely helpful comments and suggestions, Liz Blackmore and Alexandra Webster of Palgrave for their interest in this project and for their extreme generosity with their time. Finally, we thank the authors of this volume for their encouragement, patience, commitment and continuous support, without which this publication would have been impossible.

Contributors

Marco Bünte is Senior Research Fellow at the Institute of Asian Studies, German Institute of Global and Area Studies in Hamburg. He has written widely on Southeast Asian politics. His most recent book is *Democratization in Post Suharto Indonesia*.

Paul W. Chambers is Senior Research Fellow at the Institute of Political Science, University of Heidelberg, and faculty member of Payap University, Chiang Mai. His research focuses on Thai politics, civil–military relations in Southeast Asia and party politics. With Aurel Croissant and Thitinan Pongsudhirak, he is editor of *Democracy under Stress: Civil-Military Relations in South and Southeast Asia*.

Youngho Cho is a doctoral student at the Department of Political Science in the University of Missouri. He is currently working on a dissertation, examining how contemporary publics understand democracy.

Aurel Croissant teaches political science at the University of Heidelberg. His main research interests include comparative politics, Northeast and Southeast Asian politics, conflict research, democratic theory, and civil–military relations. He is author of about 150 academic books, articles and chapters in German, English, Indonesian, Russian and Spanish.

Allen Hicken is Associate Professor at Michigan University's Center for Southeast Asian Studies and Faculty Associate at the Center for Political Studies, University of California, San Diego. He is author of *Building Party Systems in Developing Democracies* and editor of the four-volume collection of articles *Politics of Modern Southeast Asia: Critical Concepts*.

Paruedee Nguitragool holds a doctoral degree in political science from the University of Freiburg. Her dissertation examines ASEAN environmental cooperation, particularly its response to the haze phenomenon haunting the region since 1997. Currently, she is a post-doctoral researcher at the Department of Political Science, University of Freiburg. Her research interests are environmental politics, international institutions, international law, international relations and political psychology.

Chong-min Park teaches political science at Korea University, Seoul. He is a member of the Asia Barometer research consortium and has published widely on political culture, values, social organizations, democratization and civil society in South Korea, Southeast Asia and the wider Asia-Pacific.

Benjamin Reilly is Director of the Centre for Democratic Institutions, Crawford School of Economics and Government at the Australian National University. His current research focuses on democratization and political engineering in the Asia-Pacific, post-conflict democracy and political parties in divided societies, electoral system design and conflict management. Among his publications is *Democracy and Diversity: Political Engineering in the Asia-Pacific*.

Roland Rich is Executive Head of the United Nations Democracy Fund. Prior to his appointment to UNDEF, he was a member of the directing staff at the Centre for Defense and Strategic Studies of the Australian Defense College. His most recent monograph is *Pacific Asia in Quest of Democracy*.

Jürgen Rüland holds a chair in political science at the University of Freiburg. He has authored or co-authored 13 monographs, edited or co-edited 19 volumes and contributed more than 140 book chapters and articles to international and German journals. His research interests include cooperation and institution-building in international relations, globalization and regionalization, international relations and security in the Asia-Pacific region, democratization, political, economic, social and cultural change in Southeast Asia

Doh Chull Shin is Professor of Political Science at the University of Missouri in Columbia, Missouri. He is the founder of the Korea Barometer and a co-founder of the Asian Barometer. For the past two decades, he has conducted comparative research on democratization and quality of life. His latest publications include *Citizens, Democracy, and Markets around the Pacific*, *How East Asians View Democracy*, and *The Quality of Life in Confucian Asia*.

Mark R. Thompson is Professor of Political Science at the University of Erlangen-Nuremberg in Germany. Among his publications are *The Anti-Marcos Struggle* and *Democratic Revolutions: Asia and Eastern Europe*. His articles have appeared in *Comparative Politics, Journal of Democracy, Third World Quarterly* and several other journals and books.

Christoph Trinn teaches comparative politics and conflict studies at the Institute of Political Science, University of Heidelberg. His main research focus is on conflict and conflict management in Asia, system theory and quantitative conflict studies. He is co-author of a German language monograph on *Cultural Conflicts since 1945*.

Andreas Ufen is Senior Research Fellow at the GIGA German Institute of Global and Area Studies, Hamburg, Germany. His research focuses on democratization, Islamization, political parties, weak states and political violence, and regional integration in Southeast Asia. His recent publications include *Democratization in Post-Suharto Indonesia*, edited with Marco Bünte.

Philip Völkel teaches comparative politics and Asian politics at the Institute of Political Science, University of Heidelberg. His main research focus is on decentralization and civil–military relations in Indonesia. He is co-author, with Aurel Croissant, of a forthcoming study on political party system institutionalization in East and Southeast Asia, *Party Politics*.

1
Introduction

Marco Bünte and Aurel Croissant

The last quarter of the twentieth century saw authoritarian regimes being replaced by democratic regimes at an astounding rate. Southeast Asia has been no exception to this global trend. Authoritarian regimes were replaced with democracies in the Philippines in 1986 and in Thailand in 1992. In 1993 the United Nations Transitional Authority (UNTAC) organized the first competitive elections in Cambodia. At the end of the 1990s, Indonesia joined the club of democracies on the downfall of its long-term president Suharto in 1998. Finally, in 2002, democratic East Timor became sovereign after UNTAC had successfully conducted presidential elections and elections for a constitutional convention in East Timor. Expectations regarding the triumph of liberal democracy in Southeast Asia, however, turned out to be premature. Many of the new democracies have been plagued by growing ethno-nationalist and communal conflicts, low levels of socio-economic development and a weak rule of law. In Cambodia and Thailand, democracy has even experienced a dramatic breakdown, with, respectively, a coup by Second Prime Minister Hun Sen in 1997 and against the government of PM Thaksin Shinawatra in 2006 (Shin and Tusalem, 2009). Furthermore, we still find a variety of political regimes below the democratic threshold: a military government in Myanmar, communist one-party rule in Vietnam and Laos, absolute monarchy in Brunei and 'electoral authoritarianism' in Cambodia, Singapore and Malaysia (Diamond, 2008; Bertelsmann Stiftung, 2009).

Moreover, the countries of Southeast Asia represent a wide variety of successful and less successful governing states. In contrast to the simplified view that authoritarian rule in the region correlates with successful governance there is actually a large variety of outcomes in terms of political, social and economic governance (Rodan et al., 2002). This collection of articles examines these variegated patterns of democratic development and governance in the region. Since the theme of this book is the crisis of democratic governance in Southeast Asia, the individual contributions mostly focus on democratic systems in the region. However, to evaluate this subject, it is necessary to develop a broader comparative perspective which also includes (albeit to different degrees) the non-democratic and 'semi-democratic' states in the region. While the individual articles deal with various sub-samples of Southeast Asian cases, each paper is designed as a comparative analysis of a small number of cases.

As this volume takes a comparative approach to the politics of Southeast Asia, it is divided into three thematic sections, each of which deals with different aspects of democratic governance in Southeast Asia. Part I examines the field of political culture, civil society and democracy. Part II provides comparative analyses of institutional designs and systems of political representation in order to explain their impact on democratic governance in the region. Part III scrutinizes questions regarding conflict management, security and human rights in Southeast Asia. Since the focus of this book is on democratic governance in Southeast Asia, we attempt in the remainder of this introduction to conceptualize democracy and governance in order to identify various facets of democratic governance before introducing the main arguments and findings of the contributions in the volume at hand.

Democracy

The first central element of the conceptual framework of this collection of articles is the concept of democracy. This is 'probably the most complex concept in political science' (Coppedge, 2002, p.35). There are countless definitions based on hundreds of years of political thinking and decades of academic debate, which have had an impact on the various traditions and schools of democratic thought. This has given way to numerous concepts such as participatory, competitive and deliberative democracy (see Held, 2006). We can draw a line between minimalist or procedural conceptions of democracy and maximalist or substantial conceptions. While the focal point of the minimalist conception is 'electoral democracy', the maximalist concept is even broader than liberal democracy and encompasses the more demanding terms of equality and social justice. The procedural minimalist definition goes back to Joseph Schumpeter who defined the democratic method as an 'institutional arrangement for arriving at political decisions in which individuals acquire the power to decide by means of a competitive struggle for the people's vote' (Schumpeter, 1975, p.242). A broader procedural understanding of democracy which has been the most influential definition of democracy in comparative politics is provided by Robert Dahl. Dahl makes 'open contestation' and 'public competition' the centre of his conception of polyarchy (Dahl, 1971, p.3). The Dahlean concept of democracy has been very influential and has been adopted by many scholars studying third-wave democratization.

More recently, a growing number of scholars have used an even broader and expanded concept of democracy under the banner of 'liberal democracy'.

These more substantial conceptions of democracy also require provisions for horizontal accountability (checks and balances), the rule of law and the absence of reserved domains for the military (see Table 1.1).

However, some if not many new democracies (and a number of old ones, too) do not fulfil all of these criteria. Rather, the empirical evidence suggests that to a significant extent the third wave of democratization could become less a triumph of political liberalism and liberal democracy, but rather a success story for 'hybrid' (Karl, 1995) or 'ambiguous regimes' (Diamond, 2002), 'defective' (Merkel, 2004) or 'illiberal democracies' (Zakaria, 1997), 'competitive' (Levitsky and Way, 2002) and 'electoral authoritarianism' (Schedler, 2006). This includes political regimes in which a democratic facade conceals an authoritarian leadership, and which therefore may be identified as 'false democracies' (Linz, 2000). Even more often, though, they include electoral democracies in which, while free and more or less fair elections take place, many segments of the population merely possess what O'Donnell calls 'low-intensity citizenship' (O'Donnell, 1999). Although *de jure* political rights, civil liberties and the institutions of constitutionalism and the rule of law are found in such political regimes, a whole battery of *de facto* restrictions – usually informal ones – curb the effective operation of the formal rules and significantly distort their value.

Although cases 'where a democratic facade covers authoritarian rule' (Linz, 2000, p.34) and low-quality democracies are not a new phenomenon (cf. Brooker, 2009, pp.233–69), they have clearly proliferated in recent years (Brownlee, 2009, p.60). This is especially true in Southeast Asia, where 'mixed' political regimes and 'defective' democracies have been an integral element of the political spectrum for a number of decades. Although there is a good deal of variation in the regime classifications provided by the latest Polity IV, Freedom House and Bertelsmann Transformation Index evaluations of the status of democracy in Southeast Asia (see Table 1.2), it is possible to differentiate three groups of political regimes in the region.

Table 1.1 Institutional criteria of liberal democracy

1. Substantial freedom of speech, expression and assembly
2. Freedom of religion as well as ethnic and cultural participation
3. Universal suffrage for adult citizens
4. Free, fair and genuinely competitive elections
5. Legal equality of all citizens under a transparent and non-retroactive rule of law
6. An independent and neutral judiciary
7. Due process of law for all individuals
8. Institutional checks on the power of elected officials (horizontal accountability)
9. State acquiescence in a vibrant civil society
10. Civilian control over the military and other state apparatuses

Source: Diamond 2008; Merkel 2004.

Table 1.2   Political regimes in Southeast Asia

Country	Polity IV (2008)[a]		Freedom house (2008)[b]			Bertelsmann transformation index (2009)[c]
	Polity score	Political regime	Political rights	Civil liberties	Political regime	Democracy score
Brunei	N/A	N/A	6	5	Not free	N/A
Cambodia	2	Anocracy	6	5	Not free	4.1
Indonesia	8	Democracy	2	3	Free (electoral democracy)	7
Laos	–7	Autocracy	7	6	Not free	2.8
Malaysia	3	Anocracy	4	4	Partly free	5.3
Myanmar	–8	Autocracy	7	7	Not free	1.7
Philippines	8	Democracy	4	3	Partly free	5.9
Singapore	–2	Anocracy	5	4	Partly free	5.4
Thailand	–1	Anocracy	5	4	Partly free	5.3
East Timor	7	Democracy	3	4	Partly free (electoral democracy)	N/A
Vietnam	–7	Autocracy	5	5	Not free	3.3

[a]The conceptual scheme of the Polity IV Project envisages a spectrum of governing authority that ranges from *fully institutionalized autocracies* through *mixed, or incoherent, authority regimes* (termed 'anocracies') to *fully institutionalized democracies*. The 'Polity score' captures this regime authority spectrum on a 21-point scale ranging from –10 (hereditary monarchy) to +10 (consolidated democracy). The Polity scores can also be converted to regime categories: we recommend a three-part categorization of 'autocracies' (–10 to –6), 'anocracies' (–5 to +5) and 'democracies' (+6 to +10). See http://www.systemicpeace.org/polity/polity4.htm.

[b]PR and CL stand for political rights and civil liberties respectively; a score of 1 represents the most free and 7 the least free rating. The ratings reflect an overall judgement based on survey results for the period from January to December 2008. In addition to providing numerical ratings, Freedom House assigns the 'electoral democracy' designation to countries that have met certain minimum standards. See http://www.freedomhouse.org/.

[c]The BTI 2010 provides quantitative measures on five criteria of democracy based on the rule of law for the period from January 2007 to January 2009. Its concept of democracy encompasses more than elections and institutions. It also includes stateness, the rule of law and the separation of powers with horizontal accountability, the strength of civil society and political participation. The BTI's Democracy Status Index is based on the ratings of five criteria and 18 indicators. Each indicator is measured on a scale ranging from one (worst score) to ten (best score). Based on the values of the democracy status index, political systems are classified as democracies, defective democracies, moderate autocracies or autocracies. See http://www.bertelsmann-transformation-index.de.

The first group consists of the long-standing 'electoral authoritarian regimes' (Schedler, 2006) in Singapore, Malaysia and Cambodia. In all three cases, formal democratic institutions coexist with authoritarian political practices. While elections are the principal means of acquiring political power, 'incumbents routinely abuse state resources, deny the opposition adequate media coverage, harass opposition candidates and their supporters, and in some cases manipulate election results' (Levitsky and Way, 2002, p.61). The salient feature of electoral authoritarianism in Malaysia, however, is that the ruling Barisan Nasional coalition faces stiff electoral challenges (as demonstrated by the 2008 election outcome).

In contrast to Malaysia, Singapore's hegemonic authoritarianism knows no significant parliamentary opposition, as the ruling People's Action Party has repeatedly won over 95 per cent of all the seats in Parliament. The political regime of Prime Minister Hun Sen and his Cambodian People's Party is located somewhere between these two forms of electoral authoritarianism. Although the dominant party allows limited standards of political competition, the CPP uses its overwhelming coercive power and resources to implement a strategy of 'intimidation by incumbency', which effectively prevents a level playing field from developing (McCargo, 2005).

The second group comprises four unambiguously authoritarian regimes. It is a heterogeneous group of single-party rule in Vietnam and Laos, military rule in Myanmar and hereditary monarchy in Brunei. While there are significant differences between the cases with regard to the question of who rules how and why, what all four regimes have in common is that they do not allow for limited political pluralism. Instead, they can correctly be classified as 'closed authoritarian regimes' (Diamond, 2002).

The third group consists of four countries which have experienced a political transition to democracy in one way or another in the last two decades or so. With the possible exception of Indonesia, however (see Chapter 3), there has not been much improvement in the democratic quality of these political regimes over this period. More than two decades since the authoritarian regime run by President Ferdinand Marcos broke down, for instance, democratic politics in the Philippines is still tumultuous. While elections have become the generally accepted method of transferring power, the elections are often overshadowed by irregularities, fraud, violence and intimidation (Patiño and Velasco, 2006). Furthermore, the country remains a hotbed of communist insurgency and ethnic violence. In addition, the armed forces exercise wide-ranging influence in key policy areas (see Chapter 11).

Similarly to the Philippines, the Thai political system is currently experiencing severe stress. Deep-reaching political conflict escalated in September 2006, when the Thai military staged a *coup d'état* against Prime Minister Thaksin Shinawatra. The return to democracy in December 2007 did little to heal existing divisions in Thai society. Furthermore, in the past six years or so, southern Thailand has seen a recrudescence of long-dormant Malay-Muslim anger against the central government.

In contrast to these two cases of 'democratic recession' in the region, Indonesia's experience of democratic reform seems to indicate a regional success story in democratization. Although many issues and challenges remain, a broad consensus exists in the scholarly literature that these reforms have contributed considerably to the deepening and consolidation of Indonesian democracy (Bünte and Ufen, 2009).

East Timor is the fourth newly democratized Southeast Asian nation. Like the political transition in Cambodia, democratization took place under the aegis of the United Nations. Unlike the Cambodian process, though, it was an integral part of a larger, multi-faceted process of decolonization and nation-building. In the first few years following the UN mandate, the nation was seen by many as a success story in UN-led nation-building. Following the events in spring 2006, when East Timor, and in particular the capital, Dili, exploded into violence, this evaluation changed substantially, however. Nevertheless, one must still acknowledge that meaningful and peaceful parliamentary and presidential elections took place in 2007, resulting in a change in government. Although the elections were hotly contested and not free of complaints, respect for democratic competition prevailed. Few other 'post-colonial' neo-democracies with ruling liberation movement-cum-political parties have experienced such a change of government after founding elections.

Governance

Governance is not only a 'notoriously slippery' concept, but also one that is subject to extreme controversy (Pierre and Peters, 2000, p.7). Since issues of governance and democracy are often debated in specialized discourses in various sub-fields of political science, there is considerable debate about its exact meaning. The multitude of definitions that exist has actually created a degree of confusion regarding the exact boundaries of the concept.

In general, we distinguish between a broader understanding of governance and a narrower one. In the widest sense, the governance concept refers to the various ways through which social life is organized and coordinated (Williamson, 1975). Government in this sense is only one of the institutions in governance; the other models of governance are markets, hierarchies and networks (Kooiman, 1993; Rhodes, 1997). Thus, in its core sense, governance is the steering and coordination of interdependent actors based on institutionalized rule systems, the 'management of interdependencies' (Benz, 2004, p.25), which in this wide sense reflects the blurring of the distinctions between state and society resulting from changes such as the development of new forms of public management, the growth of public–private partnerships, the increasing importance of policy networks, increasing globalization and the greater importance of both supranational (EU) and sub-national organizations (multi-level governance, regional governance, local governance).

A narrower understanding of governance identifies governance more closely with the traditional institutions of government: 'governance is the capacity of government to make and implement policy, in other words to steer society' (Pierre and Peters, 2000, p.1; see also Kooiman, 1993). This definition refers more to the traditional steering capacities of the state and includes the state, the private sector and civil society groups.[1]

Democratic governance is sometimes defined as the extent to which the institutional design of a democratic polity promotes political freedom and guarantees civil and political rights. The level of democratic governance shows the extent to which citizens are free to participate and act in the democratic system. Hyden and colleagues have attempted to contrive a different concept of governance. The authors adopt a rule-based rather than a result-orientated definition of the term. They define governance as referring to 'the formation and stewardship of the formal and informal rules that regulate the public realm, the arena in which state as well as economic and societal actors interact to make decisions' (Hyden and Court, 2002, p.13; Hyden et al., 2004). They further clarify that governance deals with the constitutive side of how a political system operates rather than its distributive or allocative aspects. They identify six 'institutional arenas' to understand and investigate the functional dimensions of governance: civil society, political society, government, bureaucracy, economic society and the judicial system. While this definition is directed at the definition of governance *per se*, democratic governance only differs in the evocation of different rules and arenas.

This analytic concept differs from the concept used by the World Bank (and other international organizations), which defined governance in the late 1980s as 'the exercise of political power to manage a nation's affairs' (World Bank, 1989, p.60). According to this definition, governance encompasses the form of political regime, the process by which authority is exercised in the management of a country's economic and social resources for development, and the capacity of governments to design, formulate and implement policies (World Bank, 1992, 1994, 2000). Other international organizations and donor agencies have come up with supporting definitions that resemble the World Bank's interpretation, while at the same time emphasizing special areas of good governance (Chhotray and Stoker, 2009, p.104).

Based on this interpretation of governance, researchers at the World Bank have distinguished six main dimensions of governance: (1) voice and accountability, (2) political stability and absence of violence/terrorism, (3) governance effectiveness, (4) regulatory quality, (5) rule of law, and (6) control of corruption (Kaufmann and Kraay, 2009). The World Bank Governance Indicators (WGI hereafter) provide numerical measures of these six dimensions of governance for the twelve-year period from 1996 to 2008. As Hagopian and Mainwaring (2005) point out, the first two dimensions – voice and accountability along with political stability – capture the strength of democracy, the second two – government effectiveness and regulatory quality – its effectiveness, and the last two – rule of law and control of corruption – constitutionalism.

Main arguments and findings

The twelve substantive chapters in this collection fall into three categories. The first section explores the aspects of political culture, civil society and political Islam in terms of their relationship with democratic governance. This section begins with a contribution from Doh Chull Shin and Youngho Cho. Their comparative analysis of how Southeast Asians view democracy explores the progress that has been made in democratizing mass political cultures in Southeast Asia by analysing citizens' views of democracy in Indonesia, Malaysia, the Philippines, Singapore, Thailand and Vietnam. The authors' analysis of data culled from the Asian Barometer Survey exhibits a number of worrying findings. While an overwhelming majority of Southeast Asians embrace democracy as the most preferred regime, many of these regime democrats remain either uninformed or misinformed about what makes a political system democratic. Moreover, they understand democracy in illiberal terms. Furthermore, Southeast Asians remain more attached to the authoritarian mode of governance than the liberal one. This is why authentic supporters of democracy who can play a meaningful role in the democratization process constitute a very small minority in each Southeast Asian country. Evidently, Southeast Asian countries have yet to develop democratic political cultures.

This view is supported by Chong-min Park's research on associations and social networks in Indonesia, the Philippines, Thailand, Singapore, Malaysia and Vietnam. The results of his analysis of Asian Barometer Survey data suggest that there may not be any essential connection between the density of social networks and the quality of democratic citizenship across Southeast Asia. The contra-Tocquevillian thesis that association membership is 'a woefully inadequate foundation' for democratic citizenship applies equally to Southeast Asia (Theiss-Morse and Hibbing, 2005). In fact, as Park concludes, the associations and social networks across much of Southeast Asia do not encourage the learning of civic norms and democratic values as much as the acquisition of political skills and opportunities for political participation or mobilization. If associations benefit democracy across Southeast Asia, they do not so by cultivating social trust and citizenship norms but rather by stimulating political interest and action. In so far as associations contribute to democracy in the region, they achieve this not by fostering democratic norms and procedures but by providing political skills and opportunities.

Park's conclusions are supported, to some extent, by Mark R. Thompson's analysis of the patterns of civil society and the consequences of civil society activities for democratic governance in Thailand, the Philippines and Indonesia. In his contribution, Thompson delineates different conceptions of civil society. Each conception is nested in different socio-cultural, ideological and political settings; its practices have different consequences for the role of civil society in enhancing or threatening the stability and deepening of democratic processes. Furthermore, Thompson connects his analysis of 'un'-civil societies in Southeast Asia with the debate about structural contexts and agency in Southeast Asian politics. Thompson suggests that the type of 'strategic groups' that are dominant in a society is the best way of explaining whether the country's democracy is stable or not. In the 'bourgeois polities' of the Philippines and Thailand, an alliance of big business and traditionalist strategic groups has resorted to extra-constitutional mobilization to topple populists who have used class appeals to win elections. Indonesia is a counter-example. Thompson argues that the 'enigma' of successful political transition can at least to some extent be understood by investigating the linkages between civil society and democratization. As Thompson sees it, Indonesian civil society is neither 'Gramscian', in that bourgeois elites are trying to restore hegemony in the face of a populist threat, nor 'Tocquevillian', in that professional-based NGOs are mobilized to pressure but not threaten the government. In fact, a third model of civil society has emerged in this Southeast Asian archipelago. Thompson calls this the 'Burkean' civil society: civil society is dominated by traditional nationalist and Muslim elites who have pursued largely conservative goals, both through elections and local organizing. Understanding the forms and functions of this 'Burkean' civil society and its interaction with the political society is necessary in order to see why democratic consolidation has advanced further in Indonesia than in Thailand and the Philippines.

Andreas Ufen's chapter closes the first section. His comparative historical analysis investigates the configuration of forces of political Islam in Southeast Asia – secular, Islamic and Islamist – that fight for or against democracy. This is examined against the backdrop of the evolution of Malaysia's and Indonesia's political systems. While he points to the different initial conditions of the emergence of political Islam and to the different regime trajectories in both countries, his main conclusion is that state policies in New Order Indonesia and after Suharto have allowed for a very diverse discourse and have given ample space to secular and liberal voices. Furthermore and in agreement with Thompson's analysis, Ufen argues that post-Suharto democracy has been characterized by an open civil society with very diverse actors. While this has contributed to moderate political Islam in Indonesia, in Malaysia the state has been systematically Islamizing the country and has been able to tightly control the discourse on religious issues. State sponsorship of conservative Islam and strict control of deviant civil society actors has helped to stabilize electoral authoritarianism.

Aurel Croissant opens the second section on political institutions and modes of representation in Southeast Asia by analysing constitutional choices in four Southeast Asian nations and their consequences for democratic governance. His analysis provides some evidence that the type of political institution (and, for that matter, the shift from one set of institutions to another institutional arrangement) is related to the consolidation of a country's young democratic system. But the findings presented in his chapter do not provide unanimous support for Lijphart's (1999) recommendations on constitutional choices in newly democratizing nations. While the case of Thailand confirms Lijphart's warning against the pitfalls of 'majoritarian' (or to put it more precisely, 'majoritanized') democracy for democratic quality, there is little support for Lijphart's conclusions on presidentialism and majoritarianism. The Indonesian case is instructive here. In fact, he argues that it is the 'consensualized' character of Indonesia's presidential system of governance which significantly contributes to the ability of the democratic regime to endure, to stabilize and to consolidate. On the other hand, however, the Philippine case demonstrates that we must draw a distinction between 'consensus democracy' as defined and measured by Lijphart and an 'over-fragmented' democratic system as it exists in the Philippines.

Benjamin Reilly's chapter surveys the differences between 'consociational' and 'centripetal' approaches to institutional design. After examining the key components of each model, Reilly explores their application in Southeast Asia. He demonstrates that recent democratic reforms in Southeast Asia have seen a move away from the consociational approaches of earlier decades in favour of more centripetal and majoritarian models. While ethnic balancing and coalition governments continue to resonate, specific consociational institutions are now few and far between. Rather, the evolution of electoral institutions, party systems and patterns of cabinet formation demonstrate a distinct and almost region-wide shift away from the more 'consociational' political models of the 1950s and 1960s towards 'more integrative or centripetal forms of democracy in recent years'. According to Reilly, there are at least three factors which explain this trend. One factor is the desire of incumbents to restrict the electoral prospects of opposition parties. Another factor is the political learning that resulted from the failure of so many consociational experiments with post-colonial democracy in the 1950s and 1960s, which provided powerful negative examples for contemporary reformers. This, in turn, has motivated institutional designers in some Southeast Asian countries to search for alternative institutional solutions to the problem of political integration in multi-ethnic societies.

Marco Bünte's chapter on decentralization and democracy in Southeast Asia continues the discussion on the impact of institutional reforms on democracy and governance in the region. He provides a detailed analysis of the genesis, modes and forms of decentralization in the region. In addition, he discusses the question of whether decentralization has improved democratic quality in the region. With regard to this question, Bünte shows that the decentralization processes in Southeast Asia are not as efficient in promoting democracy and good governance as they were intended to be. Decentralization has undoubtedly opened up space for positive democratic change, which might be significant if political groups such as ethnic minorities, indigenous groups, democratic political parties, politically and economically marginalized groups and NGOs could organize themselves so as to take advantage of these new openings. However, to date the politics surrounding decentralization that have occurred in the shadow of the New Order's authoritarian heritage in Indonesia, the legacy of the bureaucratic polity in Thailand and the lasting dominance of 'goons, guns and gold' in the Philippines.

The final contribution in this section, by Allen Hicken, provides an overview of the features and patterns of political party systems and the extent of their institutionalization in Thailand, Indonesia and the Philippines. Hicken argues that while party system institutionalization is generally weak in all three countries, Indonesia, the youngest democracy of the three, performs the best. Weak institutionalization is correlated with volatile structures of party competition and cooperation in Thailand, whereas the Philippine party system seems, paradoxically, to be a stabilizing influence in a situation of protracted under-institutionalization because it combines more or less stable party system patterns with weak institutionalization. Hicken then analyses some of the reasons behind the variation in party system development and institutionalization in the region. He notes that progress on some dimensions of institutionalization can have the perverse consequence of undermining gains in other dimensions and illustrates this point in an analysis of events in Thailand since 1997. Hicken's chapter concludes with a discussion of the implications of the state and trajectory of political party systems' institutionalization for democratic governance and stability in the 'newly democratized' nations of Southeast Asia.

The third section of this collection contains four contributions which deal with human rights in Southeast Asia, civil –military relations, conflict management, and the relationship between democracy and foreign policy-making. Roland Rich opens this section with an assessment of the human rights situation in Southeast Asia which allows for four conclusions. The first conclusion is that ASEAN countries have accepted the human rights discourse anchored in its United Nations context as a rhetoric in which they must engage. The fact that all the ASEAN countries have ratified at least two of the six main human rights treaties is proof of a certain level of acceptance of the global human rights system. The second conclusion is that many factors exist that demonstrate the shallow depth of attachment to the system. The third conclusion is that, on the whole, ASEAN states are doing somewhat better with respect to economic, social and cultural rights than they are in the area of civil and political rights. Fourth and last, the poor treatment of civil and political rights in most countries of Southeast Asia demonstrates that there is still some way to go before a culture of human rights compliance can be said to have taken root.

The second chapter in this section is Aurel Croissant's, Paul W. Chambers' and Philip Völkel's discussion of the thorny issue of democratization and security sector governance in Southeast Asia. The authors argue that the institutionalization of civilian control over the armed forces has in many countries remained a crucial issue. While civilian governments in some countries in Southeast Asia (for example Singapore, Malaysia, Brunei) have, in some respects, managed to keep their militaries at bay, others appear to be falling prey to the armed forces' hegemony in the political realm. Turning to case studies, the authors then disaggregate civil–military relations in Thailand, Indonesia and the Philippines into the five decision-making areas. Their analysis shows that civilian control in the three countries remains partial, fragile and contested. While the depth of military involvement in political and civilian affairs varies, the failed institutionalization of civilian control in Thailand, the prolonged crisis of civil–military relations in the Philippines, and the conditional subordination of the military under weak civilian control in Indonesia is affecting the quality of democracy in all three nations. Based on their findings, the three authors predict that at least the Philippines and Thailand will most probably be plagued by further instances of military assertion and a lack of civilian control for some time to come. Given the deep entrenchment of the militaries in the respective political systems, the manifold problems regarding the consolidation of democracy in general, and the incompetence or ineptitude of civilian governments with regard to military reforms, civilians will most likely have neither sufficient capabilities nor compelling incentives to confront the military and diminish military decision-making power in the political arena. Accordingly, any significant extension of civilian influence over the security sector remains unlikely. The prospects for gradual change in civil–military relations in Indonesia seem somewhat more promising than in the other two cases. Still, much remains to be done to bring the Indonesian military more fully under civilian control.

The issues of civil–military relations and the institutionalization of civilian control over the armed forces are closely related to the topic of internal armed conflicts and conflict management in Southeast Asia. This is the theme of Christoph Trinn's article, which focuses on the capabilities of democracies in the region to manage political conflict in general and cultural conflict in particular. Trinn's quantitative analysis discerns a (non-inverted) U-relationship between the level of democratization and the degree to which the country is affected by conflict. For the most part, democracies are affected more by (cultural) conflicts than autocratic regimes are. Mixed regime phases ('hybrid' regime periods), however, are generally least affected. This pattern is a special characteristic of Southeast Asia. In addition, democracies in Southeast Asia have particular difficulty in dealing with political conflicts focused on cultural issues because, like democracies in general, they rely on a negotiable, divisible object and have difficulty coping with absolute claims.

The last chapter in this section analyses a relationship often neglected in research on democracy and governance in Southeast Asia, namely, the relationship between democratization and foreign policy. Jürgen Rüland and

Paruedee Nguitragool examine this relationship with regard to Southeast Asia's new democracies: the Philippines, Indonesia and Thailand. The authors test the democratic peace hypothesis, which assumes that democracies do not fight wars against each other. They also look at the relationship between democracy and war, the predictability of foreign policy-making, and the relationship between democracy and regional cooperation.

In the final chapter, Aurel Croissant and Marco Bünte provide a synopsis of the observations and conclusions presented in the book and put them into the broader perspective of conflict and democratic theory. Their aim is to provide some general insights into the patterns of democratic governance in Southeast Asia that may be relevant well beyond this region. The editors and authors hope that this collection of articles will contribute to a better understanding of current trends, achievements and challenges regarding democratic governance in the area and to the development of viable strategies for coping effectively with these challenges.

Note

1. This understanding of governance emphasizes forms of governing which are characterized by the following elements: they include forms of negotiation and consensus-building and go beyond classic forms of hierarchical steering without participation of the population. Collective decision-making thus includes non-state actors in decision-making and problem-solving. Consequently, governance dismisses the idea of the state as the unitary actor and society as the precisely defined arena. Another aspect relates to the generation of stable (albeit often informal) institutions, which can be decisive for the success or failure of governance (Blumenthal and Bröchler, 2006, p.9).

References

Benz, A. (2004) 'Einleitung: Governance – Modebegriff oder nützliches sozialwissenschaftliches Konzept?',' in Benz, A. (ed.) *Governance – Regieren in komplexen Regelsystemen* (Wiesbaden: VS Verlag).

Bertelsmann Stiftung (2009) *Bertelsmann Transformation Index 2010* (Gütersloh: Verlag Bertelsmann Stiftung).

Blumenthal, J. and Bröchler, S. (2006) 'Von Government zu Governance. Analysen zu einem schwierigen Verhältnis' in Blumenthal, J. and Bröchler, S. (eds) *Von Government zu Governance. Analysen zum Regieren im modernen Staat* (Hamburg: Lit Verlag).

Brooker, P. (2009) *Non-Democratic Regimes* (New York and Basingstoke: Palgrave Macmillan).

Brownlee, J. (2009) 'Portents of Pluralism: How Hybrid Regimes Affect Democratization', *American Journal of Political Science*, 53 (3): 515–35.

Bünte, M. and Ufen, A. (2009) *Democratization in Post-Suharto Indonesia* (London: Routledge).

Chhotray, V. and Stoker, G. (2009) *Governance Theory and Practice – A Cross Disciplinary Approach* (New York and Basingstoke: Palgrave Macmillan).

Coppedge, M. (2002) 'Democracy and Dimensions. Comments on Munck and Verkuilen', *Comparative Political Studies*, 35 (1): 35–39.

Dahl, R. (1971) *Polyarchy, Participation and Opposition* (New Haven: Yale University Press).

Diamond, L. (2002) 'Thinking about Hybrid Regimes', *Journal of Democracy*, 13 (2): 21–35.

Diamond, L. (2008) *The Spirit of Democracy* (New York: The Free Press).

Hagopian, F. and Mainwaring, S. (2005) *The Third Wave of Democratization in Latin America* (New York: Cambridge University Press).

Held, D. (2006) *Models of Democracy* (Stanford: Stanford University Press).

Hyden, G. and Court, J. (2002) *Governance and Development*, World Governance Survey Discussion Paper 1, August.

Hyden, G., Court, J. and Mease, K. (2004) *Making Sense of Governance. Empirical Evidence from 16 countries* (Boulder: Lynne Rienner).

Karl, T. (1995) 'The Hybrid Regimes of Central America', *Journal of Democracy*, 6 (3): 72–86.

Kaufmann, D. and Kraay, A. (2009) *Aggregate and Individual Governance Indicators 1996–2008*, World Bank Policy Research Paper 4978.

Kooiman, J. (1993) *Modern Governance. New Government – Society Interactions* (London: Sage).

Levitsky, S. and Way, L. (2002) 'The Rise of Competitive Authoritarianism', *Journal of Democracy*, 13 (2): 36–50.

Lijphart, A. (1999) *Patterns of Democracy: Government Forms and Performance in Thirty-Six Countries* (New Haven: Yale University Press).

Linz, J.J. (2000) *Totalitarian and Authoritarian Regimes* (New York: Rienner).

McCargo, D. (2005) 'Cambodia: Getting Away with Authoritarianism?', *Journal of Democracy*, 16 (4): 98–112.

Merkel, W. (2004) 'Embedded and Defective Democracies', in Croissant, A. and Merkel, W. (eds), *Special Issue of Democratization: Consolidated or Defective Democracy? Problems of Regime Change*, 11 (5): 33–58.

O'Donnell, G. (1999) *Counterpoints: Selected Essays on Authoritarianism and Democratization* (Notre Dame: University of Notre Dame Press).

Patiño, P. and Velasco, D. (2006) 'Violence and Voting in post-1986 Philippines'. in Croissant, A., Martin, B. and Kneip, S. (eds), *The Politics of Death. Political Violence in Southeast Asia* (Muenster: Lit-Verlag).

Pierre, J. and Peters, G. (2000) *Governance, Politics and the State* (New York and Basingstoke: Palgrave Macmillan).

Rhodes, R.A.W. (1997) *Understanding Governance. Policy Networks, Governance, Reflexivity and Accountability* (Buckingham, Philadelphia: Open University Press).

Rodan, G., Hewison, K. and Robison, R. (eds)(2002) *The Political Economy of Southeast Asia. Conflict, Crisis and Change* (Melbourne: Oxford University Press).

Schedler, A. (2006) 'The Logic of Electoral Authoritarianism' in Schedler, A. (ed.), *Electoral Authoritarianism. The Dynamics of Unfree Competition* (Boulder/London: Lynne Rienner).

Schumpeter, J. (1975) *Capitalism, Socialism and Democracy* (New York: Harper and Row).

Shin, D.C. and Tusalem, R.F. (2009) 'East Asia', in Haerpfer, C. W., Bernhagen, P., Inglehart, R. and Welzel, C. (eds), *Democratization* (Oxford: Oxford University Press).

Theiss-Morse, E. and Hibbing, J.R. (2005) 'Citizenship and Civic Engagement', *Annual Review of Political Science*, 8: 227–249.

Williamson, O. (1975) *Markets and Hierarchies: Analysis and Anti-Trust* (New York: Free Press).

World Bank (1989) *Sub-Saharan Africa: From Crisis to Sustainable Development* (Washington, DC: World Bank).

World Bank (1992) *Governance and Development* (Washington, DC: World Bank).

World Bank (1994) *Governance: The World Bank Experience* (Washington, DC: World Bank).

World Bank (2000) *Reforming Public Institutions and Strengthening Governance: A World Bank Strategy* (Washington, DC: World Bank).

World Bank Governance Indicators <http://www.govindicators.org>.

Zakaria, F. (1997) 'The Rise of Illiberal Democracy', *Foreign Affairs*, 76 (6): 22–43.

2

Contours and Barriers to Democratization in Southeast Asia: A Comparative Analysis of How Southeast Asians View Democracy

Doh Chull Shin and Youngho Cho

Introduction

In the current wave of global democratization, which spread from southern Europe more than three decades ago, Southeast Asia remains one of the few regions least affected by this wave. For example, according to the 2008 Freedom House report, only two of the eleven countries in the region (Indonesia and East Timor) are electoral democracies, and only one of these two (Indonesia) is classified as a liberal democracy. The other three countries that joined the wave – Cambodia, the Philippines and Thailand – have recently stumbled and returned to non-democracies, mainly due to the inability of their people and political leaders to resolve political differences peacefully through the process of democratic politics. Other countries in the region have yet to hold free and competitive elections (Freedom House, 2008).

Why is it that so many countries in this region, unlike their peers in other regions, have failed to join the powerful wave of global democratization? Why have most of the countries that joined the wave failed to sustain democratic rule? We would like to explore these questions from the perspective of mass citizenries whose cognitive and affective orientations to democracy are known to constitute the foundation of democratic political cultures (Chu et al., 2008; Diamond and Plattner, 2008; Fukuyama, 1995; Inglehart, 2000; Inglehart and Welzel, 2005; Norris, 1999). Accordingly, the emergence and evolution of democratic culture are assumed in our study to depend on the extent to which ordinary citizens understand democracy accurately and embrace it exclusively and fully. Only those who accurately understand democracy and embrace it unconditionally and fully are deemed to be authentic supporters.

Previous public opinion research on political culture has documented that many citizens of new democracies are not *cognitively capable* of understanding or defining democracy (Bratton et al., 2005; Dalton et al., 2007; Schedler and Sarsfield, 2004). It has also documented that the acceptance of democracy does not necessarily lead to the rejection of authoritarianism or vice versa. Popular support for democracy in emerging democracies, therefore, depends on a citizenry that not only accepts it but also rejects the authoritarian and other non-democratic alternatives (Lagos, 1997, 2001; Rose and Mishler, 1994; Shin, 1999). Moreover, such affective and cognitive orientations to democracy vary not only in their level or quantity but also in their quality or patterns (McDonough et al., 1998; Shin and Wells, 2005; Shin, 2007).

The primary objective of this chapter is to explore how much progress has been made in democratizing mass political cultures in Southeast Asia by analyzing the views of democracy held by citizens in Indonesia, Malaysia, the Philippines, Singapore, Thailand, and Vietnam. We examine data culled from the Asian Barometer Survey (ABS) project, which includes four sets of questions tapping support for democracy and a pair of structured and unstructured questions tapping the meaning of democracy (see Appendix for the wording of these questions).[1] These multi-national public opinion data, which were gathered in 2006 and 2007, consist of responses collected through face-to-face interviews with randomly selected voters in ten countries in East and Southeast Asia, including Indonesia (N = 1598), Malaysia (N = 1218), the Philippines (N = 1200), Singapore (N = 1012), Thailand (N = 1546) and Vietnam (N = 1200). Findings from each of the six national sample surveys conducted in Southeast Asia were compared across the countries in the region to examine intra-regional variations in the democratization of mass political cultures. These findings were also compared with those from the ABS surveys conducted in South Korea (N = 1217) and Taiwan (N = 1587), the two most successful third-wave democracies in East Asia, to determine the relative standing of cultural democratization in the region.

This chapter is divided into five parts. The first section analyzes levels and patterns of cognitive orientations to democracy among ordinary citizens of six Southeast Asian countries in terms of their capacity to understand democracy and the specific properties they attribute to it. The second and third sections focus on levels and patterns of popular affect for democracy as, respectively, a political system in principle and a political process in practice. The fourth section identifies and compares the most and least prevalent patterns of democratic orientations among Southeast Asians by considering both their cognitive and affective orientations to democracy together. It also identifies and compares the proportion of authentic democrats, meaning those who are fully informed and unconditionally committed to democracy, in each of these countries. The final section highlights key findings and discusses their implications for democratization in Southeast Asia.

Cognitive orientations to democracy

How much progress have Southeast Asian countries made in developing democratic political cultures? To address this question, we must first examine the extent to which their citizens are informed about democracy.

Cognitive capacity

How well do Southeast Asians understand democracy? Are they capable of defining it in their own words? What properties do they name most and least often as its elements? Are they capable of weighing the various properties of democracy and identifying the most essential of these properties? We addressed these questions with a pair of questions used in the ABS, one open-ended and the other closed (see Appendix (1)). The open-ended question asked respondents to name up to three things that they think constitute democracy. The closed question asked them to consider four well-known properties of democracy and to choose the one they considered the most essential. These properties are (1) opportunities to change the government through elections; (2) freedom to criticize those in power; (3) reducing the gap between the rich and the poor; and (4) guaranteeing basic necessities.

The purpose of the first question was to determine whether the respondents were cognitively capable of conceptualizing or defining democracy in their own words, and to identify the specific content of their understanding of democracy. The purpose of the second question, on the other hand, was to determine whether the respondents were cognitively capable of discerning the relative importance of various properties of democracy and of formulating their own policy position on democratic reform. When they were able to answer both questions, we rated them as having a reasonable understanding of democracy in principle and in practice and designated them as cognitively capable.

Table 2.1 shows that 73 per cent of the respondents were able to offer such a definition. By this criterion, Southeast Asians are considerably less capable of defining democracy than their peers in South Korea and Taiwan, 87 per cent of whom offered such a definition. They are also slightly less capable than sub-Saharan Africans, 78 per cent of whom were able to offer such a definition (Bratton et al., 2005, p.66). In all of the six countries surveyed, however, clear majorities were able to define it (see Table 2.1). As in Africa and East Asia, the size of these majorities varies considerably. In Singapore, for example, nine out of ten people (90 per cent) were able to express its meaning in their own words. In Thailand, on the other hand, the corresponding proportion was less than two-thirds (64 per cent).

In Table 2.1, we also report the percentages of those who were able to answer the closed questions regarding the essentiality of four components of democracy. In every country, more than three-quarters of the respondents answered this question. This proportion is much higher than for the

Table 2.1   Levels of the cognitive capacity to understand democracy

Country	Types of questions (%)		Number of questions (%)		
	Open-ended	Closed-ended	None	One	Two
Philippines	69	95	3	31	66
Thailand	64	76	12	35	53
Indonesia	69	89	9	23	68
Singapore	90	94	3	10	87
Vietnam	83	88	7	15	78
Malaysia	68	94	4	31	65
(Pooled)	73	83	67	25	68

Source: Asian Barometer Survey II.

open-ended question. This indicates that in every Southeast Asian country, there are many people who are not able to define democracy in their own words but are able to identify what is most essential for building a democracy in their country.

To address the question of how well Southeast Asians understand democracy, we estimated their overall capacity to understand democracy by calculating the percentages of ABS respondents who answered none, one or both questions about the meaning of democracy. Table 2.1 shows that nearly one out of ten people in Thailand (12 per cent) and Indonesia (9 per cent) are *totally incapable* of understanding democracy. In the other four countries, smaller minorities of 7 per cent or less do not understand what democracy means at all. Those who are uninformed about or totally incapable of understanding democracy constitute very small minorities in the Philippines (3 per cent), Malaysia (4 per cent), and Singapore (3 per cent).

As in the case of the totally incapable, the proportion of those who are *fully capable* of defining democracy varies considerably, from a bare majority of 53 per cent in Thailand to a large majority of 87 per cent in Singapore. Only in three of the six countries – Indonesia, Singapore, and Vietnam – were more than two-thirds of the respondents fully capable of defining it and determining the relative importance of its properties. When these three countries are compared with the other three countries of the Philippines, Thailand, and Malaysia, in which less than two-thirds of the respondents could be categorized as fully capable, it would appear that exposure to modernization or to democratic politics does not powerfully shape popular understanding of democracy.

Liberal versus non-liberal conceptions

In what specific terms do Southeast Asians understand democracy? What percentages of Southeast Asians associate democracy with political freedom, political processes, and socioeconomic benefits? Figure 2.1 shows the

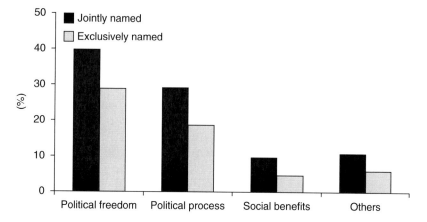

Figure 2.1   The properties of democracy Southeast Asians named exclusively and jointly

Source: Asian Barometer Survey II.

percentages of those who named each of these three properties and others as components of democracy in response to the open-ended question. When all six countries are considered together, freedom (40 per cent) is mentioned more frequently than the political process (29 per cent), social benefits (10 per cent) or other things (11 per cent). Yet, a substantial majority of three out of five (60 per cent) did not include freedom in their conceptions of democracy. Obviously, non-liberal conceptions of democracy are more common than liberal ones in Southeast Asian countries.

Moreover, freedom was not the most frequently mentioned property of democracy in all six countries (see Table 2.2). It was most frequently mentioned in four of the six countries – the Philippines, Indonesia, Singapore, and Malaysia – but only in one of these countries, Singapore, did a majority of two-thirds (66 per cent) name it as a property of democracy. In the other three countries – the Philippines, Indonesia, and Malaysia – it was mentioned most frequently by pluralities of two-fifths. In the remaining two countries – Thailand and Vietnam – substantial majorities of two-thirds or more did not include it in their notions of democracy. These findings clearly indicate that freedom and liberty do not figure prominently in conceptions of democracy among Southeast Asians.

What proportion of Southeast Asians understands democracy exclusively in terms of freedom and liberty? Figure 2.1 and Table 2.2 show that less than one-third (29 per cent) of the Southeast Asian mass publics surveyed have an exclusively liberal conception of democracy. The pertinent column of Table 2.2 shows that the percentages vary considerably, from 15 per cent in Thailand to 59 per cent in Singapore. In all of the countries but

Table 2.2 National differences in the most frequently and exclusively named properties of democracy

Country	Frequently named properties (%)				Unidimensional (%)				Multi-dimensional
	Liberty & freedom	Political process	Social benefits	Others	Liberty & freedom	Political process	Social benefits	Others	
Philippines	41	10	7	20	35	6	4	16	8
Thailand	24	42	3	8	15	31	1	5	12
Indonesia	40	34	13	13	23	15	4	4	24
Singapore	66	18	7	5	59	14	5	4	7
Vietnam	34	46	17	13	22	34	10	1	7
Malaysia	42	18	11	15	31	10	47	16	16
(Pooled)	40	29	10	11	29	19	5	6	23

Source: Asian Barometer Survey II.

Singapore, only a minority of respondents equated democracy exclusively with freedom and liberty. In Thailand, Indonesia, and Vietnam, moreover, small minorities of less than a quarter offered an exclusively liberal conception of democracy, equating it only with freedom and liberty. In Thailand and Vietnam, such liberal conceptions are outnumbered by the conceptions that equate it exclusively with political processes. These can be considered additional evidence that Southeast Asians tend to hold non-liberal conceptions of democracy.

Do Southeast Asians hold conceptions of democracy that include authoritarian political practices? To explore this question, we analyzed the latest, fifth wave of the World Values Survey (WVS) that was conducted in 56 countries, including four Southeast Asian countries – Indonesia, Malaysia, Thailand, and Vietnam. The WVS asked respondents whether they considered three authoritarian political practices – the interpretation of laws by religious leaders, the intervention of the military in politics, and the severe punishment of criminals – as essential characteristics of democracy. For Southeast Asia and six other regions, Figure 2.2 shows the percentages of those who fully subscribed to the authoritarian conceptions of democracy by designating all three of these authoritarian practices as essential characteristics of democracy. It also shows the percentages of respondents who were completely detached from all of these conceptions.

Figure 2.2 shows that of the seven regions surveyed, Southeast Asia ranks second only to the Muslim zone, composed of Egypt, Iran, Iraq and Morocco, in authoritarian conceptions of democracy. More notably, it ranks last in complete detachment from such conceptions. As many as one in

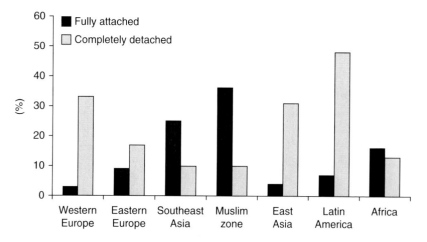

Figure 2.2   Authoritarian conceptions of democracy by cultural zones
Source: The World Values Survey V.

four (25 per cent) Southeast Asians are fully attached to authoritarian conceptions, while only one in ten (10 per cent) is completely detached from these conceptions. The corresponding figures for East Asia, which consists of China, Japan, Korea and Taiwan, are 4 and 31 per cent. According to these figures, Southeast Asians are six times more likely to be fully attached to these conceptions than East Asians (25 per cent to 4 per cent), while the latter are three times more likely to be completely detached from these than the former (31 per cent to 10 per cent). When all these findings are considered together, it is evident that authoritarian misconceptions of democracy are pervasive and pose another serious challenge to the democratization of mass political cultures in all of the Southeast Asian countries.

In summary, a substantial minority of Southeast Asians are not fully capable of understanding what constitutes democracy and are unable to determine the most important of its properties. Among those who are cognitively capable, a large majority appear to misunderstand democracy in terms of authoritarian politics. Most of the citizens of Southeast Asian countries are cognitively uninformed or misinformed about democracy. This pair of problems greatly inhibits the cultural democratization of the region.

Embracing democracy as a regime

In order to determine whether a particular country's political culture is pro-democratic, we must first measure the extent to which its citizens prefer democracy as a system of government to its alternatives. As mentioned above, we accomplished this by examining the responses to two sets of three questions asked in six countries as part of the ABS project (see Appendix (2 and 3)). By combining the affirmative responses to the three questions in each set into a four-point scale, we first estimated the extent to which each country's citizens favour democratic and authoritarian regimes respectively. We then estimated their net regime orientations by subtracting their pro-authoritarian regime orientations from their pro-democratic regime orientations.

Attachment to democracy as a regime

To estimate the general level of support for a democratic regime, we selected a set of three questions from the ABS surveys. As Appendix (2) shows, these questions address, respectively, the desirability of democracy, the suitability of democracy, and the preferability of democracy. We looked at positive or pro-democratic responses to the questions individually and collectively in order to measure democratic attachment at the regime level.

The first question asked respondents to indicate on a ten-point scale the sort of regime they found most desirable. A score of 1 indicates that a 'complete dictatorship' is favoured, while a score of 10 indicates a preference for a 'complete democracy'. The results (see Table 2.3) indicate that an absolute

Table 2.3   Attachment to democracy as a regime

Country	Domains (%)			Overall attachment (%)		
	Desire	Suitability	Preference	None	Partial	Full
Indonesia	86.4	79.8	64.3	7.6	37.2	55.3
Malaysia	86.9	81.1	70.5	4.5	37.6	57.9
Philippines	70.8	56.6	50.6	14.5	56.8	28.8
Singapore	90.7	86.3	58.9	4.0	43.0	53.1
Thailand	84.6	82.4	72.7	6.5	32.1	61.4
Vietnam	92.9	90.4	71.8	5.9	24.4	69.7
(Mean)	85.4	79.4	64.8	7.2	38.5	54.4

Source: Asian Barometer Survey II.

majority of the people in each of the six Southeast Asian countries expressed a desire for democracy by choosing a score of 6 or above. From 71 per cent in the Philippines to over 90 per cent in Singapore and Vietnam, the majority of respondents expressed a desire for democracy. Evidently, most Southeast Asians prefer, at least in principle, to live in a democratic regime.

The second ABS question asked respondents to rate the suitability of democracy on a similar ten-point scale. A score of 1 on this scale indicates 'completely unsuitable', while a score of 10 indicates 'completely suitable'. A much smaller majority in every Southeast Asian country indicated that they considered democracy suitable by choosing a rating of 6 or above on this scale. The citizens' perception of democracy's suitability is somewhat lower than their desire for democracy (79 per cent to 85 per cent). When asked whether democracy as the system of government for their country is always preferable to any other kind of government, less than two-thirds of the respondents (65 per cent) expressed a preference for democracy.

The various ratings Southeast Asians gave as to the desirability, suitability, and preferability of democracy clearly show that the level of citizen attachment to democracy as a regime greatly depends on the aspects of governance they are taking into consideration. When they view democracy merely as a political ideal, almost all of them embrace it as the best possible political system. Even when they view it as a political enterprise, most Southeast Asian citizens still believe that democracy is a viable political system. However, when asked if they prefer democracy as the means of running their country on a daily basis, a large majority of them do not always endorse it.

In addition to evaluating these items individually, we combined affirmative responses to these questions into a four-point index to measure the overall level of support for a democratic regime. On this index, a score of 0 means no support, while a score of 3 means full support. Scores of 1 and 2 indicate partial support. The last three columns of Table 2.3 contain the proportions expressing no, partial and full support for democracy at the regime level.

With the exception of the Philippines (15 per cent), all Southeast Asian countries are alike in that a small minority, less than one-tenth of the population of each country, is completely unattached to democracy (ranging from 4 per cent in Singapore to 8 per cent in Indonesia). They are also alike in that majorities express full support for democratic regimes (ranging from 53 per cent in Singapore to 70 per cent in Vietnam). Only in the Philippines do those fully attached to democracy constitute a relatively small minority of less than one-third (29 per cent). That is less than half of their counterparts in Vietnam. Why is the average level of citizen support for democracy lowest in a third-wave democracy (the Philippines), and highest in communist Vietnam? Learning theory, which suggests that the experience of democratic rule leads to greater support for democracy, is not confirmed in Southeast Asia.

Attachment to non-democratic regimes

When Southeast Asians express full support for democracy as a regime, are they fully detached from non-democratic regimes? If not, to what extent do they remain attached to these regimes? To address these questions, the ABS asked respondents whether they would favour a return to an authoritarian regime (those of one-man civilian dictatorship, military dictatorship and single-party dictatorship).

Table 2.4 shows that in five of the six countries, those favouring a return to each of these types of individual dictatorships constitute minorities. Only in Vietnam, which registered the highest level of full support for democracy, did a majority (55per cent) express an affinity for one-party dictatorship, under which they had been living for decades. It appears that many Vietnamese equate communist one-party dictatorship with democracy, remaining attached to the former while expressing affinity for the latter.

Table 2.4   Attachment to authoritarian regimes

Country	Types (%)			Overall attachment (%)		
	Civilian	One-party	Military	None	Partial	Full
Indonesia	9.8	8.2	**29.7**	64.4	33.3	2.3
Malaysia	**32.7**	19.4	9.8	58.2	37.3	4.5
Philippines	**38.5**	33.1	24.4	42.1	48.4	9.5
Singapore	**9.5**	7.5	4.2	86.6	11.6	1.9
Thailand	**21.9**	17.7	19.7	64.6	27.2	8.2
Vietnam	11.7	**55.0**	24.0	37.2	57.4	5.4
(Mean)	20.7	23.5	18.6	58.9	35.9	5.3

Source: Asian Barometer Survey II.

To estimate the overall levels of attachment to authoritarianism as a regime, we combined responses that expressed affinity for non-democracy into a four-point index scale. Scores of 0 and 3 mean, respectively, no and full attachment, while scores of 1 and 2 indicate partial attachment. In all six Southeast Asian countries, only a small minority of less than one-tenth of the population expressed full attachment to authoritarianism. Of these countries, full attachment to authoritarianism is least common in Singapore (1.9 per cent) and Indonesia (2.3 per cent) and most common in the Philippines (9.5 per cent) and Thailand (8.2 per cent). The difference between the attachment levels of these two groups of countries, however, is relatively small (no more than eight percentage points).

Those expressing no attachment to authoritarian regimes form a minority in the Philippines (42 per cent) and Vietnam (37 per cent). In the other four countries, on the other hand, they constitute majorities ranging from 58 per cent in Malaysia to 87 per cent in Singapore. Between these two groups of countries, there is a great difference in the levels of full detachment from authoritarianism, a difference of up to 50 percentage points. When these two groups of countries are compared, it is evident that full detachment from authoritarianism has more to do with the level of socioeconomic development than years of experience of democratic rule.

Net regime preferences

Having considered democracy and authoritarianism as distinct dimensions, we can now ask whether citizens prefer democracy, authoritarianism or some mixed type of regime. If they do prefer democracy, to what extent do they prefer democracy to its alternatives? To address these questions, we considered democratic and authoritarian regime types together by constructing a seven-point index (by subtracting the scores of the four-point authoritarian regime preferences index from the democratic regime preferences index).

On this seven-point net regime preference index, the three negative scores (−3, −2 and −1) indicate the preponderance of authoritarian regime preferences, while the three positive scores (+1, +2 and +3) indicate democratic regime preferences. The two extreme scores of −3 and +3 indicate complete support for authoritarian and democratic regimes respectively. A score of 0, on the other hand, indicates a balance between the two kinds of regime preferences. To summarize and highlight cross-national differences, we collapsed the negative and positive scores into two categories, authoritarian and democratic. For each country, the percentage of citizens who express a preference for an authoritarian, democratic, or mixed regime are reported in Table 2.5. It also contains the percentages of those expressing complete attachment to democracy and their mean scores on the seven-point summary index (with higher scores indicating a stronger preference for democracy).

The mean scores reported in Table 2.5 indicate that, although citizens in all six Southeast Asian countries prefer democracy to other types of regimes, the magnitude of these net preferences varies considerably across

Table 2.5 Types and magnitude of net regime preferences

Country	Preferred types (%)			Mean on 7-point index
	Authoritarian (−3, −2, −1)	Mixed (0)	Democratic (+1, +2, +3)	
Indonesia	4.9	11.6	83.4	+1.83
Malaysia	4.8	11.5	83.7	+1.77
Philippines	18.4	20.7	60.9	+0.82
Singapore	2.8	6.0	91.2	+2.15
Thailand	6.5	13.6	79.9	+1.80
Vietnam	3.7	12.1	84.3	+1.64
(Mean)	6.9	12.6	80.6	+1.64

Source: Asian Barometer Survey II.

the countries. Singapore is the only country averaging higher than 2 on the −3 to +3 index. The Philippines is the only country averaging less than 1 point on the same index. The other four countries are located in the middle, with scores higher than 1.5 but lower than 2.0.

In every Southeast Asian country except the Philippines, only a very small minority (ranging from 3 to 7 per cent of the population) preferred an authoritarian regime to a democratic regime. In addition, in every country except the Philippines, only small minorities (ranging from 6 to 14 per cent) preferred a mixed regime to democratic or authoritarian alternatives. When we consider authoritarian and mixed regime preferences jointly, however, it becomes evident that support for non-democratic regimes varies considerably across the countries. Few people in Singapore (9 per cent), for example, preferred to live in an authoritarian or mixed regime. In Thailand (20 per cent) and the Philippines (39 per cent), sizable minorities preferred such regimes. However, the most notable feature of Table 2.5 is that in all six Southeast Asian countries, including the Philippines, a large majority (over three-fifths) embraced democracy as the most preferred regime.

Embracing democracy as a political process

Now that we have examined citizens' evaluations of democracy and authoritarian regimes and found that they generally prefer democracy, we can turn to democracy as a political process and ask to what extent democracy has become the most preferred method of governing in Southeast Asia. To address this question, we selected two sets of three items, one focusing on the procedural norms of democratic governance and the other on the authoritarian practices of governance. By compiling affirmative responses to the three questions in each set into a four-point scale, we were able to estimate the extent to which each country's citizens favour democratic and authoritarian processes respectively. We then estimated their net process orientations by subtracting their pro-authoritarian process orientations from their pro-democratic regime orientations.

Orientations to democratic governance

Democratic political systems operate according to a variety of procedural norms, including the rule of law, separation of powers, and checks and balances between different branches of the government. To measure citizens' support for the rule of law, the first survey item asked respondents how strongly they agreed or disagreed with the statement 'When the country is facing a difficult situation, it is okay for the government to disregard the law in order to deal with the situation'. Only in two countries, Indonesia (68 per cent) and the Philippines (59 per cent), did a majority endorse the rule of law by disagreeing with the statement.

To discover support for the separation of powers, the ABS survey asked respondents whether they agreed or disagreed with the statement 'When judges decide important cases, they should accept the view of the executive branch'. Again, only in two countries, Indonesia (56 per cent) and Singapore (49 per cent), did a majority or near majority endorse the procedural norm of separation of powers by disagreeing with the statement.

Finally, we examined support for the norm of checks and balances between the executive and legislative branches. The ABS survey asked respondents how strongly they would agree or disagree with the statement 'If the government is constantly checked by the legislature, it cannot possibly accomplish great things'. Again, in only two countries, Indonesia (56 per cent) and Vietnam (52 per cent), did a majority endorse the norm of checks and balances by disagreeing with the statement.

To measure the overall level of support for democracy as a political process, we combined pro-democratic responses to these questions into a four-point index. As above, scores of 0 and 3, respectively, indicate no attachment and full attachment to the democratic processes. Scores of 1 and 2, on the other hand, indicate partial attachment. For each country, the percentages of the unattached, partially attached, and fully attached are reported in Table 2.6.

The most striking result is that in all six countries, only a minority, less than one-third, expressed full attachment to the democratic process. In all of the countries, significantly smaller proportions of people support democracy as a method or process of governance than as a regime.

Attachment to authoritarian governance

In light of the relatively low levels of support for democracy as a process, we wonder to what extent Southeast Asians remain attached to the procedures of authoritarian governance. To address this question, we again considered responses to three ABS items, each of which deals with a different practice specific to authoritarian rule (see Table 2.7). Pro-authoritarian responses to

Table 2.6   Attachment to democracy as a process

Country	Types (%)			Overall attachment (%)		
	Rule of law	Judicial independence	Checks and balances	None	Partial	Full
Indonesia	68.3	55.6	55.9	13.3	57.0	29.7
Malaysia	47.9	40.4	41.6	25.6	60.9	13.5
Philippines	59.3	32.3	43.1	19.3	68.2	12.6
Singapore	36.2	48.8	46.0	22.4	66.3	11.3
Thailand	33.6	27.7	38.1	43.0	46.2	10.8
Vietnam	42.7	20.2	52.1	31.7	59.5	8.8
(Mean)	48.0	37.5	46.1	25.9	59.7	14.5

Source: Asian Barometer Survey II.

Table 2.7   Attachment to authoritarianism as a process

Country	Types (%)			Overall attachment (%)		
	Paternalism	Hierarchism	Rule by morality	None	Partial	Full
Indonesia	90.0	73.7	43.7	2.8	63.6	33.6
Malaysia	84.3	62.0	48.7	5.8	62.1	32.1
Philippines	74.0	55.9	57.2	7.4	64.3	28.3
Singapore	62.6	56.5	56.7	14.3	54.1	31.6
Thailand	68.2	54.4	66.2	9.8	56.5	33.7
Vietnam	70.0	73.7	59.9	9.8	48.4	41.8
(Mean)	74.9	62.7	55.4	8.3	58.2	33.5

Source: Asian Barometer Survey II.

this set of questions indicate the levels of affinity for authoritarianism at the process level, where policies are formulated and implemented on a daily basis.

One common practice of authoritarian governance is to limit the freedom of individual citizens to participate in the political process under the pretext of protecting their interests. To measure citizens' acceptance of this practice, known as paternalism, the first ABS question asked respondents how strongly they agreed or disagreed with the statement 'The relationship between the government and the people should be like that between parents and children'. In every Southeast Asian country, a substantial majority supported the authoritarian practice of paternalism that allows political leaders to make decisions on their behalf by rejecting the democratic idea of collective self-rule.

The second question concerns the authoritarian practice of hierarchism, which deprives individual citizens of the freedom to express their disagreement with political leaders. This question asked respondents how strongly they agreed or disagreed with the statement 'Government leaders are like the head of a family; we should all follow their decisions'. Once again, in every Southeast Asian country, a majority as large as almost three-quarters of the respondents supported the practice of authoritarian governance that violates the democratic principles of competition, pluralism, and tolerance.

Finally, respondents to the ABS surveys were asked how strongly they agreed or disagreed with the statement 'If we have political leaders who are morally upright, we can let them decide everything'. Agreement with this statement indicates support for the Confucian notion of elitist government based on virtue or morality. Classical Confucians considered this form of virtuous rule superior to rule by law because the former motivates people to experience a sense of shame and behave well voluntarily. In four of the six countries – the Philippines (57 per cent), Singapore (57 per cent), Thailand (66 per cent) and Vietnam (60 per cent) – majorities endorsed the non-democratic mode of meritocracy. In Indonesia (44 per cent) and Malaysia (49 per cent), substantial minorities endorsed it.

Net process preferences

Having examined views of democratic and authoritarian practices individually, we can consider these two dimensions together to determine the particular set of political processes Southeast Asians most prefer. Do they prefer the democratic process to the authoritarian one for formulating and implementing public policies? If so, to what extent do they prefer the former to the latter? To address these questions, we again constructed a seven-point index by subtracting the four-point index measuring authoritarian process preferences from the index measuring democratic process preferences. To ease cross-national comparisons, we grouped the three negative scores (–3, –2 and –1) as evidence of the preponderance of authoritarian preferences, and three positive scores (+1, +2 and +3) as evidence of the preponderance of democratic preferences. The two extreme scores of –3 and +3 indicate, respectively, complete attachment to authoritarian and to democratic processes. A score of 0, on the other hand, indicates that the preferences of a country's population are balanced between the two.

The results presented in Table 2.8 reveal that there is a great deal of commonality in both the direction and magnitude of the mean ratings across Southeast Asia. The most notable feature of these ratings is that all the means are negative scores. These negative scores indicate that *the average citizen in every Southeast Asian country surveyed prefers authoritarian practices to democratic ones.* In every country, supporters of authoritarian governance outnumber those of democratic governance by 10 percentage points or more. The preponderance of authoritarians to democrats is least pronounced in Indonesia and Singapore, which are, respectively, the only liberal democracy

Table 2.8 Types and magnitude of net process preferences

	Preferred types (%)			Mean on 7-point index
	Authoritarian	Mixed	Democratic	
Indonesia	42.4	26.8	30.9	−0.28
Malaysia	53.5	22.8	23.6	−0.65
Philippines	52.3	23.6	24.1	−0.52
Singapore	50.7	18.2	31.1	−0.45
Thailand	59.8	20.6	19.7	−0.89
Vietnam	63.9	18.3	17.8	−0.89
(Mean)	53.8	21.7	24.5	−0.61

Source: Asian Barometer Survey II.

in the region and the richest non-democracy in the world. It is most pronounced in Vietnam, the most oppressive communist one-party state in the region. It appears that the experiences of democratic politics and socio-economic modernization orient Southeast Asians away from authoritarian governance.

Patterns of mass political orientations

Thus far, we have analyzed, separately, how ordinary people in six Southeast Asian countries react to democracy and authoritarianism, not only as regimes but also as modes of governance. The results of these analyses have revealed that they prefer democracy to authoritarianism at the regime level. In the process of governance, however, they prefer the latter to the former. To many Southeast Asians, it is evident that support for democracy at the regime level is one thing, and support for it at the process level is another. Because democracy means different things at different levels to them, we need to ascertain the different patterns of their political orientations and estimate the depth and breadth of democratic political culture in each of their countries. In examining whether democracy is preferred to non-democracy at neither, one nor both of these two levels, we discovered four patterns of political orientation: (1) democracy is not preferred at either of the two levels; (2) democracy is preferred only at the process level; (3) democracy is preferred only at the regime level; and (4) democracy is preferred at both the regime and process levels.

In Table 2.9, the prevalent pattern is reported for each country. A striking feature of the table is that a majority or large plurality in every Southeast Asian country belongs to the third pattern, in which democracy is preferred only at the regime level. Those falling into this type are called *regime democrats*: they embrace democracy as the preferred regime, while remaining attached to the authoritarian mode of governance. In every country, these

Table 2.9 Patterns of political orientations

| Patterns | Types | | Southeast Asia (%) | | | | | | Northeast Asia (%) | |
	Regime	Process	Indonesia	Malaysia	Philippines	Singapore	Thailand	Vietnam	Korea	Taiwan
Full non-democrat	No	No	14.5	13.5	29.2	7.5	17.5	14.7	6.3	15.4
Procedural democrat	No	Yes	2.1	2.8	9.9	1.3	2.7	1.1	3.1	5.2
Regime democrat	Yes	No	54.7	62.9	46.8	61.4	62.9	67.6	42.2	39.4
Full democrat	Yes	Yes	28.7	20.9	14.2	29.8	17.0	16.7	48.4	40.0

Source: Asian Barometer Survey II.

regime democrats outnumber the *non-democrats* of the first type, who do not prefer democracy neither as a regime nor as a governing process. They also outnumber the *full democrats* of the fourth type, who prefer it at both levels.

In every country, *full democrats* constitute a small minority of less than one-third. Only in Indonesia (29 per cent) and Singapore (30 per cent) do they constitute more than one-quarter of the citizens. Even in these two countries, however, they trail, by a large margin, their peers in South Korea (48 per cent) and Taiwan (40 per cent), the two most successful third-wave democracies in East Asia. While *full democrats* outnumber *non-democrats* in these two East Asian democracies, the former are outnumbered by the latter in two of the three Southeast Asian third-wave democracies (the Philippines and Thailand). Evidently the experience of democratic politics does not have much to do with the emergence of full supporters of democracy in Southeast Asia.

Those who support democracy fully and unconditionally at both the regime and process levels, however, cannot be equated with *authentic* or *informed* supporters of democracy (Schedler and Sarsfield, 2004; Sarsfield, 2007). To qualify as *authentic democratic supporters*, those full supporters must be cognitively capable of defining democracy in their own words and prioritizing its properties for further democratization. They are the kind of democrats who are knowledgeable enough to participate meaningfully in the process of democratic reform. To determine the proportion of authentic democrats in each country, we divided full democrats between the cognitively capable and incapable on the basis of their ability to understand democracy and chose the former as authentic democrats. For each of the six Southeast Asian countries, the proportion of these authentic democrats is reported in Figure 2.3. It also includes their proportion in South Korea and Taiwan as a baseline for comparison.

In Figure 2.3, we see that not all the full supporters of democracy are *authentic democrats* as defined above. In every country, including the two East Asian democracies, the former outnumber the latter by two percentage points or more. This clearly indicates that throughout East and Southeast Asia, there are people who support democracy without knowing what it is. These uninformed full supporters of democracy are most numerous in Thailand (7 per cent) and Malaysia (5 per cent), and least numerous in Singapore (3 per cent) and Vietnam (3 per cent). Even in Taiwan (35 per cent), more than one in ten full supporters of democracy is not fully informed about it.

Of the six countries in Southeast Asia, authentic democrats are most numerous in Singapore (27 per cent) and Indonesia (24 per cent), which represent, respectively, the richest country and the most democratic country in the region, suggesting that socioeconomic development and democratic rule are both conducive to the emergence of democratic political culture. In the other four countries, however, they are more numerous in Malaysia (16

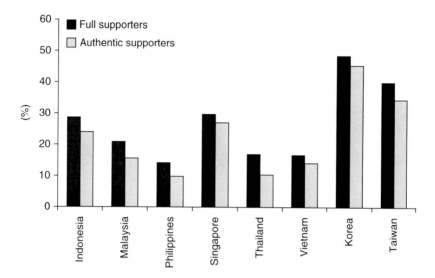

Figure 2.3   Authentic and full supporters of democracy
Source: Asian Barometer Survey II.

per cent) and Vietnam (14 per cent) than in the Philippines (10 per cent) and
Thailand (11 per cent), each of which experimented with democratic rule
for more than a decade. This finding seems to suggest that even a decade
of democratic rule does not always contribute to the significant growth of
democratic political culture.

More notable is the finding that in all six Southeast Asian countries,
authentic democrats constitute small minorities of about one-quarter of the
respondents or less, and they form much smaller minorities than their peers
in South Korea and Taiwan. This finding clearly indicates that democracy is
rooted neither broadly nor deeply in the minds of most people in Southeast
Asia. It also indicates that the region lags behind East Asia in promoting cultural democratization by transforming authoritarians into fully informed
and committed democrats.

Summary and conclusions

This study has sought to explore why Southeast Asia has lagged behind in
the current wave of democratization from the perspective of a cultural theory that recognizes mass political orientations as a force shaping the process
of democratization (Dalton and Shin, 2006; Diamond, 2008; Inglehart and
Welzel, 2005; Linz and Stepan, 1996; Bratton et al., 2005; Rose et al., 1998). In
this regard, our analysis has resulted in a number of notable findings. First, an

overwhelming majority of Southeast Asians embrace democracy as the most preferred regime (Marsh, 2006; Sinnott, 2006). Yet many of these regime democrats remain either uninformed or misinformed about what makes a political system democratic. Moreover, unlike their peers in the West and in other regions, they do not understand democracy in liberal terms; instead, they understand democracy in terms of a-liberal or authoritarian political practices. And in formulating and implementing policies, they remain more attached to the authoritarian rather than the liberal mode of governance. In every Southeast Asian country, therefore, authentic supporters of democracy, who can play a meaningful role in the democratization process, constitute a very small minority. Evidently, Southeast Asian countries have failed to democratize the age-old habits of authoritarian thinking and behaviour. They have yet to develop democratic political cultures.

Equally notable is the finding that Southeast Asians overwhelmingly perceive their current regimes to be democracies. When the ABS asked them whether their own country was a democracy, only 4 per cent replied that it was not. In every country including Singapore, which is the most advanced socioeconomically, more than nine out of ten people considered their political system a democracy. In the case of Vietnam, almost everyone (99.5 per cent) characterized it as a democracy, followed by Thailand (98 per cent), Singapore (96 per cent), Indonesia (95 per cent), Malaysia (94 per cent), and the Philippines (91 per cent). Overwhelmingly, Southeast Asians understand democracy in authoritarian terms, and, in that way, they can think of their regimes as democracies. In their minds, therefore, there is no need to transform the current regimes into democracies. There is also little variation in failing to consider the need for democratic regime change across the various segments of the population defined by levels of education and income (Shin, 2007). In Southeast Asia today, people of all stripes are united in refusing to consider such a regime change.

When these findings and the scholarly findings noted above are considered together, it becomes clear that the mass political cultures of Southeast Asian countries remain far more authoritarian than democratic. It is also clear that their political cultures are far less democratic than those of South Korea and Taiwan, the two most vigorous third-wave democracies in East Asia. If we define authentic or fully informed and unqualified support for democracy as key elements of democratic political culture, Southeast Asian countries have a long way yet to go to build democratic cultures within their nations. If their political leaders continue to supply democracy only in response to what their mass citizenry demands, these states are not likely to be transformed into liberal democracies in the foreseeable future. Instead, they are likely to become and remain illiberal electoral democracies, which were once known in the region as 'Asian democracies' (Hood, 1998; Neher, 1994; Zakaria, 2003).

Appendix

Asian Barometer survey questions

1) Conceptions of democracy

Q91   To you, what does democracy mean? What else? (ALLOW UP TO 3 RESPONSES)

Q92   People often differ in their views on the characteristic that is essential to democracy. If you have to choose only one of the things that I am going to read, which one would you choose as the most essential?

1) Opportunity to change the government through elections
2) Freedom to criticize those in power
3) A small income gap between the rich and poor
4) Basic necessities like food, clothes, and shelter etc. for everyone

2) Orientations to democracy as a regime

Q101   Here is a scale ranging from a low of 1 to a high of 10. On this scale, 1 means complete dictatorship and 10 means complete democracy. To what extent would you want our country to be democratic now? Please choose a number on this scale.

Q103   Here is a similar scale of 1 to 10 measuring the extent to which people think democracy is suitable for our country. If 1 means that democracy is completely unsuitable for our country today and 10 means that it is completely suitable, where would you place our country today?

Q121   Which of the following statements comes closest to your own opinion?

1) Democracy is always preferable to any other kind of government.
2) Under some circumstances, an authoritarian government can be preferable to a democratic one.
3) For people like me, it does not matter whether we have a democratic or a non-democratic regime.

3) Orientations to authoritarianism as a regime

There are many ways to govern a country. Would you disapprove or approve of the following alternatives? For each statement, would you say you *strongly approve, approve, disapprove*, or *strongly disapprove*?

Q124   We should get rid of parliament and have a strong leader decide things.

Q125   Only one political party is allowed to stand for election and hold office.

Q126   The military should come in to govern the country.

4) Orientations to democracy as a political process

I have here other statements. For each statement, would you say you *strongly agree, somewhat agree, somewhat disagree*, or *strongly disagree*?

Q137   When judges decide important cases, they should accept the view of the executive branch.

Q138   If the government is constantly checked [i.e. monitored and supervised] by the legislature, it cannot possibly accomplish great things.

Q.141   When the country is facing a difficult situation, it is okay for the government to disregard the law in order to deal with the situation.

5) Orientations to authoritarianism as a political process

For each statement, would you say you *strongly agree, somewhat agree, somewhat disagree*, or *strongly disagree*?

Q64   The relationship between the government and the people should be like that between parents and children.

Q134   Government leaders are like the head of a family; we should all follow their decisions.

Q139   If we have political leaders who are morally upright, we can let them decide everything.

Note

1. Further information is available at www.asianbarometer.org.

References

Bratton, M., Mattes, R. and Gyimah-Boadi, E. (2005) *Public Opinion, Democracy, and Market Reform in Africa* (New York and Cambridge: University Press).

Chu, Y., Diamond, L., Nathan, A. and Shin, D.C. (eds) (2008) *How East Asians View Democracy* (New York and Columbia: University Press).

Dalton, R. and Shin, D.C. (eds) (2006) *Citizens, Democracy and Markets around the Pacific Rim* (Oxford: Oxford University Press).

Dalton, R., Shin, D.C. and Jou, W. (2007) 'Understanding Democracy: Data from Unlikely Places', *Journal of Democracy*, 18 (4): 142–156.

Diamond, L. (2008) *The Spirits of Democracy: the Struggle to build Free Societies throughout the World* (New York: Henry Holt).

Diamond, L. and Plattner, M. (eds) (2008) *How People View Democracy* (Baltimore: Johns Hopkins University Press).

Freedom House Report (2008) <http://www.freedomhouse.org>, accessed May 1.

Fukuyama, F. (1995) 'The Primacy of Culture', *Journal of Democracy*, 6 (1): 7–14.

Hood, S. (1998) 'The Myth of Asian-Style Democracy', *Asian Survey*, 38 (9): 853–866.

Inglehart, R. (2000) 'Culture and Democracy', in Harrison, L.E. and Huntington, S.P. (eds), *Culture Matters* (New York: Basic Books).

Inglehart, R. and Welzel, C. (2005) *Modernization, Cultural Change and Democracy: The Human Development Sequence* (New York and Cambridge: University Press).

Lagos, M. (1997) 'Latin America's Smiling Mask', *Journal of Democracy*, 8 (3): 125–138.

Lagos, M. (2001) 'Between Stability and Crisis in Latin America', *Journal of Democracy*, 12 (1): 137–145.

Linz, J. and Stepan, A. (1996) *Problems of Democratic Transition and Consolidation: Southern Europe, South America, and Post-Communist Europe* (Baltimore: Johns Hopkins University Press).

Marsh, I. (2006) *Democratization, Governance and Regionalism in East and Southeast Asia* (London and New York: Routledge).

McDonough, P., Barnes, S. and Lopez Pina, A. (1998) *The Cultural Dynamics of Democratization in Spain* (Ithaca and New York: Cornell University Press).

Neher, C. (1994) 'Asian Style Democracy', *Asian Survey*, 34 (11): 949–961.

Norris, P. (ed.) (1999) *Critical Citizens* (New York and Oxford: University Press).

Rose, R. and Mishler, W. (1994) 'Mass Reactions to Regime Change in Eastern Europe', *British Journal of Political Science*, 24 (Apr): 159–182.

Rose, R., Mishler, W. and Haerpfer, C. (1998) *Democracy and its Alternatives* (Baltimore: Johns Hopkins University Press).

Sarsfield, R. (2007) 'Illuminating the Meaning of Democracy: Democratic Conceptions in Argentina and Mexico.' Presented at the Annual Meeting of the Southern Political Science Association, 3 January, New Orleans.

Schedler, A. and Sarsfield, R. (2004) *Democrats with Adjectives: Linking Direct and Indirect Measures of Democratic Support,* Afrobarometer Working Paper 45.

Shin, D.C. (1999) *Mass Politics and Culture in Democratizing Korea* (New York: Cambridge University Press).

Shin, D.C. (2007) 'Democratization: Perspectives from Global Citizenry' in Dalton, R. and Klingemann, H.D. (eds), *The Oxford Handbook of Political Behavior* (New York: Oxford University Press).

Shin, D.C. and Wells, J. (2005) 'Is Democracy the Only Game in Town?', *Journal of Democracy*, 16 (2): 88–101.

Sinnott, R. (2006) 'Political Culture and Democratic Consolidation in East and Southeast Asia', in Marsh, I. (ed.), *Democratization, Governance and Regionalism in East and Southeast Asia* (London and New York: Routledge).

Zakaria, F. (2003) *The Future of Freedom: Illiberal Democracy at Home and Abroad* (New York: W.W. Norton & Company).

3
Associations and Social Networks in Southeast Asia: Schools of Democracy?

Chong-min Park

Democratization in Southeast Asia has not followed the same path throughout the region. While strong pressure from civil society groups played a prominent role in the democratic transitions in Thailand, the Philippines and Indonesia (Franco, 2004; Aspinall, 2004; Alagappa, 2004; Karatnycky and Ackerman, 2005), the authoritarian regimes in Vietnam, Malaysia and Singapore, by contrast, have remained immune from this bottom-up trend. Although numerous non-governmental organizations and civil society groups are known to operate in the latter two countries, civil society remains dominated and manipulated by the state (Weiss, 2004; Kadir, 2004). In communist Vietnam, autonomous civil society groups are not tolerated, but mass participation in state-led official groups is extensive because of state mobilization efforts (Lockhart, 1977).

Drawing on Alexis de Tocqueville's monumental work, *On Democracy in America* (1969), many contemporary democratic theorists and researchers have emphasized the significance of associational life as a key element of successful democratization and vibrant democracy. In their pioneering work, *The Civic Culture*, Gabriel Almond and Sidney Verba (1963) held that associations imbue their members with habits of cooperation and norms of reciprocity that are conducive to civic and political engagement. Likewise, Robert Putnam (1993) has emphasized that a crucial function of voluntary associations is to generate social capital by helping members to acquire civic norms and democratic values and to thereby improve democratic institutions. In his comprehensive account of third-wave democratization, Larry Diamond (1999, p.242) further noted the critical role of civil society in democratic consolidation. He argued that civil society organizations contribute to democratic consolidation by 'inculcating not only the participatory habits, interests, and skills of democratic citizenship but also the deeper values of a democratic political culture, such as tolerance, moderation, a willingness to compromise, and a respect for opposing viewpoints'.

In an attempt to synthesize prior theory and research on the relationship between associations and democracy, Mark Warren (2001) recently distinguished three potential democratic effects of associations, claiming that they can have (1) developmental effects by cultivating democratic orientations among members, (2) public sphere effects by forming public opinion and collective judgments, and (3) institutional effects by making public decisions and implementing them. Similarly, Archon Fung (2003, p. 536) notes six types of contributions that associations can make to democracy: they include 'the intrinsic pleasures of associations, civil socialization, political education, resistance, representation, deliberation, and direct governance'. Depending on the political context they are embedded in, these types of contributions can vary widely. For instance, in non-democratic political contexts, associations may promote resistance to dominant political institutions rather than civic virtues such as respect for the rule of law or tolerance.

Building on these theoretical arguments, this chapter analyzes the potential effects of social participation on democratic development and examines whether associations and social networks serve as schools of democracy across the six Southeast Asian countries listed above. Does the neo-Tocquevillian thesis apply across Southeast Asia? Are the socially connected more likely to display the attributes of democratic citizenship than the socially disconnected? In what ways are associations and social networks likely to advance democracy in this region? These are the fundamental questions we will examine in this study.

We will carry out our investigation in two main steps. Drawing on the data from the 2005–2007 Asian Barometer Survey (ABS), we will first estimate the levels of social or civic participation in these countries by analyzing association membership and network involvement. We will next examine the potential effects of these levels of participation on two dimensions of democratic citizenship, attitudinal and behavioural. The attitudinal dimension includes civic norms and democratic orientation, whereas the behavioural dimension addresses political involvement and participation. Depending on the degree to which association membership and network involvement are linked to these dimensions of democratic citizenship, associations and social networks may be considered schools for democracy. Our findings are summarized in the conclusion.

Levels of social participation

It has been said that civil society groups flourish across much of the region in the wake of social modernization and political democratization (Alagappa, 2004). The proliferation of social associations, however, does not necessarily indicate high levels of individual participation in these groups. Unless the level of individual participation can be directly ascertained, we cannot be certain whether these groups maintain a substantial membership. We will estimate the level of social or civic participation for the citizens of each country by analyzing their association membership and network involvement.

Association membership

To measure their level of involvement in associations, the 2005–07 ABS directly asked respondents whether they were members of any organizations or formal groups. The respondents were not given a list of types of social groups; they were merely asked to name up to three of the most important groups to which they belonged. This open-ended question is in contrast to the list-type question used by other well-known surveys, such as the World Values Survey (WVS).[1] For this reason, our membership figures may be far lower than those given by the WVS. It should also be noted that our measure did not distinguish between active and passive members.

The percentage of respondents belonging to no, one or two or more social groups is reported in Table 3.1. The level of association membership varied from country to country. Vietnam (59 per cent) had the highest level, followed by Malaysia (32 per cent), Indonesia (31 per cent), the Philippines (25 per cent), and Thailand (24 per cent), in that order. Despite its high level of economic development, Singapore (10 per cent) was at the bottom of the range. As Russell Dalton (2006) has indicated, the fact that Vietnam has the highest level of group membership is evidence of state mobilization efforts. The findings suggest that the development effects of associations, if any, may apply only to small numbers of Southeast Asians, not including the Vietnamese.

The table shows that across much of Southeast Asia (except Vietnam) only small numbers of respondents reported multiple (two or more) memberships, suggesting that cross-cutting networks are limited. One respondent in ten in Indonesia and Malaysia and one in twenty in the Philippines and

Table 3.1 Levels of social participation

	Indonesia	Philippines	Thailand	Malaysia	Singapore	Vietnam
Number of association memberships						
None	68.8	73.5	75.7	68.4	90.1	40.0
One	19.3	20.3	19.1	20.5	8.1	34.6
Two and more	11.4	4.9	4.9	11.1	1.8	24.1
Involvement in informal networks						
Low	31.4	33.5	44.1	43.6	62.6	62.2
Medium	23.1	36.7	27.7	37.7	24.2	15.2
High	44.2	25.9	20.5	17.3	10.6	6.6
(N)	(1,598)	(1,200)	(1,546)	(1,218)	(1,012)	(1,200)

Source: 2005–07 Asian Barometer Surveys.

Thailand reported multiple memberships. Again, Singapore is at the bottom of the range, where one in fifty reported multiple memberships. In contrast, one in four in Vietnam belonged to two or more social groups. It is worth noting that single joiners outnumbered multiple joiners across Southeast Asia, indicating that there were far fewer cross-pressured individuals than those not cross-pressured.

A recent study has revealed that differences in economic development, religious composition, type of polity, and years of democracy result in national differences in association involvement in democratic societies (Curtis et al., 2001). Our results indicate that national levels of association membership did not follow a single pattern. For instance, the level of association membership was higher in poor Indonesia than in affluent Singapore. The level of association membership in non-democratic Malaysia rivalled that of democratic Indonesia. Singapore, the wealthiest nation in the region, displayed the lowest level of association membership, while Vietnam, the least free, exhibited the highest levels. This finding suggests that national differences in group membership across Southeast Asia may reflect both the extent of freedom and the degree of state mobilization. At the time of the survey, Indonesia was freer than the Philippines and Thailand, which were freer than Malaysia and Singapore, which in turn were freer than Vietnam.[2] On the other hand, state mobilization of membership was most extensive in Vietnam, but it was also substantial in Malaysia.

It is evident that most Southeast Asian countries are hardly 'nations of joiners'. In the Philippines and Thailand, where citizen activism was known to have played an important role in their democratic transitions, large majorities eschewed social groups. Low levels of association membership were also found in Indonesia, where civil society groups played a critical role in mobilizing civic resistance to authoritarian rule. Not surprisingly, in Singapore, where the state formally and informally discourages autonomous civil society activity, an absolute majority eschewed social groups. In Malaysia, where state-led civil society activity is encouraged, the level of association involvement was higher than in Singapore. In Vietnam, where the state engages ordinary people in official organizations, the level of group membership turned out to be the highest.

In Indonesia, the Philippines, and Thailand, the three democracies of Southeast Asia, there was a widespread absence of individual involvement in associations. Ordinary citizens in these democracies remained socially disengaged, at least formally if not informally, even though civil society groups have multiplied in the wake of democratization.

Perhaps more important than group membership is the type of group to which an individual belongs, because some types are more relevant than others for developing democratic citizenship (Stolle and Rochon, 2001; Maloney and Rossteutscher, 2007). Table 3.2 shows the distribution of membership across 19 different types of social groups, including residential

Table 3.2 Membership in social groups

	Indonesia	Philippines	Thailand	Malaysia	Singapore	Vietnam
Political parties	7.1	2.0	1.1	43.2	3.0	24.9
Residential/community associations	38.9	16.5	57.8	21.6	24.0	37.4
Religious groups	51.1	29.0	3.2	14.1	36.0	2.4
Sports/recreational clubs	8.1	1.0	2.4	12.0	11.0	4.1
Culture organizations	2.6	1.3	1.1	2.6	4.0	2.8
Charities	1.2	25.4	1.3	4.7	6.0	5.5
Public interests groups	2.2	0.3	1.9	11.2	4.0	3.6
Labor unions	1.8	1.7	0.0	3.9	9.0	4.8
Farmers unions/agricultural associations	10.8	5.0	36.3	4.4	1.0	29.4
Professional organizations	4.5	3.6	3.0	3.9	3.0	3.7
Business associations	0.4	3.3	0.3	2.3	1.0	1.6
Parent-teacher associations	1.0	2.3	1.9	6.5	4.0	5.5
Producer cooperatives	2.2	2.6	0.0	3.9	0.0	1.0
Consumer cooperatives	1.4	5.3	0.0	0.0	0.0	0.6
Alumni associations	1.6	1.0	2.4	4.4	10.0	1.0
Candidate support organizations	0.0	1.3	0.5	0.0	1.0	0.0
Other occupational organizations	8.4	4.0	8.1	0.0	2.0	4.1
Other volunteer organizations	11.0	16.5	7.5	0.0	6.0	20.8
Others (clan associations)	0.0	0.0	0.0	7.3	0.0	0.0
(N)	(491)	(303)	(372)	(384)	(100)	(703)

Note: Entries are the percentage of respondents indicating membership in each type of social groups. As up to three separate responses were coded, the percentage cannot be directly summed.

Source: 2005–07 Asian Barometer Surveys.

associations, labour unions, political parties, religious groups and sports and leisure clubs. The most popular types of social groups varied from country to country. In Indonesia, where Islam is a popular force, half of the joiners belonged to religious groups, and two-fifths had joined residential or neighbourhood associations. In the Philippines, where Catholicism is the dominant religion, approximately a quarter of the joiners belonged to a religious group, with a similar proportion belonging to religion-related charities. Among the few Singaporean joiners, a third belonged to religious groups, whereas a quarter joined residential or neighbourhood associations. In Malaysia, more than two-fifths were members of political parties, which tend to be ethnic-based, and one-fifth belonged to residential or neighbourhood associations. In Thailand, more than half belonged to residential or neighbourhood associations, while a third of farmers joined unions or agricultural associations. In Vietnam, a third of the joiners belonged to residential or neighbourhood associations, three-tenths were members of farmers' unions or agricultural associations, and a quarter joined political parties (most likely the communist party).

The popularity of residential or neighbourhood associations in Thailand and Indonesia indicates a strong tradition of communalism in those countries. Religious groups were the most popular type not only in predominantly Muslim Indonesia and the mainly Christian Philippines but also in multi-religious Singapore; however in Thailand, where most are Buddhist, religious groups were not the most popular type. In Malaysia, ethnic-based political parties were the most popular type. In Vietnam, residential and community associations, not political parties, were the most popular type. Modern interest groups such as labour unions, professional organizations and business associations, which are common in Western democracies, were the least popular types across Southeast Asia. Public involvement in environmental, human rights, and other nongovernmental civic groups, constituting new social movements, was largely negligible.

Overall, it is evident that even if the number of social groups has multiplied in the three Southeast Asian democracies in the wake of democratization, as has been alleged, these social groups have failed to maintain substantial levels of membership. In Malaysia and Vietnam, two of the three non-democracies, where autonomous civil society activity is discouraged, state-led social groups were able to maintain substantial levels of membership. Although the types of associations to which people belonged varied, the most popular types of social groups appeared to be those built on religious, ethnic, or communal identities or sentiments, particularly in countries where religious and ethnic majorities exist. Such types of associations are likely to promote primordial identities and parochial interests, rather than public identities and common interests. These bonding, not bridging, social networks are likely to foster the 'dark side' of social capital (Putnam, 2000; Warren, 2001).

Network involvement

More generally, social networks that have developed out of formal and informal social interaction constitute the structural components of social capital (Newton, 1999). Here we are focusing on informal networks of social ties that resemble the patron–client form of association still prevalent across much of Southeast Asia. To measure involvement in these types of social networks, the 2005–07 ABS asked a pair of questions. The first question read as follows: 'Some people because of their job, position in the community or contacts, are asked by others to help influence important decisions in their favour. What about you? How often are you asked to help influence important decisions in other people's favour?'. This question allows us to ascertain whether respondents have friends or acquaintances to be helped, namely, clients.[3] The second question read as follows: 'And are there people you could ask to help influence important decisions in your favour?'. This question allows us to ascertain whether respondents have friends or acquaintances to help them, namely, patrons.[4] These two questions were combined to measure the level of involvement in social networks between people with unequal status, wealth or influence, reflecting patron–client social ties or Chinese *guanxi*.

Table 3.1 shows the levels of network involvement. Indonesia had the highest level among the sample countries, with more than two-fifths (44 per cent) of respondents having high levels of informal social connections. It is followed by the Philippines (26 per cent), Thailand (21 per cent), Malaysia (17 per cent), and Singapore (11 per cent). Vietnam (7 per cent) had the lowest level of network involvement, although it had the highest level of group membership. This finding shows that involvement in networks of social ties was most prevalent in poor, democratic Indonesia, whereas in communist Vietnam and affluent, non-democratic Singapore, it was least prevalent. Other democratic and non-democratic Southeast Asian countries fell somewhere in between.

Informal networks of patron–client social ties, which tend to be buttressed by the norms of reciprocity and personal loyalty, exist between individuals of unequal status and power (Lande, 1973; Scott, 1972). These types of social networks, which 'span vertical arrangements of power, influence, wealth and prestige', are likely to promote status-bridging social capital (Wuthnow, 2002, p. 670). Networks based on favouritism such as these are likely to operate when the rule of law is weak. Notably, national levels of network involvement tend to correspond to the extent of government corruption. According to Transparency International's 2006 Corruption Perceptions Index, Indonesia was ranked 130 out of 163 countries surveyed, whereas the Philippines ranked 123. In contrast, Singapore was ranked 5, Malaysia 44 and Thailand 63. Singapore, the least corrupt of the sample countries, had low levels of network involvement, whereas Indonesia, the most corrupt, had the highest levels. An exception to this pattern, however, was Vietnam, which was ranked 111, but this might have been due to Vietnam's high social levelling and low political pluralism.

It is notable that Southeast Asians were more involved in informal networks than in formal associations. For instance, two-thirds of Indonesians and Malaysians, three-quarters of Filipinos and Thais, and nine-tenths of Singaporeans did not belong to a social group. In contrast, only a third of Indonesians and Filipinos, more than two-fifths of Malaysians and Thais, and two-thirds of Singaporeans had no networks of social ties. The only exception to this pattern was Vietnam, where two-fifths had no group membership and two-thirds had no networks of social ties. Overall, informal networks of social ties were more central to the social life of most Southeast Asians than formal associations.

Civil society, as measured by citizen involvement in voluntary associations, was not exactly strong and vibrant across Southeast Asia. However, this does not necessarily indicate that Southeast Asians are socially atomized or disconnected. It was found that majorities of ordinary people across much of Southeast Asia are at least partially embedded in informal networks of social ties.[5]

Sociodemographic differences

If association membership and network involvement provide civic and political skills and resources, inequalities in social participation would likely result in the unequal political representation of citizen interests and preferences (Verba et al., 1995). Does social participation reflect inequalities in socioeconomic resources across Southeast Asia?

The first panel of Table 3.3 presents the correlations between association membership and major demographic variables. Indicators of socioeconomic status and resources, such as education and income, were positively linked to association membership in the democracies of Indonesia and the Philippines and the non-democracy of Vietnam.

As indicators of resources or social integration, gender and age are often seen as possible determinants of social participation. First, gender was related to association membership only in Islamic Malaysia and communist Vietnam, meaning that men were more likely than women to be mobilized into social groups. Men as well as women, though, eschewed social groups across much of Southeast Asia. Second, age was related to association membership in five of six countries, except Singapore. The old were more likely to join social groups than the young, perhaps because the former tend to have more spare time or to be more integrated into society than the latter.[6] Overall, the findings suggest that inequalities in socioeconomic resources were reproduced as inequalities in group membership across much of Southeast Asia.

The second panel of Table 3.3 presents the correlations between network involvement and major demographic variables. Network involvement was related to socioeconomic resources such as education and income in the two democracies of Indonesia and the Philippines and the two non-democracies

Table 3.3 Demographic correlates of social participation

	Indonesia	Philippines	Thailand	Malaysia	Singapore	Vietnam
Number of association memberships						
Gender	Ns	Ns	Ns	0.14**	Ns	0.09**
Age	0.07**	0.14**	0.15**	0.11**	Ns	0.09**
Education	0.13**	0.10**	−0.14**	Ns	0.09**	0.06*
Income	0.13**	0.11**	−0.17**	0.06*	Ns	0.15**
Involvement in informal networks						
Gender	0.06*	Ns	0.06*	Ns	Ns	Ns
Age	Ns	Ns	Ns	−0.10**	−0.18**	Ns
Education	0.10**	0.08**	Ns	0.12**	0.27**	0.07*
Income	0.07**	0.10**	0.06*	0.12**	0.27**	Ns

Note: Entries are Pearson's correlation coefficients.
** Statistically significant at the 0.01 level.
* Statistically significant at the 0.05 level. The educated and the rich were more likely to join social groups than the uneducated and the poor. Association membership was related to income in Malaysia and to education in Singapore. Yet in Thailand, the uneducated and the poor were more likely to belong to social groups than the educated and the rich, suggesting that associations may help the socially disadvantaged, especially the rural poor, to express their interests.
Source: 2005–07 Asian Barometer Surveys.

of Malaysia and Singapore; it was related to education in Vietnam and to income in Thailand. Gender and age were not consistent determinants of network involvement, though. Only in Indonesia and Thailand were men slightly more likely than women to be embedded in informal networks. Age was negatively linked to network involvement only in Malaysia and Singapore, meaning that the young were more likely to be involved in informal networks of social ties than the old.

The results suggest that socioeconomic status and resources tend to provide individuals with access to status-bridging social networks. Social networks of patron–client ties appeared to be more central to the socially advantaged than the socially vulnerable, perhaps because the former are more likely than the latter to have high-status patrons as well as low-status clients. All the findings strongly suggest that the middle class is likely to be dominant in formal and informal associational life across most of Southeast Asia, regardless of the regime type.

Correlates of social participation

In this section, we will examine the potential effects of social participation on democratic citizenship. We have distinguished between two forms of social participation – association membership and network involvement – because they may have varying developmental effects.[7]

Social trust and citizenship norms

The first alleged attitudinal benefit of social participation is the building of civic values and norms. To assess such developmental effects, we correlated two forms of social participation with social trust[8] and good citizenship norms.[9]

The top two rows in the first panel of Table 3.4 present the correlations between association membership and civic orientations. First, in five of six democratic and non-democratic countries, association membership was found to be unrelated to social trust, suggesting that associations do not play an important role in fostering trust in others. Only in Thailand were group members more likely than non-members to display generalized trust. Second, the relationship between association membership and citizenship norms was mixed. In Malaysia, the Philippines and Thailand, group membership tended to promote citizenship norms, whereas it inhibited them in Vietnam. The potential effects of associations on social trust were largely nonexistent, whereas the effects on citizenship norms were minimal or inconsistent.

The same rows in the second panel of Table 3.4 present the correlations between network involvement and civic attitudes. First, the relationship between network involvement and social trust was found to be mixed.

In the Philippines, Singapore and Thailand, involvement in informal networks was likely to encourage trust in others, whereas it discouraged it in Vietnam. Second, in all countries (except Vietnam), network involvement was unrelated to citizenship norms. In Vietnam, network involvement was likely to reduce, rather than increase, support for citizenship norms. The potential effects of informal networks on social trust were minimal or inconsistent, whereas the effects on citizenship norms were nonexistent.

The cross-national patterns of membership effects did not distinguish democracies from non-democracies. For instance, in the Philippines and Malaysia, membership contributed to citizenship norms. In Indonesia and Singapore, it encouraged neither social trust nor citizenship norms. In Vietnam, it discouraged citizenship norms. Likewise, there was no distinction between democracies and non-democracies in the patterns of network involvement effects. In the Philippines, Thailand and Singapore, network involvement encouraged social trust. In Indonesia and Malaysia, it encouraged neither social trust nor citizenship norms. In Vietnam, it discouraged both.

The results indicate that the socializing role of associations in nurturing social trust and citizenship norms is minimal across much of Southeast Asia. Involvement in associations largely failed to foster trust in fellow citizens, a 'touchstone' of social capital. It is noteworthy that social networks of patron–client ties tended to promote trust in others in some countries, but that mobilized group membership in Vietnam undermined civic orientations. Overall, the effects of social participation on social trust and citizenship norms were generally negligible across Southeast Asia.

Table 3.4 Attitudinal and behavioral correlates of social participation

	Indonesia	Philippines	Thailand	Malaysia	Singapore	Vietnam
Number of association memberships						
Social trust	Ns	Ns	0.11**	Ns	Ns	Ns
Citizenship norms	Ns	0.14**	0.07**	0.07*	Ns	-0.14**
Support for democracy	Ns	0.09**	Ns	0.08**	Ns	Ns
Rule of law	Ns	Ns	Ns	Ns	Ns	Ns
Political efficacy	0.09**	Ns	Ns	0.18**	Ns	0.14**
Political interest	0.12**	0.07*	0.09**	0.22**	0.16**	0.17**
Voting	Ns	Ns	0.09**	0.17**	-0.09**	0.08**
Contact activity	0.29**	0.22**	0.05*	0.32**	0.20**	0.26**
Protest activity	0.14**	0.08**	Ns	0.08**	0.07*	0.09**
Involvement in informal networks						
Social trust	Ns	0.08**	0.07**	Ns	0.08*	-0.07*
Citizenship norms	Ns	Ns	Ns	Ns	Ns	-0.09**
Support for democracy	-0.09**	-0.12**	Ns	Ns	-0.09*	Ns
Rule of law	Ns	Ns	Ns	Ns	Ns	Ns
Political efficacy	0.06*	Ns	Ns	Ns	0.21**	0.12**
Political interest	0.08**	0.10**	Ns	Ns	Ns	0.08*
Voting	Ns	Ns	0.08**	Ns	Ns	Ns
Contact activity	0.23**	0.10**	0.11**	0.13**	0.17**	0.08*
Protest activity	0.19**	0.09**	Ns	Ns	0.13**	Ns

Note: Entries are Pearson's correlation coefficients.
** Statistically significant at the 0.01 level.
* Statistically significant at the 0.05 level.

Source: 2005–07 Asian Barometer Surveys.

Democratic orientations

The second alleged role of associations and social networks is to act as a source of support for democratic values and principles. To assess such developmental effects, we correlated two forms of social participation with support for democracy[10] and the rule of law.[11]

The second and third rows in the first panel of Table 3.4 present the correlations between association membership and support for democratic values and principles. First, although the meaning of democracy may differ among individuals, in four of the six countries membership in associations did not correspond to an increase in democratic aspirations. On the other hand, there was a positive, albeit weak, relationship between them in Malaysia and the Philippines, where group members were more likely than non-members to consider democracy to be legitimate and effective. Second, association membership was unrelated to support for the rule of law in all sample countries. The potential effects of formal association on democratic values and principles were largely nonexistent. Similarly, Russell Dalton (2006) found that the relationship between association membership and support for democracy was negligible or even weak in the opposite direction across Southeast Asia.

The same rows in the second panel of Table 3.2 present the correlations between network involvement and support for democratic values and principles. First, in Indonesia, the Philippines and Singapore, network involvement was linked, albeit negatively, to support for democracy, meaning that those with networks of social ties were less likely to favour democracy than those without such networks. Networks of patron–client ties were likely to undermine democratic aspirations in the new democracies of Indonesia and the Philippines. Second, network involvement was unrelated to support for the rule of law in all sample countries. The potential effects of informal networks on democratic values and principles were largely nonexistent or even detrimental.

National differences in the potential effect of group membership did not reflect the democratic–nondemocratic divide. In the democratic Philippines and non-democratic Malaysia, group membership contributed to support for democracy. Regardless of the regime form, group membership had no impact on support for the rule of law. Likewise, there was no distinction between democracies and non-democracies in the patterns of network involvement effects. In the democracies of Indonesia and the Philippines and the non-democracy of Singapore, network involvement undermined support for democracy.

Overall, there was little evidence that association membership provided a reliable source of support for democracy across most of Southeast Asia. Association membership rarely contributed to the learning of democratic values and principles in Southeast Asia, raising doubts about the role of associations as schools of democracy. It is also worth noting that networks of patron–client social ties may even undermine democratic regime orientations. All of the findings suggest that associations and social networks are not reliable sources of support for democracy, regardless of the regime form.

Political engagement

The third potential role of associations and social networks concerns the making of competent and active citizens. In particular, associations are considered to provide political skills, resources and opportunities that facilitate political participation (Verba et al., 1995; Ayala, 2000). Social networks are generally viewed as sites for political discussion, mobilization and recruitment (Iglič and Fábregas, 2007). To examine such democratic effects, we correlated two forms of social participation with attitudinal and behavioural dimensions of political engagement such as political efficacy,[12] political interest,[13] voting,[14] contact activity[15] and protest activity.[16]

The last five rows in the first panel of Table 3.4 present the correlations between association membership and political engagement. First, association membership was related to political efficacy in three of the six countries. In particular, in the non-democracies of Malaysia and Vietnam, even state-led group membership was likely to foster a feeling of political efficacy. It is worth noting that in democratic Indonesia, association membership and political engagement were weakly related, and that in the democracies of the Philippines and Thailand, they were unrelated. Second, there was a tendency for group membership to increase interest in politics, regardless of the regime type. In all of the countries, members were more likely than non-members to be concerned about public affairs and to follow news about the government and politics. Notably, the relationship was particularly strong in Malaysia, where ethnic-based political parties are the most popular type of association.

Third, the relationship between association membership and voting was largely limited and mixed. Interestingly, group membership was unrelated to voting in the democracies of Indonesia and the Philippines. By contrast, group membership was negatively linked to voting in non-democratic Singapore, meaning that members were less likely to vote than non-members. In the non-democracies of Malaysia and Vietnam, however, there was a tendency for state-led group membership to increase one's chances of voting. Fourth, association membership was strongly related to contact activity, regardless of the regime type. Group membership increased one's chances of contacting government officials, representatives of political parties and activists with non-governmental organizations. It is worth noting that group membership was more strongly related to contact activity than other modes of political participation. Finally, in the democracies of Indonesia and the Philippines, as well as in the non-democracies of Malaysia, Singapore and even Vietnam, group membership was related to protest activity, although protests in non-democracies were less likely to be elite-challenging. It is understandable that the relationship in Indonesia was stronger than that found in the non-democracies. Although protests are known as one of the key civil society activities in democratic transitions, group membership was more strongly linked to 'parochial participation' (for example, contacting) than to elite-challenging or even state-led protest activity.

All of these findings indicate that participation in social groups generally increases political engagement across Southeast Asia. Experiences of belonging and working together seem to provide skills, resources, and opportunities for political participation. The findings suggest that associations serve as a training ground for political action and that association membership is a reliable indicator of active citizenship. Even in non-democracies, association membership tended to encourage political activism.

The same rows in the second panel of Table 3.4 present the correlations between network involvement and political engagement. First, network involvement was related to political efficacy in three of the six countries. The relationship was especially strong in Singapore and modest in Vietnam. By contrast, in the three democracies, the relationship was either non-existent (the Philippines and Thailand) or weak (Indonesia). Second, in three of the six countries, network involvement was linked to political interest. The relationship was moderate in the Philippines and weak in Indonesia and Vietnam. Third, the relationship between network involvement and voting did not hold across much of Southeast Asia. The only exception was Thailand, where they were weakly related. Fourth, the relationship between network involvement and contact activity held consistently across Southeast Asia. Those with networks of social ties were more likely to be involved in contact activity than those without such networks. This was particularly the case in Indonesia. Finally, in three of the six countries, network involvement was linked to protest activity. The relationship was particularly strong in Indonesia and modest in the Philippines. Even in non-democratic Singapore, involvement in networks of social ties was likely to increase participation in a contentious activity.

The findings suggest that networks of social ties play a limited role in stimulating political activism across much of Southeast Asia. However, it is worth noting that they played a more prominent role in democratic Indonesia, where network involvement is high. Furthermore, the role of networks of social ties varied from one mode of political action to another. Network involvement was most likely to encourage contact activity.

In short, association membership had at best negligible effects on attitudinal attributes of democratic citizenship. In democracies and non-democracies alike, group membership rarely promoted trust in fellow citizens, citizenship norms, and support for democratic values and principles, yet group membership had notable effects on behavioural attributes of democratic citizenship, such as political interest and action. On the other hand, network involvement had limited effects on attitudinal attributes of democratic citizenship. It is noteworthy that network involvement inhibited support for democratic values and principles, but it tended to stimulate participation in contact activity. Overall, both forms of social participation socialized ordinary people into more active citizens but not into more civic-minded citizens.

Conclusion

In the last decade, there has been growing scholarly and policy interest in civil society as a key factor in improving the quality of democratic governance. In particular, society-oriented scholars drawing on the insights of Alexis de Tocqueville have emphasized the importance of associations as schools of democracy. They have conceived of civil society groups as fostering 'habits of hearts' associated with democratic citizenship. Does this neo-Tocquevillian thesis apply across Southeast Asia, where ethnic and religious segregation and the patron–client form of association still remain strong?

The findings of the present study suggest that there may be no essential connection between the density of social networks and the quality of democratic citizenship across Southeast Asia. The thesis that association membership is 'a woefully inadequate foundation' for democratic citizenship also applies to Southeast Asia (Theiss-Morse and Hibbing, 2005). The existence of high numbers of social groups may not necessarily strengthen democracy because it is not to be supposed that every social group nurtures civic and democratic orientations essential to liberal democracy (Bell, 1998). The democratic effects of associations and social networks vary depending on their structural and operational characteristics. The nature and content of group membership, which tends to vary depending on the political context, seem to matter. To adequately answer the question of why associations do not act as schools of democracy across Southeast Asia, we would need to know more than the numbers of associations or the level of association membership (Gutmann, 1998).

In conclusion, associations and social networks across much of Southeast Asia have contributed less to learning civic norms and democratic values than to acquiring resources and opportunities for political engagement. If associations have benefited democracy across Southeast Asia, it seems that they have done so not by cultivating civic virtues and democratic aspirations but by stimulating or mobilizing political activity. If associations have advanced democracy across Southeast Asia, it appears that they have done so by nurturing politically active citizens, not public-spirited citizens.

Notes

The survey data used here are drawn from the second wave of the Asian Barometer Survey (ABS). The author is grateful to Yun-han Chu, the ABS coordinator, and the Southeast Asian colleagues who conducted the surveys.

1. For instance, the 1999–2002 WVS asked if respondents were members of a social group in 14 different areas and an additional 'other' category.
2. There were cross-national differences in the perceived levels of freedom of association. The 2005–07 ABS showed that the percentage of those who agreed that people could join any organization they liked without fear was 90 per cent for Indonesia, 69 per cent for Thailand, 65 per cent for the Philippines, 71 per cent for Malaysia, 55 per cent for Vietnam and 46 per cent for Singapore.
3. Response categories were: 'never', 'seldom', 'occasionally' and 'often'.
4. It had four response categories: 'nobody', 'a few', 'some', and 'a lot'.
5. Regardless of the regime type, association membership was significantly, albeit weakly, related to network involvement in all six countries, suggesting that formal associations and networks of social ties were complementary, not competing.
6. There may be a curvilinear relationship between group membership and age, meaning that the young and the old are less likely to join social groups than the middle-aged. In fact, in Indonesia and Malaysia, group membership is most often found among people aged 40–49.
7. A respondent's number of association memberships was assigned one of three values: 0 (no membership), 1 (one membership) or 2 (two or more memberships). Level of network involvement was also assigned one of three values: 0 (low), 1 (medium) or 2 (high).
8. Social trust was measured by the following forced-choice single question: 'Would you say that most people can be trusted or that you must be careful in dealing with people?'.
9. Support for citizenship norms was measured by combining responses to the following two agree–disagree questions: (1) 'A citizen who does not actively participate in the affairs of his local and national community is not performing his duties'; and (2) 'Citizens should always obey laws and regulations, even if they disagree with them'.
10. Support for democracy was measured by combining responses to the following two forced-choice questions: (1) 'Democracy is always preferable to any other kind of government/ Under some circumstances, an authoritarian government can be preferable to a democratic one/ For people like me, it does not matter whether we have a democratic or a non-democratic regime'; and (2) 'Democracy is capable of solving the problems of our society/ Democracy cannot solve our society's problems'.
11. Support for the rule of law was measured by combining responses to the following two agree–disagree questions: (1) 'When the country is facing a difficult situation, it is OK for the government to disregard the law in order to deal with the situation'; and (2) 'The most important thing for political leaders is to accomplish their goals even if they have to ignore the established procedure'.
12. Political efficacy was measured by combining responses to the following two agree–disagree questions: (1) 'I think I have the ability to participate in politics'; and (2) 'Sometimes politics and government seems so complicated that a person like me can't really understand what is going on'.
13. Political interest was measured by combining responses to the following two questions: (1) 'How interested would you say you are in politics'; and (2) 'How often do you follow news about politics and government?'
14. Voting was measured by a single question that asked respondents whether they voted in the most recent national election.

15. Contact activity was measured by counting the number of the following things respondents had done in the past three years: (1) contacted government officials; (2) contacted elected officials or legislative representatives at any level; (3) contacted officials of political parties or other political organizations; and (4) contacted representatives of nongovernmental/civil society organizations.
16. Protest activity was measured by counting the number of the following things that respondents had done during the past three years: (1) refused to pay taxes or fees to the government; (2) met with others to raise an issue or sign a petition; and (3) attended a demonstration or protest march.

References

Alagappa, M. (ed.) (2004) *Civil Society and Political Change in Asia: Expanding and Contracting Democratic Space* (Stanford: Stanford University Press).

Almond, G. A. and Verba, S. (1963) *The Civic Culture* (Princeton: Princeton University Press).

Aspinall, E. (2004) 'Indonesia: Transformation of Civil Society and Democratic Breakthrough', in Alagappa, A. (ed.), *Civil Society and Political Change in Asia: Expanding and Contracting Democratic Space* (Stanford: Stanford University Press).

Ayala, L. J. (2000) 'Trained for Democracy: The Differing Effects of Voluntary and Involuntary Organizations on Political Participation', *Political Research Quarterly*, 53 (1): 99–115.

Bell, D. A. (1998) 'Civil Society versus Civic Virtue', in Gutmann, A. (ed.), *Freedom of Association* (Princeton: Princeton University Press).

Curtis, J., Baer, D.E. and Grabb, E.G. (2001) 'Nations of Joiners: Explaining Voluntary Association Membership in Democratic Societies', *American Sociological Review*, 66 (5): 783–805.

Dalton, R.J. (2006) 'Civil Society, Social Capital, and Democracy', in Dalton, D.J. and Shin, D.C. (eds), *Citizens, Democracy, and Markets around the Pacific Rim: Congruence Theory and Political Culture* (New York: Oxford University Press).

Diamond, L. (1999) *Developing Democracy: Toward Consolidation* (Baltimore: The Johns Hopkins University Press).

Franco, J.C. (2004) 'The Philippines: Fractious Civil Society and Competing Visions of Democracy', in Alagappa, A. (ed.) *Civil Society and Political Change in Asia: Expanding and Contracting Democratic Space* (Stanford: Stanford University Press).

Fung, A. (2003) 'Associations and Democracy: Between Theories, Hopes, and Realities', *Annual Review of Sociology*, 29: 515–539.

Gutmann, A. (1998) 'Freedom of Association: An Introductory Essay', in Gutmann, A. (ed.), *Freedom of Association* (Princeton: Princeton University Press).

Iglič, H. and Fábregas, F.N. (2007) 'Social networks', in van Detz, J.W., Montero, J.R. and Westholm, A. (eds) *Citizenship and Involvement in European Democracy: A Comparative Analysis* (London: Routledge).

Kadir, S. (2004) 'Singapore: Engagement and Autonomy within the Political Status Quo', in Alagappa, A. (ed.) *Civil Society and Political Change in Asia: Expanding and Contracting Democratic Space* (Stanford: Stanford University Press).

Karatnycky, A. and Ackerman, P. (2005) *How Freedom is Won: From Civic Resistance to Durable Democracy*, www.freedomhouse.org.

Lande, C.H. (1973) 'Networks and Groups in Southeast Asia: Some Observations on the Group Theory of Politics', *American Political Science Review*, 67 (1): 103–127.

Lockhart, G. (1997) 'Mass Mobilization in Contemporary Vietnam', *Asian Studies Review*, 21 (2/3): 174–179.

Maloney, W.A. and Rossteutscher, S. (eds) (2007) *Social Capital and Associations in European Democracies: A Comparative Analysis* (London: Routledge).

Newton, K. (1999) 'Social Capital and Democracy in Modern Europe', in van Deth, J.W., Maraffi, M., Newton, K. and Whiteley, P. (eds), *Social Capital and European Democracy* (London: Routledge).

Putnam, R. D. (1993) *Making Democracy Work* (Princeton: Princeton University Press).

Putnam, R.D. (2000) *Bowling Alone: The Collapse and Revival of American Community* (New York: Simon and Schuster).

Scott, J.C. (1972) 'Patron-Client Politics and Political Change in Southeast Asia', *American Political Science Review*, 66 (1): 91–113.

Stolle, D. and Rochon, T.R. (2001) 'Are All Associations Alike: Member Diversity, Associational Type and the Creation of Social Capital', in Edwards, B., Foley, M.W. and Diani, M. (eds), *Beyond Tocqueville: Civil Society and the Social Capital Debate in Comparative Perspective* (Hanover: Tufts University).

Theiss-Morse, E. and Hibbing, J.R. (2005) 'Citizenship and Civic Engagement', *Annual Review of Political Science*, 8: 227–249.

Tocqueville, A. de (1969) *Democracy in America* (Garden City: Doubleday Press).

Verba, S., Lehman Schlozman, K. and Brady, H.E. (1995) *Voice and Equality: Civic Voluntarism in American Politics* (Cambridge: Harvard University Press).

Warren, M. E. (2001) *Democracy and Association* (Princeton: Princeton University Press).

Weiss, M. (2004) 'Malaysia: Construction of Counterhegemonic Narratives and Agendas', in Alagappa, A. (ed.), *Civil Society and Political Change in Asia: Expanding and Contracting Democratic Space* (Stanford: Stanford University Press).

Wuthnow, R. (2002) 'Religious Involvement and Status-Bridging Social Capital', *Journal for the Scientific Study of Religion*, 41 (4): 669–684.

4
Moore Meets Gramsci and Burke in Southeast Asia: New Democracies and 'Civil' Societies

Mark R. Thompson

Introduction

In a recent article, John Sidel argues that Barrington Moore's class-based theory of democratization helps explain the pattern of democratic transitions and non-transitions in Southeast Asia (Sidel, 2008; Moore, 1966; also see Croissant, 2008, and Thompson, 2007).[1] Sidel suggests that Moore's thesis about a 'vigorous' and 'independent' bourgeoisie is crucial to understand whether social conditions are favourable for democratization. In a region where business is often dominated by ethnic Chinese, the extent of their integration into larger society becomes a key structural variable. The better integrated the ethnic Chinese, the greater the chances for a democratic transition.

Sidel suggests that both 'plural society' and assimilationist patterns arose in reaction to a wave of Chinese immigration to Southeast Asia in the nineteenth century. In those places where the ethnic Chinese have historically become quickly assimilated (primarily through Chinese men marrying 'native' women), and thus no longer ethnically distinguishable, a largely 'Chinese' business class has been capable of pushing for democracy. This is closest to the experience of the Philippines and Thailand, where big business played a major role in democratization in 1986 and 1992 respectively, as Sidel's thesis would predict. But in those places where a Chinese-dominated bourgeoisie was seen as an alien, 'pariah' group, it proved incapable of, or was reluctant to, challenge the state, as it already faced a hostile population. This argument seems most plausible when applied to Malaysia. Despite widespread pro-democracy protests in 1998, the Mahathir regime was able to consolidate its hold on power in the 1999 elections, largely by appealing to the fears of Chinese voters towards an opposition supposedly dominated by radical Malay Islamists, who were portrayed as hostile to Chinese interests.

Yet despite the similar 'pariah' status of its own ethnic Chinese business people, Indonesia *did* democratize, beginning in 1998 (with students and traditional Islamic as well as secular-oriented parties playing a leading role in protests that encouraged the military and ruling party Golkar to turn against Suharto and his family imperium). Even if the Indonesian case cannot be said to falsify the Moorean view of democratization (Sidel, 2008, offers an ad hoc explanation of the transition there), it does at least pose some awkward questions about it.

It is beyond the scope of this chapter to offer an alternative explanation of democratic transitions in East and Southeast Asia.[2] Rather, I want to argue that Sidel's Moorean approach provides a useful starting point for understanding the different possibilities for democratic consolidation in Southeast Asia, but I will also suggest that it is the *inverse* of Moore's thesis that holds: the stronger the bourgeoisie, the *less* the likelihood that democracy will consolidate. The 'independent' and 'vigorous' bourgeoisie of the Philippines and Thailand has had a destabilizing impact on democratic politics. In Indonesia, where the bourgeoisie is politically weaker, democracy has become more stable.

This may seem counter-intuitive until we consider the insights of another great thinker in the realm of bourgeois politics, Antonio Gramsci. Gramsci famously argued that elite groups make universalistic claims in defence of their own hegemony (Gramsci, 1971; Hedman, 2006). I will argue that big business-dominated civil society in the Philippines and Thailand is unstable given the fragility of vertical clientelist ties and the ability of populists to mobilize poor voters along horizontal, class lines. After overthrowing unpopular dictatorships, 'civil' society later mobilized against elected leaders in an effort to restore their hegemony in the Gramscian sense. In Indonesia, by contrast, traditional socio-religious cleavages hindered the rise of populism but also limited the base of support for an urban-based civil society, a combination which has helped stabilize democracy there. I term this kind of civil society, which is traditionally-oriented and lacking in strong bourgeois impulses, Burkean. The next part of this chapter offers some general thoughts on how 'civil society' can best be understood for the purposes of this argument.

Civil society and strategic groups

In Robert Putnam's influential book *Making Democracy Work* (1993), he argued that the 'density' of civil society associations is key to understanding how stable a democracy is likely to be. 'Civicness', or a sense of civic community which can be called 'civil society,' is based on a 'dense network of secondary associations' (Putnam, 1993, p.376). This is not the place to rehearse the many critiques of Putnam's work (one of my favourites is found in the introduction to Hefner, 1998). The point I wish to take up here is that Putnam's concept is curiously apolitical. How, exactly, do secondary associations relate to democratic stability? To use one of his most famous examples from the US, how do bowling leagues (often associated with sexism and racism!) strengthen democracy? We could push the example even farther and ask how Putnam would try to exclude the 'sense of community' in the Ku Klux Klan from his definition of 'civicness'.

This problem led Juan J. Linz and Alfred Stepan (1996) to distinguish 'civil' from 'political' society. In the Malaysian context, Meredith Weiss has argued that we should concentrate on the 'politicized portions of civil society' if we are to understand recent political change there. 'Politicized' civil society requires more than just 'social capital' (which Putnam often uses as a synonym for civil society); it requires 'coalitional capital'. While 'social capital bonds individuals, coalitional capital bridges collectivities,' she concludes (Weiss, 2005, p.5). A study of civil society in Thailand brings up an additional point: politically active civil society is largely 'elite' civil society; the associations that 'ordinary people' belong to are less likely to have an impact on national political developments (Albritton and Thawilwadee, 2002, pp.6–7).

When focusing on politicized, coalition-building elite civil society, it is helpful to distinguish key 'strategic groups' to offer a more differentiated, less homogenized perspective. These can be defined – in the tradition of the so-called 'Bielefeld approach' in developmental sociology – as 'collective actors striving for a share of power in society' (Berner, 2001).[3] These groups can neither be 'read' off the social structure, nor are they the result of individuals arbitrarily deciding to join forces. To use the example discussed above, whether capitalists become a strategic group in terms of political influence depends upon the (assimilationist or segregationist) social context. 'Strategic groups' is a mid-range theory that analyzes how certain organized networks of collective actors form within a particular societal framework. Rather than assuming a homogenous 'ruling class', the focus is on diversified 'leadership groups', to use Anthony Giddens's term (1983, p.119). In developing societies, subaltern groups are usually incapable of striving systematically to promote their interests because they often remain 'quasi-groups', unable to act collectively in a long-term, planned and strategic sense. They often have a 'hidden transcript' of resistance that has to be disguised in order to avoid repression by the powerful (Scott, 1990). But subalterns tend to lack the communication channels, media influence and political connections necessary to get their 'voices heard' more openly. They also do not possess a resource – material or ideal – that they can control or appropriate as the basis for making power claims. Among the 'classic' elite strategic groups, big business controls capital (other groups such as landowners and traders possess other forms of property); professionals strive for mastery of knowledge, qualifications and information; religious groups attempt to shape popular beliefs; and the military and police claim a monopoly on the legitimate use of violence (Berner, 2001). With their various resource bases, strategic groups – alone or in coalitions with others –vie with other actors and alliances for political power, economic influence and cultural hegemony.

When specifying the strategic groups that are competing for authority in politicized civil society, it is important to avoid romanticizing their actions. In a recent comparative study of civil society in Pacific Asia, Muthiah Alagappa has concluded that there is no necessary connection between civil society and democratic change. 'Civil society organizations have both expanded and contracted democratic space.... (F)requent resort to mass protest, especially massive demonstrations, legitimizes street politics and encourages politics by protest and referendum. Such actions circumvent parliamentary politics and do unintended harm' (Alagappa, 2004, pp.xi, 491). Alagappa has made the important point here that civil society can be 'uncivil' (for an elaboration of this argument, see Keane, 2004). It can turn from a pro-democratic force against dictatorship to one whose mobilization undermines electoral democracy. How *civil* post-transitional 'civil society' is, is a question in search of a comparative explanation. In short, 'civil society' can be understood in terms of the dominant, and elitist, strategic groups that struggle for control of political society and which may or may not be supportive of democracy.

Gramscian 'uncivil' society in the Philippines and Thailand

When viewing 'big business' as a strategic group, it is helpful to distinguish between the national urban bourgeoisie and provincial businessmen. As in the Philippines, Thai businessmen-politicians have often been accused of 'bossism': using money and violence to intimidate opponents, particularly in elections (Ockey, 2004). They remain largely untouched by the 'good government' discourse internalized by the urban bourgeoisie. Initially, urban business elites had strongly supported authoritarian regimes that legitimated themselves with developmental claims of 'good governance'. But urban business elites in the Philippines and Thailand turned against authoritarian developmentalist regimes in 1986 and 1992 respectively. This was less out of democratic conviction and more because of what they saw as authoritarian betrayal through neopatrimonial behaviour. The failures of the developmentalist project due to Marcos's cronyism, as well as the nepotism of the 'three tyrants' military regime (toppled in 1973) and the Suchinda military regime's corrupt money politics in 1992, led urban elites – supported by the small but growing middle class – to turn against these dictatorships.

In the Philippines, urban big business supported anti-Marcos protests materially and ideologically. They were allied in this opposition to dictatorship with the major traditionalist elite – the hierarchy of the Catholic church, most notably the Archbishop of Manila, Cardinal Jaime Sin

(Thompson, 1995, chapter 5). This alliance was formally embodied in the 'Bishops–Businessmen's Conference' organization, which coordinated oppositional efforts against the Marcos regime. 'Cause-oriented group' activists (who only called themselves 'civil society organizations' in the post-Marcos period) of various ideological shades, including those closely linked with the Communist Party of the Philippines, also played a major role in the struggle against authoritarianism (David, 2008). But after intense manoeuvring within the opposition, the mainstream broke away from the communist-lined 'national democratic forces', marginalizing them during 'people power'. The makeup of these 'middle forces' that played a major role in Corazon Aquino's election campaign against Marcos and were at the forefront of the popular uprising that followed the stolen election was very 'bourgeois', with rich businessmen and upper-class professionals dominant in the leadership (Thompson, 1995, chapter 6).

In Thailand, there was less need of the urban elite's material support (as protests were of shorter duration) than of their moral condemnation of the military regime that had shot not just at workers but also at protesting students, professionals and businessmen in the 'Black May' events of 1992. This led to outrage similar to that following the Aquino assassination in the Philippines. The 'mobile phone' mafia – as bourgeois forces were known during the uprising – was thus a crucial aspect to its success. Support for the protests from the monarchy was not initially forthcoming as the king apparently strongly backed the Suchinda military government (Handley, 2006). This pattern of royal endorsement of military rule (which had begun in the late 1950s) repeated itself with the king's endorsement of the 2006 coup against Thaksin (Hewison, 2007). Nonetheless, the king's belated intervention (after about a hundred protesters had been killed by the military) was crucial in bringing about re-democratization, with the military regime surrendering power and agreeing to new elections. As in the Philippines, an alliance of bourgeois and traditionalist strategic groups played a leading role in people power in Thailand.

But rather than promoting compromise, 'revolutionary' democratization in Manila and Bangkok against failed developmentalist regimes increased elite conflict. Weak democratic reformist governments, the prevalence of money politics, and the rise of populist leaders led business elites in both countries to turn the 'good governance' discourse against democratically elected leaders, destabilizing democracy there (Thompson, 2007). After the failure of weak reformist leaders, Corazon C. Aquino in the Philippines and Chuan Leekpai in Thailand, the democratic transition period in both countries was dominated by provincial politicians practising 'money politics' (known as 'bossism' in the Philippines and dubbed *jao pho*, or 'godfathers', in Thailand). Disillusioned, the urban bourgeois elite and its middle-class allies demobilized. They returned to the streets only after national corruption scandals by populist leaders violated their norms of political propriety.

The corrosion of the party system through money politics gave 'business populists' (Pasuk and Baker, 2005) in both countries a window of opportunity for overturning existing political structures. Though very different characters – Thaksin Shinawatra was his country's leading entrepreneur and Joseph Estrada was a famous tough-guy actor – these would-be populists shared much in common. They had both been encouraged by 'civil society'-oriented NGO activists to make appeals to poor, particularly rural, voters disadvantaged by the highly unequal levels of development in the cities and the countryside. This strategy was wildly successful, with both candidates winning landslide electoral victories against old-style politicians and thereby dramatically changing the political landscape. The key to their success lay in both circumventing traditional clientelist networks (through direct, media-made populist appeals) and centralizing them (attracting politicians to join them based on their charismatic hold on voters, as well as the money they could contribute to politicians' election campaigns). They were rent-seeking populists who themselves had become rich through state connections (Thaksin's cosy telecommunication contracts) or whose closest associates had done so (Estrada's chief financier, Eduardo Cojuangco, had made his fortune as a Marcos crony). Thaksin did help the poor (particularly through cheap credit and health care; on the latter see Kannika and Melnick, 2009), while Estrada did little for the impoverished masses in the Philippines during his short time in office. But both remained popular among the poor, even as they tarnished their reputations among elites by using state power for financial gain.

Disillusioned, NGO activists turned against the populists they had once supported. They were backed by capitalists who felt disadvantaged by the regime's self-interested entrepreneurship. Revelations by close friends-turned-enemies and major financial scandals were the triggers that led to renewed mobilization by student and NGO activists, backed by much of the big business community and by religious and moral figures such as Corazon C. Aquino and Chamlong Srimuang respectively. Once employed against dictators, the discourse of 'good governance' now came to be directed against democratically elected leaders by politically less well-connected big business leaders, elite moral guardians and their middle-class supporters.

Eva-Lotta E. Hedman (2006) has argued that such mobilization can best be understood in Gramscian terms as an attempt by a threatened elite to restore its hegemony. Challenged by populist politicians representing poor voters, urban business and NGO activist elites resorted to extra-constitutional measures to regain their predominance in the political system. Unable to win in the electoral arena, the urban bourgeois elite instead used their insurrectionary prowess and military support. Despite apparent differences (Estrada was overthrown by popular protests, Thaksin by military revolt), both regime changes essentially involved a 'people power *putsch*' of urban elites backed by military muscle against populists who had won elections largely through the support of the rural poor. It was 'People Power

II', or 'Edsa Dos', that led to the overthrow of Estrada in the Philippines in January 2001, while in Thailand there was a military coup against Thaksin in September 2006. But the role of the military in the Philippines should not be underestimated, as it was the military hierarchy's withdrawal of support that led Estrada to yield. In Thailand, a military coup would have been much more difficult, if not impossible, to launch and justify without the months of popular protest against Thaksin that preceded it.

But the restoration of 'bourgeois' rule has not brought stability to either country. In the Philippines, Gloria Macapagal-Arroyo's presidency (from early 2001 until she is slated to step down in 2010) combined neo-traditional politics with macroeconomic technocratic reforms that accelerated economic growth (at least up until the current financial crisis), with high levels of corruption (revealed in numerous scandals), and with intimidation of oppositionists (killings of leftists, kidnappings of whistle blowers). She used media appeals (her vice presidential candidate in 2004 was a famous broadcaster) along with blatant electoral fraud to fend off another populist challenge (from an even more popular movie-actor-turned-politician, the late Fernando Poe, Jr.), but the price has been an enormous 'legitimacy crisis' (Teekankee, 2006). This has resulted in the 'Arroyo Imbroglio' (Hutchcroft, 2008) that Philippine politics has been caught up in since 2005. An unpopular president has clung to power through tight control of the military hierarchy, distribution of political patronage and intimidation of leftist opponents. Several half-hearted attempts by big business, church and NGO leaders to launch another round of people power have been fiascos. The military hierarchy strongly supports the regime, while the Catholic bishops and many top business people remain ambivalent, fearing a return to populism (a fear that Estrada's strong poll ratings for the upcoming 2010 presidential elections shows may not be unfounded). In addition, a series of sex scandals in the Catholic church has weakened its moral standing (Abinales and Amorosa, 2006). Business, profiting from rapid growth (at least until the recent financial crisis), has had little incentive to fill this void.

In Thailand, the coup government and the 'tank' intellectuals supporting it were criticized for having launched a 'coup for the rich' (Ungpakorn, 2007). Military rule was weak and incompetent, leaving new elections as the only way out. After Thaksin Shinawatra's *Thai Rak Thai* (Thais Love Thais, or TRT) party was banned by the military, a successor party, the People Power Party (PPP), swept the December 2007 polls called by the retreating generals. Thaksinites quickly formed a ruling coalition in early 2008. But in late May 2008, the People's Alliance for Democracy (PAD) revived protests (from 2006) against the new pro-Thaksin government. The PAD began daily protests broadcast live continuously on satellite TV, radio and the Internet, a 'grotesque mix of reality show and a political campaign', as Kasian Techapira has aptly described it (2008). When PAD protests failed to remove the PPP government during the summer of 2008, the group resorted to more radical action at the end of August, seizing the main government compound after failing to occupy the National Broadcasting television station (in order to expand their media coverage). In late November, they won global notoriety by seizing the country's two international airports in Bangkok and occupying them for several weeks during the height of the tourist season. But it was not only the PAD's tactics which had been radicalized; they abandoned any pretence of protesting to 'save' democracy, as they had claimed to do in their earlier campaign against Thaksin. They launched a nationalist campaign around a temple at the centre of a dispute with Cambodia in order to embarrass the foreign minister, Thaksin's former lawyer, and to link the issue to Thaksin himself, whom they accused of selling out Thai interests as part of his Cambodian investments (their agitation nearly prompted a border war between the two countries). More generally, they called for a sweeping 'new politics'. This would involve an undemocratic restructuring of the political order, with 70 per cent of the seats in parliament to be appointed. Sondhi Limthongku, the PAD's most well-known leader, has openly and repeatedly said that 'representative democracy is not suitable for Thailand'. Thaksin and his allies' electoral support has remained so solid that the PAD was proposing changing the rules so as to eliminate them from the political game altogether.

Prominent business leaders appeared at PAD rallies. As one commentator has pointed out, it is revealing that leading business associations protested against the proclamation of a state of emergency by the pro-Thaksin government but not against the violent invasion of the Government House by the PAD that prompted it (Noi, 2008). The business-oriented *The Nation* (16 September 2008) wrote that PPP's populist policies were viewed 'as a waste of public money for the ruling party's short-term political popularity' and have 'reinforced fears of poor governance and unfair business treatment. This is why businesses continued to channel funds to protesters, keeping the PAD's support base strong.' Even the risk of short-term economic pain caused by the stand-off seemed worth the price to these business leaders hoping to end the cronyism, favouritism, and corruption they associate with Thaksin and the successor governments linked to him.

But the PAD has also received crucial support from factions within the military and from royalists.[4] Although the military appears divided between Thaksin and PAD factions – and reluctant to intervene again directly after the ill-fated coup of 2006 – one faction of the military close to the president of the privy council, Prem Tinsulanonda, was supportive of the protests. In an interview, Sondhi said the PAD's 'new politics' needs to be put in place before a royal succession takes place (at the time of writing, the present king is 81 and ailing). Prominent socialites and lesser members of the royal family dubbed 'the Blue Blood Jet Set' have been active in the PAD protests. This informal alliance of supporters within the military, bureaucracy and 'civil society' is characteristic of what Duncan McCargo terms the 'network monarchy' (2005).

In the end, the PAD and its supporters had to settle for a Democrat-led coalition government formed in December 2008, which formally abides by parliamentary rules even though its origins lay in a kind of judicial coup that dissolved the pro-Thaksin government and in the rumours of military and royal intervention that accompanied its formation. Like the Arroyo government in the Philippines, the new Democrat-led Thai government has not hesitated to resort to patronage politics to cement support for its new coalition, even while it was claiming to be reformist in orientation. The government has even pledged to continue with Thaksin-style subventionary populist policies; this was seen by bourgeois-traditionalist elites to be much preferable to another Thaksin-influenced government with its strong appeals to the rural poor, particularly in the north and northeast of the country. But the populist spell that Thaksin had cast over Thai politics had not been broken, as all too clearly demonstrated by the 'red shirt' (pro-Thaksin) unrest in Pattaya during a major Association of Southeast Asian Nations (ASEAN) summit, and by rioting in Bangkok in April 2009 (Montesano, 2009). For now, Thaksin and his remaining supporters (key defections from his camp had allowed the Democrats to form a government) have been driven from power by elite manipulation, much as Estrada and Poe had been overthrown or cheated in elections in the Philippines. But when the Democrat government is forced to hold elections, the Thaksin challenge may well re-emerge, as suggested by the loss of a crucial by-election in June 2009 by the Democrat-allied Bhum Jai Thai party in Sakon Nakhon to the pro-Thaksin Puea Thai party. One Thai political scientist called this the 'nightmare' of the Democrat-led coalition because it showed that Thaksin's popular support remained strong despite the massive government resources used in the campaign (quoted in Golingai, 2009). Estrada's re-emergence as a strong candidate in the Philippine presidential race (at the time of writing) – despite being previously deposed from office and convicted of corruption – shows just how strong the populist challenge also remains in the Philippines (Conde, 2009).

The root cause of political conflict in both countries remains the tension between urban big business backed by the middle class and poor, predominantly rural, voters mobilized by populists in alliance with provincial politicians. The refusal of many urban elites to accept the verdict of the poor electoral majority underlies uncivil society in Thailand and the Philippines. Protests 'in the name of civil society' have aimed at restoring 'bourgeois hegemony' in Gramscian terminology (Hedman, 2006).

'Burkean' civil society in Indonesia

Strategic group formation in Indonesia stands in stark contrast to that in the Philippines and Thailand. Given their 'alien' status, the ethnic Chinese were 'in but not of' what J.S. Furnivall (1948) famously characterized as 'plural societies', in which different ethnic groups 'mix but do not combine'. Indonesian communalism, though not as extensive as in Malaysia, also inhibited the development of a civil society led by big business. The predominantly ethnic Chinese capitalist class was subject to overt and covert discrimination under Dutch colonial rule and after independence. Stigmatized and segregated from the Muslim majority, several large Chinese business groups had a symbiotic relationship with Suharto during his long dictatorship but were at the mercy of the vagaries of his changing goals and perceived interests. Although the regime claimed to promote the growth of an 'indigenous' *pribumi* capitalist class (roughly parallel to pro-Malay affirmative action in Malaysia), Suharto often turned to *cukong* (large Chinese conglomerates) when engaged in the secretive deals that lay behind his rapidly growing 'family business' in his increasingly patrimonialized rule. A major source of popular resentment, the conspicuous wealth of key figures in the Chinese community made this minority a convenient scapegoat when the regime faced popular opposition. Suharto often instrumentalized anti-Chinese feelings by tolerating periodic pogrom-like attacks on ethnic Chinese (Sidel, 2006).

Despite its lack of support from big business, the *reformasi* opposition move-ment in Indonesia succeeded in triggering Suharto's removal from power in 1998. As in the case of the Marcos regime, the Suharto regime split under the pressure of economic crisis, with a politicized military and an increasingly unruly ruling party pushing a liberalization agenda as part of its efforts to weaken the patrimonialist core of the regime. During Suharto's long rule, fault-lines had developed between the president and his family, the 'military as institution,' and the civilian politicians in the ruling *Golkar* party. The increasing patrimonialism of the Suharto clique eventually alienated the lat-ter two groups. Both the military and Golkar leadership used the protests as a pretext to turn on Suharto and force him to resign (Aspinall, 2005).

In addition, a religious-based traditionalist strategic group emerged in Indonesia, playing a role roughly similar to that of the Catholic church in the anti-Marcos struggle in the Philippines. These 'religious virtuosos', to use Max Weber's term (1903/04), invoked religious symbols to undermine the regime's 'moral capital' (Kane, 2001), thereby jeopardizing its legitimacy. In doing so, they also thwarted Suharto's efforts to co-opt Islamic leaders in the 1990s by founding the Indonesian Association of Muslim Intellectuals, *Ikatan Cendekiawan Muslim Indonesia*, or ICMI (in which Suharto's future successor, B. J. Habibie, played the lead role). Unlike in Malaysia, where some factions of the Islamist Parti Islam Se-Malaysia (PAS) opposition party had radicalized, key Islamic groups in Indonesia were characterized by their advocacy of 'civil Islam' (Hefner, 2000; Uhlin, 1997; for a more optimistic view of PAS, see Case and Liew, 2006). The significance of traditionalist Muslim groups should not lead one to overlook the role of the national-ist tradition in Indonesian politics. This is symbolized by the former presi-dent Sukarno, whose legacy has been carried on by his daughter, Megawati Sukarnoputri, in the Indonesian Democratic Party (PDI, or officially PDI-P)

(Gerlach, forthcoming). Both national secularists and Muslim traditionalists provided invaluable support to student activists, the key strategic group behind the anti-Suharto protests (Aspinall, 2005, Chapter 5).

Without the backing of big business, student activists were not able to put as much pressure on the regime as was the case in the Philippines and Thailand, where as we have seen above, the 'bourgeois' forces dominated the opposition. The Suharto regime did not fall to an opposition onslaught; rather, reformist elements in the military seized the opportunity provided by the protests to launch an internal coup to eliminate Suharto, weaken his personal following within the military (led by his former son-in-law) and put his vice president, Habibie, into power.

In Indonesia, a populist, anti-system challenge has not emerged despite a middle class proportionately smaller than in the Philippines and Thailand. Cross-cutting traditional cultural–religious cleavages (known as *aliran*, or 'streams' in Indonesian) limit the potential of class-based populist appeals. Politics in Indonesia remains more 'traditional' and less 'bourgeois' than in the Philippines and Thailand. Indonesian parties are embedded in particular milieus where differences between nominal, secular nationalists and religious Muslims – and among the latter, differences between 'traditionalist' and 'modernist' identities – are crucial. These ethno-identities make poor Indonesian voters less vulnerable to the temptations of political patronage than their counterparts in the Philippines and Thailand. Some scholars suggest that these traditional *aliran* cleavages provide the key to understanding voting behaviour in post-Suharto Indonesia (King, 2003), while others have argued that personality politics have become more important (Liddle and Mujani, 2007). Andreas Ufen (2008) takes a middle position, suggesting that although 'Philippinization' has been increasing in Indonesian politics given the lack of clear party platforms and personalized leadership, *aliran* identities continue to significantly influence voting behaviour (Ufen, 2008).

The legislative and presidential election results from 2009 suggested that the process of *dealinarisi*, dealignment in terms of traditional cleavages, is accelerating (Sherlock, 2009). In particular, the way current president Susilo Bambang Yudhoyono was able to dominate both legislative and presidential elections suggested that the country's politics was becoming increasingly personalized. Yet, viewed *comparatively*, cultural cleavages that cross-cut class differences remain much more significant than in the Philippines and Thailand. Mietzner (2009, p.20) argues that it appears evident that Yudhoyono's emergence in 2004 was a political exception rather than a signal for the 'Philippinization' of the Indonesian party system and the decline of its socially rooted parties, '[which] have a good chance of regaining ground in the next few years'. This process is set to further stabilize Indonesia's party system, which is already much more institutionalized and socially rooted than its counterparts in other Asian democracies.

Yudhoyono has attempted to combat corruption, in part as an effort to head off an Islamist-based, populist electoral challenge. In the 2004 national elections and the 2005 local elections, the Islamist New Justice Party (PKS) performed much better than expected. Its new-found electoral strength derived from promises to combat corruption by implementing elements of Islamic law. But the party fell short of its ambitious electoral goals in the 2009 elections. In fact, it was the incumbent himself, known by his initials, SBY, who adopted a partial populist strategy, using Thaksin-style handouts to the poor (Mietzner, 2009). But here, too, there was an important difference: while this populist strategy contributed to Yudhoyono's electoral victories in 2009, it did not destroy the party system as Thaksin's electoral tsunami did in the 2001 and 2005 elections (Ufen, 2008). The continued strength of the *aliran* cleavages in Indonesia suggests that the appeals of the populist strategy will remain limited and unlikely to overturn the prevailing political system as Estrada and Thaksin succeeded in doing in the Philippines and Thailand respectively, with class-based populist appeals.

In addition, the political passivity of much of the predominantly ethnic Chinese Indonesian bourgeoisie helps explain why 'civil society' remains relatively inactive there despite a series of high-level corruption scandals. This makes it much more difficult to mobilize protests in the name of 'good governance'. Despite a series of corruption scandals, there have been few major protests since the demobilization of student activists in the first years of the transition.

It is revealing that the impeachment and removal of President Abdurrahman Wahid in 2001 after a major corruption scandal was accomplished through institutional channels, not as the result of major protests. A feared counter-mobilization of Wahid's supporters in Jakarta did not occur either (though there were pro-Wahid protests in his East Java stronghold). This appears to reflect the fact that in addition to supporting the parties linked to them through social networks, civil society activists operating within the nationalist and Islamist *'aliran'* framework have avoided staging frequent demonstrations in Jakarta in favour of concentrating on building up their local and regional associations.

Many of these organizational efforts have involved efforts to implement *sharia* law, thus raising questions about how democratic they really are. Robert Hefner (2010) has argued that in Indonesia, 'conditions that might favor democratic and human-rights-friendly interpretations of the *shari'a*' have often emerged'. He adds that such localized interpretations of human rights have proved to be largely compatible with democracy in the Indonesian context. 'Rather than being a deformation of the democratic process, this localization testifies to the inevitable and necessary accommodation of democratic and human-rights schemes to different sociocultural landscapes' (ibid.).

Civil society in Indonesia can be seen as primarily 'Burkean' in that its dominant traditionalist groups have conservative goals, aiming to strengthen their 'intermediate associations' and not engage in a revolutionary overhaul of society. In his famous polemic against the French revolution, Burke (1790) argued against sweeping transformations of society (including the elimination of what he called 'secondary institutions' such as religious groups and political parties). He instead suggested that incremental change is undertaken largely *through* such religious, party or other such institutions. Burke's philosophy involved respecting tradition and association when implementing individual rights. This distinguished Burke's views from those of 'liberal individualism'. Long-standing community norms needed to be respected despite the right of the individual to liberty. Traditions, particularly religious traditions, are collective wisdom collected over the ages and thus should be accorded due deference by would-be reformists.

These late eighteenth-century views of a British conservative correspond closely to those of religiously-oriented civil society activists in Indonesia and other predominantly Muslim countries. More generally, even where democratic views prevail, we are likely to see significant public support for the 'un-liberal' idea that religious ethics are not purely private matters, and the state should not be neutral on the promotion of the public good, not least of all as it relates to Islam. In terms of public culture, religion and state, the Muslim world's emerging democracies are likely to be *religious* democracies. Of course, the idea of non-secular democracy alarms some proponents of human rights schemes and Western liberal democracy. However, rather than contradicting democracy, the accommodation reached in such a Muslim polity is better understood as a consequence of the deepening reach of democratization into Muslim societies (Hefner, 2010).

Conclusion

To paraphrase Marcellus in *Hamlet*, there is something rotten in the state of democracy in the Philippines and Thailand. Both have had people power-style uprisings against *elected* governments (2001 in the Philippines and 2006/2008 in Thailand). In Thailand the result was a full-scale coup in 2006 and a 'slow motion' coup in 2008; in the Philippines the military-backed civilian takeover can be viewed as a 'people power *putsch*'. Elections have been marred by charges of manipulation (the Philippines in 2004) or electoral results ignored by an insurrectionist opposition (Thailand in 2008). The Freedom House survey (Freedom House 2007) has recently downgraded both countries to the status of 'partly free' (though in fact, Thailand has improved from its 'not free' status under military rule 2006–07).

In Indonesia, by contrast, there has been no major extra-constitutional threat to the government. (One president was removed constitutionally; violence during and after Suharto's fall never threatened the country's democracy directly.) Elections have been free and fair, leading to an opposition victory at the presidential and parliamentary levels in 2004. Based on this consistent constitutionalism and Huntington's (1991) 'two turnover test', it can even be argued that Indonesian democracy deserves to be classified as consolidated.[5] Such a claim is controversial and shared by few Indonesianists, who, typical of country specialists, tend to focus on problems rather than on comparative strengths. Obviously, there are many weaknesses in Indonesian democracy, particularly in terms of government efficiency (corruption) and collusion among elites (Slater, 2004). Despite this persistent patrimonialism, though, the country's democratic system has remained remarkably stable (Webber, 2006).

Democratic stability in Indonesia is quite recent (Freedom House has only rated the country as 'free' since 2006), and critics claim it is still too early to tell whether it is enjoying more than short-term stability. The early years of the Indonesian transition were plagued by massive violence (Bertrand, 2004; Sidel, 2006; van Klinken, 2007); but as Bertrand (2004) and van Klinken (2007) convincingly show, this violence was closely related to the problems of the transition itself (for a more pessimistic view, see Hadiwinata, 2009). Now that these have been (at least partially) resolved, it can be hypothesized that further major outbreaks of violence are unlikely. Moreover, Sidel (2006) argues that violence was a reaction employed by the 'losers' in intra-elite power struggles (for instance, violence against Chinese was encouraged by elements of the endangered Suharto regime; Islamist terror was a reaction to the failure of extremist Muslim parties in elections). Perhaps most significantly, the military has largely withdrawn from politics, even if further internal reforms remain necessary.

A modified Moorean approach provides a more nuanced, thickly descriptive explanation of how democracies are actually performing in Pacific Asia than one which merely equates stable democracy with a strong bourgeoisie. Inverting Moore's thesis, it was shown that in the 'bourgeois polities' of the Philippines and Thailand, an alliance of urban big business and traditionalist strategic groups resorted to extra-constitutional mobilization to topple populists who, allied with provincial politicians, had used class appeals to win elections. The argument advanced to explain this undemocratic behaviour was Gramscian in nature: that civil society tends to turn against democracy when the major cleavage is 'class', which is characteristic of the 'bourgeois' societies of the Philippines and Thailand.

In the Indonesian case it was suggested that civil society was not 'Gramscian', as the bourgeoisie was weaker due to the 'pariah' status of ethnic Chinese and because the country's elites did not face a strong populist threat as in Thailand or the Philippines. Rather, a second model of civil society emerged in this Southeast Asian archipelago – that of 'Burkean' civil society. Civil society there is dominated by traditional nationalist and Muslim elites who have pursued largely conservative goals, both through elections (in parties linked to their social milieu) and local organizing (in which they use the freedoms of democracy to attempt to implement their traditionalist agendas). Traditionalist-dominated civil society in Indonesia has been largely supportive of democracy (as Burke would have expected), while civil society in the 'bourgeois polities' of the Philippines and Thailand has been less encouraging of, or even hostile towards democratic principles (as Gramsci always suspected).

Notes

I would like to thank Marco Bünte, Aurel Croissant, Robert Hefner, Allen Hicken and Philip Völkel for their comments and suggestions for revision, as well as the participants at the conference Challenges and Prospects of Democratic Governance in Southeast Asia, German Institute of Global and Area Studies (Hamburg) and the University of Heidelberg, Heidelberg, 15–17 January 2009.

1. Not only is Sidel's thesis the starting point for this chapter, but its title is also 'Sidelian' in inspiration. See Sidel, 2001.
2. I make such an attempt in Thompson, 2010. The discussion proceeds by suggesting that a state-centred explanation of democratization in Pacific Asia is more promising than a class-based theory. Despite a weak 'bourgeois' opposition, Indonesia democratized in a manner that was in many ways reminiscent of Philippine democratization. In both countries, 'sultanization' and economic crisis derailed a 'developmentalist' project. The Marcos and Suharto regimes both collapsed in the face of rising civil societal protest (led by students in Indonesia) because of splits that had developed between neo-patrimonial rulers, and an increasingly alienated military as well as disenchanted politicians.
3. The original German text uses the word *'Herrschaft,'* which can be translated as 'rule', 'mastery', 'control', 'domination', and so on: *'kollektive Akteure, die nach Teilhabe am Herrschaftssystem einer Gesellschaft streben'.*
4. The Catholic church hierarchy in the Philippines has been a kind of 'moral equivalent' to the monarchy in Thailand. Catholic bishops, and Cardinal Sin in particular, gave their blessing to the anti-Estrada protests. With the leadership of the church divided and its standing weakened by scandal – and the military hierarchy firmly aligned with the Arroyo camp – more recent people power-style protests in the Philippines have faded.
5. What counts as consolidation depends of course upon one's definition: Indonesia has passed the 'two-turnover-test,' with Wahid peacefully succeeding Habibie after the 1999 elections, Megawati succeeding Wahid after the latter was removed constitutionally from office in 2001, and the current president Susilo Bambang Yudhoyono succeeding Megawati after defeating her in the presidential elections of 2004.

References

Abinales, P.N. and Amorosa, D.J. (2006) 'The Withering of Philippine Democracy', *Current History*, 105 (692): 290–295.
Alagappa, M. (ed.) (2004) *Civil Society and Political Change in Asia: Expanding and Contracting Democratic Space* (Stanford: Stanford University Press).

Albritton, R.W. and Thawilwadee, B. (2002) *Civil Society and the Consolidation of Democracy in Thailand*, Working Paper No. 4 – A Comparative Survey of Democracy, Governance, and Development (Tapei: Asia Barometer Office).

Aspinall, E. (2005) *Opposing Suharto: Compromise, Resistance, and Regime Change in Indonesia* (Palo Alto: Stanford University Press).

Berner, E. (2001) 'Kollektive Strategien, Herrschaft und Widerstand: Zur Relevanz einer Theorie strategischer Gruppen in der Entwicklungssoziologie', in Schrader, H., Kaiser, M. and Korff, R. (eds), *Markt, Kultur und Gesellschaft: Zur Aktualität von 25 Jahren Entwicklungsforschung* (Münster: Lit Verlag).

Betrand, J. (2004) *Nationalism and Ethnic Conflict in Indonesia* (Cambridge: Cambridge University Press).

Burke, E. (1790) 'Reflections on the Revolution in France and on the Proceedings in Certain Societies in London Relative to That Event in a Letter Intended to Have Been Sent to a Gentleman in Paris', *Harvard Classics*, 24 (3), <http://www.bartleby.com/24/3/>.

Case, W. and Liew, C.T. (2006) 'How Committed is PAS to Democracy and How Do We Know It?', *Contemporary Southeast Asia*, 28 (3): 385–406.

Conde, C.H. (2009) 'New Plot for Movie Star who was Ousted as Philippines President', *International Herald Tribune*, 29 October, p. 8.

Croissant, A. (2008) ,Politische Kräfte in Thailand. Die sozialen Ursprünge von Diktatur und Demokratie', lecture delivered at the University of Munich, 24 January.

David, R. (2008) 'When Civil Society becomes Political', *Philippine Daily Inquirer*, 8 October , <www.inquirer.net>.

Furnivall, J.S. (1948) *Colonial Policy and Practice: A Comparative Study of Burma and Netherlands India* (Cambridge: Cambridge University Press).

Freedom House (2007) *Freedom in the World 2006-2007* <http://www.freedomhouse.org/ template.cfm?page=363&year=2007>.

Gerlach, R. (forthcoming) 'Mega' Expectations: Megawati Sukarnoputri's Rise and Fall in Indonesian Politics', in Derichs, C. and Thompson, M.R. (eds), *Dynasties' Daughters and Martyrs' Widows: Female Leadership in Asia*.

Giddens, A. (1983) *The Class Structure of the Advanced Societies* (London: Hutchinson).

Golingai, P. (2009) 'Absent Thaksin Strikes Polls Blow to Ruling Coalition', *The Star*, 27 June , <www.thestar.com.my>.

Gramsci, A. (1971 [1929–35]) *Prison Notebooks: Selections*, edited by Hoare, Q. and Nowell Smith, G. (New York: International Publishers).

Hadiwinata, B. S. (2009) 'From 'Heroes' to 'Troublemakers': Civil Society and Democratization in Indonesia', in Bünte, M. and Ufen, A., *Democratization in Post-Suharto Indonesia* (London: Routledge).

Handley, P.M. (2006) *The King Never Smiles: A Biography of Thailand's Bhumibol Adulyadej* (New Haven: Yale University Press).

Hedman, E-L. (2006) *In the Name of Civil Society: From Free Election Movements to People Power in the Philippines* (Honolulu: University of Hawaii).

Hefner, R.W. (1998) *Democratic Civility: The History and Possibility of a Political Ideal* (New Brunswick: Transaction Press).

Hefner, R.W. (2000) *Civil Islam: Muslims and Democratization in Indonesia* (Princeton: Princeton University Press).

Hefner, R.W. (2010) 'Human Rights and Democracy in Islam: The Indonesian Case in Global Perspective', in Banchoff, T. and Wuthnow, R. (eds), *Religion and the Global Politics of Human Rights* (Oxford: Oxford University Press).

Hewison, K. (2007) 'The Book, the King, and the Coup', *Journal of Contemporary Asian Studies*, 38 (1): 190–211.

Huntington, S.P. (1991) *The Third Wave: Democratization in the Late Twentieth Century* (Norman: The University of Oklahoma Press).

Hutchcroft, P. (2008) 'The Arroyo Imbroglio in the Philippines', *Journal of Democracy*, 19 (1): 141–155.

Kane, J. (2001) *The Politics of Moral Capital* (Cambridge: Cambridge University Press).

Kannika D. and Melnick, G.A. (2009) 'Early Results from Thailand's 30 Baht Health Reform: Something to Smile About', *Health Affairs*, 28 (3): 457–466.

Keane, J. (2004) *Violence and Democracy* (Cambridge: Cambridge University Press).

King, D. (2003) *Half-hearted Reform: Electoral Institutions and the Struggle for Democracy in Indonesia* (Praeger: Westport).

Klinken, G. van (2007) *Communal Violence and Democratization in Indonesia: Small Town Wars* (London: Routledge).

Liddle, W. and Mujani, S.M. (2007) 'Leadership, Party and Religion: Explaining Voter Behavior in Indonesia', *Comparative Political Studies*, 40 (7): 832–857.

Linz, J.J. and Stepan, A. (1996) *Problems of Democratic Transition and Consolidation* (Baltimore: The Johns Hopkins University Press).

McCargo, D. (2005) 'Network Monarchy and Legitimacy Crisis in Thailand', *Pacific Review*, 18 (4): 499–519.

Mietzner, M. (2009) *Indonesia's 2009 Elections: Populism, Dynasties and the Consolidation of the Party System* (Sidney: Lowy Institute).

Montesano, M. (2009) 'Contextualing the Pattaya Summit Debacle: Four Days, Four Thai Pathologies', *Contemporary Southeast Asia*, 31 (2): 217–248.

Moore, B. (1966) *Social Origins of Dictatorship and Democracy: Lord and Peasant in the Making of the Modern World* (Boston: Beacon Press).

Noi, C. (2008) 'The Evolving Anatomy of the PAD', *The Nation*, 15 September , www.nationmultimedia.com.

Ockey, J. (2004) 'State, Bureaucracy and Polity in Modern Thai Politics', *Journal of Contemporary Asia*, 34 (2): 143–162.

Pasuk, P. and Baker, C. J. (2005) ''Business Populism' in Thailand', *Journal of Democracy*, 16 (2): 58–72.

Putnam, R. (1993) *Making Democracy Work: Civic Traditions in Modern Italy* (Princeton: Princeton University Press).

Scott, J.C. (1990) *Domination and the Arts of Resistance: Hidden Transcripts* (New Haven: Yale University Press).

Sherlock, S. (2009) *Indonesia's 2009 Elections: The New Electoral System and the Competing Parties,* Centre for Democratic Institutions Policy Papers on Political Governance, no. 1, ANU, Canberra, <www.cdi.anu.edu.au>.

Sidel, J.T. (2001) 'It takes a madrasah: Habermas meet Bourdieu in Southeast Asia', *Southeast Asia Research*, 9 (1): 109–122.

Sidel, J.T. (2006) *Riots, Pogroms, and Jihad: Religious Violence in Indonesia* (Ithaca: Cornell University Press).

Sidel, J.T. (2008) 'Social Origins of Dictatorship and Democracy Revisited: Colonial State and Chinese Immigrant in the Making of Modern Southeast Asia', *Comparative Politics*, 40 (2): 127–147.

Slater, D. (2004) 'Indonesia's Accountability Trap: Party Cartels and Presidential Power after Democratic Transition', *Indonesia*, 78 (October): 61–92.

Techapira, K. (2008) 'Kasian Techapira on the PAD's 'General Uprising', *Prachatai*, September, <www.prachathai.com>.

Teekankee, J.C. (2006) 'The Legitimacy Crisis of the Arroyo Government.' Talk delivered at the De la Salle School of Governance, 29 March.

Thompson, M.R. (1995) *The Anti-Marcos Struggle: Personalistic Rule and Democratic Transition in the Philippines* (New Haven: Yale University Press).

Thompson, M. R. (2007) 'The Dialectic of 'Good Governance' and Democracy in Southeast Asia: Globalized Discourses and Local Responses', *Globality Sudies,* 10 (September), <http://www.sunysb.edu/globality/Articles/no10.html>.

Thompson, M.R. (2010) 'Modernization Theory's Last Redoubt: Democratization in East and Southeast Asia', in Chu, Yin-Wah (ed.), *East Asia's New Democracies: Deepening, Reversal, Non-liberal Alternatives* (London: Routledge).

Ufen, A. (2008) 'From Aliran to Dealignment: Political Parties in Post-Suharto Indonesia', *South East Asia Research,* 16 (1): 5–41.

Uhlin, A. (1997) *Indonesia and the 'Third Wave' of Democratization* (New York: St. Martin's).

Ungpakorn, G.J. (2007) *A Coup for the Rich: Thailand's Political Crisis* (Bangkok: Workers Democracy Publishing).

Webber, D. (2006) 'A Consolidated Patrimonial Democracy? Democratization in Post-Suharto Indonesia', *Democratization,* 13 (3): 396–420.

Weber, M. (1903/1904) *The Sociology of Religion* (Boston: Beacon).

Weiss, M. (2005) *Protest and Possibilities: Civil Society and Coalitions for Political Change in Malaysia* (Stanford: Stanford University Press).

5
Political Islam and Democratization in Southeast Asia

Andreas Ufen

Some scholars underline the crucial role of Islam as a system of beliefs that blocks democratization (Huntington, 1991). They tend to stress the immutability of core ideas and their practical consequences in political processes (Lewis, 2002). A more nuanced position is held by Anderson (2004). In his view, religious tradition is not central or determining, but 'in the short term what tradition is dominant in a country may – subconsciously or as deliberately fostered by religious and/or secular leaders – help to shape the outcome of democratization processes' (Anderson, 2004, p.206). Others refute the possibility of establishing a linkage between Islam and democracy or democratization based on the core ideas of the religion. Asef Bayat, for example, argues that the compatibility of Islam with democracy 'is *not* a matter of merely philosophical speculations, but of *political struggle*. It is not as much the question of texts as the balance of power between those who want a democratic religion and those who pursue an authoritarian version' (Bayat, 2007, p.13).

In line with this assumption, this study does not deal with the discourse on religious ideas in Southeast Asia, but rather with the configuration of forces – secular, Islamic and Islamist – that are fighting for or against democracy.[1] This topic needs to be examined against the backdrop of the evolution of the political systems in Malaysia and Indonesia.

Malaysia has many 'classical' prerequisites for democracy, such as a large middle class, a low poverty rate and long-lasting, high economic growth. The country has a tradition of peaceful conflict resolution, a participatory political culture, armed forces that are effectively controlled by civilians, and no secessionist movements. Additionally, its neighbouring countries have experienced a transition from authoritarianism to electoral democracy. Malaysia has never been democratized, however. It has been described as a 'repressive-responsive regime' (Crouch, 1996) located between democracy and 'full-blown' authoritarianism. The country can also be conceptualized as a competitive electoral authoritarian regime that organizes inclusive and pluralistic elections, although these are neither fully competitive nor open

(Schedler, 2006, p.3). Such regimes differ from electoral democracies with sufficiently free and fair elections and from hegemonic electoral authoritarian regimes where elections are not competitive and opposition parties always lose (Schedler, 2002, p.47). In Malaysia, elections are not fair because of restricted political rights and civil liberties, malapportionment, gerrymandering and the financial advantages of the ruling parties (Case, 2006). The governing coalition – initially the Alliance and from the early 1970s on the BN (Barisan Nasional, National Front) – has won every election at the federal level to date (Ufen, 2009a).[2]

Indonesia was initially democratic (1949–57) and then shifted towards authoritarianism as a Guided Democracy under President Sukarno (1957–65). The subsequent New Order (1965/66–98) under Suharto was an authoritarian and Western-oriented modernization regime based mainly on military power. The profoundly centralized power structure was legitimized by (non-competitive) elections and a three-party system dominated by the ruling party, Golkar. Today, Indonesia is a presidential democracy with free and fair elections, a multi-party system and a vibrant press. Its democracy has several flaws, however. Terms such as 'defective democracy' (Croissant, 2004) or 'patrimonial democracy' (Webber, 2006) have therefore been applied to it. Nevertheless, Indonesia is today much more democratic than Malaysia, in spite of its high poverty rates, low per capita income, cultural and ethnic heterogeneity, secessionist movements, terrorism, and weak institutions as a result of the neopatrimonial legacies of the Suharto era.

What are the reasons for this? Sidel, for example, has convincingly used Barrington Moore's 'no bourgeoisie, no democracy' thesis to analyze a range of Southeast Asian countries. He states that the 'degree of vigour and independence enjoyed by a given country's bourgeoisie, understood here not in the pluralist sense of an urban middle class, but in the Marxist sense of a capitalist class' (Sidel, 2008, 1 further page (128–9)), is a decisive factor in the establishment of democracy or the entrenchment of authoritarianism. In his comparative historical analysis, Sidel underlines the importance of three interrelated determining factors in class formation, namely, 'the impact of state policies and market forces upon the assimilation and upward mobility of immigrant (mostly Chinese) merchant communities in the colonial era; the outcome of struggles for national independence after World War II; and the extent of state and foreign control over the commanding heights of the national economy since independence' (Sidel, 2008, p.129). The failure of democratization in Malaysia is thus the outcome of a structure in which both the Malaysian Chinese business class and the new Malay capitalists are highly dependent on the Barisan Nasional and/or the state. In Indonesia, in contrast, 'in mid May 1998 large-scale capital flight (and the departure of tens of thousands of Chinese businessmen) confronted the regime with the consequences of capitalist exit' (Sidel, 2008, p.141).

Slater (2009) takes issue with this focus on classes to a certain extent and highlights the role of communal elites as the 'primary possessors of nationalist and religious authority' because 'democratic mobilization is more likely to occur and to succeed in societies with politically autonomous communal elites' (Slater, 2009, p.207). In a comparison of seven Southeast Asian countries, he distinguishes between cases where democratic mobilization was successful (in the Philippines in 1986, Thailand in 1973 and 1992, and Indonesia in 1998), cases where it was unsuccessful (Myanmar in 1988 and 2007, Malaysia in 1998 and Indonesia in 1978) and cases where such mobilization has been chronically absent (Singapore and Vietnam). He concludes that communal elites who retain some measure of political autonomy provide the opposition with the necessary mobilizational thrust and symbolic power. Nationalism in Indonesia has left 'thick organizational residues', whereas in Malaysia 'nationalism provides neither a resonant frame nor a familiar framework for collective action, hamstringing democratic oppositionists' (Slater, 2009, p.212). In Malaysia, Islam has gained political hegemony and has retained only a limited degree of autonomy, whereas in Indonesia 'communal elites either assumed oppositional postures (e.g. some Islamic leaders and Sukarno's daughter) or simply withdrew their support for the authoritarian Suharto regime (i.e. the nationalist military and other Islamic leaders)' (Slater, 2009, p.226).

The cases of Malaysia and Indonesia are tricky ones in both Slater's and Sidel's account. The role of the bourgeoisie in Indonesia in 1998 does not fit smoothly into the Barrington Moore model. And according to Slater, Malaysia is an 'intermediate case', where mobilization took place but was not successful. Yet I would argue that even though the *reformasi* movement was 'easily crushed' at the beginning, the opposition in Malaysia can still achieve democratization – though probably not in the form of a democratic revolution, but rather incrementally, through a protracted transition. This was demonstrated by the 2008 elections (Ufen, 2009a). Therefore, the analysis of communal elites necessitates a closer look at specific configurations of religious groups.

In this chapter it is argued that one of the main reasons for the success of democratization in Indonesia – in contrast to Malaysia – is the way Islam has been politicized and organized there. While political Islam in Indonesia was a force partly supportive of democratization in the 1950s and is overwhelmingly conducive to democratization today, this is not the case in Malaysia, where electoral authoritarianism is stabilized by conservative state-led Islamization and by competition between UMNO (United Malays National Organization) and PAS (Parti Islam SeMalaysia, Pan-Malaysian Islamic Party) regarding which type of Islam is 'better'. This has propelled the growth of exclusivism in mainstream Islamic thinking.

The chapter depicts two different paths and proceeds as follows. In order to disentangle the complex trajectories of political Islam in Indonesia and

Malaysia, it first highlights the countries' historical legacies, the central features of state policies on Islam since independence, and the specific dynamics of party politics. The subsequent section analyses the new path taken by
the opposition in Malaysia since 1999 and in particular interprets reforms
within PAS with reference to the so-called moderation thesis.

Historical legacies

Three factors are particularly important with regard to historical legacies:
the relationship between the colonial state and Islam, the composition and
mobilization of Islamic civil society, and cleavage structures. In Malaya,
'particularly in the native states subject to indirect rule (where sultans
retained a significant measure of authority), the British encouraged cooperation between state authorities and Muslim leaders' (Hefner, 2000, p.34).
Sultans were assigned the responsibility to guard and promote the faith.
With a growing bureaucratic religious apparatus, sultans were able to effectively implement their policies. The close cooperation between colonial
rulers, the Malay aristocracy and conservative *ulama* left very few avenues
open for oppositional Muslim forces (Yegar, 1979). The sultanistic control
of Islam made it difficult for heterodox or reformist movements to flourish. A strong Islamic civil society was unable to evolve under these restrictive circumstances. Within the weak nationalist movement, neither Muslim
reform movements nor the intelligentsia with Malay education were able to
build up mass support. The only group to achieve this, to an extent, were
members of the Malay aristocracy who had received an English education
(Roff, 1994). After independence they advocated a moderate, state-centred
Islam.

Another legacy of British colonial rule was the segregation of the population into three major ethnic groups – Malays, Indians and Chinese. Religion
reinforced the partition, since Malays are Muslims by constitutional definition. These cleavages have shaped Malaysian politics heavily from the very
beginning. The ethnic and religious division entailed competing ethno-
nationalisms. Within each ethnic group, the British supported those who
appeared to least oppose a controlled transition to independence, that is,
elites fighting the political left and the Islamists. The majority of the Malays
only joined the (comparatively weak) nationalist movement in 1946, when
the Malay aristocratic elite, led by UMNO, opposed the British plan to form
a Malayan Union in which ethnic minorities were to be accorded equal citizenship rights. This Malay nationalism expressed itself as strong sentiments
against the ambitions of the other ethnic groups, and the aristocratic elite
declared itself the protector of the *Bangsa Melayu* (Malay race or nation).

In contrast, in the Dutch East Indies the Europeans 'destroyed imperial
Islam, undermined the authority of native rulers, and unwittingly reinvig-
orated popular Islam' (Hefner, 2000, p.33). Europeans controlled the state

apparatus and thereby forced many Muslim leaders to distance themselves from the government and rely on their own institutions. The dense network of mostly independent Muslim boarding schools (*pesantren*) across Java and some parts of the Outer Islands, for example, was testimony to the self-contained organization of Islam in the Dutch East Indies. The Dutch, realizing that the Christian mission in Muslim areas was doomed to fail, propagated a mere 'cultural Islam' because they feared a politicized, anti-colonial Islam. At the same time, they strengthened the syncretist traditions and indigenous belief systems (*adat*). In Indonesia, political parties and Muslim mass organizations such as Muhammadiyah (Followers of Muhammad) and Nahdatul Ulama (Renaissance of Islamic Scholars) arose long before independence. These highly politicized organizations were socially entrenched and capable of mobilizing large parts of the population.

While in Indonesia the main cleavages separating those groups that began to form political parties cut across each other in such a way as to produce a diverse political discourse, in Malaya the cleavages strengthened each other and produced a pattern according to which ethnic elites controlled the discourse and were able to implement electoral authoritarianism at the time of independence.

All these legacies shaped the trajectories of Muslim politics in Indonesia and Malaysia to a large extent. The following sections discuss the role of state policies and the specific dynamics of party politics in each of the two countries.

Patterns of state policies

Islamization is usually examined as the outcome of interactions between 'the state' and 'society'.[3] Both sides have different intentions and strategies and attempt to either promote or prevent the politicization of Islam.[4] Following this tradition, Nasr (2001), for instance, distinguishes between three typical agents of state-led Islamization: firstly, 'rejectionist secularists', who have defended the decidedly secular character of the state – with excessive force if necessary (like Algeria after the military coup in 1992 and Turkey immediately after the 'soft' coup in 1997); secondly, 'opportunist Islamizers', who have cooperated with or cautiously instrumentalized Islamic groups during specific phases, but have never considered Islam essential for expanding state power (like Egypt since 1971, Turkey from 1980 to 1997, Jordan since the 1950s, and Indonesia during the 1990s to a certain degree); and thirdly, 'thoroughgoing Islamizers' (such as Malaysia under Mahathir and Pakistan between the military coups of 1977 and 1999), where the 'Islamization of society has occurred under the aegis of the state, and in far more thoroughgoing fashion than in Egypt or Jordan' (Nasr, 2001, p.24).

Usually, scholars differentiate between inclusionary and exclusionary state policies with respect to the willingness to systematically incorporate or exclude Islamists and/or their objectives.[5] However, the policies in Malaysia and Indonesia have not followed a clearly defined blueprint; rather, they have been characterized by ambiguities and inconsistencies.

When Malaysia attained independence in 1957, Islam was merely attributed a symbolic meaning in its constitution (Mutalib, 1990, p.23). It became the 'religion of the state', but non-Muslims were accorded freedom of religion. In the 1950s and 1960s, Islamization manifested itself in the form of newly built mosques, Quran recitation contests, the spreading of Islamic symbols, etc. The Malay elite maintained Islam as a vital part of the self-conception of the state and of Malayness.

It was not until the late 1960s that the country experienced an enormous revaluation of Islam similar to that in other parts of the Muslim world. This process was accelerated by riots following the May 1969 national elections. According to government reports, 196 people, most of whom were Chinese, were killed on 13 May and in the following days of rioting. These confrontations led to the declaration of a state of emergency and resulted in a series of extensive reforms. Subsequently, the balance of power shifted, not only within the ruling coalition but also between ethnic groups in Malaysia as a whole. The pro-*bumiputera* policy within the framework of the New Economic Policy (NEP) and the New Education Policy (NEDP) – that is, affirmative action favouring Malays by providing them with privileged access to administrative positions, to universities and to state credits and concessions – was linked to a slow and cautious state-led Islamization.

This process was paralleled by the rise of Islamist groups in the early 1970s, generally known as the *dakwah* movement.[6] A huge segment of the diverse movement originated at the largest national universities, spread throughout the entire society and adopted the leading role in politicizing Islam for a few years. Its radical proponents criticized the national political elite, whom they considered to be westernized, un-Islamic, inefficient and corrupt.

It was only when Mahathir Mohamad took office as prime minister in 1981 that comprehensive state-led Islamization was carried out. As one of his first initiatives Mahathir co-opted the most prominent *dakwah* representative, Anwar Ibrahim. In the following years education was Islamized by means of additional religious instruction at schools and universities and the creation of the International Islamic University.

From the early 1980s on the regime used Islamization as an instrument to boost the Malay position in relation to ethnic minorities, especially vis-à-vis the powerful Sino-Malaysian entrepreneurs (Mutalib, 1990, p.127ff.; Hamid and Fauzi, 2007, p.457ff.). All these measures eventually ensured the creation of a religious state bureaucracy, that is, the employment of thousands of graduates from Islamic institutions by *sharia* courts, for instance, or as teachers at all levels of the educational system (Hamayotsu, 2003). Moreover, to Mahathir the state-led Islamization process represented an opportunity to convey values such as austerity, discipline, tolerance, honesty and loyalty

(Milne and Mauzy, 1983). The government attempted to Islamize the economy without jeopardizing either its effectiveness or its growing integration in the global market. It created an Islamic bank (Bank Islam Malaysia) in 1983 and an Islamic insurance company a year later. Malaysia became the first country with an elaborate Islamic banking system. Mahathir set a new course in foreign affairs by expanding Malaysia's relations with other Muslim countries and also by participating more actively in the Organization of The Islamic Conference (OIC).

This conservative Islamization continued in the 1990s. Heterodox Islamic organizations such as Darul Arqam were marginalized and criminalized.[7] The responsibilities of *sharia* courts were beefed up, and *fatwas* issued by the *muftis* of the states attained the status of binding rules.

After September 11, Mahathir used the 'war against terror' to improve the country's strained relations with the US and to stress the menace posed by militants. The government cracked down on terror suspects and tried to lay bare the insinuated linkages between radical Islamists and PAS. On top of this, Mahathir provocatively declared that Malaysia was already an Islamic state, thereby enraging liberal Muslims and the religious minorities in the country. In recent years a number of events have unsettled non-Muslims and also those Muslims who reject a conservative interpretation of their religion. These have included, among other things, the raids conducted by the Federal Territories Religious Department (JAWI) on a popular discotheque in Kuala Lumpur and the difficulties faced by civil society organizations (such as the liberal alliance known as 'Article 11') in protecting the right to freedom of religion.

In sum, government policies in Malaysia have been characterized by many continuities since at least the 1980s. This is also true of the policies of Mahathir's successors, Badawi and Najib. Badawi even introduced his own vague but moderate concept: *'Islam Hadhari'* ('Civilizational Islam'). The state has promoted a conservative Islamization process designed not only to further economic development and to safeguard Malay hegemony, but also to counter the Islamism of the opposition as represented by PAS. The conservative policy pattern combines repression and co-optation, together with the open stimulation, at times, of Islamism or Islamist actors. It stabilized electoral authoritarianism through the bolstering of Malay hegemony; the enforcement of a restricted discourse on morality, liberal values, human rights and democracy; and the institution of polarized party competition, which for a long time predominantly centred around religious issues (see below).[8]

In Indonesia, Islam is not the state religion; the 1945 constitution stipulates a 'state philosophy' – the *Pancasila* (Five Pillars) – that recognizes several religions defined as monotheistic.[9] The *Pancasila* has remained one of the few continuities of modern Indonesia, in spite of the country's vicissitudinous history. Indonesia experienced the slow institutionalization of

Islam throughout the first parliamentary democracy (1949–57). One could perceive an increasing strengthening and professionalization of interest representation for orthodox Muslims within the state apparatus. At the same time, the religious infrastructure was enhanced. The establishment of the Ministry of Religious Affairs and its growth in terms of personnel, the nationwide proliferation of *sharia* courts, and the expansion of the already significant Islamic educational sector are all indicators of this institutionalization (Boland, 1971, 105ff; Hooker, 2001; Cammack, 2007).

In the late 1950s the parliamentary democracy failed due to the strong polarization of political forces in a polity with limited legitimacy. Sukarno, the fiery secular nationalist, succeeded in pushing through his model of Guided Democracy with the support of the armed forces, the PKI (Partai Komunis Indonesia, Indonesian Communist Party), and the nationalist and secular PNI (Partai Nasional Indonesia, Indonesian Nationalist Party). The two largest Islamic parties were either degraded to junior partners (Nahdatul Ulama) or banned outright (Masyumi). During this time, the attraction of secular ideologies – nationalism, socialism and communism – was so tremendous that any dominance of political Islam was out of the question.

During the regime change from Guided Democracy to the highly authoritarian New Order in 1965–66, probably at least half a million – often only alleged – communists were killed. Many orthodox Muslims took part in the massacres. In return, they expected their interests to be adequately represented in the new regime. Instead, the New Order elites tried hard to restrain political Islam.[10] At the beginning of the 1970s a three-party system was created; it was dominated by Golkar as the hegemon and featured the PPP (Partai Persatuan Pembangunan, United Development Party) as a representative, albeit one tamed by the regime, of Muslim interests. All Islamic organizations were controlled by the regime to a considerable degree. Hence, until the 1980s, the relationship between the regime and political Islam was ambivalent.

That even the authoritarian New Order regime was incapable of fully controlling Islamic forces is best exemplified by the *dakwah* movement, which started in the early 1970s in Bandung around the campus-based Salman Mosque and spread to other universities in the following years (Latif, 2005, p.390ff.). The related *tarbiyah* (education) movement began in the early 1980s at various university campuses. While the *dakwah* groups had their strongholds at secular universities, a renewal (*pembaruan*) movement was based primarily at the quite liberal State Institutes of Islamic Studies (IAIN) and the State Islamic Universities (UIN) (Latif, 2005, p.405ff.). The *pembaruan* movement's so-called neo-modernist approach, which combined traditionalist and modernist elements, intended to indigenize and secularize Islam (Barton, 1995). What all these movements had in common was that many of their members, proponents of a political Islam, withdrew from active politics and concentrated on missionary work and opinion formation instead;

they pursued a 'cultural' rather than a 'political' Islam. This Islamization was partly due to the repression of independent student organizations, the weakening of political parties and the depoliticization of all social organizations. Moreover, the *Pancasila* was being enforced as *azas tunggal*, that is, the only authorized ideological platform for parties and mass organizations, in the early 1980s. At that time, the New Order elites were still mainly non-Muslims; syncretists influenced by old Javanese, Hindu-Buddhist and Sufi beliefs; and non-devout Muslims. The two latter groups are known as *abangan*, in contrast to the orthodox *santri*.[11]

Only in the mid- to late 1980s did the regime change its course. Suharto began tending towards the *santri* variant of Islam. Expenditures for the creation of state Islamic universities, mosques and prayer rooms were boosted. A new education law stipulated obligatory religious instruction in public and private institutions. Islamic courts were strengthened in matters of marriage, divorce and heritage (Cammack, 2007). As of 1990 Muslim girls were allowed to wear the *jilbab* (headscarf) in schools. Following the Malaysian example, the state established an Islamic bank. Orthodox Muslims rose to prominent positions within the parliament, the cabinet, the Golkar executive board and the military leadership, a process that came to be known as *penghijauan* ('greening'). In Suharto's neopatrimonial system, this 'greening' also served to weaken a military faction around head of intelligence 'Benny' Murdani. How far such instrumentalization of religion could go became evident in the last few weeks of the New Order regime, when a military faction under General Prabowo, Suharto's son-in-law, openly cooperated with Islamist groups.

Suharto's resignation in May 1998 and the succeeding transition to democracy were supported by the two large Islamic mass organizations, Nahdatul Ulama and Muhammadiyah; by numerous Muslim scholars and intellectuals; and by Islamic students' associations (Mietzner, 2009, 146ff.). With the opening up of the political system, numerous groups capable of destabilizing democratization emerged. Religious and ethnic identities have been politicized since 1998 due to increased competition for political positions and market shares. This has given rise to numerous ethno-religious conflicts; the emergence of a plethora of Islamist groups, some of which openly advocate the use of violence; and the extraordinary politicization of religion in particular regions. Moreover, survey results imply that a huge segment of the population wants an extensive, conservative or even reactionary Islamization process (Lembaga Survei Indonesia, 2007). The most prominent Islamist groups are the Islam Defenders Front (Front Pembela Islam, FPI), the Jihad Warriors (Laskar Jihad, LJ) and the terror organization Islamic Community (Jemaah Islamiyah, JI).[12] At the other end of the spectrum, peaceful fundamentalist organizations such as Hizbut Tahrir Indonesia (Indonesian Liberation Party) and Jama'ah Tabligh (Proselytizing Group) have also been able to strengthen their presence.

Parties and local executives – and surprisingly even some secularists – have made the introduction of *sharia* regulations in certain districts possible. The regulations stipulate specific clothing and behaviour for women; ban prostitution, alcohol consumption and gambling; and enforce *zakat*, the alms tax (Salim, 2007). In Aceh in September 2009, a very harsh *sharia* law with forms of punishment such as stoning was passed by the provincial parliament.

There is evidence that religious issues are politicized at the national level by the executive authority as well as in the party system. Examples of this include the education law of 2003, which discriminates against religious minorities, and the pornography law of 2008. The latter prescribes harsh prison sentences for ill-defined 'pornographic' illustrations and activities. Nonetheless, these cases are exceptions. Some ministries have, in contrast, published very progressive draft bills (Mulia and Cammack, 2007), and initiatives based unmistakably on Islamist ideas are very rare in most policy areas. The *Pancasila* remains widely accepted and was, in fact, extended in 2007 with the inclusion of Confucianism in the course of a general cultural and political reintegration of the ethnic Chinese. A range of authors therefore stress the civil character of Islam in the region.[13] Today, there are even very liberal forces such as JIL (Jaringan Islam Liberal, Liberal Islam Network).

In summary, Indonesian Islam in the 1950s was variegated and in many respects pro-democratic because of the country's historical legacies. Yet the main actors – the NU and Masyumi – still endorsed Islamist demands. Forty years later, the principal Islamic actors – NU, Muhammadiyah, PKB (Partai Kebangkitan Bangsa, National Awakening Party) and PAN (Partai Amanat Nasional, National Mandate Party) – have jettisoned these demands. This is largely the outcome of developments under the New Order regime, that is, the emergence of the *pembaruan* movement as well as the rise of a politically self-confident, devout middle class (Mujani and Liddle, 2009).

Islam in party politics

Islam has been politicized in different ways within the party systems of Indonesia and Malaysia. In post-Suharto Indonesia, even the Islamist parties support electoral democracy. In Malaysia, in contrast, PAS and UMNO have been involved in a kind of contest since the beginning of *kebangkitan Islam*, the 'rise of Islam'. Each eagerly strives to demonstrate its religious orthodoxy and simultaneously prove that the other side is deviating from 'true' Islam. This competition has been one of the major impediments to democratization. PAS – part of the *reformasi* forces – has oscillated between Islamism and a hesitant pro-democratic position since 1999.

In the 1950s the two major Islamic parties in Indonesia were Islamist. Nahdatul Ulama – a political party in itself since 1952 – and the modernist, urban-based Masyumi (Majelis Syuro Muslimin Indonesia, Consultative Council of Indonesian Muslims) propagated the idea of an Islamic state and of further implementing *sharia* laws. Yet they did so in an environment that required pragmatism and the willingness to compromise. This is why they forged numerous coalitions in the national parliament with secular parties. In fact, apart from altercations between the mainstream parties and the principally marginalized PKI, the greatest tension existed between Nahdatul Ulama and Masyumi. Their stance towards parliamentary democracy was ambivalent: on the one hand, they conformed to the rules of the democratic game; on the other, they embraced Islamist ideals. In the constituent assembly (Konstituante, 1956–59), for example, they voted for the adoption of a passage in the constitution that would force Muslims to obey *sharia* law. Besides Sukarno's *rapprochement* towards the PKI and the armed forces' intention of strongly broadening its own impact on decision-making, the ambiguity of Nahdatul Ulama and Masyumi was one of the cardinal factors responsible for the destabilization of the polity, and the impasse in the Konstituante provided a welcome opportunity for Sukarno and his allies to introduce Guided Democracy.

Ironically, the Suharto regime, mostly unwittingly, effected the moderation of political Islam. In contrast to the case in the 1950s, Muslims in the political arena have mostly backed the consolidation of democracy since 1998–99. Even the large Islamic parties PKB and PAN are secular according to their names and self-definition. In the three elections since 1998, the largest Islamist parties in the national parliament have achieved combined votes of merely 14 per cent (1999), 18 per cent (2004) and 13 per cent (2009). They have never openly advocated the establishment of an Islamic state, and their attempts to introduce the *sharia* into the constitution have failed miserably. The only Islamist party with a chance of growing into a mass party is the PKS (Partai Keadilan Sejahtera, Justice and Prosperity Party). It has campaigned against corruption and avoided a public debate on issues such as *sharia* law and an Islamic state.

In Malaysia in the 1950s and 1960s, the official, state-sponsored Islam and that represented by PAS were not as exclusive and rigid as they would later become. PAS tried to challenge the legitimacy of the government by politicizing ethnicity and emphasizing Malay nationalism. Impulses to politicize religion were still relatively weak. This began slowly in the 1970s, but at that time PAS had been part of the ruling Barisan Nasional for a few years. It was not until the early 1980s that the 'Young Turks' who had risen to prominence in the *dakwah* movement took over leading positions within PAS and set a new course for the party, explicitly denouncing the ethnic chauvinism of their predecessors in the process (Mutalib, 1990, p.113ff.; Noor, 2004, p.329ff.).

The competition between UMNO and PAS has for a long time further politicized two conservative versions of Islam, one centred on Malay interests and the strengthening of authoritarianism, the other more and more oriented towards issues such as the introduction of *sharia* and some kind of Islamic state (Malhi, 2003). Thus, party competition has long been characterized by polarization, not moderation. A strong PAS was essential to the BN since this kept the liberal forces of the opposition in check. Only since 1999, with the advent of the *reformasi* movement, have there been signs that PAS is overcoming its narrow view of Islamism; thus, a reformed Islamism may yet become the starting point for democratization.

The moderation thesis

As for the differentiation between Muslim moderates and Islamists outlined above, the compatibility of 'democracy' with the political ideas of moderates should be beyond doubt. But in many cases even Islamists may willingly or unwillingly support democratization. In the process, they themselves may become accustomed to democratic procedures and values and moderate their previous radical behaviour and world view (Wickham, 2004; Schwedler, 2006; Tezcür, 2010). With reference to European experiences, Berman (2008) propounds three arguments that speak for the realistic possibility of the moderation of Islamism in party politics. First, many parties tend to fight for the middle ground. Berman calls this the Downsian effect, according to which Islamist parties adopt more centrist platforms and tend to broaden their appeal to voters. This mechanism seems to be particularly valid if the party system is competitive and where even Islamist opposition parties have a chance of winning elections. To be sure, party competition does not necessarily engender this form of moderation. On the contrary, the dynamics of Indonesian party politics in the 1950s caused an intensification of ideological confrontation and a polarization that was brought to an end by the introduction of Sukarno's Guided Democracy. In Malaysia, the competition between PAS and UMNO about 'the better form of Islam' also caused marked polarization between Muslims and non-Muslims and between Islamists and moderate, though conservative followers of political Islam.

Nevertheless, Indonesia has been a prime example of the fight for the middle ground ever since 1998. One reason for this moderation is that political parties are largely dealigned. Loyalties to parties are weak, and there has been an upsurge of new elite networks at the local level (Ufen, 2008, p.20ff.). This dealignment is also indicated by the rise of presidential or presidentialized parties, growing intra-party authoritarianism, the prevalence of 'money politics', the lack of meaningful political platforms, and the cartelization of political parties. The identification of voters with certain parties has remained, but the ideological cement has been eroded along with the organizational base. The dividing line between traditionalist and modernist Islam has become somewhat blurred, and even the differentiation between *abangan* (nominal Muslims or syncretists) and *santri* (orthodox

Muslims) is questionable because of the expansion of orthodox Islam all over the archipelago. Primordial loyalties are weaker now than in the 1950s due to socioeconomic progress, the improvement of educational facilities, urbanization, and the impact of the mass media. Hence, parties are now far less embedded than they were in the 1950s and lack convincing ideologies (Mujani and Liddle, 2007). Islamist parties have a limited ability to mobilize supporters. In Indonesia, 'rainbow coalitions' encompassing most of the major parties generally govern the country, the provinces and the districts.

Berman (2008, p.6f.) identifies two other kindred factors that may cause the moderation of Islamism in party politics. First, the necessity of building a sophisticated party machinery is more easily managed by pragmatists than ideologists. Second, politicians, according to the 'pothole theory', have to solve common everyday problems: they have to deliver goods, fix the sewage system, raise taxes, etc. Even Islamist parties need professionals, pragmatists and able administrators when they govern. An education in *sharia* law is hardly helpful in tackling these issues.

Yet these two possible effects are hard to verify. In fact, PAS has become more radical in Kelantan and Terengganu over time. An indication of this was the attempts to introduce *hudud* laws. What is more likely is that moderation occurs in the face of weakened ruling elites. When Islamist parties see a chance to win elections and topple the government, they may tone down their radicalism in order to be able to forge coalitions with secular opposition parties. This has been the case in Malaysia since 1999. The *reformasi* movement originated at the height of the Asian crisis, following the arrest of Anwar Ibrahim, Prime Minister Mahathir's deputy.[14] At first, the establishment of a multi-ethnic and multi-religious coalition (Barisan Alternatif) tamed PAS, which agreed to work in a coalition with the predominantly Chinese and secular DAP (Democratic Action Party). Yet this cooperation was problematic from the very beginning and eventually ended in late September 2001 because PAS was unwilling to jettison its Islamist demands. The party presented a very rigid *hudud* draft law in Terengganu in July 2002, and in November 2003 it even published a 'blueprint' of an Islamic state. The *Dokumen Negara Islam* (*The Islamic State Document*) roughly describes the main objectives and characteristics of an Islamic state. It was a delayed response to Mahathir's statement on 29 September 2001 that Malaysia is an Islamic state.

Following the devastating outcome of the 2004 elections, in which the Barisan Nasional restored its hegemony, PAS shifted its course once more (Ufen, 2009a). It approached the PKR (Parti Keadilan Rakyat, People's Justice Party) and the DAP and publicly announced that it would soften its stance on the Islamic-state issue. Reformers seized important positions in the party elections in 2005 and 2007.

In the 2008 legislative elections, the opposition was, despite the limited competitiveness of the elections, unexpectedly able to strip the federal government of its two-thirds majority and to assume power in five of the 13 states. The three opposition parties (PAS, DAP and PKR) subsequently formed a new coalition, the People's Alliance (Pakatan Rakyat). The Islamic-state issue has been sidelined for the time being.

Concluding remarks

In colonial Indonesia, political Islam was deeply rooted and diverse, with no single authoritative interpretation; it was hardly controllable by the state. Islam was not state-centred. It was a basis for mass mobilization and a vital part of nationalism. In Malaya, in contrast, Islam was controlled by the sultans and the colonial power and was less pluralistic. Islam and the state were deeply intertwined, so that after independence, state policies designed to form a regime-compatible Islam were much more effective than in Indonesia.

In colonial Indonesia, cross-cutting cleavages have been institutionalized through nationalist organizations and political parties. Today these cleavages are still visible in the party system since the state apparatus and the ruling elites were never able to transform society or the discourse on Islamic issues in a way that fundamentally altered the pattern of social separation. In Malaya, ethnic and religious cleavages have reinforced each other. After independence religion was highly susceptible to manipulation by elites and became a favoured device with which to strengthen Muslim Malay hegemony over other religious and ethnic groups.

In Indonesia the role of Islam was still contested during the first parliamentary phase in the 1950s with two different models: secularism and moderate Islamism. Under Guided Democracy, Sukarno favoured his *Pancasila* state model, according to which Islam was one of several national religions. Under New Order authoritarianism, political parties and civil society forces were emasculated and, in connection with state policies, Islam was depoliticized until the 1980s. The state subsequently began to promote a slow Islamization process and co-opted sectors of civil society. It was only partially able to control some of the actors, though, who ultimately turned against the regime. State policies in New Order Indonesia and since Suharto's period in office have allowed for a very diverse discourse and given ample space to secular and liberal voices, in line with the *Pancasila* doctrine. Since 1998 the electoral democracy has been characterized by an open civil society with a wide variety of actors. Islam is only moderately politicized within the party system, probably because of the pluralization and factionalization of Islamic parties against the backdrop of party competition marked by grand coalitions or cartels. The 'secularism–Islamism' divide that shaped party politics in the 1950s was partially contained under the New Order and is relatively weak today. The outcome of this form of party politics has been incoherent, but mostly moderate state policies on the role of Islam.

In Malaya (Malaysia after 1963) the government-sponsored form of Islam was not only conservative and anti-democratic, but also anti-Islamist. The state has been systematically Islamizing the country since at least the early 1980s and has been able to tightly control the discourse on religious issues. The UMNO-led government propagates a conservative understanding of Islam that helps to stabilize the authoritarian system. Moreover, the competition with PAS is largely being exploited by UMNO in order to divide the opposition. Electoral authoritarianism has been the framework for well-managed and – all in all – coherent state policies on the role of Islam, which are accompanied by the strict control of deviant civil society actors.

Democratization has been supported by the major Islamic organizations in Indonesia. And since Suharto's fall, most Islamic parties have continued to back democracy. Indonesia is an example of a country where the political discourse is mostly dominated by pro-democratic secularist forces. In Malaysia, Islam has been politicized within the party system in an extraordinary way. Because of these peculiar dynamics, the official and the oppositionists' main versions of Islam still combine to obstruct the liberalization of the electoral authoritarian system, even though the new opposition, with a more moderate PAS, may open up the political regime incrementally.

In sum, there is no clear-cut relationship between 'Islam' and 'democracy'/'democratization'. Different variants of Islam exist, in terms of interpretations and practices, in Malaysia and Indonesia. Which of these attains the position of mainstream or hegemonic Islam depends on the configuration of forces both within the state apparatus and within society. A comparative historical analysis can help to identify the role of Islamic agents in the struggle for democracy or other regime forms.

Notes

1. Political Islam is conceptualized here as any form of politicization of Islam. Islamism is defined by the aim of creating an Islamic state with extensive *sharia* (Islamic law) legislation that encompasses not only family and civil law, but also a penal or *hudud* code. *Hudud* usually refers to the classes of punishment (capital punishment, amputation of hands or feet, and flogging) that are fixed for certain crimes, such as drinking alcohol, theft, robbery, illegal sexual intercourse, rebellion and apostasy (including blasphemy). Political Islam, thus, comprises not only Islamism but also moderate forms of Islam.
2. In the last years under British colonial rule, the Alliance – an inter-ethnic coalition of UMNO (United Malays National Organization), the MCA (Malaysian Chinese Association) and the MIC (Malaysian Indian Congress) – ran successfully for the first time in the municipal elections of 1952. The BN, the successor to the Alliance founded in the early 1970s, today consists of 13 parties, many of which solely or overwhelmingly represent specific ethnic (and in many cases, indirectly, religious) groups, that is, the Malay majority, the Chinese and Indian minorities, or the main ethnic groups in East Malaysia.
3. Parts of the following section are based on Ufen 2009b.

4. See Eickelman and Piscatori (1996); Esposito and Voll (1996); Porter (2002); Effendy (2003); Hamid and Fauzi (2007).
5. See Hamayotsu (2002), for instance.
6. On the movement, see Nagata (1984) and Anwar (1987).
7. Darul Arqam ('House of Arqam', named after one of the Prophet's companions) was founded in 1968 and led by Ashaari Muhammad. In 1972 its leaders established a commune near Kuala Lumpur. The tremendously successful organization was banned in 1994.
8. There appears to be wide backing for a conservative-orthodox interpretation of Islam. This was indicated by a survey involving over a thousand Muslim respondents that was conducted in December 2005 (see Martinez, 2006).
9. Besides Islam, these are Protestantism, Catholicism, Buddhism and Hinduism. The last two are counterfactually defined as monotheistic religions. In early 2007 Confucianism was added to this list.
10. On Islam under the New Order, see Hefner (2000), Porter (2002) and Effendy (2003).
11. Today, these terms are used much more carefully because of the expansion of orthodox Islam, the so-called *santrinisasi*, and the pluralization of Indonesian Islam. These processes have blurred some of the old divisions.
12. See van Bruinessen (2002) and International Crisis Group (2007).
13. See Hefner (2000), Azra (2006) and Assyaukanie (2009).
14. Anwar was accused of corruption and sodomy, charges which later landed him in jail for six years.

References

Anderson, J. (2004) 'Does God Matter, and If So Whose God? Religion and Democratization', *Democratization*, 11 (4): 192–217.
Anwar, Z. (1987) *Islamic revivalism in Malaysia. Dakwah among the students* (Petaling Jaya: Fajar Bakti).
Assyaukanie, L. (2009) *Islam and the Secular State in Indonesia* (Singapore: Institute of Southeast Asian Studies).
Azra, A. (2006) *Indonesia, Islam, and Democracy: Dynamics in a Global Context* (Jakarta: Solstice).
Barton, G. (1995) 'Neo-Modernism: A Vital Synthesis of Traditionalist and Modernist Islamic Thought in Indonesia', *Studia Islamica*, 2 (3): 1–75.
Bayat, A. (2007) *Making Islam Democratic. Social Movements and the Post-Islamist Turn* (Stanford: Stanford University Press).
Berman, S. (2008) 'Taming Extremist Parties: Lessons from Europe', *Journal of Democracy*, 19 (1) : 5–18.
Boland, B.J. (1971) *The Struggle of Islam in Modern Indonesia* (The Hague: Nijhoff).
Bruinessen, M. van (2002) 'Genealogies of Islamic radicalism in Indonesia', *South East Asia Research*, 10 (2): 117–154.
Cammack, M. E. (2007) 'The Indonesian Islamic Judiciary', in Feener, R.M. and Cammack, M.E. (eds), *Islamic Law in Contemporary Indonesia. Ideas and Institution* (Cambridge, MA: Harvard University Press).
Case, W. (2006) 'How do Rulers Control the Electoral Arena?' in Schedler, A. (ed.), *Electoral Authoritarianism: The Dynamics of Unfree Competition* (Boulder: Lynne Rienner).

Croissant, A. (2004) 'From Transition to Defective Democracy: Mapping Asian Democratization', *Democratization*, 11 (5): 156–178.

Crouch, H. (1996) *Government and Society in Malaysia* (Ithaca: Cornell University Press).

Effendy, B. (2003) *Islam and the State in Indonesia* (Singapore: ISEAS).

Eickelman, D. and Piscatori, J. (1996) *Muslim Politics* (Princeton: Princeton University Press).

Esposito, J. L. and Voll, J.O. (1996) *Islam and Democracy* (New York: Oxford University Press).

Hamayotsu, K. (2002) 'Islam and Nation Building in Southeast Asia: Malaysia and Indonesia in Comparative Perspective', *Pacific Affairs*, 75 (3): 353–375.

Hamayotsu, K. (2003) 'Politics of Syariah Reform: The Making of the State Religio-legal Apparatus', in Hooker, V. and Othman, N. (eds), *Malaysia: Islam, Society and Politics* (Singapore: ISEAS).

Hamid, A. and Fauzi, A. (2007) 'Patterns of State Interaction with Islamic Movements in Malaysia during the Formative Years of Islamic Resurgence', *Southeast Asian Studies*, 44 (4): 444–465.

Hefner, R. W. (2000) *Civil Islam: Muslims and Democratization in Indonesia* (Princeton: Princeton University Press).

Hooker, M.B. (2001) 'The State and Shari'a in Indonesia', in Salim, A. and Azra, A. (eds), *Shari'a and Politics in Modern Indonesia* (Singapore: ISEAS).

Huntington, S. P. (1991) *The Third Wave. Democratization in the Late Twentieth Century* (Norman and London: Oklahoma University Press).

International Crisis Group, Indonesia (2007) *Jemaah Islamiyah's Current Status* (Jakarta and Brussels).

Latif, Y. (2005) 'The Rupture of Young Muslim Intelligentsia in the Modernization of Indonesia', *Studia Islamika*, 12 (3) : 373–420.

Lembaga Survei Indonesia (2007) *Trend Orientasi Nilai-Nilai Politik Islamis vs Nilai-Nilai Politik Sekuler dan Kekuatan Islam Politik* (Jakarta: LSI).

Lewis, B. (2002) *What Went Wrong? Western Impact and Middle Eastern Response* (London: Phoenix).

Malhi, A. (2003) 'The PAS-BN Conflict in the 1990s: Islamism and Modernity', in Hooker, V. and Othman, N. (eds), *Malaysia: Islam, Society and Politics* (Singapore: ISEAS).

Martinez, P. A. (2006) *Muslim Malaysians: Living with Diversity,* Malaysiakini, August 25.

Mietzner, M. (2009) *Military Politics, Islam and the State in Indonesia: From Turbulent Transition to Democratic Consolidation* (Singapore: ISEAS).

Milne, R. S. and Mauzy, D.K. (1983) 'The Mahathir Administration: Discipline through Islam', *Pacific Affairs*, 56 (4): 617–648.

Mujani, S. and Liddle, W.R. (2007) 'Leadership, Party and Religion: Explaining Voting Behavior in Indonesia', *Comparative Political Studies*, 40 (7): 832–857.

Mujani, S. and Liddle, W.R. (2009) 'Muslim Indonesia's Secular Democracy', *Asian Survey*, 49 (4): 575–590.

Mulia, S.M. and Cammack, M.E. (2007) 'Toward a Just Marriage Law: Empowering Indonesian Women through a Counter Legal Draft to the Indonesian Compilation of Islamic Law', in Feener, R.M. and Cammack, M.E. (eds), *Islamic Law in contemporary Indonesia: ideas and institutions* (Cambridge: Harvard University Press).

Mutalib, H. (1990) *Islam and Ethnicity in Malay Politics* (Singapore: Oxford University Press).

Nagata, J.A. (1984) *The Reflowering of Malaysian Islam. Modern Religious Radicals and their Roots* (Vancouver: University of British Columbia Press).

Nasr, S.V.R. (2001) *Islamic Leviathan: Islam and the Making of State Power* (Oxford: Oxford University Press).

Noor, F.A. (2004) *Islam embedded. The historical development of the Pan-Malaysian Islamic Party PAS (1951-2003)*, 2 vols (Kuala Lumpur: Malaysian Sociological Research Institute).

Porter, D.J. (2002), *Managing Politics and Islam in Indonesia* (London and New York: Routledge).

Roff, W. R. (1994) *The Origins of Malay Nationalism* (Oxford: Oxford University Press).

Salim, A. (2007) 'Muslim Politics in Indonesia's Democratisation: The Religious Majority and the Rights of Minorities in the Post-New Order Era', in McLeod, R. and MacIntyre, A. (eds), *Indonesia. Democracy and the Promise of Good Governance* (Singapore: ISEAS).

Schedler, A. (2002) 'Elections without Democracy: The Menu of Manipulation', *Journal of Democracy*, 13 (2): 36–50.

Schedler, A. (2006) 'The Logic of Electoral Authoritarianism', in Schedler, A. (ed.) *Electoral Authoritarianism: The Dynamics of Unfree Competition* (Boulder: Lynne Rienner).

Schwedler, J. (2006) *Faith in Moderation: Islamist parties in Yemen and Jordan* (New York: Cambridge University Press).

Sidel, J. (2008) 'Social Origins of Dictatorship and Democracy Revisited: Colonial State and Chinese Immigrant in the Making of Modern Southeast Asia', *Comparative Politics*, 40 (2): 127–147.

Slater, D. (2009) 'Revolutions, Crackdowns, and Quiescence: Communal Elites and Democratic Mobilization in Southeast Asia', *American Journal of Sociology*, 115 (1): 203–254.

Tezcür, G. M. (2010) 'The Moderation Thesis Revisited. The Case of Islamic Political Actors', *Party Politics*, 16 (1): 69–88.

Ufen, A. (2008) 'From Aliran to Dealignment. Political Parties in Post-Suharto Indonesia', *South East Asia Research*, 16 (1): 6–41.

Ufen, A. (2009) 'The Transformation of Political Party Opposition in Malaysia and its Implications for the Electoral Authoritarian Regime', *Democratization*, 16 (3): 604–627.

Ufen, A. (2009b) 'Mobilizing Political Islam: Indonesia and Malaysia Compared', *Commonwealth & Comparative Politics*, 47 (3) :Webber, D. (2006) 'Consolidated Patrimonial Democracy? Democratization in Post-Suharto Indonesia', *Democratization*, 13 (3): 396–420.

Wickham, C.R. (2004) 'The Path to Moderation: Strategy and Learning in the Formation of Egypt's Wasat Party', *Comparative Politics*, 36 (2): 205–228.

Yegar, M. (1979) Islam and Islamic Institutions in British Malaya. Policies and Implementation (Jerusalem: Magnes Press).

6
Types of Democracy in Southeast Asia and Democratic Consolidation

Aurel Croissant

Introduction

What difference does the type of democracy make for democratic endurance and consolidation?[1] In his seminal studies *Democracies* (1984) and *Patterns of Democracy* (1999), Arend Lijphart argued that there are two basic types of democracy: majoritarian (or Westminster) democracy and consensus democracy. The choice of majoritarian or consensus democracy has important consequences for the actual performance of democratic regimes. In majoritarian democracies, political power is concentrated in the hands of the political majority, which allows it to control political decision-making. Majoritarian democracy is characterized by exclusiveness and the predominance of the 'winner-takes-all' principle. By contrast, consensus democracy disperses political power and maximizes the number of actors involved in decision-making. It promotes inclusiveness and facilitates power sharing among different levels of government, political institutions, and political actors. In his analysis Lijphart (1999, p.301) reached the conclusion that consensus democracies have a slightly better record on macroeconomic management and the control of violence, and clearly outperform majoritarian democracies with regard to the quality of democracy and democratic representation. Therefore, his advice to new democracies is that '[t]he consensus option is the more attractive option for countries designing their first democratic constitutions or contemplating democratic reforms' (1999, p.302).

The purpose of this chapter is to extend Lijphart's analysis to four newly democratized countries in Southeast Asia: Thailand, Indonesia, East Timor and the Philippines. At the core of the analysis are three research questions: (1) To what extent do democracies in Southeast Asia exhibit features of majoritarian or consensus democracy? (2) How do emerging democracies in Southeast Asia fit into the two-dimensional patterns of democracy identified by Lijphart? (3) Does the type of democracy matter for democratic consolidation? The rest of the chapter proceeds as follows. First, I will outline

Lijphart's approach and apply it to Southeast Asia. In the following section, we will explore how well the countries fit into Lijphart's majoritarian–consensus scheme. Next, we will discuss whether the type of democracy matters for democratic performance and consolidation in Southeast Asia. The chapter concludes with a summary of the main findings and their implications for the recent crisis of democratic governance in the region.

Democratic institutions in Southeast Asia

In this analysis, we will examine institutional patterns in Thailand, Indonesia, East Timor and the Philippines. Each of these countries has experienced a minimum of two competitive multiparty elections and has been classified as a (defective) democracy in the Bertelsmann Transformation Index 2010 (Bertelsmann Stiftung, 2009). Electoral authoritarian regimes such as Singapore, Malaysia, and Cambodia have been excluded from the analysis. The period under analysis begins with the first competitive multiparty legislative election (*founding election*) for each democracy and ends with the latest multiparty parliamentary election for which data were available at the time of writing, or in case of Thailand, with the breakdown of electoral democracy by military intervention in September 2006.

We account for constitutional amendments during the period being analyzed in Indonesia by employing an average measure of certain indicators for the entire period. Thailand, however, adopted a new constitution in October 1997. This so-called 'People's Constitution' introduced far-reaching institutional changes, such as a new electoral system and an altered structure of bicameralism, strengthened the prime minister vis-à-vis the parliament, and created numerous independent watchdog agencies, such as a new constitutional court. We have therefore split the analysis of Thailand's political institutions into two periods (see Table 6.1).

In *Patterns of Democracy* (1999), Lijphart measures the degree to which democracies fit into either the majoritarian or the consensus model by observing ten variables. These variables measure both institutions that are subject to direct constitutional design and those that emerge indirectly from the interaction between institutions and other factors (Taagepera, 2003; Roberts, 2006, p.38). For example, the number of parties in a democracy emerges from institutional (election system) and social factors (cleavage structure),

Table 6.1　Cases selected

Case	Time period	Form of government
[1] Indonesia	07 June 1999–09 April 2009	presidential
[2] East Timor	30 August 2001–08 August 2007	semi-presidential
[3] Philippines	11 May 1987–14 May 2007	presidential
[4] Thailand (1)	13 September 1992–15 October 1997	parliamentary
[5] Thailand (2)	16 October 1997–17 September 2006	parliamentary

whereas the type of bicameralism is a consequence of institutional design. Table 6.2 shows how the variables are measured.

Lijphart's correlation analysis shows that the ten variables cluster along two separate dimensions (1999, pp.243–6). The *executives–parties dimension* refers to whether power is dispersed within the central government; it is composed of variables one to five. By contrast, the *federal–unitary dimension* refers to whether power is dispersed among different political institutions; it is composed of the remaining five variables. Lijphart observes that the correlation of the variables within the dimensions is statistically significant, while the correlation between the two dimensions is not significant. Factor analysis confirms that the variables can be divided into two encompassing and exclusive factors (1999, pp.243–57).

In what follows, I will measure nine of Lijphart's ten variables for the five Southeast Asian cases from the founding election up to the most recent election (except for Thailand; see above). The single variable I will not measure is *interest group system*. Lijphart's measure of the degree of pluralism or corporatism is based on the index of interest group pluralism (Siaroff, 1998) and additional sources (Lijphart, 1999, p.178); however, for the Southeast Asian democracies, reliable data to measure interest group pluralism is not available. I will also modify Lijphart's approach as concerns the measurement of *central bank independence*. Lijphart's comprehensive index and its component indices do not provide data for the cases observed in the study at hand; I will therefore use the central bank autonomy index designed by Arnone et al. (2007). This index ranges from one to zero. The lower the index value, the lower the degree of autonomy and vice versa. For Thailand, the index value for the late 1980s is used for the first period analyzed; the 2003 value is used for the second period

Executives–parties dimension

Table 6.3 demonstrates how Southeast Asian democracies perform on the first four variables of the executives–parties dimension. On the first variable, *party system type*, Southeast Asian democracies exhibit some degree of variance; Indonesia, Thailand (1992–97), and the Philippines have quite a large number of political parties in their parliaments. By contrast, in Thailand, the data exhibits a clear trajectory toward single-party dominance between 2001 and 2006. This was a result of the rise of Thaksin Shinawatra's Thai Rak Thai (TRT) party to political hegemony between 2001 and the 2006 military coup d'état (see Hicken, Chapter 9 in this volume). The effective number of parliamentary parties dropped from 6.1 in 1992 to 1.6 in 2005. In East Timor, the effective number of parliamentary parties increased from 2.8 in 2001 to 4.4 in 2007, whereas in Indonesia the ENPP rose from 5.5 in 1999 to 7.1 in 2004; in 2009, however, the number again dropped to 6.1. Micro-parties, whose number had already markedly decreased from 14 in 1999 to 10 in 2004, were completely eradicated from parliament by the introduction of a 2.5 per cent threshold in 2009 (Croissant and Völkel, forthcoming).

Table 6.2 Variables and measurements

Variable	Majoritarian democracy	Consensus democracy	Measurement
1. Party system	Two-party system	Multiparty system	Average index of the effective number of parties in the first or only chamber of the national legislature. The formula is $ENP = 1/(\sum s_i^2)$; $s_i^2 =$ squaring each political party's share of seats in the parliament (Laakso and Taagepera, 1979).
2. Concentration of executive power	Single-party cabinets	Power sharing in broad coalition cabinets	Combined (percentage) average of the lifespan of minimal winning–single party cabinets during the period of analysis (Lijphart, 1999, pp.109ff). If cabinet posts are only filled by the party of the president or in parliamentary systems the party of the prime minister, a cabinet is classified as a single-party cabinet. If other parties participate in the government, cabinets are counted as either minimal winning cabinets or as other according to the seated proportions of the parties.
3. Executive–legislative relations	Executive dominance	Balance of power	Average cabinet duration in months during the period analyzed (1999, pp.129–34). Cabinet duration in parliamentary systems is measured based on four criteria for the termination of a cabinet – change in party composition, prime ministership, coalitional status, and new elections. In presidential and semi-presidential systems, a cabinet ends after every presidential election, the end of a presidential term, or any change in party composition or coalitional status.
4. Electoral disproportionality	Majoritarian and disproportional systems of election	Proportional representation	Averaged Gallagher index of disproportionality. The index involves taking the square root of half the sum of the squares of the difference between the percentage of votes and the percentage of seats (as whole numbers) for each of the political parties. The index ranges from 0 to 100. The lower the index value, the lower the disproportionality and vice versa (Gallagher, 1991). 'Other parties' as a whole category are excluded.

5. Interest group system	Pluralism	Corporatism	Degree of pluralism or corporatism based on Alan Siaroff's index of interest group pluralism (Siaroff, 1998) and Lijphart's measures on the basis of expert judgments.
6. Degree of centralization	Unitary–centralized government	Federal–decentralized government	Federalism–decentralization index, proposed by Lijphart. Countries are measured on a scale from 1.0 to 5.0, with 1.0 representing unitary–centralized states and 5.0 indicating federal–decentralized countries (Lijphart, 1999, p.189).
7. Bicameralism	Unicameral system	Strong bicameralism	Lijphart's index of bicameralism, ranging from 4.0 (strong bicameralism, including symmetrical distribution of legislative powers and incongruent representation of segments of the electorate), 3.0 (medium-strength bicameralism of symmetrical and congruent chambers or asymmetric and incongruent chambers), 2.0 (weak bicameralism with asymmetrical, congruent chambers), to 1.0 (unicameral systems) (1999, pp.205–13).
8. Constitutional rigidity	Constitutional flexibility	Constitutional rigidity	Lijphart's index of constitutional rigidity, ranging from 1.0 (parliamentary plurality), 2.0 (plurality to two-thirds majority), 3.0 (two-thirds majority), to 4.0 (supermajorities of more than a two-thirds majority are required for amending the constitution) (1999, pp.219–20).
9. Judicial review	No judicial review	Strong judicial review	Lijphart's index of judicial review. It differentiates between non-existent judicial review exercised by either a constitutional court or supreme court (1.0 points), weak judicial review (2.0), moderate judicial review (3.0), or strong judicial review (4.0) (1999, pp.225–8).
10. Central bank independence	Central bank controlled by the executive	Independent central bank	Lijphart's comprehensive index of central bank independence, composed of three individual indices (1999, pp.236–40).

Source: Lijphart (1999).

Table 6.3 Executives–parties dimension

	Effective number of parliamentary parties	Minimal winning one-party cabinets (%)	Index of executive dominance (in years)	Index of disproportionality
Indonesia	6.4	5.9	1.19	4.56
East Timor	3.6	85.6	1.96	4.47
Philippines	4.49	0	2.85	5.23
Thailand 1	5.6	33	0.54	3.26
Thailand 2	2.3	17.7	1.81	11.1

Source: Data for the effective number of parties and the index of disproportionality are taken from Croissant and Völkel (forthcoming). Percentages of minimal winning one-party cabinets and the index of executive dominance were calculated by the author based on data from *Keesing's World News Archive* (various issues), Chambers (2003, 2008), and national newspapers.

On measures of concentration of executive power, government power in Thailand until 1997, in the Philippines and especially in Indonesia has tended to be dispersed among coalition parties. These countries consistently have oversized multiparty coalitions. In Indonesia, the National Unity Cabinet of President Wahid (1999–2001), the Rainbow Coalition of President Megawati (2001–04), and the United Indonesia Cabinet of President Susilo Bambang Yudhoyono (since 2004) all belong to this type of oversized cabinet (see Reilly, Chapter 7 in this volume). The Philippines has also had instances of presidents forming oversized cabinets, but unlike in Indonesia, these coalitions are formed as pre-election alliances of political groupings (Ufen, 2008, p.334). In Thailand before 2001, oversized multiparty cabinets of five or more parties were the rule (Chambers, 2003). These cabinets tended to be short-lived, with frequent changes in the party composition of coalitions and cabinet reshuffles. Prior to Thaksin, a popularly elected coalition government had not managed to serve a full four-year parliamentary term. Although the number of parties declined with the 2001 election, oversized coalitions continued to govern until 2004, when the Thai Rak Thai party of Premier Thaksin formed a single-party government (Chambers, 2006). East Timor is the only semi-presidential system in Southeast Asia. The president is elected by popular vote for a single five-year term. He appoints as prime minister the leader of the majority party or the coalition of parties in parliament and has the power to dissolve the parliament, but only with the consent of the political parties sitting in the parliament (Art. 86). He can dismiss the government and remove the PM from office only if parliament has rejected his or her programme two consecutive times (Art. 86). Under this semi-presidential structure, the Fretilin party formed a single-party government from 2001 to 2007. Following the 30 June 2007 election, the CNRT (National Congress for Timorese Reconstruction) allied itself with three other parties to form an oversized coalition cabinet.

In his analysis, Lijphart (1999, pp.12ff.) uses the length of the average cabinet duration in months as an indicator of the third variable, *degree of executive dominance*. Compared to other Southeast Asian nations, the Philippines has experienced a high degree of cabinet durability and, hence, a strong degree of executive dominance over the Congress. However, the index value gives a partly inaccurate impression of the degree of executive dominance in the Philippines, as the president is potentially weaker due to weak discipline among the major Philippine political parties (Rüland et al., 2005, pp.226–42). Furthermore, presidential authority is considerably stronger in budgetary policy-making than in other policy areas where the Congress is more influential (Kasuya, 2009). In East Timor, which is ranked second in terms of Lijphart's indicator of executive dominance, conflicts between Prime Minister Alkatiri of Fretilin and the former Fretilin leader and chairman of the oppositional CNRT, President Gusmão (2002–07), created serious issues of contention between the two institutions. On two occasions, the president demanded the dismissal of a cabinet minister, on both occasions without effect. This system of 'conflictual cohabitation' (Shoesmith, 2007, p.229) only came to an end with the crisis of 2006, when PM Alkatiri, facing strong pressure from President Gusmão and the international community, had to step down. In the following 2007 election, the CNRT coalition won both the presidential race and the parliamentary election, which eliminated cohabitation.

The parliamentary system in Thailand (1992–97) and presidentialism in Indonesia are characterized by rather transient cabinets, which indicates a rough balance of power between parliament and the executive. Among other things, the low index of executive dominance in Indonesia reflects the political instability during the years 1999 to 2001 (King, 2004). In Thailand (until 1997), the cabinet's weakness vis-à-vis the parliament was, to a certain extent, a consequence of intra-party factionalism and the weak cohesion of the political parties (Chambers, 2008). After the 1997 constitutional amendment, and especially after the 2001 legislative election, the balance of power shifted to strong executive dominance during the administration of Prime Minister Thaksin (2001–06).

Some scholars criticize Lijphart's measure, claiming that cabinet duration is not an appropriate indicator for measuring the patterns of dominance and the balance of power between the two institutions (Taagepera, 2003). An alternative measure to capture formal executive dominance over the legislature was developed by Matthew Shugart and John Carey (1992). They measure the strength of presidents in two dimensions. In the dimension of the legislative powers of presidents, their coding integrates package and partial veto, decrees, initiation of legislation, budgetary powers and referenda provisions. The second dimension comprises non-legislative powers, such as presidential authority over cabinet formation and cabinet dismissal, censure, and the presidential power to dissolve parliament (1992, pp.150–4). Shugart and Carey also provide a method for measuring the strength of presidential powers in each dimension. They have adopted a four-point scale for each of the six items in the first dimension and for each of the four powers in the second dimension. The higher the score, the stronger the president's authority (for details, see ibid., p.150).

As we can see from Table 6.4, the Shugart and Carey index is at odds with Lijphart's cabinet duration variable. When measured against the formal indicators of constitutional power developed by Shugart and Carey, the president in Indonesia is the strongest executive both in terms of legislative and non-legislative powers, whereas the president in East Timor has only minimal constitutional authority. However, the Shugart and Carey index only captures the *formal* powers of the presidents. When considering the real pattern of the executive–legislative relationship in Indonesia – and, as mentioned, in the Philippines – one has to take into account that the president's influence over the legislature also depends on the strength of the ruling party or parties in parliament, the degree of party discipline and the status of the presidential party vis-à-vis its coalition partners. In this context, Indonesia's score on the Lijphart scale still reflects to some extent the existing balance of power between the executive and legislative branches of government. Since the transition to democracy, the submissive legislature of the authoritarian New Order regime of President Suharto (1966–98) has evolved into a competitive parliament that actively

Table 6.4   Constitutional powers of popularly elected presidents in Southeast Asia

	East Timor*	Indonesia**	Philippines
Legislative powers	3	8	5
Package veto	1	4	2
Partial veto	0	0	3
Decree	0	2	0
Exclusive initiation of legislation	0	1	0
Budgetary powers	0	1	0
Proposal of referenda	2	0	0
Nonlegislative powers	2	12	11
Cabinet formation	0	4	3
Cabinet dismissal	1	4	4
Censure	0	4	4
Dissolution of parliament	1	0	0

*The president may veto a bill (Art. 85), but parliament can override it within 90 days by an absolute majority (Art. 88). He can call a referendum following a proposal by parliament or government (Art. 66).
**After the third and fourth constitutional amendments (November 2001/August 2002).

Sources: compiled by the author based on King (2004, p.64), Shugart and Carey (1992, p.154), Constitution of East Timor.

constrains the decision-making authority of the president and forces him to adopt an inclusive style of governance (Ziegenhain, 2008).

The last variable in the first dimension is the type of *electoral system*. The typical electoral system in consensus democracy is the PR (proportional representation) system; majoritarian democracy typically uses the single-member constituency plurality system (Lijphart, 1999, p.143). In his contribution to this volume, Reilly shows that there has been a region-wide convergence in recent years, with the Philippines, Thailand and other East Asian nations choosing 'mixed-member' electoral systems during the last two decades. Still, there is significant variation in the region's electoral systems. East Timor conducted its first election with a mixed-member *proportional* system (MMPS) but switched to a system of proportional representation with closed party lists and a 3 per cent threshold in 2007. Indonesia started with a proportional representation system with closed lists in 1999, then switched to open lists in 2004, and recently introduced a 2.5 per cent threshold for the 2009 elections.

As demonstrated in Table 6.3, the average degree of electoral disproportionality (Gallagher Index) ranges from a low 3.26 per cent for Thailand's multi-member district plurality system during the period 1992–97 to a high 11.1 per cent in post-1997 Thailand. Although PR systems in Indonesia and East Timor exhibit a lower degree of disproportionality than the mixed-member majoritarian system in the Philippines, there is no strikingly clear line dividing the PR systems from the plurality and segmented systems, except for Thailand's post-1997 mixed-member *majoritarian* system.

Federal–unitary dimension

The five variables in Lijphart's second dimension focus on the dispersion of political power between separate institutions. Despite its name, not all structures in this dimension are necessarily ingredients of federalism. For example, strong central bank autonomy, extensive judicial review, and constitutional rigidity also exist in unitary–centralized states. Therefore it would be more accurate to label this second dimension the 'divided-power dimension' (Lijphart, 1999, p.5).

Southeast Asian scores on all five of the variables can be found in Table 6.5. With regard to the *federalism* variable, all five cases fall on the majoritarian end of the scale. Though most unitary states have retreated from authoritarian centralization by introducing decentralization schemes in the past two decades, only the Philippines and Indonesia have devolved real decision-making authority (see Bünte, Chapter 8 in this volume).

There is also considerable variation in *cameral structure* among the countries. East Timor has a unicameral system, while all of the other cases have a bicameral system. The Philippine Congress consists of the Senate and the House of Representatives. The 24 senators are popularly elected in a

Table 6.5   Federal–unitary dimension

	Federalism [1.0–5.0]	Bicameralism [1.0–4.0]	Constitutional rigidity [1.0–4.0]	Judicial review [1.0–4.0]	Central bank autonomy [0.0–1.0]
Indonesia	2	2	2	2	0.69
East Timor	1	1	3	2	0.38
Philippines	2	3	2	3	0.63
Thailand 1	1	3	2	1	0.36
Thailand 2	1	2	2	2	0.44

Sources: Data gathered from the individual countries' constitutions, Arnone et al. (2007), Croissant (forthcoming), Rüland et al. (2005) and Nickson et al. (2008).

nationwide constituency by plurality, whereas the members of the House are elected in 212 single-member districts and as Sectoral Representatives through the party list system. The House has the exclusive power to propose legislation relating to appropriations, revenues, tariffs and increasing the public debt. In addition, the House can initiate bills of local application. On other matters of legislation, the authority of the Senate equals that of the House of Representatives. In Thailand before 1997, the appointed Senate functioned as a powerful instrument for the civil bureaucracy and the military to check the political process in the directly elected House of Representatives. With the constitutional reform of 1997, Senators were for the first time popularly elected on a non-partisan basis. At the same time, the Senate's legislative powers remained limited. Furthermore, the actual political performance of the upper house was constrained by its weak internal organization and lack of resources and by the frequent political interventions of the Thaksin government in senatorial affairs (Chambers, 2009, pp.19–20).

The second chamber in the Indonesian legislature is also quite weak. Before 2004, the People's Consultative Assembly (*Majelis Permusyawaratan Rakyat* or MPR) was the highest governing body in Indonesia. The MPR elected the president and had the right to amend the constitution, but it did not participate in the legislative process. With the introduction of the popular election of the president in 2004, the Assembly lost most of its relevance. In the same year, the Regional Representative Council (*Dewan Perwakilan Daerah* or DPD) was established to represent the provinces in national politics. Regional representatives are popularly elected in provincial constituencies on a non-partisan basis. The Council's legislative powers are restricted to bills on regional affairs, central–local government relations, resource management and the financial balance between the centre and the regions. The DPD can propose such bills to the first chamber and must be heard on any regional bill proposed by the People's Representative Council (Ziegenhain, 2008).

Turning to *constitutional rigidity*, we can see from Table 6.5 that Southeast Asian countries have opted for moderately difficult to amend constitutions. In Indonesia, two-thirds of the members of the People's Consultative Assembly must be present, but any proposed amendment requires a majority. In East Timor, a two-thirds majority of parliament can amend the constitution, and in Thailand, until 2006, amendments to the constitution required approval by a plurality of both the Senate and the House of Representatives. Rules for constitutional change in the Philippines are more complicated. Under the 1987 constitution, there are three methods of amendment: people's initiative, constituent assembly, and constitutional convention. The different modes of constitutional change require quorums from different assemblies. Each mode includes a referendum, in which the proposed amendment must receive a majority of votes in order to be adopted.

All of the countries in the region have some form of *judicial review*. Thailand's 1991 constitution had a provision for an ad hoc constitutional tribunal, whose members were drawn from the leadership of various political, administrative and judicial bodies, and which was vested with the power of preventive and concrete review. It was only with the adoption of the 'People's Constitution' in October 1997 that an independent constitutional court was established. Indonesia established a constitutional court in August 2003. In 1987, the Philippines returned to the pre-Marcos system of centralized judicial review with a supreme court at the top of the judicial system. In East Timor, the Supreme Court is vested with the exclusive power of preventive and abstract review of the 'unconstitutionality of normative and legislative acts by the organs of the State' (Art. 126).

The Philippine Supreme Court has been quite active and has frequently overruled parliamentary legislation and executive orders in the past. Although not as strong, Indonesia's constitutional court has succeeded in establishing itself as a legitimate and active 'guardian of human rights' (Croissant, forthcoming). This, however, contrasts with the experiences of the 1997 Constitutional Court in Thailand. While the Court did play a prominent role as the guarantor of government accountability in its early years, it failed to call the authoritarian and manipulative Thaksin government of 2001 to 2006 to account in any meaningful way. Instead of acting as the guardian of the constitution, the Court became increasingly marginalized by the government (Chaowana and Hoerth, 2008, p.321).

Finally, *central bank independenc* is the weakest in East Timor and Thailand; in the Philippines, the degree of central bank autonomy is higher; and in Indonesia, the central bank enjoys the greatest level of independence (see Table 6.5).

Southeast Asia situated on Lijphart's two-dimensional conceptual map of democracy

One of Lijphart's main conclusions is that these variables of majoritarian–consensus democracy cluster along two separate dimensions. Recent analyses of new democracies in Eastern Europe (Roberts, 2006; Fortin, 2008) and Asia (Croissant and Schächter, 2010) have tested this conclusion. Taken together, their findings suggest that emerging democracies follow 'different dynamics than Lijphart's established democracies' (Roberts, 2006, p.48; Croissant and Schächter, 2010, pp.186–7). The majority of democracies in both Asia and Eastern Europe appear to be hybrids, mixing features of consensus and majoritarian democracy in ways that are not easy to reconcile with Lijphart's categories. For example, these studies found fewer (and weaker) relations between the variables in each of the two dimensions. Moreover, they revealed a number of statistically significant correlations between indicators of the first and the second dimensions, although according to Lijphart (1999, pp.245–6), they should be independent.

The aim of this section, however, is not to test whether Lijphart's variables cluster along two separate dimensions but to investigate where the emerging democracies in Southeast Asia are situated between majoritarian and consensus democracy. In order to place each of the 36 cases in his data set on a two-dimensional conceptual map of democracy, Lijphart standardized all five variables in each dimension and averaged them to produce a summary measure of the executives–parties dimension and the federal–unitary dimension (1999, p.248).[2] To situate the five Southeast Asian countries on Lijphart's map, I have used data for 46 democracies – 36 from Lijphart's data set, five (Nepal, Bangladesh, Mongolia, South Korea and Taiwan) from Croissant and Schächter (2010), and the five cases from this article. Because I did not measure Lijphart's interest group system, I repeated the calculation of factor values in both dimensions for Lijphart's 36 countries, plus the other five Asian countries, excluding this variable.[3] Moreover, the signs of the variables were adjusted so that high values on each variable represent majoritarianism, while low values indicate consensus.

The Philippines and Indonesia are positioned in the lower-left field (II), displaying strong consensual features on the federal–unitary dimension and particularly strong consensual features on the executives–parties dimension. Indonesia is the clearest consensual type in Asia on the executives–parties dimension. The Philippines also exhibits consensus elements on the executives–parties dimension (in particular, frequent coalition cabinets, multipartism, and moderately disproportional plurality elections) along with consensus traits, albeit somewhat more strongly, on the divided-power dimension (in particular, stronger bicameralism and judicial review).

Thailand before October 1997 represents the combination of consensus elements on the executives–parties dimension and majoritarianism on the federal–unitary dimension. The contrast between Thailand's two positions on the conceptual map demonstrates a sizeable shift toward greater majoritarianism since 1997, which situates Thailand during the second period next to East Timor. This change reflects the impact of constitutional reform on the executives–parties dimension – in particular, the drastic increase in electoral disproportionality and the emergence of the single-party dominance of the TRT party, which gave rise to executive dominance. At the same time, the creation of new institutional checks and balances accounts for the modest shift in the second dimension, separation of powers.

At first glance, our results seem at odds with recent research findings about the types of democracy in Asia. For example, Reilly argues that in the Asia Pacific, and especially in Southeast Asia, 'the cumulative impact' of constitutional reforms 'has seen a shift away from the broadly 'consociational' political models of the immediate post-independence period toward more integrative or centripetal forms of democracy in recent years' (Reilly, Chapter 7 in this volume). Furthermore, he provides empirical evidence that there is 'an Asian model of democracy' emerging that 'is in some ways moving closer to the Anglo-American model of two-party democracy' (Reilly, 2007, p.1367). Our findings do not necessarily contradict these assessments. First of all, the period analyzed in this chapter is shorter than Reilly's, who compares institutional reforms in recent years with the institutional models that were prevalent in Southeast Asia in the 1950s and 1960s. Second, the positions of democracies on the conceptual map in Figure 6.1 are the *averages* of the positions over the period under analysis. These averages conceal any large or small changes that may have taken place during the period analyzed. In fact, Thailand, the only country case we split into two periods, confirms Reilly's argument of a recent change 'characterized by aggregative electoral politics, centrist political competition and [a] nascent two-party system' (2007, p.1351). Third, Reilly (2007, p.1367) acknowledges that Indonesia and the Philippines are the two main exceptions to the pronounced movement toward more majoritarian politics in the Asia-Pacific region. The position of both cases on the map in Figure 6.1 confirms this conclusion.

What difference does the type of democratic institution make for democratic consolidation?

Another question remains pertaining to the consequences of democratic institutions and constitutional choices. Lijphart's study investigates the impact of different patterns of democracy on the political, economic and social performance of *established* democracies. More recently, the third wave of democratization has stimulated inquiry into the impact of consensus and majoritarian institutions on democratic consolidation. Wolfgang Merkel, for example, linked consensus democracy and democratic consolidation

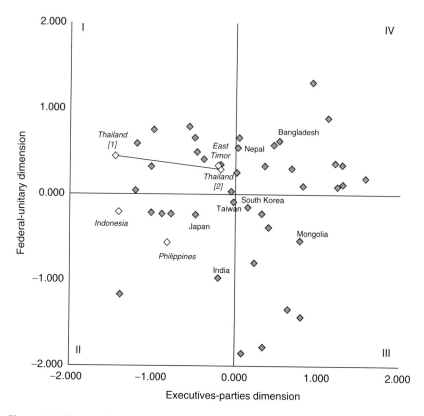

Figure 6.1 The position of Asian cases in Lijphart's democracy matrix

through the notion of 'social and political inclusion', by which he means that no 'structural' minority group (racial, ethnic, linguistic or religious minorities) nor any relevant political minorities should be barred from or be at a disadvantage in gaining institutional access to political power (Merkel, 1998; see also Ágh, 2001). Similarly, Mair notes that 'the likelihood of successful consolidation of democracy depends, in large part on the willingness of the protagonists to encourage a culture of compromise and accommodation. Winners should not take all' (Mair, 1998, p.197). Consensus institutions are more representative, more inclusive, and tend to feature higher degrees of compromise and accommodation than majoritarian institutions, and are hence more conducive to the integration of diverse segments of society into the democratic system. This is especially important in plural societies, where a higher degree of inclusiveness not only provides better incentives for political elites to develop a sense of restrained partisanship and an underlying consensus on political game rules, but also contributes to broader support for and legitimacy of the democratic system among the mass citizenry (Lijphart, 1999, pp.32–4; Merkel, 1998; Norris, 2008, p.210).

Other research has focused mainly on the different consequences of presidential and parliamentary systems and electoral rules (PR or plurality rule), and has tended to lead to claims of the superiority of parliamentary or PR systems (see Lijphart, 2008a [1991], 2008b [1994]; Linz, 1994). On the other hand, Lijphart asserts that presidentialism is a highly majoritarian form of government because it concentrates 'executive power to an even greater degree than does a one-party parliamentary cabinet – not just in a single *party* but in a single *person*' (Lijphart, 2008a, p.162; emphasis Lijphart's). While consensus institutions subject elected governments and legislative majorities to formal and informal checks and balances that ensure that democracy is not degenerating into 'elected dictatorship' (Hailsham, 1976), majoritarian systems lack such mechanisms. While Lijphart (2008b) sees 'majoritarian' presidentialism as especially prone to turning democracies into 'elective dictatorships', other authors point to how Westminster-style parliamentary systems are more likely to lead to this scenario, because parliamentary supremacy can easily be abused by governments, especially when the rule of law, the media and civil society and other constitutional constraints of 'separationism' are weak (Sajó, 1999, p.160; Cameron et al., 2006).

However, recent comparative research demonstrates that the results are closely conditioned by case selection: for example, Lijphart's recommendation of PR or parliamentary systems rests primarily on his research on democratic performance in established democracies and might be biased by the inclusion of very small and homogeneous societies in Scandinavia, whereas his characterization of presidentialism is strongly influenced by the US model (see Foweraker and Landman, 2002, p.47). Comparative research on presidentialism outside the US, though, clearly demonstrates that most presidential systems have PR electoral rules and are multiparty. Government coalitions are not exceptional in presidential systems, and legislative coalitions are pervasive (Cheibub, 2007).

In fact, the Southeast Asian countries are only partially congruent with Lijphart's view, especially regarding the difficult combination of presidentialism and majoritarianism. This does not apply to Indonesia and the Philippines, where the presidential executive is embedded in network structures of 'veto points' (Immergut, 1990) that check executive power and counterbalance the menace of 'elective dictatorship'; the consequences for regime endurance and the consolidation of democracy, however, differ considerably. On the one hand, the experience of post-Suharto Indonesia demonstrates the virtues of 'consensualized' presidentialism with its strong features of consensus institutions, especially in the first dimension, executives–parties. Since the transition to democracy in 1999, there has been no extra-constitutional threat to the government. Despite remaining challenges on its way to more transparent, clean and effective governance, the democratic institutions seem healthy, with a working system of genuine checks and balances among the branches of government, stable political parties, a relative high level of support for democracy and low popular attraction to political extremism. Although it is probably too early to call Indonesia a consolidated democracy, the political system has achieved remarkable stability (Bünte and Ufen, 2009; Mietzner, 2009). The conditional success of democratic transition in Indonesia was supported by the political elite's ability to produce and maintain public support, by civilian consensus on the need to keep the military out of politics, and by the political actors' adherence to essential democratic norms and procedures. Inclusionary coalition politics, compromise, and accommodation among party elites have become largely uncontested parameters for the political process in that country.

In contrast to Indonesia, the political regime in the Philippines appears as a fragmented, not consensus, democracy. 'Fragmented' democracy is a 'distorted version of the consensus democracy', with an overdriven separation of powers, an overlapping system of institutional 'checks and balances', the asymmetrical character of intermediary actors caused by the marginalization of social actors by the political parties, and the weakness of civic associations and civic attitudes at the micro-level (Ágh, 2001, pp.94–5). In fact, while the Philippine constitutional system features strong 'divided power' institutions and multipartism, many scholars express doubts about the ability of the political parties to represent their electorates, to act on behalf of their constituents, and to enact the policies they have pledged to enact. Furthermore, the inchoate character of the national party system means that political parties find it difficult to build close links with voters. Given that political parties come and go, it is difficult to imagine that parties can cooperate and realize that the main advantage of consensus government is its higher degree of compromise and accommodation, because this requires some political certainty (Mair, 1998).

The case of East Timor, on the other hand, shows the limits of power-dividing semi-presidentialism and PR arrangements in a political setting that is shaped by disunified elites and a lack of shared commitments to democracy (Guterres, 2006). After independence, an old distinction between people from the east and west of East Timor re-emerged, carrying a degree of political significance and adding to the existing political fault lines stemming from differences in generational, ideological and organizational backgrounds (Simonsen, 2006, p.590). Between 2001 and 2007, East Timor's democratic regime featured divisive politics, marginalized opposition and Fretilin's control of government and parliament as the party in power (Guterres, 2006, p.292; Shoesmith, 2007, p.224).

Post-1997 Thailand provides the clearest example of parliamentary systems where majoritarianism has given rise to 'elected dictatorships'.

Thailand's transformation into 'elected authoritarianism' (Thitinan, 2008) during the government of Prime Minister Thaksin Shinawatra (2001–06) was closely associated with the institutional reforms of 1997. The new constitution weakened the existing institutional arrangements in the executives–parties dimension by supporting the executive over the legislature, by strengthening the prime minister and the cabinet over individual party and faction leaders, and by shifting party-system development from multipartism toward a predominant party system (Kuhonta, 2008, p.375). At the same time, the Thaksin government pursued a policy of confrontation not only with political actors but also with social actors – often accompanied by official declarations on the necessity of the concentration of power in the hands of the government and on its popular mandate and legitimation to do so. This not only ran counter to the 'People's Constitution's' goal of more participatory governance but also challenged the increasing pluralization of Thai civil society and deepened the existing political fissures (Thitinan, 2008).

The efforts to turn Thailand into a majoritarian democracy and to establish a presidential-style democracy in a parliamentary disguise threatened the informal network of monarchy, bureaucracy, military and civilian elites that had previously formed a counterbalance to the elected politicians (McCargo, 2005). In this context, the new 2007 constitution can be seen as another (perhaps ill-fated) attempt to use constitutional arrangements to structure political outcomes. The 2007 constitution, using electoral engineering, again discourages a concentration of political parties and an agglomeration of the party leaders' prowess, and encourages a revival of intra-party factionalism. While the constitution weakens both the control of political party executives over parliamentary leadership positions and the position of the prime minister vis-à-vis parliament, political parties and party factions, the new charter also strengthened the prerogatives and autonomy of nonelected or only partly elected state organs packed with military appointees, such as the Election Commission, the Senate, and the Constitutional Court (Kuhonta, 2008).

By way of conclusion

The insights gained from only five cases are too limited for far-reaching conclusions about the question of which type of democracy is the more attractive option for new democracies. Furthermore, my analysis did not investigate some of the main measures of democratic performance that were analyzed, for instance, by Lijphart and in other studies on the impact of constitutional designs for socioeconomic performance on democratic regimes. The comparative analysis of democratic institutions in this chapter focused on the relationship between types of political institutions and the quality and consolidation of democracy in Southeast Asia, but not much on the actual policy performance of the four countries under consideration. I are therefore not in a position here to comment on the question of whether institutional variation in the region makes a difference in the actual policy performance of democracies. Given the difficulties of drawing causal inferences about the impact of constitutional design on policy performance, and of differentiating its effects from those of contextual conditions such as geography, population size, economic wealth, political culture and international contexts (Foweraker and Landman, 2002; Cheibub, 2007), as well as the short time that has elapsed since some of the countries democratized, I believe that it is safer not to posit that there is a relationship between the type of democratic institutions and the performance of democratic regimes measured in terms of, for example, human development levels, economic growth, inflation or social and environmental policies (Lijphart 1999, pp.258–300).

However, my analysis provides some evidence that the type of political institution (and, for that matter, the shift from one set of institutions to another institutional arrangement) is related to the consolidation of a country's young democratic system. But the findings presented in this chapter do not provide unanimous support for Lijphart's recommendations on constitutional choices in newly democratizing nations. While the case of Thailand confirms Lijphart's warning against the pitfalls of 'majoritarian' (or, to put it more precisely, 'majoritanized') democracy for democratic quality, there is little support for Lijphart's conclusions on presidentialism and majoritarianism. The Indonesian case is instructive here. In fact, we argue that it is the 'consensualized' character of Indonesia's presidential system of governance which significantly contributes to the ability of the democratic regime to endure, to stabilize and to consolidate. On the other hand, however, the Philippine case demonstrates that we must draw a distinction between 'consensus democracy' as defined and measured by Lijphart and an 'over-fragmented' democratic system as it exists in the Philippines.

Notes

1. Democratic consolidation is a notoriously slippery and contested concept in political science (Schedler, 1997). However, political scientists seem to agree that there are at least three different aspects of consolidation: the institutionalization of democratic norms, rules, and procedures; the stabilization of democratic institutions; and the legitimation of the democratic regime. According to Morlino, consolidation means that the institutions and procedures that have been established during the transition to democracy are going to be 'effective', and the political action of the relevant political, social and economic actors is tied lastingly to these regulations of the new democratic regime. In this sense, successful consolidation can be understood, as suggested by Morlino, as an adaptation of democratic rules and procedures by the relevant actors of a democratic order that leads to 'persistence and a stable democracy' (Morlino 1998, p.15).

2. This operation does not contradict the fact that some studies failed to identify Lijphart's patterns. By averaging all of Lijphart's variables, the possible lack of patterns is obscured (Roberts, 2006, p.54).
3. Lijphart provides data for both the 1945–96 and 1971–96 periods. We used the dataset for the 1945–1996 period. The updated periods for the remaining five democracies in Asia are as follows: Bangladesh 1991–2007; Mongolia 1990–2007; Nepal 1981–2005; South Korea 1988–2008; and Taiwan 1992–2008.

References

Ágh, A. (2001) 'Early Consolidation and Performance Crisis: The Majoritarian-Consensus Debate in Hungary', *West European Politics*, 24 (3): 89–112.

Arnone, M., Laurens, B.J., Segalotto, J.F. and Sommer, M. (2007) *Central Bank Autonomy. Lessons from Global Trends*, IMF Working Paper WP/07/88, Washington DC.

Bertelsmann Stiftung (2009) *Bertelsmann Transformation Index 2010* (Gütersloh: Verlag Bertelsmann Stiftung).

Bünte, M. and Ufen, A. (eds) (2009) *Democratization in Post-Suharto Indonesia* (London: Routledge).

Cameron, M.A., Blanaru, A.M. and Burns, L.M. (2006) *Constitutions and the Rule of Law. Between Delegative Democracy and Elective Dictatorship*, unpublished manuscript.

Chambers, P. (2003) *Factions, Parties, Coalition Change, and Cabinet Durability in Thailand, 1979–2001*, unpublished PhD thesis.

Chambers, P. (2006) 'Consolidation of Thaksinocracy and Crisis of Democracy. Thailand's 2005 Election', in Croissant, A. and Martin, B. (eds), *Between Consolidation and Crisis. Elections and Democracy in Five Nations in Southeast Asia* (Muenster: Lit Verlag).

Chambers, P. (2008) 'Factions, Parties and the Durability of Parliaments, Coalitions and Cabinets: The Case of Thailand (1979–2001)', *Party Politics,* 14 (3): 299–323.

Chambers, P. (2009) 'Superfluous, Mischievous or Emancipating? Thailand's Evolving Senate Today', *Journal of Current Southeast Asian Affairs,* 28 (3): 3–38.

Chaowana, T. and Hoerth, J. (2008) 'Thailand', in Hill, C. and Menzel, J. (eds) *Constitutionalism in Southeast Asia* (Singapore: KAS).

Cheibub, J. A. (2007) *Presidentialism, Parliamentarism, and Democracy* (Cambridge: Cambridge University Press).

Croissant, A. (2006) 'Conclusion: Electoral Politics in Southeast Asia', in Croissant, A. and Martin, B. (eds), *Between Consolidation and Crisis. Elections and Democracy in Five Nations in Southeast Asia* (Muenster: LIT Verlag).

Croissant, A. (forthcoming) 'Provisions, Practices and Performances of Constitutional Review in Democratizing East Asia', *Pacific Review*.

Croissant, A. and Schächter, T. (2010) 'Institutional Patterns in the New Democracies of Asia. Forms, Origins and Consequences', *Japanese Journal of Political Science*, 11 (2): 173–197.

Croissant, A. and Völkel, P. (forthcoming) 'Party System Types and Party System Institutionalization. Comparing New Democracies in East and Southeast Asia', *Party Politics*.

Fortin, J. (2008) 'Patterns of Democracy?', *ZfVP*, 2: 198–220.

Foweraker, J. and Landman, T. (2002) 'Constitutional Design and Democratic Performance', *Democratization,* 9 (2): 43–66.

Gallagher, M. (1991) 'Proportionality, Disproportionality and Electoral Systems', *Electoral Studies*, 10 (1): 33–51.

Guterres, F. (2006) *Elites and Prospects of Democracy in East Timor*, unpublished PhD thesis.

Hailsham, Lord (1976) *Elective Dictatorship. The Richard Dimbleby Lecture* (London: BBC).

Immergut, E. (1990) 'Institutions, Veto Points, and Policy Results:A Comparative Analysis of Health Care', *Journal of Public Policy*, 10 (4): 391–416.

Kasuya, Y. (2009) *Presidential Bandwagon. Parties and Party Systems in the Philippines* (Manila: Anvil).

Keesing's Worldwide (various years) *Keesing's Record of World Events/ Keesing's, Contemporary Archive*, London.

King, B. A. (2004) *Empowering the Presidency: Interests and Perceptions in Indonesia's Constitutional Reforms, 1999–2002*, unpublished PhD thesis.

Kuhonta, E.M. (2008) 'The Paradox of Thailand's 1997 "People's Constitution": Be Careful What You Wish for', *Asian Survey*, 48 (3): 373–392.

Laakso, M. and Taagepera, R. (1979) 'Effective Number of Parties. A Measure with Application to West Europe', *Comparative Politics*, 12 (1): 3–27.

Lijphart, A. (1984) *Democracies. Patterns of Majoritarian and Consensus Government in Twenty-One Countries* (New Haven: Yale University Press).

Lijphart, A. (1999) *Patterns of Democracy. Government Forms and Performance in Thirty-Six Countries* (New Haven: Yale University Press).

Lijphart, A. (2008a) [1991] 'Constitutional Choices for New Democracies', in Lijphart, A. (ed.), *Thinking About Democracy. Power Sharing and Majority Rule in Theory and Practice* (London and New York: Routledge).

Lijphart, A. (2008b) [1994] 'Presidentialism and Majoritarian Democracy: Theoretical Observations', in Lijphart, A. (ed.), *Thinking About Democracy. Power Sharing and Majority Rule in Theory and Practice* (London and New York: Routledge).

Linz, J.J. (1994) 'Presidential or Parliamentary Democracy: Does It Make a Difference?', in Linz, J.J. and Valenzuela, A. (eds), *The Failure of Presidential Democracy* (Boulder and London: Westview Press).

Mair, P. (1998) *Party System Change* (Oxford: Clarendon Press).

McCargo, D. (2005) 'Network Monarchy and Legitimacy Crisis in Thailand', *The Pacific Review*, 18 (4): 499–519.

Merkel, W. (1998) 'The Consolidation of Postautocratic Regimes: A Multilevel Model', *Democratization*, 5 (3): 33–65.

Mietzner, M. (2009) *Military Politics, Islam, and the State in Indonesia: From. Turbulent Transition to Democratic Consolidation* (Singapore: ISEAS).

Morlino, L. (1998) *Democracy between Consolidation and Crisis. Parties, Groups, and Citizens in Southern Europe* (Oxford: Oxford University Press).

Nickson, A., Devas, N., Brillantes, A.B., Cabo, W.L. and Celestino, A. (2008) 'Asia-Pacific', in World Bank, *Decentralization and Local Democracy in the World. First Global Report by United Cities and Local Governments 2008* (New York: World Bank).

Norris, P. (2008) *Driving Democracy. Do Power-Sharing Institutions Work?* (Cambridge: Cambridge University Press).

Reilly, B. (2007) 'Democratization and Electoral Reform in the Asia-Pacific Region: Is There an "Asian Model" of Democracy?' *Comparative Political Studies*, 40 (11): 1350–1371.

Roberts, A. (2006) 'What Kind of Democracy Is Emerging in Eastern Europe?', *Post-Soviet Affairs*, 22 (1): 37–64.

Rüland, J., Jürgenmeyer, C., Nelson, M.H. and Ziegenhain, P. (2005) *Parliaments and Political Change in Asia* (Singapore: Institute of Southeast Asian Studies).

Sajó, A. (1999) *Limiting Government. An Introduction to Constitutionalism* (Budapest and London: CEU Press).

Schedler, A. (1997) 'What is Democratic Consolidation?', *Journal of Democracy*, 9 (2): 91–107.

Shoesmith, D. (2007) 'Semi-presidentialism and the Democratic Transition in a New, Small State', in Elgie, R. and Moestrup, S. (eds) *Semi-presidentialism outside Europe. A Comparative Study* (London: Routledge).

Shugart, M. S. and Carey, J. (1992) *Presidents and Assemblies* (Cambridge: Cambridge University Press).

Siaroff, A. (1998) 'Corporatism in 24 Industrial Democracies. Meaning and Measurement', *EJPR*, 36: 175–205.

Simonsen, S. G. (2006) 'The Authoritarian Temptation in East Timor: Nationbuilding and the Need for Inclusive Governance', *Asian Survey*, 46 (4): 575–596.

Taagepera, R. (2003) 'Arend Lijphart's Dimensions of Democracy. Logical Connections and Institutional Design', *Political Studies*, 51 (1): 1–19.

Thitinan, P. (2008) 'Thailand since the Coup', *Journal of Democracy*, 19 (4): 140–153.

Ufen, A. (2008) 'Political Party and Party System Institutionalisation in Southeast Asia: Lessons for Democratic Consolidation in Indonesia, the Philippines and Thailand', *The Pacific Review*, 21 (3): 327–350.

Ziegenhain, P. (2008) *The Indonesian Parliament and Democratization* (Singapore: Institute of Southeast Asian Studies).

7
Political Reform and the Demise of Consociationalism in Southeast Asia

Benjamin Reilly

Southeast Asia has undergone a significant political transformation over the past two decades. Until 1986, not a single Southeast Asian state could be classified as genuinely democratic. Today, Indonesia is the world's third largest democracy, East Timor has emerged as Asia's newest democratic state, and the Philippines and Thailand remain nominal, if deeply troubled, democracies, Thailand having returned to unstable civilian rule following the 2006 coup, while defective democracy continues in the Philippines. All of these Southeast Asian countries also meet Huntington's 'two-turnover test' of democratic development (Huntington, 1991, 1 further page (266–7)) – that is, they have experienced at least two peaceful turnovers of power via the electoral process. By contrast, there have been no turnovers of power in the long-standing 'semi-democracies' of Malaysia and Singapore, although both maintain regular and mostly fraud-free elections, albeit with heavy restrictions on opposition movements backed by a compliant judiciary and a pro-government press. A third Southeast Asian state, Cambodia, could also be seen as a borderline member of this 'semi-democratic' group: while there have been no turnovers of power since the UN-sponsored polls of 1993, competitive elections do take place, although marred by significant voting irregularities, intimidation, and violence.

Complicating this picture, nearly all of these countries have also experienced deepening ethno-regional or religious cleavages in recent years. Social diversity is most pronounced in Indonesia, the region's largest state, which encompasses a large and pluralistic Islamic majority as well as Christians, Hindus and adherents of other religions, a small but economically powerful Chinese minority, and hundreds of diverse local ethno-regional identities. Malaysia is divided not only between the majority *bumiputera* (literally 'sons of the soil') Malays and indigenous groups (comprising 62 per cent of the population in total) and the large Chinese and smaller Indian minorities, but also between peninsular Malaysia and the more fragmented eastern states of Sabah and Sarawak on the island of Borneo. The Philippines is split at a national religious level between its Catholic majority and a Muslim minority concentrated in the southern region of Mindanao, and is linguistically fragmented, too. In Thailand, recent years have seen a growing rural–urban cleavage between the affluent middle-class population of Bangkok and the poorer regions of the north – a process which seems likely to further intensify in the short term.

The consequences for Southeast Asia's political development of this multilayered cultural, regional and religious diversity have been profound (Pei, 1998). Democracy in Indonesia, for instance, has been recurrently hampered by the consequences of party fragmentation, both in recent years following the collapse of the Suharto regime, and earlier, during the country's initial democratic interlude in the 1950s, when shifting coalitions of secular, Islamic, nationalist and communal parties led to six changes of government in seven years, providing a ready pretext for the declaration of martial law by President Sukarno in 1957. Similarly, the Philippines has long suffered the consequences of its fragmented social landscape of *cacique* plantation owners, local strongmen, regional warlords and peasants – highly ephemeral and personalized political parties, clientelistic and patrimonial politics and an ongoing crisis of underdevelopment. The restricted political systems of Malaysia and Singapore evolved partly as a result of a perceived need to control the political expression of ethnicity; the management of communal relations has remained a cornerstone of politics in both states (Crouch, 1996; Rodan, 1996). Even Thailand, which often claims to be culturally homogeneous, has seen a marked politicization of ethnicity in recent years, not just in the Muslim 'deep south' but also between the center and the northeast.

As these cases suggest, there appears to be a symbiotic interrelationship between democratization and the politicization of ethnicity. Around the world, democratic openings often have the effect of bringing ethnic identities to the forefront, as political parties frequently form around identity issues in the absence of meaningful ideological or policy schisms. At the same time, political liberalization also opens up opportunities for redesigning political institutions to manage such differences. Both processes have been evident in Southeast Asia over the past decade. In different ways, and at different points in time, democratic reforms in Indonesia, Thailand, and the Philippines have introduced political institutions designed to encourage more nationally focused party politics and reduce the appeal of sectional or localized movements, even as new democratic freedoms encouraged such movements to develop. The semi-democracies of Cambodia, Malaysia and Singapore have also introduced modest reforms in this direction, although with the pre-eminent aim of strengthening incumbent governments.

Drawing on a book-length study of political engineering in Asia and the Pacific, I argue that the cumulative impact of these various reforms has resulted in a shift away from the broadly 'consociational' political models of the immediate post-independence period towards more integrative or centripetal forms of democracy in recent years (Reilly, 2006). Across a range of different countries and contexts, Southeast Asian reformers have sought to forge more stable political systems while simultaneously limiting room for potential challengers to the established order. As a result, the experiments of earlier decades with consociational approaches to democracy – featuring communal political parties, proportional representation elections and grand coalition governments – have increasingly been left behind in favour of new strategies designed to transcend or impede, rather than communicate and reinforce, the political expression of social cleavages.

Consociationalism

Two contrasting normative and empirical models of democracy have dominated much of the debate on the issue of how best to ensure stability in ethnically diverse societies. One is the scholarly orthodoxy of *consociationalism*, which relies on elite cooperation between leaders of different communities. Because majoritarian, 'winner-takes-all' political models can lead to ethnic minorities being denied parliamentary representation, it is often argued that such systems are unsuitable for ethnically diverse societies. For example, simple majority rule when applied in an ethnically bifurcated society can easily entrench one party or group's dominance over all others. Because of this, proponents of ethnic power sharing in plural societies often advocate institutions and practices which encourage interethnic balancing in public office, proportional representation of all significant cleavages in parliament, and sharing of power between these various segments in government. Consociationalism is the most established and well-developed of such models.[1]

Consociational prescriptions are based on the principle that each ethnic polity should enjoy a significant degree of autonomy and a right of veto over matters directly affecting the welfare of its members. Emphasizing the need for elite cooperation if democracy is to survive deep ethnic cleavages, consociational agreements entail a balance of power within government between clearly defined social segments, brokered by identifiable ethnic leaders representing distinct social groups. Arend Lijphart, the scholar most associated with the consociational model, developed this prescription from a detailed examination of the features of power-sharing democracy in European countries such as the Netherlands, Belgium and Switzerland, but there is disagreement over the extent to which these measures can be applied to other regions (Reilly, 2001). However, there is little doubt that consociationalism represents the dominant model of power sharing for 'plural societies' – that is, in Lijphart's terminology, 'societies that are sharply divided along religious, ideological, linguistic, cultural, ethnic or racial lines into virtually separate subsocieties with their own political parties, interest groups, and media of communication' (Lijphart, 1984, p.22).

Consociational reforms often focus on core democratic institutions such as political parties, electoral systems and cabinet governments, and on the territorial division of state powers. In each case, the focus is on defining and strengthening the autonomy of communal components of the society in question. In terms of political parties, for example, consociational approaches favour parties that represent social cleavages explicitly, via what Pippa Norris has characterized as 'bonding' rather than 'bridging' strategies – that is, parties that 'focus upon gaining votes from a narrower homebase among particular segmented sectors of the electorate' (Norris, 2004, p.10). The ideal party system for consociationalists is one in which parties are based on clear social cleavages so that all significant groups, including minorities, can seek representation through their own communal party organizations. Only through parties that draw their support from clear and relatively exclusive segmental cleavages, contend consociationalists, can political elites negotiate delicate ethnic issues effectively (Lijphart, 1995).

To ensure the fair representation of such communal parties, consociational prescriptions invariably recommend proportional representation (PR) electoral systems, with a particular preference for large-district party list systems to ensure a close parity between the proportion of the vote won by a party and its parliamentary representation. Optimally, 'closed' party lists that do not enable voters to select individual candidates (thus strengthening the autonomy of party leaders), combined with large multi-member electoral districts (to maximize the proportionality of outcomes), are favoured. The ideal consociational electoral system would be held under PR rules in one country-wide electoral district, so as to maximize representation between contending party lists (Lijphart, 1990).

A final step in the consociational package is the formation of multiparty governments in which a spectrum of parties and groups are represented so as to ensure inclusion and representation of communal interests. This allows the full gamut of social diversity to thus be represented via power-sharing cabinets in which all significant voices are given a share of executive power, and in which minorities have the right of veto over important issues directly affecting their own communities. Indeed, a core consociational practice is the formation of 'grand coalition' governments in which all elected parties are included in the cabinet in proportion to their numbers in parliament. While opposition parties have always been present, Malaysia's ethnically balanced government is frequently cited as Southeast Asia's clearest example of this kind of cross-ethnic power sharing (Case, 1996).

While there are no ideal types, Southeast Asia's initial post-colonial democratic experiments of the 1950s often displayed strong consociational features. In Burma, for example, 'the principle of institutional separation by ethnicity was ingrained during the colonial period' (Holliday, 2008, p.1050). As such, Burma's 1947 constitution provided for a combination of ethnically based states, ethnic 'councils' to look after the interests of intermixed or dispersed minorities, and reserved parliamentary seats for specified groups (Furnivall, 1948, p.169). Indonesia's short-lived incarnation as a parliamentary democracy in the 1950s was also strongly consociational (Lijphart, 1977). A list PR electoral system was combined with guaranteed representation for specified numbers of Chinese, European, and Arab minorities,[2] and religious-communal parties were routinely included in (short-lived) grand coalition governments on the assumption that 'ethnic and other demands would be articulated through the party system and conflicts would be settled through negotiation and compromise in the parliament' (Liddle, 2002, p.286).

Despite lacking PR and some other institutions often associated with consociationalism, Malaysia's consociational democracy under the Alliance lasted until the race riots of 1969 and has continued as a 'coercive consociation' ever since.[3] Singapore, despite its paternalistic and repressive politics, has also been identified as operating according to consociational principles, according to some country experts (Ganesan, 1996). Even Cambodia has at times been included in the consociational club, via the 1991 Paris Peace Accords and subsequent UN-sponsored elections, which brought the country's rival groups together on the basis of 'the consociational agreements of pro-monarchy and pro-Hun Sen forces' (Shin, 2008, p.103), the form if not the substance of which was continued in the coalition government formed after the 1993 elections.

The one shared feature of all these examples of consociational practice is that they proved incompatible with open, competitive democracy. In Indonesia, the elected 1955 parliament delivered not just a reflection of the country's social diversity but also an extreme form of political gridlock that led directly to the end of democracy in 1957 and to four decades of authoritarian rule. Burma's post-independence democracy survived for 14 turbulent years until 1962, before being overthrown in a military coup that had strong ethnic motivations. Likewise, in the increasingly quasi-authoritarian political systems of both Malaysia and Singapore, the management of communal relations has remained a cornerstone of politics in both states. Cambodia's political settlement began to unwind almost before the end of the 1993 elections and collapsed completely in 1997, when incumbent leader Hun Sen routed his erstwhile power-sharing partner in government, the royalist FUNCINPEC party. The eclipse of democracy in all of these cases, and its replacement with forms of resilient semi-democracy (in Singapore and Malaysia, and to some extent Cambodia) or outright authoritarianism (in Indonesia and Burma in the 1960s), has presented a powerful negative example for Southeast Asia's contemporary political engineers.

Centripetalism

Centripetalism represents an alternative approach to political engineering for ethnically plural democracies. So called 'because the explicit aim is to engineer a centripetal spin to the political system – to pull the parties towards moderate, compromising policies and to discover and reinforce the centre of a deeply divided political spectrum' (Sisk, 1995, p.19), centripetalism emphasizes the importance of institutions that encourage integration, not separation, across ethno-political divides. Contrary to consociational recommendations, centripetalists maintain that the best way to manage democracy in divided societies is not to simply replicate existing ethnic divisions in the legislature and other representative organs, but rather to *depoliticize* ethnicity by putting in place institutional incentives for politicians and their supporters to act in an accommodatory manner towards rival groups. Scholars such as Donald Horowitz have consistently advocated the need for political institutions that encourage cross-ethnic behaviour, such as electoral systems that enable the pooling of votes across ethnic lines (Horowitz, 1985).

In an earlier book on electoral engineering for divided societies, I defined centripetalism as a political system or strategy designed to focus competition at the moderate centre rather than the extremes and identified three facilitating components:

1. the presentation of *electoral incentives* for campaigning politicians to attract votes from a range of ethnic groups other than their own, thus encouraging candidates to moderate their political rhetoric and broaden their policy positions on potentially divisive issues;
2. the presence of multiethnic *arenas of bargaining* such as parliamentary and executive forums, in which political actors representing different communities have an incentive to come together and cut deals on reciprocal electoral support, and hence perhaps on other more substantial policy issues as well; and
3. the development of *centrist, aggregative, and multiethnic political parties* or coalitions of parties that can present credible cross-ethnic appeals and policy options to the electorate (Reilly, 2001, p.11).

Like consociationalism, centripetal proposals for conflict management tend to focus on parties, elections and representative bodies. However, the institutional recommendations of centripetalists often run sharply counter to those of consociationalists. For instance, rather than focusing on the fair representation of ethnically defined political parties, centripetalists place a premium on promoting multiethnic parties and cross-ethnic activity. To achieve this, electoral processes can be structured so as to require successful candidates to gain support across different regions of a country, thus helping to break down the appeal of narrow parochialism or regionalism. One example is the 'distribution requirement' for presidential elections in Indonesia, where winning candidates must gain at least 20 per cent of the vote in at least half of all provinces in the first round of elections to avoid a run-off. This requires presidential candidates to gain votes across the archipelago rather than relying on regionally concentrated support. This requirement was easily surmounted in 2009 by Indonesian president Susilo Bambang Yudhoyono, a classic moderate and centrist politician of the type advocated by centripetalists.

Another option is to encourage candidates to transcend ethnic appeals during elections. Methods to prompt this vary widely. Some are surprisingly simple: electoral arrangements in the Philippines (where senators are elected on a nationwide basis, making cross-national support almost essential) and in East Timor (where parliamentarians are similarly elected from across the country as a whole rather than from local districts) should, in theory, encourage a focus on national rather than regional or sectoral interests (Wurfel, 2004, p.220). But these only provide relatively weak incentives for cross-ethnic voting. Another limited approach can be found in Singapore, where party lists for most seats must include candidates from designated ethnic minorities on their ticket, and voters must choose between entire lists rather than individual candidates – arrangements that effectively require some measure of cross-ethnic voting, while still guaranteeing the ongoing political dominance of the ruling People's Action Party.

More important differences between consociational and centripetal approaches can be found in their contrasting recommendations regarding political parties. As already discussed, consociationalists advocate the presence of ethnically based parties and party systems, and see a virtue in having a multiplicity of parties representing all significant social groups. By contrast, centripetalists ideally favour an aggregative party system, in which 'one or two broadly based, centrist parties fight for the middle ground' (Diamond, 1996, p.239), and therefore tend to endorse the development of multiethnic parties or party coalitions based on a few large parties. Indonesia's legal requirement that all political parties must demonstrate a nationwide organizational base before they are eligible to take part in elections is an example of this kind of centripetal approach. Each registered political party wishing to compete in national elections has to first establish branches across a set proportion of provinces (initially one-third, then two-thirds, and now 60 per cent of all provinces), as well as offices in at least half of the districts or municipalities within these provinces. This decision has proved highly consequential: as Edward Aspinall has observed, in responding to this law, Indonesian parties 'have proven remarkably adept at acting at encouraging cross-ethnic bargaining, or even at minimizing the role of ethnicity in politics' (Aspinall, 2010).

The bias in favour of national parties in Indonesia is today so strong that regional parties are even banned from competing in elections to the *regional* assemblies, where again only national-level parties are permitted. As Dwight King notes, 'where previously the number of election contestants was stipulated by law, permitting only three, now they were limited on the basis of insufficient geographical coverage and depth of penetration of their organizations' (King, 2003, p.51). Indonesia's current party rules are thus one of the most extreme versions of centripetal incentives to be found anywhere in the world. However, an exception to this rule was made for Aceh under the terms of the 2005 peace deal there. At the provincial legislative elections in Aceh held in April 2009, the local party representing the former rebels secured an impressive victory, a precedent which may make it difficult to maintain restrictions on local parties in other regions such as Papua (Hillman, 2010).

While these examples of centripetal reform are focused on political institutions, non-institutional factors are also important. For example, while consociationalism assumes that enlightened elites are the driving force behind interethnic moderation in divided societies, centripetalism places more faith in the behaviour of campaigning politicians and their supporters on the ground and assumes that voters will follow the lead of their political leaders and pool votes across ethnic lines when asked to. In Malaysia, for example, the long-standing centripetal practice of vote pooling across ethnic lines has been a mainstay of national politics for decades and was a major factor in the government's victory in 1999 at the height of the Asian economic crisis, when the rural Malay vote deserted the ruling coalition (Ahmad, 2000). More recently, the tables were turned when non-Malays proved to be a key swing vote behind Anwar Ibrahim's Reform Coalition in the breakthrough 2008 elections (Maznah, 2008).

The Southeast Asian experience

What does the Southeast Asian experience reveal about the relative appeal of consociational or centripetal models of democratic institutional design? While aspects of both models have been applied at different times, in recent years Southeast Asian states have shown a preference for centripetal forms of political engineering and a shift away from consociational models. As Allen Hicken observes, most contemporary reforms 'have favoured centripetal institutions and political parties. [...] The vast majority of Southeast Asian states have opted for institutions and regulations consistent with aggregative goals' (Hicken, 2008, 1 further page (74–5)).

Several trends are evident. First, countries with proportional representation electoral systems, such as Indonesia and Cambodia, have emphasized majority-enhancing reforms. To do this, both have drastically reduced their systems' proportionality of outcomes. In 2004, for example, Indonesia abandoned the long-standing use of provincial boundaries as electoral districts and introduced much smaller constituencies capped at a maximum of 12 members per district. This raised the threshold for electoral victory considerably, making it much more difficult for small parties to win seats than in previous elections, when districts were based on entire provinces (Sherlock,

2004, p.4). In 2009, the proportionality of the electoral system was further reduced with the adoption of open list voting (which tends to be less proportional in its effects than closed list PR, as well as diluting the ability of party leaders to control their internal seat allocations) and the introduction of a 2.5 per cent electoral threshold (thus eliminating the dozens of small 'mosquito' parties which had been a feature of previous parliaments).

A similar pattern has been evident in Cambodia, where reforms have sharply reduced the proportionality of the PR electoral system inherited from the UN. In 1998, the electoral formula used to convert votes into seats was changed to the 'highest average' method at the provincial level rather than the nationwide 'largest remainder' system used in 1993 – a change that discriminated against smaller parties. As in Indonesia, calls for greater local accountability also saw district boundaries adjusted and smaller constituencies created, with the result that over one-third of all Cambodian parliamentarians now represent single-member districts.[4] As in Indonesia, the net effect of these changes has been a sharp decline in the proportionality of electoral outcomes and the elimination of many small political parties, to the advantage of the larger incumbent parties. In both countries, the overall impact of these changes has been to make electoral politics considerably more *majoritarian* than previously.

Elsewhere, 'mixed' electoral systems that combine elements of both plurality and proportional voting have been the vogue, again with a strongly majoritarian weighting. The Philippines was the first Asian democracy to adopt this model, with 20 per cent of the legislature chosen from a national list designed to represent 'sectoral interests' and marginalized groups such as women, youth, labour, the urban poor, farmers and fishermen. First implemented in 1998, the party list regulations restrict each group's representation to a maximum of three seats. The effect of these rules appears to have been widespread confusion, and the list seats have been dogged by problems, with less than half of the winning list candidates taking up their seats in recent elections. Observers, such as Aurel Croissant, for instance, argue that the party list seats have actually exacerbated problems of electoral disproportionality and minority underrepresentation (Croissant, 2002, p.329).

The most recent example of mixed-member majoritarianism comes from Thailand, where the electoral system has come almost full circle over the past decade. Thailand's reformist 1997 constitution abandoned the long-established block vote system, in which candidates from the same party competed with each other in small multi-member electorates, in favour of a mixed model comprising 400 seats elected from single-member districts and another 100 chosen by PR from a national list. In combination with a 5 per cent list threshold (to weed out splinter parties) and rules requiring party membership for all MPs (to reduce pre-election party hopping), these reforms were designed to strengthen the party system and ensure political stability. This they did, all too well: the electoral and party reforms coincided with (and helped facilitate) the emergence of Thaksin Shinawatra, one of Thailand's richest men, and his Thai Rak Thai (TRT) party as the country's dominant political force (Hicken, 2006).

The military coup of 2006 which removed Thaksin from power saw the abrogation of the 1997 constitution and the promulgation of a new 'People's Charter' constitution that removed many of these incentives for strong parties and stable government. In an apparent attempt to undermine the possibility of TRT or its offshoots ever returning to power, the electoral system reverted to the old (and discredited) block vote model of multimember constituencies, which studies have found to be one of the least proportional of all electoral systems. However, in a novel twist, this was combined with the maintenance of 80 list seats elected by PR on a regional, rather than a national basis – a move designed to dilute the voting power of the northern provinces where Thaksin's support was strongest (Pongsudhirak, 2008). This unlikely and unwieldy combination of divergent institutional models is likely to have the odd effect of both refragmenting the party system while simultaneously undercutting equitable representation.

Finally, in the resilient semi-democracies of Malaysia and Singapore, a succession of technical changes has tilted the electoral playing field increasingly in favour of incumbents. Both countries continue to use the standard Westminster model of plurality elections, but constituency boundaries are gerrymandered to favour pro-government communities. In addition, in a deviation from its British heritage, most of Singapore's parliamentary representatives are today elected from multi-member Group Representation Constituencies (GRCs). First introduced in 1988, there are now 14 multi-member GRCs of between five and six seats elected by a 'party block' vote – a system which entails multi- rather than single-member districts, but in which electors cast one vote for predetermined party lists rather than for candidates. The party that wins a simple plurality of votes wins *all* the seats available, thus making Singapore's one of the most 'mega-majoritarian' national electoral systems anywhere in the world.[5] While providing a nominal level of multiethnic representation and interethnic vote pooling as described earlier, the real effect of the growth of GRCs has been to extend the already huge overrepresentation of the governing People's Action Party, which regularly wins over 90 per cent of seats in parliament. Some have argued that the enshrinement of race as a form of political representation also serves to marginalize class consciousness and thereby further weakens the capacity for anti-government collective action (Huat, 2007).

Table 7.1 sets out the changes in electoral systems across Southeast Asia. In almost all cases, electoral reforms have seen the introduction of new systems that are substantially more majoritarian and less proportional than their predecessors.

Table 7.1 Electoral-system changes in Southeast Asia

Country	Former electoral system	New electoral system
Cambodia	closed list PR, with large districts (largest remainder method) (1993)	closed list PR, with smaller districts (highest average method) (1998)
Indonesia	closed list PR, with large districts (1999)	open list PR, with smaller districts (2004/9)
Philippines	plurality/block (1986)	mixed plurality–PR, with three-seat PR limit (1998)
Thailand	mixed plurality–PR (1997)	mixed block–PR (2007)
Singapore	plurality in mostly single-member districts (pre-1988)	party block in mostly multi-member districts (post-1988)

How do we explain the pronounced move away from electoral proportionality and toward majoritarianism across Southeast Asia? One factor is clearly the desire of incumbents to minimize the threat of political fragmentation by restricting the electoral prospects of opposition parties. But more lofty aims have also been present: political reformers in countries such as post-Suharto Indonesia and post-1997 Thailand hoped to encourage more cohesive political parties that could appeal to national rather than regional or local constituencies. Indeed, when attempts to shape the development of their party systems themselves are examined, it is clear that in addition to using electoral system design to try to change the way political parties function, many Southeast Asian states have also attempted to reform their party systems more directly through overt engineering of the rules governing the formation, organization, and behaviour of political parties.

The Indonesian example described above is the clearest example of this approach. In addition to restricting the ability of regional parties to contest elections, Indonesia's new party laws also attempt to limit party numbers by introducing systemic pressures for smaller parties to amalgamate with each other. Following the 1999 election, parties that failed to gain more than 2 per cent of seats in the lower house of parliament or 3 per cent of seats in regional assemblies had to merge with other parties to surmount these thresholds in order to contest future elections – a provision which resulted in a number of smaller parties amalgamating prior to the 2004 elections. The introduction of a 2.5 per cent electoral threshold for the 2009 election further magnified this trend, with the overall number of parties in parliament dropping sharply (from 21 parties in 1999 to 17 in 2004 and just nine political parties in the 2009 parliament, easily the lowest number in Indonesia's democratic history). A similar trend was evident in Thailand's 1997 constitution, which introduced a range of reforms to strengthen the party system and combat fissiparous tendencies. These led to a sharp decline in the number of parliamentary parties in Thailand, which, combined with the electoral reforms discussed above, clearly assisted the TRT in capturing and controlling the government – in coalition after 2001, and alone after 2004.[6]

Compare this with the Philippines, whose 1987 constitution was also based on the desire for a more inclusive and responsive political system, but which included no reductive constraints upon party proliferation. There, party numbers have steadily increased since the return to democracy in 1986, especially compared with the experience of the pre-Marcos democratic period from 1946 to 1969. Since 1986, party fragmentation has grown to more than double the level of that of the 1946–69 period – an ironic outcome, as an underlying aim of the 1986 constitution was to improve political stability (Hicken, 2006).

A final deviation from consociationalism has been in the area of executive government formation. As discussed earlier, the grand coalition cabinet in which all significant parties are represented is a key pillar of consociational politics. But while oversized executives have been the rule rather than the exception in much of Southeast Asia, true grand coalitions have been less common. My research has identified just three Southeast Asian countries in which grand coalition cabinets have been employed in contemporary politics: Cambodia (where the 1993 constitution required a two-thirds vote of parliament for the investiture of new governments), Indonesia (most notably under the post-Suharto presidency of Abdurrahman Wahid between 1999 and 2001), and in the most well-institutionalized arrangement, at various times in Malaysia as part of the long-ruling, cross-ethnic coalition (particularly under the pre-1969 Alliance, but also to some extent in today's Barisan Nasional). However, such all-encompassing governing coalitions have increasingly been rejected in recent years.

In Cambodia, for instance, mandated power sharing via a two-thirds majority requirement for government formation was introduced after the 1993 election by the incumbent Cambodian People's Party (CPP) as a safeguard against their marginalization from power. With no party commanding a working majority, and under CPP's threats of a civil war if it was excluded from government, the United Nations brokered a deal that saw the installation of a power-sharing coalition featuring 'co-prime ministers' from the two major parties, CPP and FUNCINPEC. This arrangement proved to be highly unstable in practice and fell apart in 1997 when the CPP forces of the 'second prime minister', Hun Sen, overthrew those of the 'first prime minister', Prince Norodom Ranariddh. The shaky CPP–FUNCINPEC coalition was revived again after the 1998 and (after much wrangling) 2004 elections – not through any rapprochement between the party leaders, but solely due to the two-thirds requirement for government formation that had earlier been inscribed, at the CPP's insistence, into the constitution. With observers branding it 'a significant obstacle to forming elected government and to political stability' (Albritton, 2004, p.102), the two-thirds rule was finally abandoned in 2006 when the CPP dropped FUNCINPEC and joined with a renewed Sam Rainsey Party in order to vote through the lower threshold of a bare majority vote for government formation. This ended Cambodia's pretence of grand coalition power sharing, making it likely that a single party will form future governments and further solidifying Hun Sen's grasp on power.

In Indonesia, all of the governments since the return to democracy in 1999 have been oversized multiparty coalitions, effectively co-opting most of the opposition into the government (Slater, 2004). However, enthusiasm for genuine grand coalitions has declined over time. The only true grand coalitions in the modern era were the short-lived transitional administrations formed by Indonesia's first democratically chosen president, Abdurrahman Wahid, in 1999–2000. But Wahid's so-called 'National Unity Cabinets' proved highly unstable in practice, with a bewildering array of ministers appointed and then removed over the 22 months of Wahid's presidency. Wahid's replacement, his former vice president, Megawati Sukarnoputri, maintained the practice of oversized coalitions but did not attempt to replicate the grand coalition model. This approach was continued by her successor, Yudhoyono, who formed what he called an 'Indonesian unity' cabinet following his election in 2004, but without co-opting all of the parties in parliament. Yudhoyono's 2009 cabinet included six of the nine parliamentary parties, but also featured a significant opposition centred on PDI-P. In sum, while *kabinet pelangi* ('rainbow cabinets') remain the order of the day in Indonesia, there also appears to be a clear trend away from grand coalitions, with each elected government over the past decade containing successively fewer parties.

Conclusion

Overall, recent democratic reforms in Southeast Asia have seen a move away from the consociational approaches of earlier decades in favour of more centripetal and majoritarian models. While the broad practices of ethnic balancing and coalition government building continue to resonate, the use of specific consociational *institutions* such as grand coalition cabinets, ethnically based political parties and proportional representation elections have declined. Across Southeast Asia, electoral systems have become less proportional, party laws have attempted to coerce aggregative rather than particularistic political parties, and attempts to mandate grand coalition power-sharing governments have largely been abandoned. Even in areas not examined in this chapter, such as minority rights initiatives or moves to grant special autonomy to ethnically distinct regions in Indonesia and the Philippines, Southeast Asian governments have tended to shy away from explicit recognition of ethnic groups and have rejected approaches based on group rights or minority vetoes.

Why has consociationalism lost its appeal? There are many possible explanations, but one reason is surely the comprehensive failure of so many consociational experiments with post-colonial democracy in the 1950s and 1960s – including the overthrow of introduced democratic systems in Burma and Indonesia, as well as the erosion of competitive democracy and its replacement with quasi-authoritarian rule in Singapore and Malaysia. In all of these cases, the inability of introduced post-colonial political systems to cope with the realities of ethnic politics played a role in their downfall and has provided a powerful negative example for contemporary reformers.

There is also the key issue of democratic development over time. Several examinations of the empirical record of consociationalism in divided societies have concluded that it may work better as an interim device than over the longer term: 'if consociational structures are entrenched in plural societies which do show potential for the withering away of ethnic voting, then the very institutions designed to alleviate tensions may merely entrench the perception that all politics must be ethnic politics' (Reilly and Reynolds, 1999, p.31). Similar conclusions have been reached in recent book-length studies of power sharing in post-conflict societies (Roeder and Rothchild, 2005) and in transitions from war to democracy (Jarstad and Sisk, 2008). This raises the question of whether consociational models of politics have a limited life span, as ethnic allegiances become less predominant and the political evolution toward more 'normal' politics takes place.

The Malaysian case is instructive here. Although consociational practices have been a feature of Malaysian politics for decades, recent political evolution has opened up the possibility of a more competitive model of multiethnic democracy. Demands for greater political openness and a shift away from ethnic politics have accompanied the country's economic development, with increasing criticism that the control of social conflict has come at the cost of flagrant gerrymandering and malapportionment, suppression of basic freedoms, and intimidation of political opposition, all aimed at ensuring that the ruling coalition remains in power. Recently, the foundations of the Malaysian model have started to crack. The 2008 general elections were a watershed event: for the first time since 1969, the United Malays National Organization (UMNO) no longer commands the two-thirds parliamentary majority necessary to freely amend the constitution and also lost power to the Islamist PAS in a number of key states. While the Barisan retained a working parliamentary majority, a surge of cross-ethnic support for the reformist Parti Keadilan Rakyat, led by former Deputy Prime Minister Anwar Ibrahim, saw it become the second largest party in parliament. Numerous commentators hailed these events as signaling the beginning of the end of the old model of ethnic politics in Malaysia, and (perhaps) a new era of two-party politics.[7]

These events have raised the possibility of a first ever change of government in Malaysia in the not too distant future. Were this to happen, it could mark a decisive break with the long-dominant trade-off on which Malaysian politics has been based, namely, the use of restrictions on open democracy, along with pro-Malay affirmative action, to control ethnic mobilization and potential social conflict. While ethnic balancing is likely to remain import-ant, regardless of which coalition is in power, the success of Keadilan may herald a shift in Malaysian voter support toward pan-ethnic politics in the future. Of course, speculation about future political development is a highly uncertain process, and at the time of writing, many other outcomes are pos-sible. But if a move toward a more open, multiethnic and pluralistic model of politics were to occur, it would likely represent a final and decisive step in the demise of consociationalism not just in Malaysia, but across Southeast Asia more generally.

Notes

Thanks to the participants in the University of Heidelberg workshop as well as Robert Cribb, Donald Horowitz, and Edmund Malesky for their helpful comments on earlier drafts of this chapter; the usual caveats apply. I also gratefully acknow-ledge the fellowship support provided by the National Endowment for Democracy in Washington, DC.

1. The literature on consociationalism is voluminous. Major works include Arend Lijphart (1968), *The Politics of Accommodation: Pluralism and Democracy in the Netherlands* (Berkeley CA: University of California Press); Eric A. Nordlinger (1972), *Conflict Regulation in Divided Societies* (Cambridge MA: Center for International Affairs, Harvard University); Kenneth McRae, ed. (1974), *Consociational Democracy: Political Accommodation in Segmented Societies* (Toronto: McLelland and Stewart); Arend Lijphart (1977), *Democracy in Plural Societies: A Comparative Exploration* (New Haven CT: Yale University Press).
2. See Allen Hicken and Yuko Kasuya, 'A guide to the constitutional structures and electoral systems of east, south and southeast Asia', *Electoral Studies*, 22 (2003): 135.
3. The phrase comes from Diane Mauzy (1983) 'Malay political hegemony and "coer-cive consociationalism" ', in John McGarry and Brendan O'Leary (eds), *The Politics of Ethnic Conflict Regulation* (London and New York: Routledge).
4. At the time of writing, there were eight single-member constituencies in Cambodia, up from six in 1993.
5. See Andrew Reynolds, Ben Reilly and Andrew Ellis (2005) *Electoral System Design: the New International IDEA Handbook* (Stockholm: IDEA), for a discussion of this.
6. For a discussion, see Erik Kuhonta (2008) 'The Paradox of Thailand's 1997 "People's Constitution": Be Careful What You Wish For', *Asian Survey*, 48: 373–92.
7. See, for example, Mohamad Maznah (2008) 'Malaysia – democracy and the end of ethnic politics?', *Australian Journal of International Affairs*, 62 (4): 441–59.

References

Ahmad, Z.H., Kim, K.K., Nathan, K.S., Singh, H., Weiss, M. and Funston, J. (2000) *Trends in Malaysia: Election Assessment* (Singapore: Institute for Southeast Asian Studies).

Albritton, R.B. (2004) 'Cambodia in 2003: On the Road to Democratic Consolidation', *Asian Survey*, 44 (1): 102.

Aspinall, E. (2010) *Democratization and the Weakening of Ethnic Politics in Indonesia*, paper presented to the annual meeting of the American Association for Asian Studies, Philadelphia PA, 26 March.

Case W. (1996) *Elites and Regimes in Malaysia: Revisiting a Consociational Democracy* (Monash: Monash Asia Institute).

Croissant, A. (2002) 'Electoral Politics in Southeast and East Asia: A Comparative Perspective', in Croissant, A., Bruns, G. and John, M. (eds), *Electoral Politics in Southeast and East Asia* (Singapore: Friedrich Ebert Stiftung).

Crouch, H. (1996) *Government and Society in Malaysia* (Ithaca NY: Cornell University Press).

Diamond, L. (1996) 'Toward Democratic Consolidation', in L. Diamond and M. F. Plattner (eds), *The Global Resurgence of Democracy* (Baltimore and London: Johns Hopkins University Press).

Furnivall, J.S. (1948) *Colonial Policy and Practice: A Comparative Study of Burma and Netherlands India* (Cambridge: Cambridge University Press).

Ganesan, N. (1996) 'Democracy in Singapore', *Asian Journal of Political Science*, 4 (2): 63–79.

Hicken, A. (2006) 'Party Fabrication: Constitutional Reform and the Rise of Thai Rak Thai', *Journal of East Asian Studies*, 6 (3): 381–408.

Hicken, A. (2008) 'Political Engineering and Party Regulation in Southeast Asia', in Reilly, B. and Nordlund, P. (eds), *Political Parties in Conflict-Prone Societies: Regulation, Engineering and Democratic Development* (Tokyo: United Nations University Press).

Hillman, B. (2010) *Political Parties and Post-Conflict Transition: The Results and Implications of the 2009 Parliamentary Elections in Aceh*, Policy Paper 1/10, (Canberra, Centre for Democratic Institutions).

Holliday, I. (2008) 'Voting and Violence in Myanmar: Nation Building for a Transition to Democracy', *Asian Survey*, 68 (6): 1050.

Horowitz, D.L. (1985) *Ethnic Groups in Conflict* (Berkeley: University of California Press).

Huat, C.B. (2007) 'Political Culturalism, Representation, and the People's Action Party of Singapore', *Democratization*, 14 (5): 911–927.

Huntington, S. P. (1991) *The Third Wave: Democratization in the Late Twentieth Century* (Norman OK: University of Oklahoma Press).

Jarstad, A.K. and Sisk, T.D. (eds) (2008), *From War to Democracy: Dilemmas of Peacebuilding* (Cambridge: Cambridge University Press).

King, D.Y. (2003) *Half-Hearted Reform: Electoral Institutions and the Struggle for Democracy in Indonesia* (Westport CT and London: Praeger).

Kuhonta, E. (2008) 'The Paradox of Thailand's 1997 'People's Constitution': Be Careful What You Wish For', *Asian Survey*, 48 (3): 373–392.

Liddle, W. (2002) 'Coercion, Co-optation, and the Management of Ethnic Relations in Indonesia', in A. Reynolds (ed.), *The Architecture of Democracy: Constitutional Design, Conflict Management and Democracy* (Oxford: Oxford University Press).

Lijphart, A. (1968) *The Politics of Accommodation: Pluralism and Democracy in the Netherlands* (Berkeley CA: University of California Press).

Lijphart, A. (1977) *Democracy in Plural Societies: A Comparative Exploration* (New Haven CT: Yale University Press).

Lijphart, A. (1984) *Democracies: Patterns of Majoritarian and Consensus Government in Twenty-One Countries* (New Haven CT and London: Yale University Press).

Lijphart, A. (1990) 'Electoral Systems, Party Systems and Conflict Management in Segmented Societies', in R.A. Schreirer (ed.), *Critical Choices for South Africa: An Agenda for the 1990s* (Cape Town: Oxford University Press).

Lijphart, A. (1995) 'Self-determination Versus Pre-determination of Ethnic Minorities in Power-sharing Systems', in W. Kymlicka (ed.), *The Rights of Minority Cultures* (Oxford: Oxford University Press).

Maznah, M. (2008) 'Malaysia – Democracy and the End of Ethnic Politics?', *Australian Journal of International Affairs*, 62 (4): 441–459.

McGarry, J. and O'Leary, B. (eds) (1993) *The Politics of Ethnic Conflict Regulation* (London and New York: Routledge).

McRae, K. (ed.) (1974) *Consociational Democracy: Political Accommodation in Segmented Societies* (Toronto: McLelland and Stewart).

Nordlinger, E. A. (1972) *Conflict Regulation in Divided Societies* (Cambridge MA: Center for International Affairs, Harvard University).

Norris, P. (2004) *Electoral Engineering: Voting Rules and Political Behavior* (Cambridge: Cambridge University Press).

Pei, M. (1998) 'The Fall and Rise of Democracy in East Asia', in L. Diamond and M. F. Plattner (eds), *Democracy in East Asia* (Baltimore and London: Johns Hopkins University Press).

Pongsudhirak, T. (2008) 'Thailand since the Coup', *Journal of Democracy*, 19 (4): 140–153.

Reilly, B. (2001) *Democracy in Divided Societies: Electoral Engineering for Conflict Management* (Cambridge: Cambridge University Press).

Reilly, B. (2006) *Democracy and Diversity: Political Engineering in the Asia-Pacific* (Oxford: Oxford University Press).

Reilly, B. and Reynolds, A. (1999) *Electoral Systems and Conflict in Divided Societies* (Washington DC: National Academy Press).

Reynolds, A., Reilly, B. and Ellis, A. (2005) *Electoral System Design: the New International IDEA Handbook* (Stockholm: IDEA).

Rodan, G. (1996) 'Elections without Representation: the Singapore Experience under the PAP', in R. H. Taylor (ed.), *The Politics of Elections in Southeast Asia* (Cambridge: Cambridge University Press).

Roeder, P.G. and Rothchild, D.S. (eds) (2005) *Sustainable Peace: Power and Democracy after Civil Wars* (Ithaca NY: Cornell University Press).

Sherlock, S. (2004) *Consolidation and Change: The Indonesian Parliament after the 2004 Elections* (Canberra: Centre for Democratic Institutions).

Shin D.C. (2008) 'The Third Wave in East Asia: Comparative and Dynamic Perspectives', *Taiwan Journal of Democracy*, 4 (2): 103.

Sisk, T.D. (1995) *Democratization in South Africa: The Elusive Social Contract* (Princeton NJ: Princeton University Press).

Slater, D. (2004) 'Indonesia's Accountability Trap: Party Cartels and Presidential Power after Democratic Transition', *Indonesia*, 78 (1): 61–92.

Wurfel, D. (2004) 'Democracy, Nationalism and Ethnic Identity: The Philippines and East Timor Compared', in Susan J. Henders (ed.), *Democratization and Identity: Regimes and Ethnicity in East and Southeast Asia* (Lanham MD: Lexington Books).

8
Decentralization and Democratic Governance in Southeast Asia: Theoretical Views, Conceptual Pitfalls and Empirical Ambiguities

Marco Bünte

Introduction

In the last two decades, many developing and transitional countries have experimented with decentralization reforms. This wave of decentralization, which has now reached most of the countries in Latin America, Africa, Asia and Eastern Europe, began in the 1970s, picked up momentum in the 1980s and accelerated in the 1990s. Since more than 95 per cent of countries worldwide had elected sub-national governments or were experimenting with reforms of central–local relations at the turn of the century, the World Bank called decentralization a 'global and regional phenomenon' (World Bank, 2000, p.107). Much of Southeast Asia stood in contrast to this global trend for a long time; before the 1990s, most countries had highly centralized polities. Today, even non-democratic states such as Vietnam and China are experimenting with reform of their central–local relations in order to enhance the legitimacy and effectiveness of their political systems. This regional wave of political and administrative decentralization has been induced by a variety of pressures, including poor governmental performance, urbanization, democratization and societal demands. Further incentives for undertaking decentralization also came from international development organizations such as the World Bank, USAID and the German GTZ.

The aim of this chapter is to give an overview of recent decentralization reforms and explore whether and how decentralization impacts on democratic governance in the region. I argue that the relationship between decentralization and democratization is problematic at best in most of democratic Southeast Asia. Decentralization reforms have succeeded in those cases where the bureaucracies have been seriously weakened in the regime coalition due to democratizing pressure from below. In contrast, decentralization has failed in those cases where strong bureaucracies exist in the regime coalition. Decentralization was only able to succeed where conservative status quo forces could be engaged in reform. The impact of decentralization on democratic governance is far from clear, however. Since decentralization in the region has often been accompanied by elite capture, growing corruption, limited political participation and violent contestation, the promises mentioned in the discourse on democratic governance have so far not become reality. The Southeast Asian cases echo the pessimism outlined in the literature on decentralization. My argumentation proceeds in three steps. In the first part, I shall address the conceptual and theoretical issues raised in the discourse on decentralization and propose my own theoretical argument. In order to contribute to this volume's cross-national comparative analysis on democratic governance, the second and third parts analyze the region's decentralization initiatives from a comparative perspective. The aim of the second section is to sketch and explain the different decentralization strategies by referring to the political and structural context of decentralization reforms. The third section describes the impact these have on democratic governance in the region.

Decentralization and democratic governance

The concept of democratic decentralization

The relationship between decentralization, democratization and political participation has been debated ever since Alexis de Tocqueville's study of *Democracy in America* (1835) and John Stuart Mill's *Considerations on Representative Government* (1861). In the past quarter of a century, decentralization has become an integral element in the standard template of democracy promoters around the world. The popularity of decentralization reforms results from their assumed consequences and intended effects. It is supposed that decentralization supports the modernization of public administration, that it leads to economic growth and poverty reduction and that it contributes to democratic consolidation (Rondinelli and Cheema, 2007; Cohen and Peterson, 1999, p.20). However, the exact nature of this relationship is still not clear and the value of decentralization and the consequences it has for the broader democratic system and society at large are far from uncontroversial (Treisman, 2007). At least two reasons account for this. First, the controversy can be attributed to the lack of theoretical knowledge about the proper relationship between decentralization and democracy. Up until very recently, most of the theoretical literature on democratization and democratic consolidation has focused on the national government in the centre. Concepts of democracy applied in democratization studies do not consider democratic decentralization or local democracy a relevant component of a democratic political regime. Accordingly, few authors establish a link between transition theory and decentralization reforms.[1] Democratization is usually only treated as a process taking place at the macro level. Secondly, decentralization is a 'complex concept' and catch-all term for what proves in practice to be a highly differentiated and differently motivated range of political, economic and administrative practices and institutional reforms. At least three different processes or facets of decentralization must be identified here and each form can be distinguished according to the extent to which power and authority are being transferred (Rondinelli, 1981; Cohen and Peterson, 1999):

- *Deconcentration* is the shifting of administrative responsibilities from central ministries to lower-level branch offices. It refers to the decentralization of policy administration or implementation and could include the establishment of field offices of national departments and the transfer of some decision-making to the field staff. Different policies continue to be made at the central level. Deconcentrated local governments often lack authority over the scope or quality of local services and how these are provided. In the case of deconcentration, local officials are not elected.
- *Delegation* includes some transfer of decision-making authority; it is the transfer of managerial responsibility for a specially defined function outside the usual central government structure.
- *Devolution* is the most comprehensive form of decentralization. It means the shifting of power to independent or semi-independent local units that are responsible for providing a set of public services and imposing fees and taxes to finance these services. Responsibility comes through the mechanism of local elections. Devolution thus aims at giving citizens more influence over local-government policies.

As Table 8.1 demonstrates, however, these three forms of decentralization do not automatically include democratization. Deconcentration and delegation, in particular, are measures to improve the effectiveness of the central government, a move designed to strengthen the latter's output legitimacy. Thus, only a specific form of decentralization – called 'political decentralization' or 'democratic decentralization' in the literature (Manor, 1999; Blair, 2000) – is inherently related to democratization.

The promises and pitfalls of democratic decentralization

Democratic decentralization means the devolution of decision-making authority to local citizens or their democratically elected representatives. Firstly, this implies the existence of working sub-national legislatures and executives, which have to be accountable to the local demos for their actions. Secondly, it implies the presence of extra-parliamentary mechanisms of accountability and control such as a vibrant civil society and a free press. Advocates of democratic decentralization emphasize a number of

Table 8.1   Forms of decentralization

Nature of delegation	Basis of delegation		Decentralization as democratization
	Territorial	Functional	
Within formal political structures	Devolution	Interest-group representation	When authority and power are given to autonomous local-level units of the elected leadership
Within public administrative or parastatal structures	Deconcentration	Establishment of parastatals	No
From state to private sector	Privatization	Privatization of national functions	No

Source: Adapted from Turner (1999) and Hutchcroft (2001).

assumed positive consequences of democratic decentralization. These can be summarized in five arguments.

First of all, the liberal tradition, which has its origins in the Federalist Papers, mainly stresses the importance of vertical checks and balances resulting from decentralization and elected sub-national governments (Madison, 1999, p.270; Hamilton, 2001, p.282). In this view, administrative decentralization and local democracy are instruments for dispersing political power and authority, which prevents the emergence of democratic despotism at the national level as well as the local tyranny of the majority against political, sectoral or ethnic minorities. Secondly, the communitarian or conservative tradition goes back to Alexis de Tocqueville. The great French philosopher and analyst of modern democracy saw administrative centralism as the main threat to individual liberty and political freedom in any democratic society. According to de Tocqueville, local self-rule and township democracy was the key to democratic freedom (de Tocqueville, 1969, p.192). Political – and especially administrative – decentralization contributes to the emergence and preservation of a vibrant civil society as it provides the institutional context for greater civic participation in public affairs, which not only enhances levels of accountability, but also contributes to the necessary viable civic culture within local communities as well as society as a whole. Thirdly, following the arguments of Alexis de Tocqueville, Robert Putnam and others have emphasized the idea that democratic governance requires a solid foundation in well-functioning institutions of participatory self-governance (Putnam, 1993). More specifically, this view imagines the enhancement of levels of transparency and accountability and the development of good-governance practices (Crook and Manor, 1998; Blair, 2000).

The idea is that local needs will be identified better as a result of decentralization. They will be given higher priority and local leaders will be more directly under the scrutiny of their respective communities. A central idea here is that democratic governance requires a sound foundation in well-functioning local institutions that could conceivably thrive in a decentralized environment.

Fourthly, in development studies it is strongly suggested that decentralization is likely to help to alleviate bottlenecks in decision-making that are often caused by central government planning and control of important economic and social activities (Kimeny and Meagher, 2004). The link between successful decentralization and democratic decision-making is assumed to be fairly clear: decentralization can help national government ministries reach larger numbers of local areas with services. These services are able to meet local demands more effectively and are also provided at a lower cost than centralized services. Decentralized governments 'are more responsive to the needs of the poor than central governments and thus are more likely to conceive and implement pro-poor policies' (Crook, 2003, p.77). Democracy at the local level can play an important role in local government accountability. Decentralization also allows greater political representation of diverse political, ethnic, religious and cultural groups in decision-making. Decentralization is also an appropriate solution to the problems of communal conflict and ethnic separatism in culturally fragmented societies. By promoting a certain degree of political and administrative autonomy for ethnic groups, decentralization strengthens regime stability and allows democracy to work in multi-ethnic societies (Brancati, 2009). A fifth point is the argument of inverse timing of democratization. Initiating democracy at the local level may well prove an important way to begin the transition to national democracy. Because the stakes are lower, local elections are clearly easier to implement and sustain than national ones (cf. Weingast, 2006).

On the other hand, it can be argued that implementing decentralization involves certain trade-offs. More specifically, the literature mentions five possible perils of decentralization within the context of democratization. Firstly, Weingast emphasizes a potential liability of democracy he calls the 'tragic brilliance mechanism' of an authoritarian regime (Weingast, 2006). The tragic brilliance mechanism implies that for democracy to serve as a mechanism of freedom and choice, it must be embedded in institutions that provide working checks and balances against the local government's misuse of discretionary authority to threaten particular voters who vote for the opposition. Yet there is a danger that decentralization reforms will be captured by powerful local elites in the absence of a strong, independent civil society and a working judicial system that can be counterposed to those elites that have little to gain from local governance characterized by greater participation of and accountability to local constituencies (McCarthy, 2004). Secondly, for local democracy to work, it must be embedded in a series of institutions that affect the incentives of political officials. When the absence of limit conditions is combined with the 'tragic brilliance' mechanisms so that basic services depend on whom citizens support in elections, citizens' freedom of choice is proscribed and democracy serves more as a mechanism of social control than of personal choice. Thirdly, democracy at the local level can only increase accountability if it allows local citizens to make choices of competing visions about policies and throw out corrupt or ineffective local officials (Bardhan and Mookherjee, 2006). Local governments often allow local elites and narrow interests to have more influence, enshrine homogenous groups in power and provide an opportunity for local elites to simply capture the benefits of decentralization, however. As critics argue, there is little recognition in the dominant discourse on decentralization that local elites have succeeded in occupying key positions of political power in many countries, which has allowed them to block the expansion of meaningful participation. Whether or not democratic processes are captured by vested interests may depend on a variety of factors such as the electoral system, the media landscape and the different costs associated with organizing group behaviour. The costs of information and organization for interest groups may be lower in smaller jurisdictions because their interests tend to be more homogeneous. Taking those factors into account, it comes as no surprise that local governments often appear more vulnerable to capture than do national governments. With similar considerations in mind, Bardharn and Mookherjee conclude that the lower the level of government, the greater the extent of capture by vested interests (Bardhan and Mookherjee, 2000, p.135).

Fourthly, even though a decentralized state may be more efficient and responsive to local needs or the interests of minorities, it may also be more fragmented and inefficient because of insufficient planning, co-ordination and administrative capacities or funding. Decentralization may not strengthen the state, but actually weaken it as it can create multiple steering problems. Furthermore, where bureaucracies are disorganized and problems of nepotism, patronage and corruption are endemic, decentralization may not heal this problem, but deepen it. Paradoxically, to avoid shifting a set of problems along a centralized–decentralized axis and radicalizing problems of state incapacity, decentralization needs to be balanced with the strengthening of central governments and national bureaucracies. Fifthly, while decentralization policy narratives are often dressed up in the clothes of technical governance issues, decentralization is a highly political and complex process affected by multiple struggles between diverse social interests (Hadiz, 2004). In the real world, the actual balance between central and regional authority is far less about a conscious division of labour than about concrete struggles over political and economic resources. Although the design of decentralization is important, particular constellations of power and interests impose limits on the policy options available to decision-makers. Bad policies and faulty management are often not the main reason that decentralization processes fall prey to predatory politics. Thus, successful democratic decentralization requires more than just good policies, planning and resources – it also calls for the political will and power to tip the balance in favour of meaningful local democratization.

It seems that both the affirmative and critical line of reasoning may be valid, but they very much depend on the modalities of decentralization and the political context that political actors face. Focusing on decentralization processes in young democracies in Southeast Asia, the Asian experiences suggest that the relationship between decentralization and democracy is problematic at best in many cases. With particular reference to Indonesia and the Philippines, it can be shown that predatory forces and interests can capture the process and institutions of decentralization. In such cases, decentralization is likely to have little bearing in terms of promoting a governance agenda based on participation transparency and accountability, as assumed in the recent discourse on co-operation regarding decentralization and international development.

Democratic decentralization in Southeast Asia – forms and strategies of decentralization and their impact on democratic governance

Forms and strategies of decentralization in Southeast Asia

Southeast Asia is a late developer as far as decentralization is concerned. Historically, most of the states in the region were highly centralistic and decentralization reforms were not initiated until the 1990s. Even Malaysia, a long-term federal state, is quite centralistic in character (Case, 2007). Table 8.2 provides an overview of the various initiatives of democratization decentralization in the regioin. In general, the approaches to decentralization in Southeast Asia can be divided into three broad categories: 'fast starters', 'incrementalists' and 'cautious movers' (World Bank, 2005, p.6). The fast starters (Indonesia and the Philippines) have rapidly introduced major structural, institutional and fiscal reforms in response to a sudden and far-reaching political stimulus. Sweeping decentralization reforms were introduced in the Philippines in the late 1980s after the fall of Marcos, and in Indonesia they came into being due to a 'big bang' in 1999 in the aftermath of Suharto's fall and the financial crisis. These fast starters introduced the basic elements of the decentralization framework in their revised constitutions, enacted far-reaching decentralization laws, installed democratic elections at the local level and quickly opted for a substantial resource-sharing formula. Considerable follow-up policies and legislative work to create a fully coherent and functional system remained in place in the following years to maintain the decentralization impetus. The Philippine Local Government Code (LGC) of 1991 has consequently been typified as one of the most in-depth

Table 8.2   Overview of democratic decentralization initiatives in Southeast Asia

Country legal framework	Mode	Basis for decentralization	Fields and primary levels assigned	Formal institutions of local democracy
Cambodia Law on Commune Elections, 2001	Cautious	*Deconcentration* (to a lesser extent devolution	Commune-level (4th tier)	Commune elections
Indonesia Law 22/1999 and 25/1999	'Big Bang' decentralization	*Devolution*	Environment, health, natural resources, public works to district level (3rd tier)	Local elections on all levels (provincial, district heads and assemblies)
Philippines Local Government Code, 1991	'Big Bang' decentralization	*Devolution*	Health, social services, environment, agriculture, education, tourism, to Barangay level (4th tier)	Local elections
Thailand Decentralization Act, 1999	Cautious	*Deconcentration* (to a lesser extent devolution)	Tambon level (3rd tier)	Elections of TAO

Source: Own.

and extensive decentralization initiatives in Southeast Asia that addressed the decades-old problem of a highly centralized political-administrative system, with most significant political and administrative decisions being concentrated in Manila (Turner, 1999). The LGC devolved responsibilities in the fields of health, social services, the environment, agriculture, education, tourism and other services to the local level. Moreover, it increased the financial resources available to local governments by broadening their tax powers and providing them with a specific share of national taxes. In a similar vein, Indonesia's 'big bang' decentralization has been characterized as a complete overhaul of the political system, with new responsibilities and fiscal resources being devolved to the several hundred district governments (Bünte, 2004). Law 22/1999 assigned new responsibilities in the fields of education, the environment, health, natural resources management and public works to the district level, while Law 25 developed a new fiscal framework between the centre and the regions and mandated that 25 per cent of domestic revenues should be transferred to local governments.

The incrementalists have taken a more piecemeal approach to decentralization. In China or Vietnam, for instance, the government made ad hoc policy decisions and passed legislation directly affecting sub-national governments (some decentralizing, some recentralizing), although decentralization is not an officially documented policy (Vasavakul, 1999). The cautious movers (Thailand and Cambodia) have established significant elements of decentralization at the formal policy and legislative levels, but only limited progress has been made on implementation. In Thailand, for instance, there has been considerable opposition to even modest moves towards decentralization ever since the early 1990s. Existing decentralization initiatives stipulated in the decentralization framework of the 1997 constitution and the laws of 1999 were undermined by the more centralizing scheme of creating unelected 'CEO governors' (Mutebi, 2004). In Cambodia, efforts regarding greater devolution have fallen behind the concrete measures of deconcentration that have been progressing since 2001 (Turner, 2002).

How can these findings be explained? The difference in these approaches can mainly be attributed to the interplay of three factors: firstly, the mode of transition to democracy and the strength of the bureaucracy in the regime coalition; secondly, the intensity of provincial separatism and communal tensions at the local level and the push for decentralization from below; and thirdly, the extent of conflict between bureaucratic and non-bureaucratic players at the central level, especially during the implementation phase, which made decentralization either succeed or fail. In both Indonesia and the Philippines, the authoritarian regime coalition has been seriously weakened by democratization, and bureaucratic elements came under intense pressure to alter central–local relations. Pressure to undergo decentralization came from below in both countries. In Indonesia, regional and local leaders began voicing their discontent about the perceived excesses of centralized rule and started demanding greater regional control over political and economic affairs after Suharto's fall in May 1998. Hundreds of local officials had to resign due to pressure from the reform movement. Consequently, decentralization became an important element in the reform agenda proposed by democracy activists (Erb et al., 2005, p.6). Supporters of decentralization equated centralized governance with the old authoritarian regime and viewed decentralization as a necessary process by which civilian involvement in public affairs could be enhanced (Törnquist, 2006). The Habibie government, which lacked popular legitimacy of free elections, responded to these developments with the promulgation of a policy of regional autonomy as part of the broader reform agenda of democratization. Habibie's move can thus be seen as a political manoeuvre undertaken to improve his election prospects. Still associated with his former patron, Suharto, and the New Order, and lacking a solid support base both within his party and the New Order, Habibie was keen to distance himself from the Suharto regime and gain recognition as a political reformer. He also wanted to underline his credibility in the eyes of the international community, which was calling for good governance and political reforms at the time (Bünte, 2009). The decentralization laws 22/1999 and 25/1999 were passed in Parliament in great haste and with a minimum of public debate. Despite their possessing little information about the consequences of decentralization, political party members grabbed at any opportunity to present themselves as being reform-orientated. Most politicians voted for the decentralization laws even though decentralization stood to threaten their interests as national-level actors and elites of highly centralized political parties.

In the Philippines, the push for decentralization in the post-authoritarian transition period came from provincial and local government officials themselves (Angeles and Magno, 2004, p.218). They were supported in their bid for decentralization by the national executive and legislature. The centralism of the Marcos era was equated with his authoritarianism and consequently democratization was associated with decentralized political structures. President Aquino provided strong support for decentralization in order to bring democracy to lower levels of government, and most of the senators (and a few Congressmen) also supported the move since they needed the backing of local executives in their bids for national office. The Speaker of the House, Ramon Mitra, appeared to believe that by shepherding the Code through the House of Representatives, he would gain the support of local politicians in his attempt to succeed President Aquino in 1992. The opposition in the House and the deadlock in Congress might have been overcome thanks to the pressure of these political players, and the Local Government Code could then have been passed as well (Hutchcroft, 2004).

There have only been modest moves towards decentralization in Thailand and Cambodia. In Thailand, there has been considerable opposition to even small steps towards decentralization since democratization took place in 1992. The resistance of the bureaucracy has been hard to overcome. After the May protest in Bangkok in 1992, almost every major political party had promised on its electoral platform to undertake some initial steps regarding political and fiscal decentralization, steps that were deemed necessary given Thailand's long history of centralism (Medhi, 1995, p.343). In the end, however, decentralization reforms caught the attention of political players and bureaucrats in their search for political power. The Chuan administration introduced a bill in 1994 that pushed for all posts at local government level to be filled in accordance with elections and established the sub-districts as the appropriate legal body for achieving this and the Tambon Administrative Organization (TAO) as a new form of local government. These changes, however, met with fierce resistance from the Ministry of the Interior, a powerful body that controls all aspects of local administration.[2] Consequently, even minor reforms were watered down in the first few years following democratization. The Thai government did not attempt any serious renegotiation of central–local relations; there was no pressure from below either. Thailand's pro-democracy movement paired the reform of the overall system with the development of an initial decentralization framework. This movement culminated in the passage of the People's Constitution in 1997, which mandated further decentralization of the political system (Medhi, 1995). While even minor attempts at transferring power to sub-national levels have been thwarted by nationalist bureaucrats and conservative politicians in Thailand, the initiatives for decentralization in Cambodia came from the state itself. The rationale for decentralization has been to strengthen the presence and legitimacy of the state at the local level after decades of conflict and turmoil. Since the rural areas have always been the political backbone of the ruling Cambodian People's Party (CPP), the party supported the direct election of commune councils after 2001 (Turner, 2002).

The three factors mentioned above proved to be even more important during the implementation phase (see Table 8.3). Although seriously weakened after democratization, the bureaucracy was able to derail decentralization by resisting it during the implementation period. While the resistance of senior bureaucrats was overcome in Indonesia and the Philippines, the decentralization provisions of the Thai constitution of 1997 and the Decentralization Act of 1999 have still not been fully implemented yet. In Indonesia and the Philippines, the implementation of the decentralization framework remained a protracted struggle between the central government ministries and local governments. The problems in implementing the Philippine Local Government Code ranged from a lack of resources and capabilities at the local level to the continued resistance of central ministries. The main success factor was the commitment of the Ramos administration, which helped to resolve bureaucratic conflicts and monitor the implementation (Hutchcroft, 2004, p.310). In Indonesia, decentralization remained one of the most important and heavily contested policies of the post-Suharto era. Both decentralization laws contained major weaknesses and needed a multitude of implementing regulations that were to be written under President Wahid (1999–2001) and President Megawati (2001–04). What started with a 'big bang' ultimately became a protracted process of decentralization in which centre-based political elites with vested interests in the surrounding regions and their counterparts in these outlying areas fought over the scope of authority to be devolved to the local level (Bünte, 2009, p.108). Neither the central nor the local governments adhered to the decentralization laws set up in law 22/1999. In the absence of a strong rule of law, the legal framework was often abused by newly formed alliances involving politicians, bureaucrats and private interests for pursuing rent-seeking activities. Confronted with many decentralization-related problems,[3] nationalist politicians slowed the autonomy process down. In an effort to gain further control of the restive governments, a new decentralization law (32/2004) directed authorities back to the central government, which was granted more power to intervene in local affairs.

In contrast, Thai decentralization has been in a dilemma ever since the inauguration of Prime Minister Thaksin Shinawatra in 2001. His election, however, also meant a radical departure from the more democratic politics

Table 8.3   Democratic decentralization in Southeast Asia

	Mode of democratic transition	Mode of politico-bureaucratic interactions	Crisis of national integration/ push from below	Mode and scope of decentralization
Indonesia	Breakdown of regime coalition of bureaucrats and military elites	Bureaucratic and military elites temporarily sidelined	High	Big Bang/ extensive
Philippines	Breakdown of regime coalition – bureaucracy under pressure	Non-bureaucratic elites dominant	High	Big Bang/ extensive
Thailand	Controlled from above	Bureaucratic elements dominant	Weak	Cautious/low
Cambodia	Breakdown	Political elites dominant	Weak	Cautious/low

Source: Own.

of the late 1990s, which had culminated in the promulgation of the new constitution in 1997 and the Decentralization Act in 1999. Thaksin's more business-orientated, strong-arm leadership also meant a renunciation of Thai decentralization policies. Thaksin used his influence to initiate the recentralization scheme of 'CEO governors', which enhanced the powers of elected governors, who were supposed to act like corporate CEOs with full management authority and have the final say on all branches of local government, including budgets and personnel (Mutebi, 2004, p.46).

All in all, the scope of decentralization and transfer of power to sub-national units has been quite extensive in the Philippines and Indonesia and quite low in Cambodia and Thailand. This is also reflected in the willingness to transfer significant financial resources to local governments. As Table 8.4 indicates, sub-national expenditures and functions have been enhanced considerably in less than a decade.

Decentralization and democratic governance in Southeast Asia

A comparative analysis of the impact of decentralization on democratic governance will focus on the broadening of public participation (beyond local elections), the involvement of civil society in local politics and the operation of local accountability mechanisms. Existing evidence from Southeast Asia suggests that the relationship between decentralization and democratization is problematic at best in the young democracies. With particular reference to Indonesia and the Philippines, it can be argued that decentralization has broadened formal routes of citizens' participation in local

Table 8.4   Fiscal decentralization in Southeast Asia

Country	Expenditure decentralization (sub-national spending as a percentage of national spending)
Cambodia (2003)	17
Indonesia (2002)	32
Philippines (2001)	26
Thailand (2001)	10
Vietnam (2002)	48

Source: World Bank (2005).

politics and established channels of direct involvement and monitoring of civil society organizations. This achievement, however, has to be seen against the increasingly oligarchic character of local politics, the continuing involvement of local bosses, which has been accompanied by illiberal practices such as increasing corruption, a lack of transparency and mounting violence. Consequently, it can be argued that predatory forces and interests have captured the processes and institutions of democratic governance in the young democracies of Southeast Asia (especially the Philippines and Indonesia).

In the Philippines, the evidence of effective participation in local government is mixed. The legal framework made the Local Government Code a good vehicle by which to advance local democratization and deepen national democracy (Brilliantes, 1997). The LGC initiated democratic mechanisms that ought to enhance local citizens' participation and community empowerment. It provided for the active participation of local NGOs and civil society, which were given the opportunity of participating in local development councils and holding local governments accountable for their deeds. Since the transition from authoritarianism to democracy gave birth to a robust civil society composed of a multitude of NGOs and social movements, there was the initial hope that civil society could act as an agent of control regarding local government affairs (Panganiban, 1995). NGOs are, indeed, said to be very active in local governance, especially in the education and health sector (Azfar et al., 2004, p.222). However, despite the involvement of NGOs in local politics, participation is often merely a ritual. According to a World Bank assessment of decentralization, only 30 to 50 per cent of local governments have actually established Local Development Councils, and less than a third of all local governments have made development plans that include meaningful civil society participation (Turner, 1999). Moreover, 33 per cent of the civil society organizations were found to be either appointed or selected by local chief executives (Turner, 1999, p.119). Although the LGC provided for a sectoral representation of women, workers and other marginalized groups (like the poor and disabled), these groups did not enhance the representativeness of local politics since most of them were co-opted by the local elite. The LGC also established mechanisms for recalling elected officials whose performance in office had been unsatisfactory and provided for local initiatives and referenda. These provisions, however, have only seldom been used by civil society (Angeles and Magno, 2004, p.228). In general, we can find a number of regions where civil society plays an active role in local politics. In other areas, however, local governance simply relies on political democracy with limited amounts of direct participation (Ishi et al., 2007, p.369). This judgement has to be seen against the continuing influence of local strongmen in politics. One can find localities throughout the Philippines where one politician – or one family – has held office and built up a monopolistic position in the local economy over the course of many years. Local families have often employed patronage, violence and intimidation to consolidate their position. The overall oligarchic character of local politics has been further consolidated and the effects of decentralization, which in this context means the empowerment of local strongmen, have been captured. The phenomenon of 'bossism', which has been discussed from different angles in various localities (Anderson, 1988; Sidel, 1999), is not only the cause of the democratic deficit, but is also responsible for the country's weak state capacity, lack of order and ungovernability.

In Indonesia, the verdict on decentralization and local democracy is still pending after ten years. Taking into account the huge regional diversity of the archipelago and the differing historical, cultural and economic local conditions in each region, it is no wonder that there is no clear picture about the impact of the decentralization process on local democracy so far. Scholars' evaluation ranges from optimistic to cautious or even pessimistic (Malley, 2003; Schulte Nordholt and Van Klinken, 2007; Hadiz, 2007; Bünte, 2009; Sulistiyanto and Erb 2009). The latest studies point to the intricacies posed by the historical legacy of the Suharto era, the restructuring of the New Order elites and rise of local bosses and their abuse of state power in addition to the side effects of decentralization, namely ethnic and religious mobilization, violence and administrative and political fragmentation (Schulte Nordholt, 2004). The early years of local autonomy were haunted by the legacy of Suharto's New Order regime, which systematically undercut political opposition, severely weakened civil society and established an intricate system of economic and political patronage. Existing institutions that could enforce checks and balances and accountability at the local level such as local parliaments (DPRD), political parties, the media and civil society organizations have structural and performance weaknesses that prevent them from fully exercising their roles. Local councillors are primarily accountable to their parties, and these in turn largely lacked broad-based representative policy platforms. Councillors are also largely disconnected from their communities and face weak electoral incentives to react to constituency aspirations. Numerous cases of charges of corruption brought against local councillors and local officials are indicative of these shortcomings.

While the general participation of civil society has not been enhanced, the politico-administrative elite of the New Order has managed to adapt to the decentralized rules and adjust to the democratized framework. The growing competition for local power has radically facilitated money politics and the use of intimidation and violence (Malley, 2003). In the early years of decentralization in Indonesia (1999–2004), the whole political process was overshadowed by money politics. Since government projects have been decentralized (land use, community development projects), local legislators have attempted to mobilize local residents to protest against these projects with the aim of extracting money for mediating between protesting 'citizens' and the local administration (Honna, 2006, p.84). This form of 'parochial mobilization' (Honna, 2006, p.5) of these civic protests demonstrates the ambiguity of increased participation and protests, which are often mobilized by *preman*, local thugs or power brokers with strong connections to the underworld, and thus reveal the dark side of civil society. Overall, it is clear that the last few years have witnessed the rise to power and prominence of local mafias, networks and clans around the country (Hadiz, 2007; Bünte, 2009).

The predatory networks in Indonesia are very different from the pattern of local bossism in the Philippines (and in Thailand)[4] since the emergence of local strongmen is prevented by strong assemblies, strong centralized parties and the party system (Sidel, 2004). Nevertheless, it has become clear that decentralization has not caused local democracy to flourish. While local state institutions were captured by the entrenched elite in the early years of decentralization, the direct election of local government heads (and governors) introduced along with law 33/2004 gave a reform impetus to improve the overall accountability of local government heads. Recent studies, however, have shown that the new electoral rules have not drastically changed the composition of the political and economic elites at the local level. While entrenched elites have continued to dominate electoral competition, voters have dramatically enhanced their bargaining power by throwing out unpopular incumbents and electing more competent figures in their stead: approximately 40 per cent of the office holders in Indonesia were replaced by candidates with more attractive performance records. Regional elections thus have a positive impact on Indonesia's young democracy (Mietzner, 2009; Sulistiyanto and Erb, 2009). Decentralization has also been accompanied by various side-effects, which have had negative implications for democratic local governance. Ethnic and religious mobilization driven by elite contestation has led to the rise of communal conflicts.[5] Moreover, religious discrimination has been enhanced by the issuance of local religious by-laws (so-called *Perda Sharia*). According to a mainstream reading, political elites have adopted Sharia by-laws to overcome serious legitimacy problems, particularly given the public's increasing identification of the local political class with corruption and unethical rent-seeking (McGibbon, 2006, p.334). While this reading sees religious by-laws as a populist move aimed at winning the votes of the conservative Indonesian Muslim community, another interpretation suggests that religious by-laws are an attempt by local politicians to tap into another source of revenue for local politicians (Buehler, 2008).

All in all, one has to admit that the promises of democratic decentralization have not been realized in Southeast Asia so far. Although decentralization could enhance civil society's participation in some localities, the overall result seems to be negative. It can also be added that decentralization has been followed by a decentralization of corruption in both Indonesia and the Philippines (Azfar et al., 2004, p.233). The reason for this can be found in the restructuring of patrimonial networks after democratization and decentralization and the weakness of strong monitoring institutions in civil society. Even in Thailand, where the overall move towards decentralization has been slow and the extent of decentralization has been limited, the main beneficiaries have been local politicians with vested interests. Here, local politics is still the prerogative of families and clans, and watchdog agencies are very weak (Achakorn, 2007; Nelson, 2005).

Conclusion

After many decades of centralism, Southeast Asian states have embarked on the decentralization of their state structures. The approaches that Southeast Asian states have taken to decentralization have varied: while some have opted for comprehensive decentralization, including a complete overhaul of their political and administrative structure, others have been more cautious in their reforms. This chapter has shown that far-reaching decentralization evolved from a combination of local, national and international pressure to initiate a reform of central–local relations. This chapter has demonstrated that for decentralization to succeed, a clear reform coalition is necessary that also guides its implementation. This has frequently been the case after a breakdown or weakening of the authoritarian regime coalition when the bureaucracy was seriously weakened. In cases where such a reform coalition is absent, decentralization has met with fierce resistance from status quo forces with an interest in rent-seeking activities. These forces often act as veto players with the aim of derailing the whole process. One of the guiding *leitmotifs* of decentralization policy has been to bring democracy closer to the people. Although decentralization has had a big impact on governance structures at the local level, it has not automatically led to more participation. It has undoubtedly created space for democratic change, which might be significant if political groups such as ethnic minorities, democratic parties, politically and economically marginalized groups and NGOs could organize themselves so as to take advantage of these new openings. Nevertheless, to date, these promises have not been met. With regard to the relationship between decentralization and democratization, we can learn some important lessons from the case of Southeast Asia.

First of all, democratic decentralization does not automatically serve as a tool to deepen democracy at the sub-national level and needs to be embedded in institutions that provide working checks and balances against the local governments' misuse of discretionary authority. A strong and independent civil society and a strong judicial system may function as an alternative tool to accountability. In the absence of a strong and independent civil society and a working judicial system that can be counterposed to those elites who have little to gain from local governance characterized by greater participation and by accountability to local constitutions, decentralization will most certainly be captured by powerful local elites.

Secondly, decentralization in former neo-patrimonial systems can lead to the decentralization of corruption. While the impact of democracy on clientelism and neo-patrimonial structures itself depends on the depth of democratization and the existence of interest groups, strong political parties and civil society at the local level, decentralization only redirects existing informal structures. Without strong watchdog agencies corruption can become endemic and thrive at the local level.

Thirdly, as existing research on bossism in Thailand, the Philippines and Indonesia indicates (Sidel, 2004; Hutchcroft, 2004), it is essentially the interplay between national and local forces that provides incentives for the rise of local strongmen. Such powerful people are found in places where national institutions are weak, where political parties and party systems are weakly institutionalized, and where the local political economy allows the rise of figures who are not constrained by a strong local society. Much more comparative research needs to be done in order to fully comprehend the evolution and rise of local strongmen.

Notes

1. Diamond (1999, pp.117–61) is an exception.
2. Chavalit Yongchaiyudh, the Minister of the Interior at the time, prevented the election of sub-district and village heads in order to secure the support of these officials in the next election. These officers generally serve as vote canvassers for electoral candidates at all levels.
3. These problems included a multitude of new taxes and regulations which were (illegally) put in place and reinforced trade restrictions. Moreover, problems in implementation arose since there was a growing contradiction between sectoral laws and regulations; there were also problems in supervision due to the weakened role of the governors.
4. Local power does not seem to be monopolized by individual strongmen as in the Philippines, but instead seems to be more loosely defined and rather fluid

around clusters and cliques of businessmen, politicians and officials (the New
Order elite).
5. Schulte Nordholt (2007) points out that all major communal conflicts (e.g. Poso/
Central Sulawesi, Ambon/Moluccas and Sampit/Kalimantan) started as district-
level conflicts. Whenever these conflicts have erupted, radical Islamic groups
have been quick to exploit them.

References

Achakorn, W. (2007) 'Decentralization and Its Effect on Provincial Political Power in
Thailand', *Asian and African Studies*, 6 (2): 454–470.
Anderson, B. (1988) 'Cacique Democracy in the Philippines, Origins and Dreams',
New Left Review, 169, May-June: 3–31.
Angeles, L. and Magno, F. (2004) 'The Philippines Decentralization, Local Govern-
ments and Citizen Action', in Oxhorn, P. et al. (eds), *Decentralization, Democratic
Governance, and Civil Society in Comparative Perspective: Africa, Asia, and Latin Amer-
ica* (Baltimore: Johns Hopkins University Press).
Azfar, O., Gurgur, T. and Meagher, P. (2004) 'Political Disciplines on Local Government:
Evidence from the Philippines', in Kimenyi, M.S. and Meagher, P. (eds) *Devolution
and Development, Governance Prospects in Decentralizing States* (Aldershot: Ashgate).
Bardhan, P. and Mookherjee, D. (2000) 'Capture and Governance at Local and
National Levels', *The American Economic Review*, 90 (2): 135–139.
Bardhan, P. and Mookherjee, D. (2006) *Decentralization and Local Governance in
Developing Countries. A comparative perspective* (Cambridge/London: MIT Press).
Blair, H. (2000) 'Participation and Accountability at the Periphery: Democratic Local
Governance in Six Countries', *World Development*, 28 (1): 65–81.
Brancati, D. (2009) *Peace by Design. Managing Ethnic Conflict through Decentralization*
(Oxford, New York: Oxford University Press).
Brilliantes, A. (1997) 'Redemocratization and Decentralization in the Philippines:
The Increasing Leadership Role of NGOs', *International Review of Administrative
Sciences*, 60 (4): 575–586.
Buehler, M. (2008) 'The Rise of Shari'a by-laws in Indonesian districts: An indication
for changing patterns of power accumulation and political corruption', *South East
Asia Research*, 16 (2): 255–285.
Bünte, M. (2004) 'Indonesia's Big Bang revisited', in Nelson, M. (ed.), *Thai Politics:
Global and Local Perspectives*, KPI Yearbook No. 2, Bangkok.
Bünte, M. (2009) 'Indonesia's protracted decentralization: Contested Reforms and
their unintended consequences', in Bünte, M. and Ufen, A. (eds), *Democratization
in Post-Suharto Indonesia* (London: Routledge).
Case, W. (2007) 'Semi-democracy and Minimalist Federalism in Malaysia', in
Baogang, H., Galligan, B. and Inoguchi, T. (eds), *Federalism in Asia* (Cheltenham:
Edward Elgar Publishers).
Cohen, J. and Peterson, S. (1999) *Administrative Decentralization, Strategies for Develop-
ing Countries* (West Hartford: Kumarian Press).
Crook, R. C. (2003) 'Decentralization and poverty reduction in Africa: the politics of
central-local relations', *Public Administration and Development*, 21: 149–157.
Crook, R.C. and Manor, J. (1998) *Democracy and Decentralisation in South Asia and
West Africa: Participation, Accountability and Performance* (Cambridge: Cambridge
University Press).
Diamond, L. (1999) *Developing Democracy Toward Consolidation* (Baltimore/London:
Johns Hopkins University Press).

Erb, M., Sulistyanto, P. and Faucher, C. (2005) *Regionalism in Post-Suharto Indonesia* (London: Routledge).

Hadiz, V. (2004) 'Decentralisation and Democracy in Indonesia: A Critique of Neo-Institutionalist Perspectives', *Development and Change*, 35 (4): 697–718.

Hadiz, V. (2007) 'The Localization of Power in Southeast Asia', *Democratization*, 14 (5): 873–892.

Hamilton, A. (2001) [1769–1804] *Writings* (New York: Library of America).

Honna, J. (2006) 'Local Civil–Military Relation During the First Phase of Democratic Transition, 1999-2004: A Comparison of West, Central and East Java', *Indonesia*, 82 (October): 75–95.

Hutchcroft, P.D. (2001) 'Centralization and Decentralization in Administration and Politics: Assessing Territorial Dimensions of Authority and Power', *Governance: An International Journal of Policy and Administration*, 14: 23–53.

Hutchcroft, P.D. (2004) 'Paradoxes of Decentralization. The Political Dynamics behind the Passage of the 1991 Local Government Code of the Philippines', in Nelson, M. (ed.), *Thai Politics: Global and Local Perspectives*, KPI Yearbook No. 2, Bangkok.

Ishi, R., Hossain, F. and Rees, C. (2007) 'Participation in Decentralized Local Governance: Two Contrasting Cases from the Philippines', *Public Organization Review*, 7 (4): 359–373.

Kimeny, M.S. and Meagher, P. (2004) *Devolution and Development, Governance Prospects in Decentralizing States* (Aldershot: Ashgate).

Madison, J. (1999) *Madison: Writings*, ed. by Jack N. Rakove (New York: Library of America).

Malley, M. (2003) 'New Rules, Old Structures and the Limits of Democratic Decentralization', in Aspinall, E. and Fealey, G. (eds), *Local Power and Politics in Indonesia: Decentralization and Democratisation* (Singapore: ISEAS).

Manor, J. (1999) *The Political Economy of Democratic Decentralization* (Washington, DC: World Bank).

McCarthy, J. F. (2004) *Changing to Gray: Decentralization and the Emergence of Volatile Socio-legal Configurations in Central Kalimantan, Indonesia*, Asia Research Centre, Murdoch University, Working Paper 101.

McGibbon, R. (2006) 'Indonesian politics in 2006: stability, compromise and shifting contests over ideology', *Bulletin of Indonesian Economic Studies*, 42 (3): 321–340.

Medhi K. (1995) 'The Political Economy of Decentralization in Thailand', *Southeast Asian Affairs*, 22: 343–361.

Mietzner, M. (2009) 'Indonesia and the pitfalls of low-quality democracy: A case study of the gubernatorial elections in North Sulawesi', in Bünte, M. and Ufen, A. (eds), *Democratization in Post-Suharto Indonesia* (London: Routledge).

Mill, J.M. (1861) *Considerations on Representative Government* (London: Parker).

Mutebi, A. (2004) 'Recentralizing while Decentralizing: Centre-Local Relations and "CEO" Governors in Thailand', *The Asia Pacific Journal of Public Administration*, 26 (1): 33–53.

Nelson, M. (2005): *Analyzing Provincial Political Structures in Thailand: phuak, trakun, and hua khanaen*, SEARC Working Paper Series 79, City University of Hong Kong, Southeast Asia Research Centre.

Panganiban, E. (1995) 'Democratic Decentralization in Contemporary Times: A New Local Government Code of the Philippines', *Philippine Journal of Public Administration*, 39 (2): 121–238.

Putnam, R. (1993) *Making Democracy Work: Civil Traditions in Modern Italy* (Princeton: Princeton University Press).

Rondinelli, D. (1981) 'Government Decentralization in Comparative Perspective: Theory and Practice in Developing Countries', *International Review of Administrative Science*, 47 (2): 133–145.

Rondinelli, D. and Cheema, S. (2007) *Decentralizing Governance – Emerging Concepts and Practices* (New York: Brookings).

Schulte Nordholt, H. (2004) 'Decentralisation in Indonesia: Less State, More Democracy?', in Hariss, J., Stokke, K. and Törnquist, O. (eds), *Politicising Democracy, the New Local Politics of Democratization* (London: Palgrave).

Schulte Nordholt, H. (2007) *Communal Conflict and Decentralization in Indonesia*, ACPACS Paper Series 7 (Brisbane: ACPACS).

Schulte Nordholt, H. and van Klinken, G. (2007) *Renegotiating Boundaries. Local Politics in Post-Suharto Indonesia* (Leiden: KITLV Press).

Sidel, J. (1999) *Capital, Coercion and Crime: Bossism in the Philippines* (Stanford: Stanford University Press).

Sidel, J. (2004) 'Bossism and Democracy in the Philippines, Thailand and Indonesia: Towards an alternative understanding of local strongmen', in Harriss, J., Stokke, K. and Törnquist, O. (eds), *Politicising Democracy: The New Local Politics of Democratisation* (London: Palgrave Macmillan).

Sulistiyanto, P. and Erb, M. (2009) *Deepening Democracy in Indonesia? Direct Local Elections for Local Leaders (Pilkada)* (Singapore: ISEAS).

Tocqueville, A. de (1969) [1835] *Democracy in America* (New York: Harper Perennial).

Törnquist, O. (2006) 'Assessing Democracy from Below: A Framework and Indonesian Pilot Study', *Democratization*, 13 (2): 227–255.

Treisman, D. (2007) *The Architecture of Government. Rethinking Political Decentralization* (Cambridge: CUP).

Turner, M. (1999) 'Philippines: From Centralism to Localism', in Turner, M. (ed.), *Centre-Local Relations in Asia-Pacific: Convergence or Divergence* (London: Palgrave Macmillan).

Turner, M. (2002) 'Whatever happened to Deconcentration? Recent Initiatives in Cambodia', *Public Administration and Development*, 22 (4): 353–364.

Vasavakul, T. (1999) 'Rethinking the Philosophy of Central-Local Relations in Post-Central-Planning in Vietnam', in Turner, M. (ed.), *Central-Local Relations in Asia-Pacific: Convergence or Divergence* (London: Palgrave Macmillan).

Weingast, B. (2006) *Second Generation Fiscal Federalism: Implications for Decentralized Democratic governance and Economic Development*, Working Paper, Hoover Institution, Stanford University, http://politicalscience.stanford.edu/ faculty/documents/ Weingast-second%20 generation%20fiscal%20federalism.pdf.

World Bank (2000) *Entering the 21st century*, World Development Report 1999/2000 (Washington, DC: World Bank).

World Bank (2005) *East Asia Decentralizes. Making Local Government Work* (Washington, DC: World Bank).

9
Coming Up Short? Party System Institutionalization in Southeast Asia

Allen Hicken

Introduction

As the title of this volume suggests, democracy and democratic govern-ance face severe challenges in Southeast Asia. One may rightly view the Indonesian transition as, at the very least, a partial success story, but any measure of triumphalism is tempered by the reality of ongoing challenges in Indonesia and the lingering malaise in the Philippines, to say nothing of the recent democratic setbacks in Thailand. At the same time, Myanmar, Vietnam, Cambodia, Singapore and Malaysia seem no closer to 'full' dem-ocracy than they did ten or even 20 years ago. Certainly there is little in the Southeast Asian context to support the notion of a gradual, steady regional convergence towards democracy.

Yet while Southeast Asia complicates arguments describing a global convergence on some democratic 'end of history', it is clear that there is a widespread acceptance of and enthusiasm for democratic norms and institutions – at least as an abstract ideal. In recent surveys, more than three-quarters of Indonesian and Thai respondents expressed strong support for democracy (East Asian Barometer). This compares favourably to attitudes in other regions of the world, including Western democracies (see Shin and Cho, Chapter 2 in this volume, for an in-depth analysis of Asian attitudes towards democracy). The case of the Philippines is intriguing; only 55 per cent of Filipino respondents reported themselves satisfied with democracy. These results suggest that in the face of prolonged poor performance on the part of democratic regimes, enthusiasm for democracy may begin to ebb (ibid.).

Indeed, this is common across developing democracies. Respondents' views of democracy as an ideal often diverge sharply from their assessment of the fruits of their particular democracy. Surveys suggest that some of this disillusionment can be traced to people's widespread distrust of and even antipathy toward the building blocks of modern democracy – political par-ties. In many developing democracies, less than half of respondents have any confidence or trust in their country's political parties (see Table 9.1). In Southeast Asia, only 44 per cent of Indonesians, 33 per cent of Filipinos and 56 per cent of Thais have any confidence in their countries' parties.

Ironically, it seems that in the eyes of many people, political parties, the hallmark of modern democratic government (as expressed in Schattschneider's famous quote), have become one of the biggest obstacles to democratic consolidation and good governance.[1] In the words of one Thai politician, 'political parties are the weakest link in the system' (Thai Politicians, 1999).[2]

What is the status of the parties and party systems in Southeast Asia? To what extent are they the weakest link instead of being a democratic cornerstone? In this chapter, I provide a partial answer to these questions. Focusing on the parties and party systems in Thailand, Indonesia and the Philippines, I will first discuss the characteristics and patterns of the party systems and party development in each country, paying particular attention to the issue of party system institutionalization and discussing why we observe variation in the degree of institutionalization across countries and over time. I will argue that while institutionalization is generally weak in all three countries, Indonesia, the youngest democracy of the three, performs the best. I will then analyze some of the reasons behind the lack of institutionalization in all three countries. I will conclude this chapter with a brief discussion of the implications of the trajectory and state of institutionalization for democratic governance and stability.

Party and party system institutionalization

(Why) does it matter?

There is a large literature in comparative politics on party and party system institutionalization.[3] This literature began with an attempt to explain why party institutionalization is necessary for establishing political stability

Table 9.1   Confidence in political parties

Region	Confidence/trust in political parties (average %)
W. Europe/N. America (most recent year available)	75
Latin America (2007)	20
Africa (2005)	48
Asia (most recent year available)	42
Indonesia (2006)	44
Philippines (2005)	33
Thailand (2006)	56

Sources: W. Europe/N. America, Asia, World Values Survey; Latin America, Latinobarometer; Africa, Afrobarometer; Thailand, Indonesia, and the Philippines, East Asian Barometer.

(Huntington, 1968). Scholars, for instance, Huntington, argued that institutionalized parties provide the organizational structure necessary to incorporate and stabilize social demands, thereby ensuring effective governance. More recent studies have broadened their focus from individual parties to the party *system* as a whole (for instance, Mainwaring and Scully, 1995). This is in part a recognition of the reality that while some degree of party institutionalization is a necessary condition for party *system* institutionalization, it is certainly not a sufficient condition – well-institutionalized parties can exist within systems that remain largely underinstitutionalized.

Part of the shift towards an emphasis on party systems also reflects a growing interest in the effect of institutionalization on democratic consolidation. There is a good deal of agreement, based on theoretical grounds, that party system institutionalizations *should* affect the prospects for democratic consolidation (see, for example, Sartori, 1976; Diamond, 1999; Mainwaring, 2006; Mainwaring and Scully, 1995). To quote Larry Diamond, '[s]ome degree of party system institutionalization – of parties with effective, autonomous organizations, and developed, relatively stable linkages to voting blocks and social organizations – seems an important condition for democratic consolidation' (Diamond, 1999, pp.97–8). The logic behind this argument is fairly straightforward. First, a lack of party system institutionalization undermines the ability of the electorate to hold politicians accountable by making it harder to determine collective responsibility and to assign collective punishment (Mainwaring and Torcal, 2006; Hicken, 2007). Second, in underinstitutionalized party systems, the lack of credible organizational counterweights to traditional, non-democratic forces reduces the probability that new democracies will successfully consolidate. Finally, where the party system is weakly institutionalized, the fluidity of the party system offers opportunities for individuals from outside the existing party system to win office and subsequently to centralize power (ibid.). The underperformance of democratic government in weakly institutionalized party systems can generate a demand for 'stronger' leadership, which can take on a decidedly undemocratic tint.

While the theoretical case for a causal link between institutionalization and consolidation is plausible, the empirical record paints a decidedly less conclusive picture. Some scholars do find evidence that institutionalization is related to the level of democracy in Africa (Kuenzi and Lambright, 2005); that a lack of institutionalization makes countries more prone to personalism and more vulnerable to potentially destabilizing 'outsiders' (Mainwaring and Torcal, 2006); and that underinstitutionalization interferes with many of the institutional incentives that are assumed to operate within democracies (Moser, 1999, 2001). However, other studies fail to find any straightforward relationship between party system institutionalization and democratic consolidation (for example, Markowski, 2000; Tóka, 1997; Croissant and Völkel, forthcoming; Stockton, 2001).

Yet it would be premature to dismiss the connection between institution-alization and consolidation completely. For example, there is some evidence that the relationship between institutionalization and consolidation exists, but that it is nonlinear (Tan, 2001). Under certain circumstances, high levels of institutionalization may actually be inimical to democracy, particularly where party group ties are so calcified as to undermine effective account-ability and competition (Hicken, 2007). Others reverse direction of caus-ation and argue that party system institutionalization emerges as the *result* (or final stage) of democratic consolidation rather than as a necessary pre-condition (Markowski, 2000). Finally, it is possible that party system insti-tutionalization has an *indirect* effect on consolidation via its direct effect on the quality of democracy and democratic governance. A number of studies associate institutionalization with better democratic governance, includ-ing more programmatic representation, greater stability of interests, better accountability and more attention to public goods (for instance, Mainwaring and Torcal, 2006; Tóka, 1997; Darby et al., 2004). It is clear, then, that the connection between party system institutionalization and democracy con-tinues to be debated among scholars. In this light, analyses of party system institutionalization in Southeast Asia can play a helpful role in challenging (or confirming) existing theories, extending empirical knowledge, and sug-gesting new and interesting hypotheses.

Defining party system institutionalization

The existing literature defines institutionalization in a variety of ways (see Huntington, 1968; Welfling, 1973; Panebianco, 1988; Mainwaring and Scully, 1995; Levitsky, 1998; Randall and Svasand, 2002). I argue here that a helpful way to bring these disparate definitions together is to think of institutionalization as consisting of an external–systemic dimension and an internal–organizational dimension. Starting with the *external–systemic* dimension, party systems that are more institutionalized share two char-acteristics. First, there is stability in the rules and the pattern of interparty competition. Second, political actors view parties as a legitimate and neces-sary part of the democratic process.[4] By contrast, in weakly institutionalized party systems, we see a high degree of instability in the pattern of party competition. Both 'birth' and 'death' rates are high – new political parties regularly enter the system, while existing parties exit. There is also a high degree of electoral volatility – the fortunes of individual parties vary greatly from election to election. Finally, political actors in weakly institutionalized systems view parties as at best superfluous, and at worst a threat. To measure the stability of interparty competition, I have relied on estimates of elect-oral volatility, as well as the rate at which parties exit and enter the system. Assessing the degree to which political actors view parties as legitimate and necessary is more challenging. I have looked for evidence of this in the degree to which major actors that rival political party politicians for control of the political system and who challenge the legitimacy of political parties to run government remain in the political system. I have also made use of public opinion data on voter attitudes about political parties.

Shifting gears, the *internal–organizational* dimension concerns the nature of party organization itself and the parties' links with the broader society. To begin with, where parties are institutionalized, they exhibit a high degree of what Levitsky calls value infusion (Levitsky, 1998), with strong links between parties and identifiable societal interests and groups of voters. Parties are 'rooted' in society to the extent that '[m]ost voters identify with a party and vote for it most of the time, and some interest associations are closely linked to parties' (Mainwaring and Torcal, 2006, p.7). Party membership is valuable in and of itself and not just as a means to an end; we can differentiate one party from another on the basis of its constituencies and policy platform. Where parties are not institutionalized, political parties have weak roots in society; voters and politicians have few lasting attachments to particular parties; there are no enduring links between parties and interest groups; and parties have no distinct policy or ideological identities. Indicators of the degree of value infusion include electoral volatility, the extent to which voters split their votes across parties when given the opportunity to do so, and the prevalence of party switching. Also useful are estimates of the degree to which parties have close ties to identifiable social groups, the degree to which voters express an attachment to a particular political party, and the extent to which voters view elections as a meaningful choice between different parties.

A second characteristic falling under the internal–organizational dimension is organizational routinization.[5] Institutionalized parties have entrenched organizations and established patterns of interactions. Parties are relatively cohesive and disciplined and are independent and autonomous from any charismatic leaders or particular financiers (Levitsky, 1998). Where parties are weakly institutionalized, they tend to be thinly organized, temporary alliances of convenience and are often extensions of or subservient to powerful party leaders. Again, I use electoral volatility as a rough but reasonable proxy for routinization – for example, volatility should be higher where parties rise and fall with the fortunes of individual leaders. The extent to which parties undertake efforts to build a party organization via party branches and membership is another indicator. Finally, assessments of the degree of party cohesion and discipline are another way to gauge routinization.

The different dimensions of party system institutionalization as well as the indicators for each dimension are summarized in Table 9.2, which also contains a summary of how the indicators are operationalized, with details to follow in the text.

Table 9.2   Party system institutionalization

	Indicators	Operationalization
External–systemic dimension		
Stable pattern of interparty competition	* Electoral volatility * New party entry * Party exits	* Pedersen Index * Party birth rate * Party death rate
Parties viewed as legitimate and necessary	* Major rivals * Party Confidence	* % of population that had a great deal of or some confidence in political parties * Anti-party actions by rival institutions
Internal–organizational dimension		
High degree of value infusion	* Electoral volatility * Voter loyalty * Party ID * Party difference * Party ties to groups	* Pedersen Index * Prevalence of split-ticket voting * % of population that identifies with a political party * Frequency voters think elections offer a real choice between different parties or candidates * Literature consensus on extent of formal and informal ties
High degree of organizational routinization	* Electoral volatility * Party branches * Party membership * Party age	* Pedersen Index * Average number of party branches * Average number of party members * % of parties ≥ 10 years (at least 10% of seats) *% of Parties ≥ 25 years (at least 10% of seats)

Party system institutionalization in Southeast Asia

So how do Indonesia, Thailand and the Philippines fare in terms of degree of institutionalization? Let us consider each of the dimensions in turn.

External–systemic dimension: Stability of interparty competition

One commonly used indicator of the stability or volatility of the party system from election to election is the measure of electoral volatility. Electoral volatility captures the degree to which there is variation in aggregate party vote shares from one election to another. Where there is a stable pattern of interparty competition, we expect to see a low volatility score, indicating that the same set of parties receives consistent levels of support from election to election. High levels of electoral volatility reflect instability in the voters' preferences from election to election and/or elite-driven changes to the party system, such as the demise of existing parties, the birth of new parties, party mergers, party splits, and so on. Electoral volatility is not a perfect measure by any means – tracing party vote shares can prove extremely complicated where there are lots of party mergers or splits, or where a candidate's party affiliation is difficult to assess.[6] The latter is particularly a challenge in the Philippines, where candidates will often claim multiple party affiliations. The very fact that party labels are so fluid in the Philippines is telling. Nonetheless, it is possible to come up with reasonable estimates of volatility based on some simple assumptions.[7] It is also important to note that electoral volatility does not allow us to track the sources of instability – fickle voters or ephemeral parties (Hicken and Kuhonts, forthcoming).

Electoral volatility is calculated by taking the sum of the net change in the percentage of votes gained or lost by each party from one election to the next and dividing it by two ($\Sigma \ |v_{it} - v_{it+1}|$) / 2). A score of 100 signifies that the set of parties winning votes is completely different from one election to the next. A score of 0 means that the same parties received exactly the same percentage of votes across two different elections. The higher the volatility score, the less stable the pattern of party competition.

The average volatility scores for Indonesia, Thailand and the Philippines are displayed in Table 9.3. For comparative purposes, I have also listed the volatility scores for four other Asian democracies, along with the average volatility for each of the major world regions. Because of the long authoritarian interlude in the Philippines, I have reported numbers for each democratic period separately. The electoral volatility score for the last election for which data were available are also reported in Table 9.3. For Thailand, the volatility scores are an average of the scores for the 11 elections between 1979 and 2007. The entry 'Philippines (pre-martial law)' covers the seven elections prior to martial law; the sample for the entry 'Philippines (post-Marcos)' is more limited since the necessary vote share data are available only for the 1992, 1995 and 1998 elections. To compensate for this deficiency, I have also calculated electoral volatility for the Philippines using seat share data, which is available for all of the post-Marcos elections. The Indonesian score reflects the average of volatility in Indonesia's three post-Suharto elections in 1999, 2004 and 2009.

Two things stand out in Table 9.3. First, the party systems of Thailand, Indonesia and the Philippines are very fluid; the fortunes of the individual parties tend to vary greatly from election to election. In other words, the results of past elections by and large are not a good predictor of future

Table 9.3   Comparative electoral volatility

	Years	Number of elections	Volatility: Last election	Average volatility
W. Europe/N. America	–	–	–	10.4
Eastern Europe/Former Soviet Union	–	–	–	44.1
Latin America	–	–	–	25.6
Africa	–	–	–	11.9
Asia	–	–	–	22.1
Indonesia	1999–2009	3	29.8	27.5
Philippines (pre-martial law)	**1946–1969**	**7**	**18.0**	**18.5**
Philippines (post-Marcos)	**1992–1998**	**3**	**28.2**	**37.3**[8]
Thailand	**1979–2007**	**11**	**71.2**	**39.6**
India	1951–2004	14	13.6	25.7
South Korea	1988–2004	5	24.9	29.1
Taiwan	1992–2004	5	10.5	16.2
Japan	1947–2005	22	8.5	16.6

Sources: Hicken and Kuhonta forthcoming; Mainwaring and Zoco, 2007; Birnir, 2007 (Africa).

election results – for instance, in the case of Thailand, the results of a past election can be used to predict the result of the next election with less than 61 per cent accuracy. Second, and more surprising, is the fact that among the three transitioning democracies in Southeast Asia, it is Indonesia, the youngest and least experienced democracy, that currently exhibits the most stability with a volatility score of 27.5.[9]

Average volatility is a useful indicator, but it does not allow us to determine whether there has been any change over time. As discussed below, some have argued that the voters' ties to political parties develop gradually over time, bringing greater stability to electoral competition. If this were true, we would expect electoral volatility to improve (decrease) over time. Do we see evidence of this? The short answer is no. In none of the countries is a clear downward trend evident. In Indonesia, volatility actually increases by about 4 points between the first and second elections, and the second and third elections. In the Philippines, electoral volatility did decline steadily for the first few post-independence elections, but increased substantially in the two elections prior to martial law. Since the fall of Marcos, there has been a much higher rate of electoral volatility than prior to martial law,[10] and, although we see an initial drop in volatility after the first couple of elections, the party system has yet to stabilize. In Thailand, there is also scant evidence of increased stability in the pattern of interparty competition over time. In fact, volatility in the 2007 election hit an all-time high score of 71. Note, though, that Thai democracy has experienced a large number of systemic shocks, including a military coup and subsequent social unrest in 1991–92, sweeping constitutional reforms and a severe economic crisis in 1997, and a military coup in 2006. Volatility shoots up after each of these events, which is a typical outcome in the face of such shocks (Hicken and Kuhonta, forthcoming). In the case of the 2007 election, an increase in volatility was a mathematical certainty once the coup group outlawed the electorally dominant Thai Rak Thai party, forcing its supporters to form or join new parties. The recent Thai experience will be discussed in more detail in the final section of this chapter.

One question that arises from the use of volatility is the source of that volatility. As mentioned previously, high volatility can be driven either by high variability in party vote shares from election to election, or by high entry and exit rates, or a combination of the two. We can tease out which one of these effects is at work by looking at the rate at which parties enter and depart the party system. The party birth and death rates for the three countries are displayed in Table 9.4. Looking at the raw birth rate numbers, the amount of party turnover appears to be significant across all three countries – around 40 per cent of the parties in each election are new parties. In Thailand and the Philippines, a similar percentage of parties fails to compete in the next election. None of Indonesia's major parties disbanded between the first and second, or the second and third, democratic elections. The story is more complicated, however, if we consider the relative size of the parties that enter and exit the party system. While there is a good deal of party turnover in the Philippines, these parties are very small – the average combined vote share for new and exiting parties in each election is 3 and 5 per cent respectively. At the other end of the extreme, parties that exit and enter the system in Thailand tend on average to control a significant share of the votes – as much as 25 per cent in the case of new parties in Thailand. What this tells us is that much of the electoral volatility in Thailand is

Table 9.4 Party birth and death rates[11]

	Birth rate	Death rate	Combined vote share for new parties	Combined vote share for exiting parties
Indonesia (1999–2009)*	0.38	0.0	14%	0%
Philippines (1946–69; 1992–98)	0.41	0.44	3%	5%
Thailand (1979–2007)	0.41	0.35	25%	16%

*Parties garnering at least 1 per cent of the votes.

Source: Author's calculations.

driven by party exits and entries, while volatility in the Philippines is almost entirely a product of shifting party fortunes from election to election.[12]

External–systemic dimension: Legitimacy

One of the most telling indications of a lack of institutionalization is the lingering doubt about whether the major actors view political parties as a legitimate and necessary part of political life. Of course, we need to exercise some care to not conflate the legitimacy of the party system with the legitimacy of democracy. Conceptually, these are distinct but related concepts. The most direct measure of party system legitimacy available is the level of trust in a country's political parties. As discussed in the introduction, a majority of Filipino (67 per cent) and Indonesian (56 per cent) respondents report little or no confidence in their country's political parties. In Thailand trust in parties is higher (56 per cent), but voters still rank parties below almost every other institution in terms of trustworthiness – lower than the military, lower than the police, and lower than the bureaucracy (KPI, 2003).

There is also the question of whether there are viable institutional alternatives to political parties or whether parties are seen as the only legitimate means to political power. In practical terms, it becomes very difficult to separate support for political parties from support for democracy since anti-party actions on the part of major actors often takes the form of anti-democratic actions (for example, coups). We see the strongest animus towards political parties in Thailand. For years, the Senate was maintained as an unelected bastion against the influence of political parties. Even when the 1997 Constitution transformed the Senate into a completely elected body, senators were prohibited from belonging to a political party, suggesting that constitutional drafters still viewed the Senate as a necessary check against the power of party politicians. In the wake of the 2006 coup, the lack of trust in political parties was once again clearly manifest. First, the Senate was transformed into a partially elected, partially appointed body designed to operate outside the control of party politicians (Hicken, 2007). Second, coup leaders lobbied hard, but unsuccessfully, to insert a provision into the revised constitution which would allow for the selection of a non-elected prime minister.

In Indonesia, the same level of antipathy displayed by major actors toward political parties is thus far largely absent, and, not inconsequentially, Indonesia presently seems furthest removed from the threat of an extra-constitutional seizure of power.[13] By contrast, military intervention and coup threats continue to be a prominent feature of Filipino politics, with near-constant rumours of coup plots and actual military interventions in 1986 and 2000 to resolve political stalemates. However, in the case of the Philippines, it is harder to separate anti-party sentiments from more general anti-democratic sentiments.

Internal–organizational dimension:
Value infusion and organizational routinization

How deeply rooted and organizationally strong are the parties in Thailand, the Philippines and Indonesia? One indication of the weak links between parties and cohesive societal interests in Thailand and the Philippines is the high volatility scores discussed previously. The relatively lower volatility score for Indonesia suggests that parties, while still weak, are relatively more deeply rooted than their Thai or Philippine counterparts.

Another indication of the low degree of value infusion within most parties is the lack of party loyalty manifested by large numbers of voters, even within a single election. In Thailand, where prior to 2001 there were multiple seats in each constituency and voters could cast votes for as many candidates as there were seats, one indication of a strong link between parties and voters would be the extent to which voters were loyal to all of the candidates on a party's ticket. Instead, what we observe is that most voters chose to split their votes between candidates from different parties (Hicken, 2009). Likewise in the Philippines, voters frequently split their votes between candidates from different parties, whether between presidential and vice presidential candidates, or between the 12 candidates for the Senate (ibid.). Even in Indonesia, we often see a large discrepancy between the share of votes a presidential candidate receives and the share of votes the candidate's party receives in proximate legislative elections. For example, in 2004 Susilo Bambang Yudhoyono (SBY) garnered 33.6 per cent of the votes in the first round of the presidential elections, while his party, Partai Demokrat, received only 7.45 per cent of the votes in the legislative (DPR) election.[14] In 2009, SBY received 61 per cent of the votes while his party won only 21 per cent.

Another indicator of value infusion among voters is the extent to which voters report having a party identity. Here again, the connections between voters and political parties seem somewhat tenuous. In the most recent East Asian Barometer surveys, the percentage of respondents who report that they don't feel close to any political party is 58 per cent for the Philippines, 64 per cent for Indonesia, and 72 per cent for Thailand (East Asian Barometer). The decline in the number of Indonesian voters who feel close to a political party in the decade since the fall of Suharto is also striking; 58 per cent of Indonesians felt close to a particular party in a 2004 survey. This figure declined steadily until in a July 2009 survey, only 23 per cent of respondents reported an attachment to a political party (Mujani and Liddle, forthcoming).

Where split ticket voting and party identification are indicators of the degree of mass connections with parties, the degree to which politicians remain loyal to their parties reveals the extent of value infusion among the political elite. Like voters, politicians in Thailand and the Philippines are politically promiscuous. Party switching is a common occurrence in both countries, and in the Philippines, politicians often claim affiliation with multiple parties simultaneously. By comparison, party switching is a rare event in Indonesia, even after the opening of the party system after decades of circumscribed party competition (Tan, 2004).

Another indicator of value infusion is the extent to which political parties are clearly associated with particular societal interests. Two questions are especially germane: To what extent do parties rely on different or distinct constituencies? Can we differentiate one party from another on the basis of its policy platform? In both Thailand and the Philippines, the ties between parties and identifiable societal interests have traditionally been very weak. Parties are generally ephemeral alliances of locally focused politicians, rather than cohesive national political parties with distinct policy visions. In fact, one of the defining characteristics of these party systems is the enduring lack of policy or ideological vision among most political parties. Survey evidence bears this out, particularly for the Philippines. When asked how often elections offer voters a real choice between parties or candidates, only 39 per cent of Philippine voters reported that elections offer a real choice 'always' or 'most of the time'. The corresponding number is higher in Thailand at 66 per cent, while an impressive 81 per cent of respondents in Indonesia felt elections offer a real choice (ibid.).

There are, of course, some exceptions to the general pattern of indistinguishable party platforms and weak party labels (Hicken, 2006). In Thailand, for example, the Democrat Party has roots in southern Thailand, and in recent elections the Thai Rak Thai (TRT) party and its successor, Palang Prachachon (PPP), manifested strong links with poorer, rural voters, particularly in Thailand's north and northeast. Whether these links will endure the dissolution of both the TRT and PPP is an intriguing question. In the Philippines, there are a few parties on the left, as well as parties running for party list seats that tend to have clearer ties to identifiable constituencies and party platforms that are programmatically distinct. However, these parties have performed poorly at the polls (in the case of the left) or are constitutionally prohibited from having more than three seats in the House (in the case of party list parties).

In Indonesia, parties have stronger associations with particular regions and societal interests than in either Thailand or the Philippines; for example, two of the country's oldest and largest parties are strongly rooted in particular regions – the PDI-P in Java, and Golkar off Java (Tan, 2004). Some have argued that Indonesian parties also remain rooted in enduring religious, class, and regional cleavages (*aliran*) (King, 2003). In this line of argument, these *aliran* continue to act as a cue to voting decisions and are the basis for many party identities. The most obvious examples are the PKB and PAN parties, which are based in Indonesia's two largest Islamic mass organizations – the traditionalist NU, and the modernist Muhammadiyah. However, there are clear indications of the increasing dealignment of Indonesian parties despite the *aliran* attachments (Ufen, 2008a), as well as a marked trend toward greater personalism in politics (Mujani and Liddle, 2007). Voters' attachment to charismatic leaders is beginning to play a much bigger part in shaping their decisions than sociological variables such as *aliran*.

In terms of organizational routinization, parties in Thailand and the Philippines have yet to develop party organizations that 'matter'. Parties function almost solely as electoral vehicles for powerful individuals and are noticeably devoid of any lasting autonomous organizational structures. Parties are also highly factionalized, and this factionalism has predictable effects on government stability, party cohesion, and government effectiveness (see Chambers, 2003; Hicken, 2009). Inbetween elections, parties cease to operate to all intents and purposes, with very little in the way of ongoing connections to party 'members'; for example, a study of ten Filipino parties found that, although every party considered mass member recruitment a top priority, none of the ten parties was able to produce a membership list, suggesting that 'political party memberships [...] are as fluid as the party system itself' (Carlos, 1997, p.220). Likewise, few Thai parties have a meaningful network of party branches. Where branches exist, these tend to function less as party offices than as campaign headquarters or constituency offices for members of parliament. The internal governance structure of parties is also notoriously weak. Members who deviate from the party line (when there is one) are rarely sanctioned.

Indonesia's parties tend to have stronger organizations and higher levels of party cohesion (Ufen, 2008). This reflects the greater power that party leaders have over backbenchers due to their control of access to the party list and their ability to replace wayward MPs. However, we should take care not to overstate the case for Indonesia. Party organizations may be stronger relative to their counterparts in Thailand and the Philippines, but party organizational capacities still remain underdeveloped, and recent changes to the electoral law will likely weaken party leaders' control of backbenchers. There is also significant variation across political parties in Indonesia. Golkar, with its party branches throughout the Indonesian archipelago, has the most developed organization. Under Suharto, the two sanctioned opposition parties, the PDI (now PDI-P) and PPP, were not allowed to establish party branches. Post-Suharto, they have yet to develop the kind of national branch network Golkar possesses. Likewise new parties, such as SBY's Partai Demokrat, largely remain organizationally thin, personal electoral vehicles for powerful politicians.

To summarize the parties and party systems in Thailand and the Philippines: each exhibits low levels of institutionalization. Parties are organizationally weak and lack strong links with voters or social groups. Party fortunes fluctuate greatly from election to election, and their political parties have yet to be fully accepted as legitimate and necessary by key members of the power elite. By comparison, there is a somewhat greater degree of stability to interparty competition in Indonesia, where parties are more deeply rooted in existing societal cleavages. Nonetheless, institutionalization is still incomplete (Tan, 2001), and there are indications that these roots are not as deep as they once were.

Causes of institutionalization

Why have the political parties and party systems thus far failed to fully institutionalize, particularly in Thailand and the Philippines? One common explanation in the parties literature is the argument that institutionalization is a process that takes time to develop. Several elections may be needed for voters to develop attachments to parties, for parties to create lasting organizational structures, and for actors to adjust to the incentives of a new political system. Although this sounds plausible, and we observe in Table 9.3 that developing democracies tend to have higher rates of average volatility than developed democracies, the Southeast Asian cases suggest some caution is warranted. It is the youngest democracy, Indonesia, that is the most institutionalized, while the Philippines and Thailand, each now with long histories of democratic elections, have made relatively little progress in institutionalization.[15]

More compelling for the Southeast Asian cases are the explanations that focus on incentives and catalysts. Each of these countries transitioned or retransitioned to democracy during the so-called third wave. The environment in which candidates and parties must compete in these late democracies is very different from earlier transitions; namely, the availability of relatively affordable mass communication technologies enables parties and candidates to mobilize large numbers of voters without the costly investment in party organization and grassroots networks that parties in earlier eras had developed (Mainwaring and Zoco, 2007). In other words, alternative mobilization strategies undermine the incentives to create institutionalized parties. Note, however, that while this helps explain why these Southeast Asian party systems are less institutionalized than their Western counterparts, it does not help us account for differences between the Southeast Asian cases. For that we must look elsewhere.

Certain kinds of political institutions can also affect institutionalization (Hicken and Kuhonta, forthcoming). The electoral system has a substantial impact on the nature of the party system. Electoral rules that place a premium on candidate-based electoral strategies (as opposed to party-based strategies) undermine the development of strong and distinct party labels. Thailand and the Philippines have both implemented electoral systems that are associated with weak political parties and underdeveloped party labels. Specifically, both countries have used a block vote electoral system (Thailand for its House, and the Philippines for its Senate) that pits candidates from the same party against each other – thereby undermining the value of the party label as a tool for candidates and a cue for voters. The ease with which politicians are allowed to switch parties in the two countries and the Philippine party leaders' lack of control over who runs on their party ticket also further hamper institutionalization. By contrast, Indonesia's closed list PR system – used for the first two legislative elections – tends to be associated with stronger parties and more distinct party labels. In that light, we would expect the switch to open list PR for the 2009 elections to hamper further institutionalization.

Finally, scholars have identified a number of catalysts to institutionalization. These include 1) deep-seated reinforcing cleavages, which provide a base for strongly rooted parties (Birnir, 2007); 2) independence or suffrage struggles, which tend to forge strong links between mobilizing parties and citizens (Mainwaring and Zoco, 2007); 3) the presence of a strong partisan left, which can spur grassroots organizing and the development of competing party platforms (Hicken, 2008); and 4) strong institutionalized ruling parties during authoritarian periods (Hicken and Kuhonta, forthcoming). These four catalysts have been largely absent in Thailand and the Philippines, but present to some extent in Indonesia. Regional and socioreligious cleavages have helped shape the party system in Indonesia, though their influence may be waning; they were particularly pronounced during the struggle for independence, when different mass movements formed along social cleavages, giving rise to mass-based political parties. More specifically, both the PNI and PKI were products of the nationalist struggle and became the two most important political parties during Indonesia's brief democratic experience in the 1950s. The communist PKI party, once a major force, was utterly destroyed by Suharto in the late 1960s.[16] However, the ideological and organizational threat represented by the PKI helped spur Suharto to create the state-backed Golkar 'party' as a counterweight. The presence of this strong party, with a national organization that reached down to the local level, helped serve as an anchor to the new democratic party system after Suharto fell from power (Hicken and Kuhonta, forthcoming). By contrast, societal cleavages have generally not translated into partisan cleavages in either the Philippines or Thailand, as discussed previously. In addition, a mass-based nationalist movement never developed in Thailand, which managed to retain its independence, or in the Philippines, where a roadmap for independence from the US was established early on and where many of the ruling elite were invested in the status quo. Both Thailand and the Philippines experienced significant leftist insurgencies, but for a variety of reasons, this did not generally translate into a strong electoral challenge from leftist political parties.[17] Finally, neither the various military leaders in Thailand nor Marcos in the Philippines went to the trouble of creating Golkar-like party organizations to support and perpetuate their rule. As a result, when those authoritarian governments fell, the party system lacked any sort of organizational anchor and contained higher levels of uncertainty.

Conclusion: Institutionalization and democratic governance

This review of party system institutionalization in Southeast Asia highlights the complex, multidimensional nature of institutionalization. I have
focused on four dimensions: the stability of interparty competition, the
degree of party system legitimacy, the degree of value infusion, and the
degree of organization routinization. There is no perfect indicator for any of
the dimensions, and a lack of comparable data can be a challenge, but this
approach is a useful start. Going forward, more work needs to be done both
on the empirical front – collecting data and devising new measures – and
on the theoretical front.

I have argued in this chapter that a defining characteristic of the
Indonesian, Philippine and Thai party systems to date is their lack of institutionalization. Strikingly, the Philippines, with its long history of democratic elections, is, by many measures, the *least* institutionalized. Despite
the suggestion of recent improvements, the Thai case is also underinstitutionalized, even after its 30 years of experience with democratic elections.
The region's youngest democracy, Indonesia, exhibits the highest degree of
value infusion and the lowest level of volatility, but by comparative standards it is still relatively underinstitutionalized and is perhaps becoming
more so. At the very least, these three cases underscore the fact that institutionalization does not automatically follow from democratic elections.

If we accept the argument that institutionalization is poor in Southeast
Asia, we must again return to the question of whether it matters, and if so,
how and why? After all, there are some long-lasting (if not high-function-
ing) democracies that roll along with low levels of institutionalization (for
example, India). So why should we care?[18] To begin with, underinstitutionalized party systems are generally a hindrance to democratic consolidation
and good governance. Institutionalized parties serve as 'long coalitions'
that allow for a balance between short-term political expediency and long-
er-term good governance (Bawn and Rosenbluth, 2006). Where parties and
party systems are underinstitutionalized, politicians will tend to have narrow constituencies and short time horizons – both of which are inimical
to the provision of public goods and policies. In fact, a common complaint
about the political systems in Thailand and the Philippines is the responsiveness of government to narrow, particularistic interests at the expense of
the provision of broader public goods.

A lack of party system institutionalization can also undermine the ability of voters to hold politicians individually and collectively accountable
by hindering voters' ability to identify who is to blame or to credit for
governance outcomes and undermining their capacity to pursue collective electoral punishment or reward (Mainwaring and Torcal, 2006; Powell,
2000). This is manifest in Thailand, where parties have traditionally been
ephemeral; when a party's electoral fortunes looked bleak, it would simply

disappear, and its constituent parts would be reconstituted as new parties or incorporated into existing parties. Politicians and factions that were part of governments accused of corruption or incompetence were still able to return under a new party banner, owing their election not to the party, but to their development of local support networks. Likewise in the Philippines, the propensity of politicians to switch parties after the election, generally to the president's party or coalition, effectively weakens the ability of voters to hold legislative parties collectively accountable.

Finally, where party institutionalization is low, the combination of disillusionment with the extant system and weak party loyalties (both of which we see evidence of in Southeast Asia) may provide opportunities for anti-system or anti-party politicians to rise to power (Mainwaring and Torcal, 2006). SBY and Marcos are examples of this phenomenon and illustrate the potential danger such mavericks can pose to democracy. While some outsider politicians have pursued agendas in harmony (or at least not in direct conflict) with democratic norms and institutions (for example, SBY), other charismatic anti-party or anti-establishment individuals have worked to undermine democratic norms and institutions (for example, Marcos). In short, the underperformance of democratic government in weakly institutionalized party systems can produce ambivalence in some voters about the relative merits of the democratic status quo versus strong, decisive, albeit less democratic, leadership.

Notes

1. 'Political parties created democracy... [M]odern democracy is unthinkable save in terms of the parties' (Schattschneider, 1942).
2. See Mainwaring (2006) for a similar diagnosis of what ails Andean democracies.
3. This paragraph draws on Hicken and Kuhonta (forthcoming).
4. Note that this definition applies to institutionalization in democratic settings. Party institutionalization in non-democratic or semi-democratic settings is a different but related concept (see Slater, 2003; Brownlee, 2008; Hicken and Kuhonta, forthcoming).
5. Compare Levitsky's discussion of behavioural routinization (1998).
6. Where possible, I follow Mainwaring and Zoco's rules about how to treat such situations (2007).
7. Specifically, where candidates claimed multiple party affiliations, I have used the largest party of which they were a member to calculate volatility. Because the largest parties are also likely to be around over several elections, any bias is likely to be in the direction of understating the level of volatility.
8. If we calculate volatility using seat rather than vote shares (seat share data are available for all of the post-Marcos elections), the average volatility is 37.9.
9. For more on the stability of Indonesia's party system, see Mietzner (2008).
10. This is in part a reflection of the demise of the stable two-party system post-Marcos (Hicken, 2009).
11. Birth rate is the share of parties receiving votes that ran for the first time in a given election. Death rate is the numbers in Table 9.4 (first two columns) are not % of

parties that receive votes in election *t* but do not win votes in election *t+1*. For Indonesia and the Philippines, data for smaller parties are lumped together in an 'other' category, which is excluded from the calculation of birth and death rates.

12. We see a similar story if we weight the birth and death rates by party size. The size-weighted birth and death rates for the Philippines are near 0, compared to a birth rate of 0.13 and death rate of 0.09 in Thailand. Indonesia's size-weighted birth and death rates are 0.06 and 0 respectively.

13. Perversely, this is due in part to the fact that the military's continuing role in economic activities means that it is more content under democratic governments than its counterparts in Thailand and the Philippines (Beeson, 2008).

14. Note that the discrepancy between SBY and PD vote shares could also be fuelled by the fact that SBY's running mate was Jusuf Kalla, former and now once again head of Golkar. Presumably, some supporters of Golkar in the DPR election threw their support behind the SBY–Kalla ticket in the presidential election.

15. This is consistent with findings in the broader literature; for example, Mainwaring and Torcal (2006), Mainwaring and Zoco (2007), and Reich (2004) find no evidence of a decline in volatility and the number of parties over time.

16. Suharto forced the PNI to merge with other political parties to form the PDI, one of the two officially sanctioned opposition parties in Suharto's Indonesia.

17. These reasons include hostility towards the left, a product of the violent insurgencies and the Cold War environment; institutions such as restrictive electoral systems; and the strategic decisions of leftist leaders (for example, the decision of the Communist Party to boycott the 1986 presidential election in the Philippines).

18. For more on these arguments, see Hicken (2008a).

References

Afrobarometer <www.afrobarometer.org> (accessed January 2009).

Bawn, K. and Rosenbluth, F. (2006) 'Short versus Long Coalitions: Electoral Accountability and the Size of the Public Sector', *American Journal of Political Science*, 50 (2): 251–265.

Beeson, M. (2008) 'Civil-Military Relations in Indonesia and the Philippines: Will the Thai Coup Prove Contagious?', *Armed Forces and Society,* 34 (3): 474–490.

Birnir, J.K. (2007) *Ethnicity and Electoral Politics* (New York: Cambridge University Press).

Brownlee, J. (2008) 'Bound to Rule: Party Institutions and Regime Trajectories in Malaysia and the Philippines', *Journal of Southeast Asian Studies*, 8 (1): 89–118.

Carlos, C.R. (1997) *Dynamics of political parties in the Philippines* (Makati City, Konrad Adenauer Foundation).

Chambers, P. (2003) *Factions, Parties, Coalition Change, and Cabinet Durability in Thailand: 1979-2001*, PhD dissertation, Northern Illinois University.

Croissant, A. and Völkel, P. (forthcoming) 'Party System Types and Party System Institutionalization', *Party Politics*.

Darby, J., Li, C. and Muscatelli, V.A. (2004) 'Political uncertainty, public expenditure and Growth', *European Journal of Political Economy*, 20 (1): 153–179.

Diamond, L. (1999) *Developing Democracy, towards consolidation* (Baltimore: Johns Hopkins University Press).

East Asia Barometer, <http://www.asianbarometer.org/> (accessed January 2009).

Hicken, A. (2006) 'Stuck in the Mud: Parties and Party Systems in Democratic Southeast Asia', *Taiwan Journal of Democracy*, 2 (2): 23–46.

Hicken, A. (2007) 'The 2007 Thai Constitution: A Return to Politics Past', *Crossroads*, 19 (1): 128–160.

Hicken, A. (2008a) 'Developing Democracies in Southeast Asia: Theorizing the Role of Parties and Elections', in Kuhonta, E., Slater, D. and Vu, T. (eds), *Southeast Asia and Political Science: Theory, Region, and Method* (Stanford: Stanford University Press).

Hicken, A. (2008b) 'Political Engineering and Party Regulation in Southeast Asia', in Reilly, B. et al., (eds), *Political Parties in Conflict-Prone Societies: Regulation, Engineering and Democratic Development* (United Nations University Press).

Hicken, A. (2009) *Building Party Systems in Developing Democracies* (New York: Cambridge University Press).

Hicken, A. and Kuhonta, E.M. (forthcoming) 'Reexamining Party System Institutionalization through Asian Lenses', *Comparative Political Studies.*

Huntington, S.P. (1968) *Political Order in Changing Societies* (New Haven: Yale University Press).

King, D.Y. (2003) *Half-Hearted Reform. Electoral Institutions and the Struggle for Democracy in Indonesia* (Westport: Praeger).

KPI (King Prajadhipok's Institute) (2003) *Public Opinion Survey on the Performance of the National Assembly, Government, Public Independent Organizations, and Other Issues, King Prajadhipok's Institute*, <http://www.kpi.ac.th/RD/e_pub_open.htm>.

Kuenzi, M. and Lambright, G. (2005) 'Party Systems and Democratic Consolidation in Africa's Electoral Regimes', *Party Politics*, 11 (4): 423–446.

Latinobarometro, <http://www.latinobarometro.org/> (accessed January 2009).

Levitsky, S. (1998) 'Institutionalization and Peronism: the concept, the case and the case for unpacking the concept', *Party Politics*, 4 (1): 77–92.

Mainwaring, S. (ed.) (2006) *The Crisis of Democratic Representation in the Andes* (Stanford: Stanford University Press).

Mainwaring, S. and Scully, T. (1995) 'Introduction', in Mainwaring, S. and Scully, T. (eds), *Building Democratic Institutions: Party Systems in Latin America* (Stanford: Stanford University Press).

Mainwaring, S. and Torcal, M. (2006) 'Party System Institutionalization and Party System Theory after the Third Wave of Democratization', in Katz, R.S. and Crotty, W. (eds), *Handbook of Political Parties* (London: Sage Publications).

Mainwaring, S. and Zoco, E. (2007) 'Historical Sequences and the Stabilization of Interparty Competition: Electoral Volatility in Old and New Democracies', *Party Politics*, 13 (2): 155–178.

Markowski, R. (2000) *Party System Institutionalization in New Democracies: Poland – A Trend-Setter with No Followers,* paper presented and discussed at the conference 'Re-thinking Democracy in the New Millennium' organized by the University of Houston, 16–19 February.

Mietzner, M. (2008) 'Stable but Unpopular: Political Parties after Suharto', *IIAS Newsletter* 47, Spring.

Moser, R. (1999) 'Electoral Systems and the Number of Parties in Post-Communist States, *World Politics*, 51 (3): 359–384.

Moser, R. (2001) *Unexpected Outcomes: Electoral Systems, Political Parties, and Representation in Russia* (Pittsburgh: University of Pittsburgh Press).

Mujani S. and Liddle, R. W. (2007) 'Leadership, Party and Religion: Explaining Voting Behavior in Indonesia', *Comparative Political Studies,* 40 (7): 858–885.

Mujani, S. and Liddle, R.W. (forthcoming) 'Voters and the Indonesian Democracy', unpublished manuscript.

Panebianco, A. (1988) *Political Parties: Organization and Power* (Cambridge: Cambridge University Press).

Pedersen, M.N. (1983) 'Changing Patterns of Electoral Volatility in European Party Systems, 1948–1977: Explorations in Explanation', in Daalder, H. and Mair, P. (eds), *Western European Party Systems: Continuity and Change* (Beverly Hills: Sage).

Powell, G. B. (2000) *Elections as Instruments of Democracy* (New Haven: Yale University Press).

Randall, V. and Svasand, L. (2002) 'Party Institutionalization in New Democracies', *Party Politics*, 8 (1): 5–29.

Reich, G. (2004) 'The Evolution of new Party Systems: Are Early Elections Exceptional?', *Electoral Studies*, 23 (2): 232–250.

Sartori, G. (1976) *Parties and Party Systems: A Framework for Analysis* (Cambridge: Cambridge University Press).

Schattschneider, E.E. (1942) *Party Government* (New York: Farrar and Rinehart).

Slater, D. (2003) 'Iron Cage in an Iron Fist: Authoritarian Institutions and the Personalization of Power in Malaysia', *Comparative Politics*, 36 (1): 81–101.

Stockton, H. (2001) 'Political Parties, Party Systems, and Democracy in East Asia: Lessons from Latin America', *Comparative Political Studies*, 34 (1): 94–119.

Tan, P.J. (2001) *Political Parties and the Consolidation of Democracy in Indonesia,* Panduan Parlement Indonesia (Indonesian Parliament Guide), Jakarta, API, 117–146.

Tan, P.J. (2004) *Party Rooting, Political Operators, and Instability in Indonesia: A Consideration of Party System Institutionalization in a Communally Charged Society,* paper presented to the Southern Political Science Association, New Orleans, 10 January.

Tóka, G. (1997) 'Political Parties and Democratic Consolidation in East Central Europe', *Studies in Public Policy*, 279.

Ufen, A. (2008) 'Political Party and Party System Institutionalization in Southeast Asia: Lessons for Democratic Consolidation in Indonesia, the Philippines and Thailand', *The Pacific Review*, 21 (3): 327–350.

Ufen, A. (2008a) 'From Aliran to Dealignment: Political Parties in post-Suharto Indonesia', *South East Asia Research*, 16 (1): 5–41.

Welfling, M.B. (1973) *Political Institutionalization: Comparative Analyses of African Party Systems* (Beverly Hills: Sage Publications).

World Values Survey, <http://www.worldvaluessurvey.org/> (accessed January 2009).

10
An Appreciation of the Human Rights Situation in Southeast Asia

Roland Rich

Introduction

The issue of human rights has taken a central place in international relations, though not without conflict, contestation and confusion as to how to apply them. At the heart of the problem lies the methodological issue of how to determine and, if possible, measure human rights compliance. This chapter describes a number of methods employed in this regard and concludes that each one has its limitations. An additional method of appreciating the human rights situation is proposed. While the methodologies discussed are universally applicable, this chapter will focus on the situation in Southeast Asia as a useful case study that encompasses a range of national situations and practices.

How to determine the extent of human rights compliance?

The issue of measuring human rights compliance is a particularly difficult one; this reflects the political nature of the process from the points of view of both the observer and the observed. The tendency of observers to resort to a 'name and shame' tactic in trying to increase compliance naturally leads to resistance on the part of the observed, which makes the government-level discourse on these issues, often conducted in debates on resolutions in the United Nations, an imprecise source from which to confidently draw conclusions.

This has led to other forms of measurement that often take a factual or numerical form. These may also have certain limitations, but they provide the best starting point for an investigation of the issues. This chapter will look at three such tools: ratification of international instruments, 'expert' assessment of compliance and regional mechanisms for the promotion and protection of human rights.

Focusing on ratification of human rights treaties

Depending on the school of international relations one follows, treaties may or may not have much value in appreciating the on-the-ground realities of compliance with human rights norms. Realists tend to downplay their significance, while constructivists point to their normative role in shaping state behaviour. Regardless of the view one adopts, an examination of the level of support for major international treaties is a useful way to enter the debate.[1] The first facts to look for concern ratification by the ASEAN states of the six major international human rights treaties, as shown in Table 10.1.

At first glance, the results look quite impressive. Of the 60 possible ratifications, ASEAN countries can claim 43, or 72 per cent. Furthermore, there has been a complete acceptance in the ASEAN countries of Convention on the Elimination of All Forms of Discrimination against Women (CEDAW) and the Convention on the Rights of the Child (CRC). Finally, four of the ten ASEAN countries have ratified all six treaties (though Cambodia expressed objections to provisions in three of the six treaties). On the negative side, however, Malaysia, Myanmar[2] and Singapore have only ratified CEDAW and CRC and have therefore, along with Brunei, failed to accept the two major international covenants (International Covenant on Civil and Political Rights (ICCPR) and International Covenant on Economic, Social, and Cultural Rights (ICESCR)) that, between them, put into treaty form the fundamental concepts of the Universal Declaration of Human Rights.

Each of these treaties has compliance mechanisms, the main one being the creation of a treaty committee to examine periodic reports submitted by parties to the treaties on the level of compliance with their provisions.[3] The quality of these reports and the amount of consultation with the public while they are being drafted, in effect allowing a society to take its own temperature in relation to these human rights, are the most interesting aspects but are difficult to measure. A simple measure, however, is compliance with the clear obligation to submit reports on time, as compiled in Table 10.2.

Table 10.2 shows us that the ASEAN countries have submitted 123 of the 193 required reports, a score of 64 per cent. Part of the explanation may derive from limited state capacities to draft these difficult documents. ICESCR, for example, contains many obligations that require a report containing relatively sophisticated statistics on economic indicators; Cambodia, Indonesia, and Thailand have never filed a report with the committee of ICESCR. And although Malaysia has accepted only two of the six treaties, it was nine years late in submitting its report under CRC. Consequently, this rough test of compliance may say more about the countries' bureaucratic inadequacy than any lack of commitment to protecting human rights.

It is the next table, Table 10.3, that raises doubts about that commitment. International law is based on the consent of states to be bound by its strictures, yet experience has shown that the mere official promise of respecting treaties is not sufficient to instill confidence that the terms will be complied with. Indeed, one recent study has, surprisingly, claimed the opposite – that because there is 'not a single treaty for which ratification seems to be reliably associated with better human rights practices and several for

Table 10.1 Dates of ratification of six major human rights treaties

Treaty	International Covenant on Civil and Political Rights (ICCPR)	International Covenant on Economic, Social, and Cultural Rights (ICESCR)	International Convention on the Elimination of All Forms of Racial Discrimination (ICERD)	Convention on the Elimination of All Forms of Discrimination against Women (CEDAW)	Convention Against Torture and Other Cruel, Inhuman and Degrading Treatment or Punishment (CAT)	Convention on the Rights of the Child (CRC)
Brunei Dar.	–	–	07 Mar. 1969	24 May 2006	–	24 May 2006
Cambodia	26 May 1992*	26 May 1992*	28 Nov. 1983	15 Oct. 1992*	15 Oct. 1992	15 Oct. 1992
Indonesia	23 Feb. 2006	23 Feb. 2006	25 June 1999	13 Sept. 1984	28 Oct. 1998	05 Sept. 1990
Laos	signed	13 Feb. 2007	22 Feb. 1974	14 Aug. 1981	–	08 May 1991
Malaysia	–	–	–	05 July 1995	–	17 Feb. 1995
Myanmar	–	–	–	22 July 1997	–	15 July 1991
Philippines	23 Oct. 1986	07 June 1974	15 Sept. 1967	05 Aug. 1981	18 June 1986	21 Aug. 1990
Singapore	–	–	–	05 Oct. 1995	–	05 Oct. 1995
Thailand	29 Oct. 1996	05 Sept. 1999	28 Jan. 2003	09 Aug. 1985	02 Oct. 2007	27 Mar. 1992
Vietnam	24 Sept. 1982	24 Sept. 1982	09 June 1982	17 Feb. 1982	–	28 Feb. 1990

*With objections.

Table 10.2   Submission of HR treaty reports by ASEAN countries

Country	Reports submitted	Reports late or outstanding
Brunei Darussalam	1	3
Cambodia	13	18
Indonesia	9	8
Laos	21	6
Malaysia	3	2
Myanmar	5	1
Philippines	31	16
Singapore	4	2
Thailand	9	7
Vietnam	27	7

Table 10.3   ASEAN Countries' acceptance of compliance mechanisms

Optional Protocols and Declarations *	Optional Protocol on the International Covenant on Civil and Political Rights (ICCPR-OP1)	Optional Protocol on the Convention on the Elimination of All Forms of Discrimination against Women (OP-CEDAW)	Optional Protocol on the Convention Against Torture and other cruel, inhuman and degrading treatment or punishment (OP-CAT)	Convention of elimination of all forms of racial discrimination (Article 14 Declaration)
Brunei Darussalam	–	–	–	–
Cambodia	Signed	signed	30 March 2007	–
Indonesia	–	signed	–	–
Laos	–	–	–	–
Malaysia	–	–	–	–
Myanmar	–	–	–	–
Philippines	22 Aug. 1989	12 Nov. 2003	–	–
Singapore	–	–	–	–
Thailand	–	14 June 2000	–	–
Vietnam	–	–	–	–

*Optional Protocol to ICESCR not yet in force.

which it appears to be associated with worse practices, it would be premature to dismiss the possibility that human rights treaties may sometimes lead to poorer human rights practices within the countries that ratify them' (Hathaway, 2002, p.1940). Because of this reality, enforcement processes going beyond the periodic report mechanism have been established for the human rights treaties.

Four of the six treaties have mechanisms that allow for far more intrusive means of dealing with a nation's lack of compliance, including expert investigations within a country and the possibility of giving a nation's citizens the right to file a complaint about that nation's conduct directly with a supranational body, one of the committees established under the various treaties. Here then is a far sterner test of commitment to the provisions of the treaty. If a nation is prepared to allow these intrusive means of enforcement, it is demonstrating its commitment in a way that a promise alone cannot do, no matter how formal or legal.

The compliance position of the ASEAN countries is quite compromised. Of the 40 possible acceptances, only three mechanisms have thus far been ratified by only three countries, with three additional signatures signalling an intention to be legally bound at a later stage. The reasoning behind the lack of acceptance may lie, in part, beyond human rights issues. Some states may believe that these mechanisms are so intrusive as to compromise the principles of sovereignty. The legal response to this belief is simple: there is no compromise of sovereignty if a nation draws on its sovereign right to voluntarily give its consent. The political response may be more complex. Nevertheless, on this particularly exacting measure of commitment, the countries of Southeast Asia do not emerge in a particularly good light.

Focusing on breaches of human rights

Focusing on breaches of human rights has been the traditional means by which critics of government action or inaction have marshalled the evidence to support their arguments. Civil society groups dedicated to the respect of human rights – such as Human Rights Watch, Amnesty International or the International Commission of Jurists – criticize government behaviour in their reports and publications. This is certainly a powerful way of appreciating the situation in each country, but it suffers from the obvious problem that the more closed and secretive a country is, the more difficult it is to catalogue government actions amounting to a breach of human rights. In Pacific Asia, there would be little argument that the Democratic People's Republic of Korea boasts the worst human rights record, yet the closed nature of the society allows for only sparse evidence of that reality. Nevertheless, the defector accounts certainly tell a story about the depth of the problem in that country.[4] Even with this limitation, measuring the number of breaches remains a useful tool; the most cited measure is that published each year by Freedom House.

The Freedom House guide to human rights in ASEAN countries, as shown in Table 10.4, does not paint a particularly encouraging picture. Each of the ten ASEAN countries has received scores on two measures over the past ten years, yielding a total of 200 scores. Of these, only 13 are in the 'free' category, 100 in the 'partly free' category and 87 in the 'not free' category. The pendulum is therefore on the wrong side of centre, but is it moving in the right direction? The answer is not clear. Some countries are moving in a positive direction. There has been a slight improvement in Brunei, Cambodia, and Vietnam, but their political rights scores remain in the 'not free' category.

Table 10.4 Freedom house scores, 1998–2007*

Country	1998 PR	1998 CL	1999 PR	1999 CL	2000 PR	2000 CL	2001 PR	2001 CL	2002 PR	2002 CL	2003 PR	2003 CL	2004 PR	2004 CL	2005 PR	2005 CL	2006 PR	2006 CL	2007 PR	2007 CL
Brunei	7	5	7	5	7	5	7	5	6	5	6	5	6	5	6	5	6	5	6	5
Cambodia	6	6	6	6	6	6	6	5	6	5	6	5	6	5	6	5	6	5	6	5
Indonesia	6	4	4	4	3	4	3	4	3	4	3	4	3	4	2	3	2	3	2	3
Laos	7	6	7	6	7	6	7	6	7	6	7	6	7	6	7	6	7	6	7	6
Malaysia	5	5	5	5	5	5	5	5	5	5	5	4	4	4	4	4	4	4	4	4
Myanmar	7	7	7	7	7	7	7	7	7	7	7	7	7	7	7	7	7	7	7	7
Philippines	2	3	2	3	2	3	2	3	2	3	2	3	2	3	3	3	3	3	4	3
Singapore	5	5	5	5	5	5	5	5	5	4	5	4	5	4	5	4	5	4	5	4
Thailand	2	3	2	3	2	3	2	3	2	3	2	3	2	3	3	3	7	4	6	4
Vietnam	7	7	7	7	7	6	7	6	7	6	7	6	7	6	7	5	7	5	7	5

*Freedom House Index, PR = Political Rights, CL = Civil Liberties; Status: 1.0 to 2.5 = free; 3.0 to 5.0 = partly free; 5.5 to 7.0 = not free.

Source: Drawn from Freedom House http://www.freedomhouse.org/template.cfm?page=1

Malaysia and Singapore have also seen slight improvement, but neither has achieved a score of 3 (at the 'free' end of the 'partly free' range) on any measure in any of the last ten years. Laos has not had any changes in its 'not free' score, and Myanmar has had the lowest score on both measures in every year. Moreover, the Philippines and Thailand have regressed. Both were in the 'free' category for political rights until 2005, when they slipped into the 'partly free' category. Thailand dipped even further in 2006, the year of its military coup, when it scored the lowest possible mark on this measure. The most positive story, though, comes from Indonesia, which has shown a steady improvement since the fall of Suharto, with a sufficiently high score on the political rights measure to be listed as 'free'.

Focusing on economic, social and cultural rights

Human rights are indivisible; simply focusing on breaches of civil and political rights does not explain the full picture. Economic, social, and cultural rights are equally important and can at times hold the key to an improvement in civil rights. It is important to assess the ASEAN countries' performance under this category as well. One shorthand way of doing so is to look at three key measures concerning the right to a primary school education, levels of child mortality and levels of adult literacy, as compiled in Table 10.5.

A far more satisfying picture emerges from these statistics. All of the ASEAN countries, with the exception of Laos, are above the world average for primary school enrolment; all but Cambodia, Laos and Myanmar are below the world average for child mortality; and all but Laos are above the adult

Table 10.5   Economic, social and cultural rights

Country	Net primary school enrollment rate (2005) (%)	Under-five mortality rate (per 1,000 live births, 2005)	Adult literacy rate (based on national estimates, 1995–2005) (%)
Brunei	93	9	92.7
Cambodia	99	143	73.6
Indonesia	96	36	90.4
Laos	84	79	68.7
Malaysia	95	12	88.7
Myanmar	90	105	89.9
Philippines	94	33	92.6
Singapore	98 (est.)	3	92.5
Thailand	88	21	92.6
Vietnam	88	19	90.3
Global average	86.4 (2006)	76	83.9

Source: UNDP 2005–07 http://portal.unesco.org/education/en/ev.php-URL_ID=53553&URL_DO=DO_TOPIC&URL_SECTION=201.html

literacy average. Indeed many citizens enjoy First World conditions in parts of Southeast Asia. This is a great credit to the governments concerned.

Focusing on human development

The Human Development Index (HDI) in Table 10.6 provides a way of measuring the impact of all human rights, and because it incorporates both the civil and political aspects, as well as economic, social and cultural rights, it provides a more comprehensive measure than the Freedom House scores.

The first point we can make is that, with one exception, each of the five years saw an improvement in human development in each of the ten countries. The one exception is in Thailand in 2005, when deep political problems affected people's quality of life, leading to a slight drop in Thailand's HDI score. From a comparative perspective, the picture is mixed. The Southeast Asian average HDI score for 2005 is 0.741, which puts it below Europe, Latin America and the Arab States, but well above South Asia and Sub-Saharan Africa. Among the ASEAN countries, Cambodia, Laos and Myanmar hover around the 0.600 mark while the others are all above the 0.7 mark.

Focusing on regional mechanisms

Another way of examining the human rights situation in Southeast Asia may be to look at additional regional mechanisms for the promotion and

Table 10.6   Human development index

Country or region	2001	2002	2003	2004	2005
Brunei Darussalam	0.872	0.867	0.866	0.871	0.894
Cambodia	0.556	0.568	0.571	0.583	0.598
Indonesia	0.682	0.692	0.697	0.711	0.728
Laos	0.525	0.534	0.545	0.553	0.601
Malaysia	0.790	0.793	0.796	0.805	0.811
Myanmar	0.549	0.551	0.578	0.581	0.583
Philippines	0.751	0.753	0.758	0.763	0.771
Singapore	0.884	0.902	0.907	0.916	0.922
Thailand	0.768	0.768	0.778	0.784	0.781
Vietnam	0.688	0.691	0.704	0.709	0.733
Averages					
ASEAN	0.706	0.711	0.720	0.727	0.741
OECD	0.905	0.911	0.892	0.923	0.924
Central/Eastern Europe + CIS	0.787	0.796	0.802	0.802	0.893
Latin America/Caribbean	0.777	0.777	0.797	0.795	0.818
East Asia/Pacific	0.722	0.740	0.768	0.760	0.773
Arab States	0.662	0.651	0.679	0.680	0.767
South Asia	0.582	0.584	0.628	0.599	0.616
Sub-Saharan Africa	0.468	0.465	0.515	0.472	0.511

Source: UNDP http://www.undp.org/

protection of human rights and to assess how effective they may be. Other regions of the world have certainly made great advances in establishing strong regional mechanisms. The model against which all other mechanisms are judged is the European Convention on Human Rights and the European Court of Human Rights that enforces it. These mechanisms have become so well established and effective that Buergenthal argues that the court has 'for all practical purposes become the constitutional court of Western Europe' (Buergenthal, 1997, p.716).

The evolution of the inter-American human rights system demonstrates the intrinsic link between protecting human rights and democratization. The structures of the regional mechanisms have been in place for quite a while, but it is only with the process of democratization that the Inter-American Court of Human Rights and the Inter-American Commission on Human Rights came to play a far more active role. Unlike Europe, however, Latin America does not purport to be a regional integration body, and the support for regional mechanisms is correspondingly weaker. Furthermore, democratization remains an ongoing process nearing the consolidation stage only in some parts of the continent, thus also contributing to a correspondingly weaker regional response.

The adoption in June 1998 of the Protocol to the African Charter on Human and Peoples' Rights on the Establishment of an African Court on Human and Peoples' Rights marks Africa as the third region to attempt to put in place a judicial regional mechanism. Because both the African Charter and the African Commission charged with receiving individual complaints had been regarded as weak and ineffectual, there was a push for a human rights court (Matua, 1999). Matua concluded, however, that 'the Court promises to be a disappointment unless state parties revisit the African Charter and strengthen many of its substantive provisions' (Matua, 1999, p.363).

Until very recently, there was no comparable mechanism among the ASEAN countries and no discussion of establishing any type of judicial structure. Article 14 of the ASEAN Charter allows for a type of supranational human rights institution in accordance with terms of reference to be drafted by its foreign ministers. The Eminent Persons Group charged with drafting the blueprint for the ASEAN Charter supported plans to establish an ASEAN Commission on Women and Children based on the very practical idea that as each ASEAN member had ratified both CEDAW and CRC, there should be no impediment to establishing an ASEAN Commission to deal with these issues. Inevitably, the devil is in the detail, and in this case, in the reservations member nations held about these two treaties. Brunei, Malaysia, Singapore and Thailand have entered substantive reservations to CEDAW, including to some articles that the CEDAW Committee considers essential (Linton, 2008, p.463). The same four countries entered cross-cutting reservations to CRC that drew negative comments from the Committee for the Rights of the Child and that also drew formal objections from ten parties to the treaty (Linton, 2008, pp.473 ff.). Subsequently, it is not clear to which obligations the reserving states have subscribed, making the establishment of a body to oversee the discharge of these specific obligations problematic.

On 20 July 2009, the Foreign Ministers chose to establish a broader ASEAN Intergovernmental Commission on Human Rights (AICHR).[5] The hesitant quality of this initiative can be discerned from the principal purpose included in its terms of reference (Terms of Reference of ASEAN Intergovernmental Commission on Human Rights, http://www.aseansec.org/DOC-TOR-AICHR.pdf):

> To promote human rights within the regional context, bearing in mind national and regional particularities and mutual respect for different historical, cultural and religious backgrounds, and taking into account the balance between rights and responsibilities. (Ibid. Para. 1.4)

This formulation of the AICHR's principal purpose validates a culturally relative perspective on human rights and resurrects a discredited notion that, under international law, governments should specify their citizens' responsibilities. Among its principles is the vague 'non-confrontational approach' to protecting human rights (Ibid. Para. 2.4) and the even vaguer requirement of avoiding 'politicization' (Ibid. Para. 2.2). Perhaps the most telling part of the terms of reference is what is missing. There is no mechanism for investigation, for receiving complaints, or for the judicial determination of adherence to the norms. The functions of the AICHR are limited to carrying out studies, developing frameworks, enhancing public awareness, providing advisory services and other worthy means of promoting human rights (Ibid. Para. 4). What is missing are effective mechanisms to protect human rights. One possible encouraging concept is the acceptance of an 'evolutionary approach' (Ibid. Para. 2.5), suggesting that the last word may not yet have been heard on this issue. Nevertheless, at this stage, ASEAN does not compare well to the other regions.

An alternative way to appreciate commitment to human rights

Each of the above means of measuring compliance with human rights norms has a certain utility, along with its limitations. Government articulation, especially through formal treaty action, provides a measure of official commitment to human rights, which then allows citizens to demand that their governments live up to these commitments. It is important, however, to examine the treaty commitments beyond simply counting up the ratifications, taking into account issues such as reservations, adherence to reporting obligations and openness to compliance mechanisms. On that basis, the results among ASEAN countries are mixed. Measuring breaches by means of the score card approach also produces mixed results, with only one ASEAN country in the top echelon in the Freedom House survey, while three other countries are in the 'partly free' category and the other six in the 'not free' category. The ASEAN countries, however, tend to score quite well in the Human Development Index approach.

These approaches provide a useful overview of the situation, either by considering government commitment (or a lack thereof) or by averaging out economic and social conditions. What they provide in terms of overview, though, they lack in terms of a fine-grained appreciation of the situation on the ground. That appreciation can be gained from a deep case study approach to each individual country. Such studies, however, are difficult to use comparatively as they focus on the particularities of each polity. But perhaps one way to combine the benefits of the case study approach with the benefits of the comparative methodology would be to narrow the focus of the case studies by looking at broadly comparable cases.

The selection of comparable cases presents its own difficulties. Were the ten ASEAN countries identical in social structure, one could perhaps focus on issues such as the treatment of tribal peoples or religious minorities, but the social variations throughout ASEAN makes this approach problematic. Perhaps the way forward, therefore, is not to identify any particular group but instead to ask the following question: Which are the most reviled groups in each society, and how are their human rights protected? This question presents itself in terms similar to those used when talking about issues related to protecting speech. In open societies, it is invariably unworthy or offensive speech, not reasoned or balanced speech, that needs action for its protection.[6] Similarly, it is not the elite or the privileged that need the protection of human rights norms, but the outcasts, the reviled, and the despised in a society. This recognition leads to a potential methodology for comparative analysis, namely, comparing the human rights protection accorded to the most reviled in each society. While this method requires a certain subjectivity in determining who are the most reviled, by choosing groups that are clearly oppressed, the methodology remains useful from a comparative perspective.

Political opponents

In systems disallowing public policy contestation, whether Leninist (Vietnam and Laos) or military (Myanmar), the groups most reviled by the incumbents are those opposing their monopoly on power. Human rights protection is not effectively extended to these groups. Take, for example, the Vietnamese Communist Party:

> Opposition parties, independent media and labor unions, and religious groups that operate outside of Vietnamese Communist Party control are banned. In 2007, authorities have increasingly suppressed activists, organizations, and political parties that surfaced in 2006 when the government temporarily eased restrictions prior to hosting the Asia Pacific Economic Cooperation summit. (Richardson, 2007)

Opponents of the military regime in Myanmar can also expect no protection:

> It's no secret that Burma's military rulers show no respect for law, but these last few weeks show a more concentrated crackdown on dissent clearly aimed at intimidating the population. These peaceful activists should not be on trial in the first place, let alone thrown in prison for years after unfair trials. (Pearson, 2008)

One therefore need not look further in Myanmar, Laos or Vietnam.

There is also a category of countries with single-party dominance that permit opposition parties to function. Singapore and Cambodia fit into this category. Robert Amsterdam (quoted in Hiatt, 2008) compiled this timeline of the treatment by the authorities in Singapore of their most reviled political opponent, Dr Chee Soon Juan, which speaks for itself:

1999: Jailed for speaking in public without a permit.
1999: Jailed for speaking in public without a permit.
1999: Fined for selling books without a permit.
2002: Fined for speaking about the ban on Muslim girls wearing headscarves.
2002: Jailed for holding a May Day rally.
2006: Jailed for saying that the judiciary is not independent.
2006: Jailed for speaking in public without a permit.
2006: Jailed for attempting to leave Singapore without a permit.
2008: Jailed for saying that the judiciary is not independent.[7]

As for Cambodia, Human Rights Watch said that 'the Cambodian election is taking place against a backdrop of massive violence in previous elections, with no one ever held to account for political killings' (Adams, 2008a).

We can therefore confidently conclude that in half of the ASEAN countries, the political opposition are given only minimal human rights protection. Brunei's relatively benign record on human rights is largely due to its small size and large wealth. Few conclusions can be drawn from its example, which would be made especially clear if a less enlightened Sultan should come to power. Malaysia presents a rather different picture. While opposition parties are allowed to operate and have won many seats in state and federal elections, reviled opponents are dealt with under the Internal Security Act (ISA), a draconian piece of legislation inherited from the British colonists. In 2004, Human Rights Watch published the report *In the Name of Security: Counterterrorism and Human Rights Abuses Under Malaysia's Internal Security Act*, which documented the near-complete denial of due process rights to detainees in the first several weeks of detention, as well as the physical and psychological abuse of ISA detainees who allegedly belong to Islamist militant groups. In 2006, it published *Convicted Before Trial: Indefinite Detention Under Malaysia's Emergency Ordinance*, detailing how the Malaysian government has detained criminal suspects indefinitely without charge or trial, subjected them to beatings and ill treatment while in detention, and rearrested them upon their court-ordered release (Human Rights Watch, 2006). The Malaysian government is armed with the means to deal with its most reviled opponents, and it has not been recalcitrant in using them. It is noteworthy that the Human Rights Commission of Malaysia has called for the repeal of the ISA (Asia Pacific Forum, 2008).

Reviled social elements

For the purposes of this brief survey, the practices of the region's three leading democracies, Indonesia, the Philippines and – although the appropriateness of calling it a democracy has been called into question – Thailand, are of most interest. By and large, the major political parties and their partisans operate without government persecution, though a qualification will be added to this statement in relation to the Philippines in the context of its leftist political parties; doubts have also arisen about the freedom of Thaksin supporters to engage freely in Thai politics. A commitment to respecting human rights is not generally extended to the treatment of the politically reviled. Our focus will therefore shift to the socially reviled.

A pattern of dealing with social problems without reference to human rights norms or the rule of law was starkly evident in Indonesia during Suharto's presidency. When criminality came to be perceived as a particular problem, Suharto authorized extrajudicial methods to deal with it. During the period 1983–85, some five thousand suspects were executed in the streets of various Indonesian cities, their bodies left there for others to contemplate (Schwartz, 1994). In his 1991 autobiography, Suharto admitted responsibility and explained that 'this was meant as shock therapy so that people would realize that loathsome acts would meet with strong action' (Schwartz, 1994, p.249). The executions were not hidden from the public, as they were intended as a public message, and there was little criticism of the practice, unsurprising in a nation ruled by a regime that did not value freedom of expression. This type of extrajudicial conduct is not unexpected in an authoritarian setting but is unacceptable in a democratic context.

That is why it was so reprehensible for the Thai government under Thaksin Shinawatra to resort to such practices. The National Human Rights Commission of Thailand found that the Thaksin government's campaign against 'drug pushers' had led to thousands of deaths (National Human Rights Commission of Thailand, 2003). Human Rights Watch put the number of deaths between February and June 2003 at 2275 (Adams, 2004), a remarkable circumstance in a nation with a free media and many outspoken social activists. What is most remarkable is how little complaint there was in Thailand at the time, giving the impression that Thai society as a whole approved of the government's actions. Indeed, some Thais criticized the National Human Rights Commission for blowing the whistle on this issue and thus painting Thailand in a bad light internationally.[8]

In the Philippines, extrajudicial executions have become a fact of life, no longer tied to short-term campaigns, and an enduring feature of political and criminal life (United States Department of State, 2005). One report has claimed that in Davao City alone, over 70 criminals were executed with the blessing of the mayor in the first three months of 2005 (Conde, 2005). The campaign against 'leftists' is particularly noteworthy and was the subject of a UN investigation, which found:

> Over the past six years, there has been a spate of extrajudicial executions of leftist activists, including human rights defenders, trade unionists, land reform advocates, and others. The victims have disproportionately belonged to organizations that are members of Bagong Alyansang Makabayn [*sic*] (Bayan), or the 'New Patriotic Alliance', or that are otherwise associated with the 'national democratic' ideology also espoused by the Communist Party of the Philippines/New Peoples Army/National Democratic Front. These killings have eliminated civil society leaders, intimidated a vast number of civil society actors, and narrowed the country's political discourse. Responses to the problem have been framed by lists produced by civil society organizations. The most widely cited list is that of Karapatan, which contains 885 names. (United Nations Human Rights Council, 2008, pp.7ff.)

Philip Alston, the UN Special Rapporteur, went on to note that 'the military is in a state of denial concerning the numerous extrajudicial executions in which its soldiers are implicated' (United Nations Human Rights Council, 2008, p.13) and that '[t]here is impunity for extrajudicial executions. No one has been convicted in the cases involving leftist activists' (United Nations Human Rights Council, 2008, p.17). An indirect but powerful confirmation of Alston's findings was provided by the nation's Supreme Court:

> In the wake of a disturbing wave of unexplained killings of civilian activists and media personnel, and to put an end to these, which have been stalking our legal landscape, our Supreme Court issued on 1 March 2007 Administrative Order No. 25-2007, designating 99 regional trial courts across the country to 'specially and preferentially' hear, try, and decide cases involving extralegal killings and enforced disappearances. (Justice Consuelo Ynares-Santiago, 2008)

In the Philippines, at least, there has been an outcry against these killings from parts of civil society, the courts and some elements of the executive and legislative branches. Thus, while some parts of the establishment consider the 'leftists' the most politically reviled elements in society, there are other segments of society that are prepared to speak out in defence of their human rights, even though they do not share their political views.

Perhaps the most interesting country in the group is Indonesia, where deep societal and governance changes are proceeding within a rhetoric and context of significant democratization. This does not mean that ordinary people in Indonesia enjoy a more fulfilling human rights situation than the people in neighbouring countries; indeed, the 1997 financial crisis hit Indonesia hard, and the immediate post-Suharto years were not noted as examples of good governance. If there is a criticism to be made of the Indonesian government's record on human rights, however, it would be directed at its omissions rather than commissions; more specifically, citizens may be even more vulnerable to political violence now than in the Suharto New Order period:

> The collapse of the New Order and the resulting fragmentation of its patronage networks have prompted a decline in state-sponsored violence, but at the same time the number of non-state groups employing violence and intimidation as a political, social, and economic strategy has increased. (Wilson, 2006, p.265)

Political violence has been democratized and decentralized to such an extent that the non-authoritarian government of Indonesia lacks the wherewithal to quickly come to grips with the problem, and in some cases may also lack the political will to do so. It is the acts of commission, however, that are of most interest for the present method of appreciating the human rights situation in Indonesia. Who are the reviled in Indonesian society? The likely response is that the state and society of Indonesia revile those who challenge its status as a unitary state and those who openly challenge the basic tenets of Islamic orthodoxy; this then leads to the question of what human rights protection such individuals enjoy.

With the East Timor issue now cast in a historical context and the post-tsunami Aceh question apparently on its way to being resolved, the groups that most overtly challenge the unitary state and their place within it come from Papua, which is possibly the final outpost of New Order methods for dealing with members of the independence movement (Human Rights Watch, 2009), the most common means of which is to treat them as serious criminals (Human Rights Watch, 2007). From a historical, ethnic, and social perspective, the Papuan situation is complex, but it must be said that the most vocal criticism of the official treatment of Papuans comes from voices outside of Indonesia rather than from the handful of local NGOs who stand up for the human rights of those Papuans protesting their membership in the Republic. Papuan separatists accordingly enjoy very limited human rights protection vis-à-vis the state.

Indonesia is a country tolerant of all monotheistic religions in accordance with its national doctrine of *pancasila*, but that tolerance has been tested in the case of Islamic schismatic cults, as has been recently evidenced by the official reaction to the Ahmadiyah faith, which was founded in what is now Pakistan in 1889 by Mirza Ghulam Ahmad and which differs from orthodox Islam on the issue of whether Muhammad was indeed the 'final' prophet. The Ahmadiyah community is banned in Pakistan and Saudi Arabia and has come under attack in Bangladesh. There are approximately 200,000 Ahmadis in Indonesia, and they have occasionally come under attack from mobs (Adams, 2008b). On 9 June 2008, Religious Affairs Minister Maftuh Basyuni, Home Minister Mardiyanto, and Attorney General Hendarman Supandji signed a decree ordering the Ahmadiyah community to 'stop spreading interpretations and activities which deviate from the principal teachings of Islam', including 'the spreading of the belief that there is another prophet with his own teachings after Prophet Mohammed'.[9] Violations of the decree are subject to up to five years imprisonment. Indonesian human rights groups have argued against these proscriptions and have been supported by many international voices. In response, President Susilo Bambang Yudhoyono is reviewing the decree, and no implementing action has yet been taken.

The treatment of Papuans and Ahmadis provides a litmus test for human rights in Indonesia. The jury is still out, but the fact that the issues are at least under discussion is a first positive step. Indonesians' overcoming their revulsion and allowing Papuan separatists freedom of speech and Ahmadis freedom of worship will far more eloquently provide an appreciation of the human rights situation in Indonesia than their lodging of ratification instruments of international treaties.

Conclusions

The first conclusion we are able to draw is that ASEAN countries have accepted the human rights discourse anchored in its United Nations context as a rhetoric in which they must engage. The fact that all of the ASEAN countries have ratified at least two of the six major human rights treaties is evidence of a certain level of acceptance of the global human rights system, but there are many factors indicating the shallow depth of attachment to the system. Four of the ten nations have not accepted the two major covenants; their record of diligence in reporting on the human rights situation is spotty at best; half of the ASEAN nations have compromised their treaty ratifications with reservations and objections that bring into question the extent of the obligations they have entered into; and very few of the voluntary compliance mechanisms built into the treaties have been embraced by ASEAN countries. As a whole, ASEAN states are doing somewhat better in the area of recognizing economic, social and cultural rights than in recognizing civil and political rights, as demonstrated by their relatively strong scores on primary school enrolment, literacy and child mortality compared to their relatively poor scores on the Freedom House scale; the former scores are pulling up the human development index scores for the region as a whole. While these broad conclusions are open, they do not provide a sufficiently accurate means of appreciating the human rights situation in Southeast Asia in themselves.

It comes as little surprise that the appreciation of the human rights situation in Southeast Asia parallels the process of democratization among its member states. This is true for negative as well as positive processes. The absence of any of the processes of democracy is mirrored by the absence of the protection of human rights, with Myanmar sadly providing the most telling example. The more advanced the processes of democratization in a country, the more likely that the citizens of that country will enjoy a greater degree of protection of their human rights. Surprisingly, the best example of this phenomenon among ASEAN countries, thought in the recent past to be Thailand or the Philippines, may now be Indonesia.

In the ten years since the fall of Suharto, Indonesia has changed from an authoritarian and centralized developmental state to a relatively open, complex and decentralized state moving steadily towards democratization though facing many deep social and governance problems. The improvement in its human rights situation in terms of strengthening domestic institutions for the protection of human rights, as well as adhering to international instruments for that purpose, runs parallel to its process of democratization. Indonesia's democratic emergence is highly significant, as the weight of history and demography continues to make it the leading nation of the region. Indonesia has now reached the point where it has the confidence to espouse democratization regionally, for instance with the launch of the Bali Democracy Forum in December 2008 (Jakarta Post, 2008).

Appreciating respect for human rights around the world through the prism of the protections afforded to the most reviled elements of society produces a finely grained comparative instrument. It can be applied to nations of the north and south, east and west, and to developed and developing countries as readily as to the ASEAN countries. While it tends to focus on civil and political rights, these should be seen as indicators of the broader human rights picture. The poor treatment of the most reviled elements in each of the ten countries in Southeast Asia indicates that there is still some way to go before a culture of human rights compliance can be said to have taken root. Political opponents in the non-democratic states are deprived of their basic rights, and even in the more democratic polities, the socially reviled benefit from little in the way of human rights protection. The treatment of those reviled elements of society in Indonesia requires continuing monitoring, because this provides a litmus test of the progress Indonesia has made in this field and serves as an example to the other states in the region.

Notes

1. All statistics on treaty matters are drawn from the website of the UN Office of the High Commissioner for Human Rights. http://www.ohchr.org/EN/Pages/WelcomePage.aspx
2. The term Myanmar is used when formal treaty membership is being described, while Burma is used when speaking of the country in less formal terms.
3. Now complemented by the Universal Periodic Reports.
4. See the Seoul-based Network for North Korean Democracy and Human Rights (NKnet) journal *Keys.* http://nknet.org/eng/board/jbbs_list.php?id=e_pds
5. ASEAN Secretariat, Press Release 'Another step forward for regional human rights cooperation', 20 July 2009, http://www.aseansec.org/PR-Another-Step-Forward-for-Regional-HR-Cooperation.pdf
6. Bringing to mind what George Orwell once said: 'If liberty means anything at all, it means the right to tell people what they do not want to hear.'
7. Compiled by Robert Amsterdam; quoted in Fred Hiatt, 'A Public Enemy in Singapore', *Washington Post,* 8 December 2008, p. 19.
8. In several conversations with the author at that time.
9. For the English translation of the decree, see http://www.thepersecution.org/world/ indonesia/docs/ skb.html

References

Adams, B. (2004) *Thailand: Anti-Drug Campaign Reaches New Low. More Than 50 Organizations Sign Letter of Protest,* 6 October, <http://hrw.org/english/docs/2004/10/05 /thaila9445.htm>.
Adams, B. (2008a) *Cambodia: Threats, Intimidation Mar Campaign. Unequal Media Access Hampers Opposition Parties,* 24 July, <http://www.hrw.org.en/news/2008/07/24/cambodia-threats-intimidation-mar campaign>.
Adams,B. (2008b) *Indonesia: Reverse Ban on Ahmadiyah Sect,* 10 June, <http://www.hrw.org/english/docs/2008/06/10/indone19073.htm>
ASEAN Secretariat (2009) *Another step forward for regional human rights cooperation,* Press Release, 9 July, <http://www.aseansec.org/PR-Another-Step-Foward-for-Regional-HR-Cooperation.pdf>.
Asia Pacific Forum (2008) *Malaysia: Repeal ISA and amend Act 597, says Suhakam,* 15 December, <http://www.asiapacificforum.net/news/malaysia-repeal-isa-and-amend-act-597-sayssuhakam.html>.
Buergenthal, T. (1997) 'The Normative and Institutional Evolution of Human Rights', *Human Rights Quarterly,* 19 (4): 703–723.
Conde, C.H. (2005) 'Philippine death squads extend their reach', *International Herald Tribune,* 23 March.
Freedom House (various years) <http://freedomhouse/org/template.cfm?page=1>.
Hathaway, O.A. (2002) 'Do Human Rights Treaties Make a Difference?', *The Yale Law Journal,* 111 (8): 1935–2042.
Hiatt, F. (2008) 'A Public Enemy in Singapore', *Washington Post,* 8 December, p. 19.
Human Rights Watch (2006) *Convicted Before Trial. Indefinite Detention Under Malaysia's Emergency Ordinance,* Press Release, 23 August, <http://www.hrw.org/en/reports/2006/08/23/convicted-trial-O>.
Human Rights Watch (2007) *Protest and Punishment: Political Prisoners in Papua,* 20 February, <http://www.hrw.org.en/reports/2007/02/20/protest-and-punishment>.

Human Rights Watch (2004) *In the Name of Security: Counterterrorism and Human Rights Abuses Under Malaysia's Internal Security Act*, <http://www.hrw.org/en/reports/2004/05/24/name-security-0>.

Human Rights Watch (2009) *What Did I Do Wrong? – Abuses by Indonesian Special Forces against Papuans in Merauke*, 24 June, <http://www.hrw.org/en/node/84044/>.

Jakarta Post (2008) *Yudhoyono opens Bali democracy forum*, 16 December, <http://www.thejakartapost.com>.

Justice Consuelo Ynares-Santiago (2008) *Impunity and the Constitution: Power and Political Will*, http://www.supremecourt.gov.ph/publications/benchmark/2008/05/050824.php>.

Linton, S. (2008) 'ASEAN States, Their Reservations to Human Rights Treaties and the Proposed ASEAN Commission on Women and Children', *Human Rights Quarterly*, 30 (2): 436–493.

Matua, M. (1999) 'The African Human Rights Court: A Two- Legged Stool?' *Human Rights Quarterly*, 21 (2): 342–363.

National Human Rights Commission of Thailand (2003) 'The government's war on drugs in right(s) perspective', *Right Angle*, 2 (2), <http://www.nhrc.or.th/en/publications/Eng% 20Right%20Angle% 20V2N2.pdf>.

Network for North Korean Democracy and Human Rights (NKnet) <http://nknet.org/eng /board/jbss_list.php?id=e_pds>.

Pearson, E. (2008) *Burma: Free Activists Sentenced by Unfair Courts. Draconian Laws Invoked Against September 2007 Protestors*, 11 November, <http://www.hrworg/en/content/burma-free-activists-sentenced-unfair-courts>.

Richardson, S. (2007) *Testimony on the Human Rights Situation in Vietnam. House Committee on Foreign Affairs Subcommittee on International Organization, Human Rights and Oversight*, 5 November, <http://www.hrw.org/en/news/2007/11/05/testimony-human-rights-situation-vietnam>.

Schwartz, A. (1994) *A Nation in Waiting: Indonesia in the 1990s* (Boulder: Westview Press).

Terms of Reference of ASEAN Intergovernmental Commission on Human Rights <http://www.aseansec.org/DOC-TOR-AICHR.pdf>.

United Nations Development Program (various years) <http://portal.unesco.org/education /en/ev.phpURL_ID=53553&URL_SECTION=201. html>.

United Nations Human Rights Council (2008) *Report of the Special Rapporteur on extra-judicial, summary or arbitrary executions*.

United Nations Office of the High Commissioner for Human Rights <http://www.ohchr.org/EN/Pages/ WelcomePage.aspx>.

United States Department of State (2005) *Philippines. Bureau of Democracy, Human Rights, and Labor 2004*, 28 February, <http://www.state.gov/g/drl/rls/hrrpt/2004/41657.htm>.

Wilson, I. (2006) 'The changing contours of organized violence in post-New Order Indonesia', *Critical Asian Studies*, 38 (2): 265–297.

11
Democracy, the Military and Security Sector Governance in Indonesia, the Philippines and Thailand

Aurel Croissant, Paul W. Chambers and Philip Völkel

Introduction

This chapter discusses the thorny issue of democratization and civilian control over the military in Southeast Asia. Studies of political regime types around the world demonstrate that with the third wave of democratization, few countries remain under direct military rule (Siaroff, 2009, pp.92–3). Moreover, the number of military coups d'état has dramatically decreased since the 1980s (Belkin and Schofer, 2003). Southeast Asia, however, seems to deviate to some extent from this trend. Military dictatorship in Myanmar seems unshakable. The September 2006 coup in Thailand and approximately ten attempted but failed coup attempts in the Philippines since 1986 indicate that 'the military coup is not a problem of the political past, but a continuing danger, even for electoral democracies that have persisted for over a decade' (Barracca, 2007, p.138). Civil–military relations in Indonesia and East Timor, while not as unstable as in neighbouring countries, are also strained.

This chapter aims to discuss three major questions: (1) What patterns of civil–military relations exist in the region? (2) How is civilian control exercised in emerging democracies? (3) What are the consequences for the broader democratic polity? With these questions in mind, this chapter proceeds as follows. Section one covers the recent literature on civil–military relations and security sector governance, in which we offer a justification for the focus on the 'classical' research question of civilian control and present a new multidimensional concept of civilian control of the military. This is followed by a comparative overview of civil–military relations in Southeast Asia. Turning then to case studies, in part three we investigate the failed institutionalization of civilian control in Thailand, the prolonged crisis of civil–military relations in the Philippines, and the conditional subordination of the military under weak civilian control in Indonesia. In part four, we discuss how limited or absent civilian control affects democracy in these states. In the final part, we summarize our main findings and provide some tentative conclusions.

The conceptual framework

Comparative research on civil–military relations before the 1980s primarily aimed at explaining military intervention in politics, military coups and military regimes. With the third wave of democratization, scholarly attention shifted from 'coup politics' to processes for establishing and institutionalizing civilian control in newly democratized nations. Over the last few years, however, civil–military research has shifted its attention from military putsches, military rule and civilian control to the study of '(democratic) security sector governance' and security sector reform. The concept of the security sector refers to all of the institutions possessing a monopoly on legitimate coercive power, ranging from regular military units, paramilitary forces and intelligence services to the police, the judiciary, quasi-private security guards and even contracted private security providers (Lambert, 2009, p.320). The research agenda of the security sector governance literature focuses on the way the security sector is governed at the sub-national, national and international levels. It reflects a comprehensive notion of security, embracing both military and non-military dimensions and encompassing both state and human security. In this vein, Heiner Hänggi (2004) presented the concept of 'democratic governance of the security sector' as an ideal-type model of security sector governance. The normative ideal of democratic security sector governance includes not only the effective control of the military by democratically elected civilian authorities but also, among other things, parliamentary oversight, transparent decision-making, civil society participation, effectiveness and efficiency in defence policy-making, ensuring that military training is in line with the norms and values of democratic societies, and providing human security. The related approach of security sector reform, then, conceptualizes the process of achieving this normative ideal (Beeson and Bellamy, 2008, p.24).

The security sector governance literature has enhanced our understanding of security sector reforms within emerging and established democracies. Moreover, it offers valuable insights for national policy makers and political practitioners in the areas of international development cooperation and democracy promotion.

However, the usefulness of this paradigm for the study of civil–military relations in Southeast Asia and its consequences for democratic governance and consolidation is limited. While it is true that the challenges of democratic governance necessarily go beyond narrow questions of civilian control of the military, the concept of security sector governance has yet to be proven a realistic alternative to the narrower conceptions of civilian or democratic control. The concept itself entails so many issues of traditional and non-traditional (human) security, involves such a plethora of domestic and international, state and non-state actors, and covers so many security-related and non-security policy areas that it does not provide enough structure and heuristic leverage for empirical analysis. Another problem with using the framework lies in its lack of a causal theory from which hypotheses concerning the mechanisms that 'link' the factors found to be relevant (the independent variables) to the observed outcomes (the dependent variable, civil–military security sector governance) can be derived and empirically tested. This criticism also includes the lack of a systematic theoretical reference to the 'agent-structure problem' (Mahoney and Snyder, 1999) in the study of civil–military relations, which is not solely a shortcoming of this framework, but which is of particular relevance for this approach because security sector governance and reform is understood, per definition, as being genuinely agency-centred. In fact, the few systematic attempts to analyze security sector governance in Southeast Asia (Beeson et al., 2006; Beeson and Bellamy, 2008) focus mostly on the issue of (democratic) civilian control of the military; only very rarely (for example, Tan and Chew, 2008) do studies transcend the core issues of traditional civil–military relations.

Accordingly, we use the more traditional civilian control approach, which is based on a narrow definition of the armed forces as the top military officers and of civilians as the political elites occupying key national government positions in a state. We describe civil–military relations as a continuum, with 'civilian control' and 'military rule' as the endpoints of the scale. Cases in which political decision-making power is divided between civilians and the military are positioned somewhere along the spectrum of the continuum.[1] Civilian control is thus defined as civilians having the exclusive authority to decide on national politics and their implementation. Under civilian control, civilians can freely choose to delegate decision-making power and the implementation of certain policies to the military, but the military has no autonomous decision-making power outside those areas specifically defined by civilians. Furthermore, it is the civilians alone who determine which particular policies, or policy aspects, the military will implement; the civilians also define the boundaries between policy- making and policy implementation. Moreover, civilian authorities must possess sanctioning power vis-à-vis the military, and they can – in principle – revise their decisions at any time.[2]

In order to analytically capture all of the possible distributions of decision-making power between civilians and the military, we have delineated five different decision-making areas within civil–military relations (see also Colton, 1979; Trinkunas, 2005). Full-fledged civilian control requires that civilian authorities enjoy uncontested decision-making power in all five areas, while in the ideal-type military regime, soldiers control all five areas.

1. The area of *Elite Recruitment* defines the rules, criteria and processes for recruiting, selecting and legitimizing political office holders, meaning the degree of openness of the political processes to competition, and the degree of participation, or in other words, the inclusiveness of political competition (Dahl, 1971, pp.4–6). Civilian control in this area is constrained when, for example, representation in the cabinet and parliament is reserved for military officers, or when the military controls aspects of the electoral process.
2. *Public Policy* comprises the rules and procedures for the processes of policy-making and policy implementation with regard to all national policies except the narrowly understood aspects of security and defence policy. In order to determine the level of civilian control over policy-making, the extent to which the armed forces can assert their interests in the processes of agenda setting, policy formulation, and policy adoption must be analyzed. While all policy issues are important for gauging the degree of civilian control over this area, the influence of the military, formal or informal, on the national budget is particularly relevant.
3. *Internal Security* entails the decisions made and concrete actions taken with regard to the preservation and restoration of law and order, including counterinsurgency operations, counterterrorism and domestic intelligence gathering, regular law enforcement and border control (Collier, 1999; Trinkunas, 2005). Measures of the degree of civilian control over this area include the extent to which civilians formulate the goals of and decide on the methods for upholding internal security, and the degree of military control over non-military organizations for maintaining internal security and providing law enforcement.
4. *National Defence* includes all aspects of defence policy, ranging from the development of security doctrines to the deployment of troops abroad and conducting war. Civilian control over this area can be gauged by analyzing the degree to which civilians can effectively devise and decide on defence policy and the extent to which they are able to effectively oversee the military's implementation of defence policies.
5. The area of *Military Organization* comprises decisions regarding all of the organizational aspects of the military institution, including the 'hardware' – in other words, the military's institutional, financial and technological resources – and the 'software' – for instance, decisions on military doctrine, education and personnel selection – of military organization (Bland, 2001; Cottey et al., 2002). Measures of the degree of civilian control over this area are the extent of civilians' authority to decide on the 'hardware' and 'software' of military organization, and the degree to

which civilians can establish the boundaries of military autonomy in deciding on these military internal affairs.

Our definition of civilian control does not equate civilian control with democratic control. Even if there is a tendency to civil–military convergence in non-democratic regimes, civilian control can exist under autocracy. Furthermore, effective civilian control neither implies 'good' security sector governance, nor does it necessarily enhance security. It simply ensures that civilians alone are responsible for political decision-making (Trinkunas, 2005, p.8). For liberal democracy to persist, however, the armed forces must be subordinated to the authority of democratically elected civilian governments (Dahl, 1989; Linz and Stepan, 1996). By disaggregating civilian control into separate areas and evaluating who has the power to make decisions in each of these areas, our conceptual framework allows for nuance in the analysis and assessment of the overall patterns of civilian control in individual cases or across sets of cases, in democracies and non-democratic regimes, both cross-sectionally and longitudinally.

Mapping civil–military relations in Southeast Asia

Southeast Asia offers a rich tapestry of different categories of civil–military relations. Although not fully congruent with our multidimensional concept of civilian control, Alan Siaroff's (2009) continuum for measuring the degree of military intervention into a state's political and civilian affairs provides a good starting point for mapping the variety of civil–military relations in the region. Within this conceptual scheme, he envisages a continuum of civil–military relations that ranges from 'civilian supremacy' and 'civilian control' (in contrast to the first category, civilians lack expertise in military affairs, do not hold the military to account for past human rights violations, and cannot control its internal affairs), across the intermediate categories of 'conditional subordination' and 'military tutelage', to military control and military rule.

Siaroff's classification of civil–military relations is based on a set of eleven indicators that are measured on a scale of one to ten; the higher the numerical score, the more comprehensive the civilian control (Siaroff, 2009, pp.89–92). Table 11.1 outlines the categories to which the Southeast Asian nations belong, according to Siaroff. To allow comparison with other Asian states, the table also displays the categorization of selected countries in East Asia.

As we have noted, civilian control can exist under autocracy. In fact, the cross-tabulation of regime classifications based on the conceptual scheme of the Polity IV project and Siaroff's categorizations demonstrates that regime type is not a good predictor of the types of civil–military relations to be found in East and Southeast Asia. North Korea, China and Singapore are in

Table 11.1 Categories of civil–military relations and regime types in East and Southeast Asia (2007)

	Civilian supremacy (10)	Civilian control (8)	Conditional subordination (6)	Military tutelage (4)	Military control (2)	Military rule (0)
Democracy	Japan South Korea Taiwan	East Timor Philippines	Indonesia			
Anocracy	Singapore	Malaysia	Cambodia		Thailand	
Autocracy	China North Korea	Vietnam	Laos			Myanmar

Source: Regime classification according to Polity IV data (Marshall and Jaggers, 2009); six-fold country categorization of civil–military relations according to Siaroff (2009, p.92); no data for Brunei.

the same category of civil–military relations as the liberal democracies in Japan, South Korea and Taiwan. Furthermore, Siaroff's category of 'civilian control' comprises democracies such as East Timor and the Philippines, but also Malaysia and Vietnam. In addition, Indonesia, Cambodia and Laos are listed as cases of conditional subordination of the military under civilian authority, whereas only Thailand (2006–07) and Myanmar are included in the categories of military control and military rule respectively.

While the next part of this chapter will provide a more nuanced analysis of civilian control in Indonesia, Thailand and the Philippines, the state of civil–military relations in the other Southeast Asian nations will be briefly commented on, as the situation in some cases is more complex than Siaroff's categorization might suggest. Of course, Myanmar is a clear case of military rule. Unlike other Southeast Asian countries that have experienced rule by the armed forces, Myanmar has been under uninterrupted military control for almost five decades Even though there have been power struggles for supreme power, the military has remained united and as long as the military junta is able to maintain internal unity , the military will certainly remain the dominant political force in the country (Min, 2010).

In contrast to Myanmar, civil–military relations in Singapore, Malaysia, Vietnam, Laos and Cambodia are characterized by a relatively low risk of military rule. In non-communist hegemonic party systems, such as in Singapore, Malaysia and Cambodia, control is exercised by a personal ruler (Prime Minister Hun Sen of Cambodia), includes the fusion of civil–military roles (Singapore) or is safeguarded by informal networking between military officers and the dominant government party (Malaysia). Notwithstanding the 'supremacy' or (conditional) control of civilians over the militaries in these countries, the armed forces are not apolitical. For example, in post-civil war Cambodia, the ruling Cambodian People's Party relies on the military for political support. At the same time, the armed forces function predominantly as a 'large income-generating and electoral machine, which created slush funds for commanders, cementing their loyalty to the center and financial and political support for the government while keeping the opposition weak' (Hughes, 2009, p.107). In Malaysia, the armed forces (MAF) are one of the country's key symbols of Malay identity (Crouch, 1997). Since the country gained its independence in 1957, the MAF has remained a predominantly Malay institution, with its highest echelons filled almost exclusively by ethnic Malays. Although subordinate to the civilian authorities, the UMNO leadership rewards the political loyalty of military officers (after their retirement) with positions in state enterprises, public offices and party politics (Beeson and Bellamy, 2008, p.81).

In Singapore, the distinction between non-military and military functions is even less clear. Since the 1980s, military officers have become involved in several types of political and administrative activities, including cabinet posts, senior positions in the public sector and direct representation at the highest levels of the ruling People's Action Party (Huxley, 2000, pp.230–6). The military thereby became a 'part of the ruling class' and 'a source of recruits for renewing the ranks of the PAP government' (ibid., pp.241, 245).

While active military personnel in Singapore are prohibited from joining any political party, even the PAP, in Vietnam and Laos, the higher echelons of the party–military leadership are inextricably intertwined; many party leaders are also career soldiers (Thayer, 1995). As in other communist countries, Vietnam and Laos have an iron triangle of party–army–state relations, where military elites occupy high-level positions in the military and party. However, the militaries in both countries tend to engage more actively in economic activities and in the political decision-making process than has been the case in the former communist regimes of Eastern Europe and the Soviet Union. While the opaque nature of policy-making in Vietnam makes it difficult to assess how much influence the military actually has, scholars generally agree that it is a considerable amount (Manyin, 2005, pp.317–8). Judging from its presence in politics, the state and the economy, the Laotian military plays an even more prominent role. Military officers occupy many top positions in governmental administration and ministries, still dominate the 11-member Politburo of the ruling Lao People's Revolutionary Party (LPRP) and are deeply involved in legitimate as well as illicit economic activities (Freeman, 2006, pp.138–9).

Two conclusions can be drawn from this brief overview. First, as of 2010, civil–military relations in Myanmar are distinguished from those in all other Southeast Asian states by direct military rule. In the remaining non-democratic states in the region, 'autocratic civilian control' is embedded into a pattern of civil–military relations in which civil and military spheres are separated only formally, whereas in reality, civilian and military elites converge into one ruling coalition (see also Beeson et al., 2006, p.456). Second, notwithstanding the ongoing evolution of civil–military relations in the states discussed here, the central elements of civil–military interaction and the fundamental pattern of distribution of decision-making authority between 'civilians' and 'soldiers' have remained remarkably stable for the past two to three decades. Both the existence and the stability of a concordance model of civil–military relations distinguishes the situation in many Southeast Asian autocracies from the experiences of the three emerging democracies that will be discussed next – Indonesia, the Philippines, and Thailand.

Civil–military relations in three emerging democracies

Thailand, the Philippines and Indonesia are the three major emerging democracies in contemporary Southeast Asia. In this section, we examine the status of civilian control and important developments that have occurred since democratization using the above framework of decision-making areas. We will demonstrate that even today, after two decades of democratic development, military officers continue to exercise political influence, thereby jeopardizing the democratic process.

Elite recruitment

Soldiers in all three countries have played an active part in elite recruitment after democratization, but to varying degrees and following different paths. After democratization in Thailand in 1992, an end was put to the participation of active-duty officers in the cabinet and the representation of military officers in the Senate was greatly reduced. Democracy returned after the collapse of civilian rule during the military regime of 2006–07, but the military continued to influence government formation: military leaders helped to cobble together the current ruling coalition after the fall of a pro-Thaksin government in 2008, and the number of soldier-Senators also increased again (Chambers, 2010, pp.58–64). Moreover, the military grants monetary support to the parties close to it, thereby distorting electoral competition (*The Nation*, 21 December 2007).

  In contrast, soldiers in the Philippines have exerted political sway more indirectly. Although active-duty soldiers are barred from taking civilian posts in the government or the legislature, military officers succeeded in exerting political influence when acting coherently and allied with civilians, such as during the toppling of President Estrada, when the alliance transferred its allegiance from him to Vice President Gloria Macapagal-Arroyo in 2001 or in allegedly manipulating the 2004 and 2007 election results in her favour (Landé, 2001; Hutchcroft, 2008). During the turbulent years of the Wahid presidency (1999–2001), the military initially regained influence over elite recruitment that it had lost in the late years of the Soeharto era (O'Rourke, 2002, p.317; Malley, 2008, p.26), mirroring the exit of Estrada in the Philippines. The military also wielded its influence, in part, by holding seats in the legislature that were reserved for military members; these, however, were abolished with the election of 2004. While retired officers accounted for a significant part of the first two democratic cabinets (16 per cent under Wahid and 12 per cent under Megawati), under Yudhoyono this number has decreased (6 per cent in 2010),[3] parallelling the waning military influence on the election of the president himself.

Public policy

Civilian control over the formulation and implementation of public policies has been achieved more successfully across all three countries. Since the early 1990s, Thailand has seen improved civilian supremacy over most policy fields, except for during the military regime in 2006–07. This transition was facilitated by the influence of political parties, decentralization and the constitutions of 1997 and 2007, placing most policies under elected civilians' scrutiny. In the Philippines, the 1987 constitution de-prioritizes the Defence Department relative to other ministries and grants Congress control over all appropriations. However, the military still exerts informal control over local administrations (Hall, 2009). Similarly, decentralization reforms in Indonesia have brought many issues within reach of local military commanders, who often participate in local decision-making processes (Honna, 2006, p.83)[4] and pull funding that would otherwise be available for civilian purposes (Jansen, 2008, p.446). This growing sub-national influence also undermines the successful abolition of the dual-function doctrine in 1999 that justified a sociopolitical, as well as a traditional, security role for the military. While direct military influence on public policies through the legislature is minor, military concerns are sometimes taken into account in the drafting process, as in 1999 when political power in Indonesia was decentralized to the district rather than the provincial level for fear of strengthening secessionist movements (Hofmann, 2004, p.18).

Internal security

Elected governments in all three states have thus far not been able to end the military domination of internal security and domestic intelligence. A paradigmatic case is Thailand, where soldiers traditionally oversaw internal security through the Internal Security Operations Command (ISOC). From democratization in 1992 to the 2006 military coup, military authority over ISOC declined; however, the military government in 2006–07 re-established army control of this key institution. In addition, the new Internal Security Act greatly strengthens military leverage vis-à-vis civilians and, simultaneously, weakens parliamentary control (Chambers, 2010, pp.66–73). While on paper the Philippines has undergone important reforms since 1987, with the establishment of a Human Rights Commission, the separation of the police and armed forces, and new monitoring powers for Congress (Hernandez, 2007, pp.86–7), soldiers have generally succeeded in informally exerting control over this area. They have done so under the guise of counter-insurgency operations that resulted in numerous extrajudicial killings, leading to an all-out military campaign without civilian surveillance after 2006 (Beeson, 2008, pp.484–5). In Indonesia, BAIS, the Armed Forces Strategic Intelligence Agency, remains involved in domestic intelligence gathering, and the nominally civilian National Intelligence Agency (Badan Intelijen Nasional, or BIN) is still manned extensively by military personnel (Jemadu, 2007; Putra, 2007). The separation of military and national police – initiated in 1999 – remained superficial as the restructuring of missions to eliminate overlapping areas of responsibility was never fully implemented (Human Rights Watch, 2006); rather, with President Yudhoyono ordering the military to participate in the 'war on terror', the military was again able to expand its influence on internal security operations (Wandelt, 2007, p.269). Moreover, even important decisions with security implications, such as the enactment of the Helsinki peace accord with the rebels in Aceh, only became possible after Yudhoyono staffed the military leadership with loyalists (Miller, 2009, p.160).

National defence

Across all three countries, civilians have some authority over defence issues but lack both surveillance mechanisms and active civilian involvement in reforms. Although defence ministers in Thailand since the 1990s (except during the 2006–07 period of military rule) must be civilians, most have been retired generals with close ties to active-duty personnel. Such alliances have allowed the military to influence the Ministry of Defence and to informally manipulate defence policy. Moreover, the civilianized National Security Council is parallelled by a military-dominated Defence Council in the Ministry of Defence, thereby creating institutional redundancies that undermine civilian control (Chambers, 2010, pp.73–6).

The Philippines has a more robust institutional framework for the civilian control of defence policy-making. The 1987 constitution enshrines presidential authority over external military deployments, and active-duty officers are barred from even advisory positions. Presidents Estrada (1998–2001) and Arroyo (since 2001) each appointed civilian defence secretaries without military connections and civilian national security advisers. Yet since the Ramos presidency (1992–98), a growing number of retired soldiers have been appointed to defence-related civilian posts, thereby intensifying informal military influence (Hernandez, 2007, p.93; Gloria, 2003). Similarly, Indonesia's ministers of defence have been civilians since 1999; however, the Ministry of Defence is still staffed with active military personnel. Even more importantly, the powerful coordinating minister for politics and security has always been a recently retired military officer. Furthermore, civilians lack independent monitoring capabilities, hindering their control of national defence. While the result of past reforms has been an improvement in formal civilian control, it is unclear whether civilians could prevail should they decide to push further.

Military organization

Like the other decision-making areas in Thailand, military organization has seen declining civilian control after it had peaked in the late 1990s, when Thaksin successfully gained control over defence spending, ensuring that military requests would pass through him alone (McCargo and Ukrist, 2005, p.137), and also interfered successfully in military reshuffles. Since 2007, soldiers have informally pressured civilian governments to augment military budgets, and the military has regained control over personnel issues (Chambers, 2010, pp.76–82). In contrast, Philippine military organization is under civilian control, with the 1987 constitution giving Congress the power to determine military appropriations and senior military appointments, as well as fixing the retirement age for soldiers. A modernization programme that aims to better equip and professionalize the armed forces is led by civilian officials, and while military education remains under the armed forces' control, there have been attempts to integrate democratic values into the curriculum (De Castro, 2005).

Even though Indonesia is closer to the Philippines than Thailand in this area, as in defence reform, progress towards greater civilian control of military organization happened under the auspices of the military. While President Wahid had an active hand in filling higher military positions (Honna, 2003, p.186), only President Susilo Bambang Yudhoyono has succeeded in asserting control over personnel management (Malley, 2008, p.263). Still, sensitive issues, like a long-overdue reform of military justice or the implementation of a law that orders the military to civilianize their business assets, have not been pursued with enough rigour by civilian politicians (Human Rights Watch, 2010), and procurement decisions are sometimes disregarded by military officers (Human Rights Watch, 2006, p.72; Human Rights Watch, 2010; *Jakarta Post*, 28 January 2010).

The military and democracy

Civilian control of the military has long been considered a necessary condition for democratic rule and the consolidation of nascent democracies (Dahl, 1989; Schmitter and Karl, 1991; Linz and Stepan, 1996). However, the survey across decision-making areas discussed above shows that civilian control is still being challenged by the military in all three Southeast Asian countries.

Whereas the absence of civilian control over the military is in itself a democratic defect by reducing civilians' legitimate power to govern, it can also indirectly have detrimental effects on other aspects of democracy, as demonstrated in particular by the case of post-2007 Thailand. Albeit not to the same extent as in Thailand, ineffective civilian control compromises the quality of democracy in Indonesia and the Philippines as well. In all three cases, these problems particularly concern the integrity of the electoral dimension of democracy, political rights, civil liberties and human rights, as well as the effectiveness of the rule of law.

As mentioned above, Thailand's 2007 constitution reserves some seats in the empowered senate for retired members of the military, excluding those seats from democratic contestation (Chambers, 2009, p.26). In addition, military financial contributions to selected parties have potentially skewed election results, while a lack of military security for the Thaksin-friendly post-coup government contributed to its downfall. The election commission offers no redress for disadvantaged candidates either, since its staff was appointed mainly by the military-backed coup government of Prime Minister Surayud.[5] Another consequence of military tutelage is that it severely infringes on the political rights of association and information. The military's heightened control over ISOC has given soldiers the power to obstruct political opposition, which they did during pro-Thaksin 'Red Shirt' demonstrations in 2009–10. The military exercises extensive control over the media, with 245 of the country's 524 radio stations in their hands and 'one of the harshest' internet crime laws in the world, enacted by the military-appointed Surayud government. Soldiers also manipulated the media to influence the 2007 general election (Pasuk and Baker, 2009, pp.309–10). Moreover, the Internal Security Act (ISA) empowers the military to arrest and detain citizens without a judicial warrant; soldiers acting under the ISA are also exempt from being prosecuted for human rights abuses. The fact that the letter of ISA can be invoked without necessitating the declaration of a state of emergency has led human rights groups to fear an expansion of arbitrary military rule (Human Rights Watch, 2007). Moreover, soldiers and military-directed paramilitary forces have been accused of numerous human rights violations in the southern border provinces – extrajudicial killings, disappearances, torture – and none of the purported perpetrators have been prosecuted (International Commission of Jurists, 2010, p.iii). Military influence also infringes heavily on the separation of powers, the working of the judicial system, and the rule of law. While Thaksin-friendly politicians and parties have almost always faced legal troubles, few charges have stuck against anti-Thaksin politicians and parties (Kitti, 2010, p.204). In June 2007, for example, the Interim Constitutional Tribunal decided to dissolve Thaksin's Thai Rak Thai (TRT) party and revoked the electoral rights of the party's more than 100 Executive Committee members on the legal basis of Declaration No. 27 promulgated by the military junta in 2006 (Croissant, forthcoming). In 2008, the constitutional court, in what many observers see as a military-backed political decision, responded to a complaint submitted by the military-backed Senate by removing elected Prime Minister Samak Sundaravej of the Palang Prachachon Party (PPP), the largest of the TRT remnants, from office. He was replaced by Somchai Wongsawat, Thaksin Shinawatra's brother-in-law. Prime Minister Somchai was then forced to vacate the office in December 2008 when the court disbanded the PPP.

As in Thailand, the Philippine military has supported civilian politicians, though much more indirectly and on a smaller scale; for example, the ouster of President Estrada in 2001 was instigated by civilian elites directing civilian demonstrators but was successful only when the military withdrew their support for him. Likewise, military top brass, acting in alliance with President Arroyo, helped to influence the 2004 and 2007 elections (Patiño and Velasco, 2006; Hutchcroft, 2008). The military is therefore abetting civilians in their attempts to manipulate the electoral regime, rather than doing it of their own accord. Furthermore, in carrying out civilian orders when quashing demonstrations, such as the protests against President Estrada's ouster, and the involvement of armed groups allegedly linked with the military in extrajudicial killings and other human rights violations (Alston, 2007), the military has contributed to the drastic decline in the standards of electoral democracy, political freedoms and human rights in the Philippines in recent years. Despite the repeated allegations by national and international organizations of the extrajudicial killings of left-wing political activists and the targeting of civil society groups under the pretext of fighting communist front organizations, it appears that such military behaviour continues with impunity (Hernandez, 2007, p.87; Hernandez and Kraft, 2010, pp.126–9). In addition, military involvement in the so-called 'war on terror' has led to an expansion of military prerogatives in counter-insurgency and counter-terrorism without adequate civilian surveillance and parliamentary oversight. Finally, the fight against separatist insurgencies in the countryside, as in Thailand, remains under military control and often leads to extrajudicial killings, especially in Mindanao (Buendia, 2006; Hernandez et al., 2010).

In contrast to the situation in Thailand, the Indonesian armed forces neither openly take a partisan position in party politics, nor do they consistently take the same side in an electoral competition. Still, the presence of former military officers on many presidential tickets led to some attempts by local commanders to pressure voters during the 2009 elections (Carter Center, 2009); however, military influence in local and provincial elections has been pronounced. Since former soldiers have been less successful as candidates in recent elections (Mietzner, 2009, p.347), the military now gives local commanders the autonomy to choose candidates to support instead (Honna, 2006, p.95).

In accordance with their less prominent position in the national political system, the Indonesian armed forces violate political liberties to a much smaller degree than their Thai counterparts. Human rights abuses in crisis zones such as Timor-Leste (Robinson, 2010) – before its independence

– and West Papua and Aceh (Miller, 2009) continue but have ebbed in recent years, in addition to which, turf wars between members of the military and the police frequently endanger the physical integrity of civilians in Indonesia when these become violent (Human Rights Watch, 2006, p.67). Occasionally, soldiers or intelligence officers commit acts of violence against human rights or independence activists (Kingsbury, 2008; Malley, 2002). Attempts to intimidate political opponents or protesters at the local level have been reported (Honna, 2006), but they do not seem to hinder the frequent expression of political protest during demonstrations. Freedom of the press is not significantly curtailed by the military, so the media, together with an active NGO sector, often contribute to the exposure of military scandals (see also Human Rights Watch, 2006; Miller, 2009, p.76). Local military officers, though, frequently use their abundant funds from legitimate and illegitimate business activities to bribe other officials, especially judges (*Jakarta Post*, 10 February 2010), thereby aggravating existing problems in this partial regime.

Conclusion

It is clear from the above that the Thai military in the early twenty-first century still acts like a self-proclaimed guardian of king and nation. Even following the end of direct military rule in late 2007, soldiers have continued to exert great power. Indeed, it seems the armed forces today have found their perfect niche, having become Thailand's crucial clandestine political player. In the Philippines, soldiers have influenced politics and society, as multiple insurgencies have provided an excuse for greater scope for the armed forces to be involved in politics. Given the general fragility of civilian governments, the military has achieved significant influence in the domestic political arena. In contrast to Thailand, however, the Philippine military intervenes in a more indirect and latent fashion.

In Indonesia, there is an increasingly slim chance of the armed forces returning to direct rule, as soldiers have mostly departed from the political arena; however, the degree to which civilian control over the military has been established remains problematic. Indeed, after more than ten years of military reforms, the armed forces remain an important political force, especially at the sub-national level, where they have expanded their role and used parallel structures down to the local level in which to embed themselves alongside civilian politicians, picking and choosing allies on a case by case basis. In addition, the military continues to exercise a strong degree of autonomy vis-à-vis the civilian government, but existing problems in restructuring the military in Indonesia seem to be caused more by the unwillingness of civilians to press for substantial reform than by the military actively resisting civilian attempts to reduce military influence in political and civilian affairs.

What can be learned from this analysis? We propose four main conclusions. First, the most obvious finding is that the transition from authoritarian rule to electoral democracy in Southeast Asia did not lead to full-scale
civilian control. Rather, civilian control remains partial, fragile and contested – to a much stronger degree than, for example, in the resilient electoral
autocracies of Singapore or Malaysia. Second, it seems plausible to assume
that at least the Philippines and Thailand will most probably be plagued
by further instances of military assertion and a lack of civilian control for
some time to come. Given the deep entrenchment of the militaries in the
respective political systems, the manifold problems of the consolidation of
democracy in general, and the incompetence of civilian governments with
regard to military reforms, civilians will most likely have neither sufficient
capabilities nor compelling incentives to confront the military and diminish military decision-making power in the political arena. Accordingly, any
significant extension of civilian influence over the security sector remains
unlikely. The prospect for a gradual change in civil–military relations in
Indonesia seems somewhat more promising than in the other two cases.
Still, much remains to be done to bring the Indonesian military more fully
under civilian control.

A third conclusion proposes that the successful crafting of civilian control within processes of democratic liberalization depends very much on
the ability of civilian elites to maintain high levels of public support. A
military finds it harder to resist pressure for change in civil–military relations and to push for non-democratic prerogatives when political elites are
visibly backed by a wide array of electorally strong political forces (see also
Barracca, 2007). This, obviously, is a weakness in civilian leverage over the
military in Thailand and the Philippines, but it strengthens the position of
civilians vis-à-vis the military in Indonesia.

Fourth, the Thai case is a reminder that militaries find it easier to block
transitions from military autonomy to civilian supremacy if the democratic government fails to produce effective government, or if important groups desert the pro-democracy coalition. Despite the many failings
of democracy in the Philippines, most of the relevant civilian factions
stick to the established, oligarchic elite consensus. This is certainly one
of the main reasons why the Philippine military 'does not really seek to
capture political power for itself (despite all the instances of attempted
coups), and instead institutionally (through the upper ranks of the military leadership) aligns itself with certain political factions' (Hernandez
et al., 2010, p.130). Similarly, one if not *the* most remarkable achievement
of democratic consolidation in Indonesia is that adherence to essential
democratic norms and procedures and inclusionary coalition politics by
political party elites have become largely uncontested parameters for the
political process in that country. Indeed, both the failure of civilians to
attain control over the military in Thailand and the still conditional but

(given the initial conditions in 1999) surprisingly solid subordination of the military in Indonesia remind us of the utmost significance of consensus among civilian elites to not rely on the military to protect their interests against other political and social groups or elites (Mietzner, 2009). Only in emerging democracies where this is the case will there be a high probability of stable and healthy civil–military relations with long-term prospects.

Notes

1. This follows thoughts drawn from Croissant et al. (forthcoming).
2. See also Kemp and Hudlin (1992); Pion-Berlin (1992); Bland (1999); Feaver (1996); and Welch (1976).
3. Authors' calculation with data from the *Jakarta Post* (24 August 2000, 10 August 2001, 22 October 2009).
4. The Indonesian military has a territorial structure that lies parallel to civilian governmental layers, down to the village level, dating back to the independence struggle against the Dutch (Lowry, 1996).
5. Personal interview with Lt. Gen. Peerapong Manakit, 16 February 2009.

References

Alagappa, M. (2001) 'Investigating and Explaining Change: An Analytical Framework' in Alagappa, M. (ed.), *Coercion and Governance: The Declining Political Role of the Military in Asia* (Stanford: Stanford University Press).

Alston, P. (2007) *Special Rapporteur of the United Nations Human Rights Council on Extrajudicial,Ssummary or Arbitrary Executions,* Press Statement, 21 February, Manila, <http://pcij.org/blog/wp-docs/alston_press_statement.pdf>.

Barracca, S. (2007) 'Military Coups in the Post-cold War Era: Pakistan, Ecuador and Venezuela', *Third World Quarterly,* 28 (1): 1360–2241.

Beeson, M. (2008) 'Civil-Military Relations in Indonesia and the Philippines: Will the Thai Coup Prove Contagious?', *Armed Forces and Society,* 34 (3): 474–490.

Beeson, M. and Bellamy, A. J. (2008) *Securing Southeast Asia. ThePolitics of Security Sector Reform* (New York: Routledge).

Beeson, M., Bellamy, A.J. and Hughes, B. (2006) 'Taming the Tigers? Reforming the Security Sector in Southeast Asia', *The Pacific Review,* 19 (4): 449–472.

Belkin, A. and Schofer, E. (2003) 'Toward a Structural Understanding of Coup Risk', *Journal of Conflict Resolution,* 47 (5): 594–620.

Bland, D.L. (1999) 'A Unified Theory of Civil-Military Relations', *Armed Forces & Society,* 26 (1): 7–25.

Bland, D.L. (2001) 'Patterns in Liberal Democratic Civil-Military Relations', *Armed Forces & Society,* 27 (4): 525–540.

Buendia, R. (2006) 'Mindanao Conflict in the Philippines: Ethno-Religious War or Economic Conflict?' in Croissant, A., Martin, B. and Kneip, S. (eds), *The Politics of Death: Political Violence in Southeast Asia* (Berlin: Lit Verlag).

Carter Center (2009) *Final Report of the Carter Center. Limited Observation Mission to the Legislative Elections in Indonesia,* 9 April, (Atlanta: One Copenhill).

Chambers, P.W. (2009) 'Superfluous, Mischievous or Emancipating? Thailand's Evolving Senate Today', *Journal of Current Southeast Asian Affairs,* 28 (3): 3–80.

Chambers, P.W. (2010) 'U-Turn to the Past? The Resurgence of the Military in Contemporary Thai Politics', in Chambers, P. and Croissant, A. (eds), *Democracy under Stress: Civil-Military Relations in South and Southeast Asia* (Bangkok: ISIS).

Collier, K. (1999) *The Armed Forces and Internal Security in Asia: Preventing the Abuse of Power,* East-West Center Occasional Papers, Politics and Security Series 2, <http://scholarspace.manoa.hawaii.edu/bitstream/10125/3451/1/PSop002.pdf>.

Colton, T.J. (1979) *Commissars, Commanders, and Civilian Authority: The Structure of Soviet Military Politics* (Cambridge: Harvard University Press).

Cottey, A., Edmunds, T. and Forster, A. (2002) 'The Second Generation Problematic: Rethinking Democracy and Civil-Military Relations', *Armed Forces & Society*, 29 (1): 31–56.

Croissant, A. (2010) 'Provisions, Practices and Performances of Constitutional Review in Democratizing East Asia' *The Pacific Review*, 23(5): 548–578.

Croissant, A., Kühn, D., Chambers, P. and Wolf. S.O. (2010) 'Beyond the Fallacy of Coupism: Conceptualizing Civilian Control of the Military in Emerging Democracies', *Democratization*, 17(5): 948–978.

Crouch, H. (1997) 'Civil-Military Relations in Southeast Asia', in Diamond, L. et al. (eds), *Consolidating the Third Wave Democracies: Themes and Perspectives* (Baltimore: Johns Hopkins University Press).

Dahl, R.A. (1971) *Polyarchy: Participation and Opposition* (New Haven: Yale University Press).

Dahl, R.A. (1989) *Democracy and Its Critics* (New Haven: Yale University Press).

De Castro, R. (2005) 'The Dilemma Between Democratic Control Versus Military Reforms: The Case of the AFP Modernization Program, 1991–2004', *Journal of Security Sector Management*, 3 (1): 1–24.

Feaver, P.D. (1996) 'The Civil-Military Problematique: Huntington, Janowitz, and the Question of Civilian Control', *Armed Forces & Society*, 23 (2): 149–178.

Freeman, N.J. (2006) 'Laos', in Funston, J. (ed.), *Government and politics in Southeast Asia*, (Singapore: ISEAS).

Gloria, G. (2003) *We Were Soldiers* (Quezon City: Friedrich Ebert Stiftung).

Hall, R., (2009) Personal interview, 11 November.

Hänggi, H. (2004) 'Conceptualising Security Sector Reform and Reconstruction', in Bryden, A. and Hänggi, H. (eds), *Reform and Reconstruction of the Security Sector* (Münster: Lit Verlag).

Hernandez, C. (2007) 'The Military in Philippine Politics: Retrospect and Prospects' in Severino, R. and Salazar, L.C. (eds) *Whither the Philippines in the 21st Century* (Singapore: ISEAS)

Hernandez, K.M.G., Hermann, J. and Kraft, S. (2010) 'Armed Forces as Veto Power: Civil-Military Relations in the Philippines', in Chambers, P. and Croissant, A. (eds), *Democracy under Stress: Civil-Military Relations in South and Southeast Asia* (Bangkok: ISIS).

Hofmann, S.R. (2004) 'Islam and Democracy: Micro-Level Indications of Compatibility', *Comparative Political Studies*, 37 (6): 652.

Honna, J. (2003) *Military politics and Democratization in Indonesia* (London: Routledge).

Honna, J. (2006) 'Local civil-military relations during the first phase of democratic transition, 1999–2004: A comparison of West, Central, and East Java', *Indonesia* 82 (October): 75–96.

Hughes, C. (2009) *Dependent communities: aid and politics in Cambodia and East Timor* (Ithaca: Cornell University Press).

Human Rights Watch (2006) *Too high a price: The Human Rights Cost of the Indonesian Military's Economic Activities* (New York).

Human Rights Watch (2007) *Thailand: Internal Security Act Threatens Democracy and Human Rights: Government Proposes Draconian Steps to Institutionalize Military Control* (New York).

Human Rights Watch (2010) *Unkept Promise: Failure to End Military Business Activity in Indonesia* (New York).

Hutchcroft, P. (2008) 'The Arroyo Imbroglio in the Philippines', *Journal of Democracy*, 19 (1): 141–155.

Huxley, T. (2000) *Defending the Lion City. The Armed Forces of Singapore* (St. Leonards NSW: Allen and Unwin).

International Commission of Jurists (2010) *Thailand's International Security Act: Risking the Rule of Law?*, February.

Jakarta Post (2000) 'Gus Dur picks 26-member Cabinet', 24 August, <http://www.thejakartapost.com/news/2000/08/24/gus-dur-picks-26membercabinet.html>.

Jakarta Post (2001) 'Megawati names rainbow cabinet', 10 August, <http://www.thejakartapost.com/news/2001/08/10/megawati-names-rainbow-cabinet.html>.

Jakarta Post (2009) 'United Indonesia Cabinet 2009–2014', 22 October, <http://www.thejakartapost.com/news/2009/10/22/united-indonesia-cabinet-20092014.html>.

Jakarta Post (2010) 'PDI-P deems govt failed on defense issues in its first 100 days' 28 January, <http://www.thejakartapost.com/news/2010/01/28/pdip-deems-govt-faileddefense-issues-its-first-100-days.html>.

Jansen, D. (2008) 'Relations among security and law enforcement institutions in Indonesia', *Contemporary Southeast Asia*, 30 (3): 429–454.

Jemadu, A. (2007) 'Terrorism, intelligence reform and the protection of civil liberties', in Hadiwinata, B.S. and Schuck, C. (eds), *Democracy in Indonesia: The Challenge of Consolidation* (Baden-Baden: Nomos).

Kemp, K.W. and Hudlin, C. (1992) 'Civil Supremacy over the Military: Its Nature and Limits', *Armed Forces & Society*, 19 (1): 7–26.

Kingsbury, D. (2008) 'Indonesia in 2007: Unmet Expectations, Despite Improvement', *Asian Survey*, 48 (1): 38–46.

Kitti P. (2010) 'Thailand in 2009: Colored by Turbulence', *Asian Survey*, 50 (1): 203–210.

Lambert, A. (2009) *Democratic Civilian Control of Armed Forces in the Post-Cold War Era* (Münster: Lit Verlag).

Landé, C.H. (2001) 'The Return of 'People Power' in the Philippines', *Journal of Democracy*, 12 (April): 88–102.

Linz, J.J. and Stepan, A.C. (eds) (1996) *Problems of Democratic Transition and Consolidation: Southern Europe, South America, and Post-Communist Europe* (Baltimore: Johns Hopkins University Press).

Lowry, R. (1996) *The armed forces of Indonesia* (St Leonards: Allen & Unwin).

Macan-Markar, M. (2010) 'Thailand: Army Asserts Foreign Policy Role', IPS, 7 January, <http://www.humanrights-geneva.info/spip.php?article7179>.

Macan-Markar, M. (2010) 'With Hmong Expulsion, Thai Army Asserts Foreign Policy Role', Irrawaddy, 6 January, <http://www.irrawaddy.org/article.php?art_id=17532>.

McCargo, D. and Ukrist, P. (2005) *The Thaksinization of Thailand* (Copenhagen: NIAS Press).

Mahoney, J. and Snyder, R. (1999) 'Rethinking Agency and Structure in the Study of Regime Change', *Studies in Comparative International Development*, 34 (2): 3–32.

Malley, M.S. (2002) 'Indonesia in 2001: Restoring Stability in Jakarta', *Asian Survey*, 42 (1): 124–132.

Malley, M.S. (2008) 'Democratization and the challenge of defense reform in Indonesia', in Bruneau, T.C. and Trinkunas, H.A. (eds), *Global Politics of Defense Reform* (New York: Palgrave Macmillan).

Manakit, Peerapong (2009) Personal interview, 16 February.

Manyin, M. (2005) 'Vietnam: Focused Domestically, Adrift Internationally', in Carpenter, W.M., and Wiencek, D. G. (eds), *Asian Security Handbook. Terrorism and the New Security Environment* (Armonk, NY: M.E. Sharpe).

Marshall, M.G. and Jaggers, K. (2009) *Polity IV Project: Political Regime Characteristics and Transitions, 1800–2008* (Arlington:Polity IV Project).

Mietzner, M. (2009) 'Indonesia and the Pitfalls of Low-Quality Democracy: A Case Study of the Gubernatorial Elections in North Sulawesi', in Bünte, M. and Ufen, A. (eds), *Democratization in Post-Suharto Indonesia* (London: Routledge).

Miller, M.A. (2009) *Rebellion and Reform in Indonesia: Jakarta's Security and Aautonomy Policies in Aceh* (London: Routledge).

Min, W. (2010) 'Under an Iron Heel: Civil-Military Relations in Burma/Myanmar', in Chambers, P. and Croissant, A. (eds), *Democracy under Stress: Civil-Military Relations in South and Southeast Asia* (Bangkok: ISIS).

O'Donnell, G. and Schmitter, P.C. (1986) 'Transition from Authoritarian Rule: Tentative Conclusions about Uncertain Democracies', in O'Donnell, G., Schmitter, P.C. and Whitehead, L. (eds), *Transition from Authoritarian Rule. Prospects for Democracy* (Baltimore: Johns Hopkins University Press).

O'Rourke, K. (2002) *Reformasi: The struggle for power in post-Soeharto Indonesia* (Crows Nest: Allen & Unwin).

Pasuk P. and Baker, C. (2009) *Thaksin* (Chiang Mai: Silkworm Books).

Patiño, P. and Velasco, D. (2006) 'Violence and voting in post-1986 Philippines', in Croissant, A., Martin, B. and Kneip, S. (eds), *The Politics of Death: Political Violence in Southeast Asia* (Berlin: Lit Verlag).

Pion-Berlin, D. (2009) 'Defense Organization and Civil-military Relations in Latin America', *Armed Forces & Society*, 35 (3): 562–586.

Putra, R.D. (2007) 'Strategic Intelligence Agency (BAIS)', in Sukadis, B. (ed.), *Almanac on Indonesien Security Sector Reform* (Geneva: Center for the Democratic Control of Armed Forces).

Robinson, G. (2010) *If you leave us here, we will die. How genocide was stopped in East Timor* (Princeton: Princeton University Press).

Schmitter, P. and Karl, T. (1991) 'What Democracy Is and Is Not', *Journal of Democracy*, 2 (3): 75–88.

Siaroff, A. (2009) *Comparing Political Regimes* (Toronto: Toronto University Press).

Tan, S.S. and Chew, A. (2008) 'Governing Singapore's Security Sector: Problems, Prospects and Paradox', *Contemporary Southeast Asia*, 30 (2): 241–263.

Thayer, C.A. (1995) *The Vietnam People's Army under Doi Moi* (Singapore: ISEAS).

The Nation (2007) 'Rights group questions 'free and fair' elections in Thailand', 21 December <http://www.nationmultimedia.com>.

Trinkunas, H.A. (2005) *Crafting Civilian Control of the Military in Venezuela: A Comparative Perspective* (Chapel Hill: University of North Carolina Press).

Wandelt, I. (2007) 'Security Sector Reform in Indonesia. Military vs. Civil Supremacy', in Hadiwinata, B.S. and Schuck, C. (eds), *Democracy in Indonesia. The Challenge of Consolidation* (Baden-Baden: Nomos).

Welch, C.E. (1976) 'Civilian Control of the Military: Myth and Reality', in Welch, C.E. (ed.), *Civilian Control of the Military: Theory and Cases from Developing Countries* (Albany: State University of New York Press).

12
Democratic Conflict Management Capabilities in Southeast Asia

Christoph Trinn

Introduction

During the last six decades, Southeast Asia has seen several instances of violent domestic political conflict. This can be attributed to deep-seated political and social problems in many countries of the region. While some countries like Singapore and Malaysia have been successful in terms of maintaining political stability, generating economic wealth and creating societies largely free from political violence, these can be juxtaposed with many states that have been marred by historical patterns of violent conflict. Among the contemporary conflicts most prevalent in both academic discussion and media attention have been the separatist war in Aceh, Indonesia; the Moro rebellion in the south of the Philippines and especially the Abu Sayyaf insurgency; the Islamist separatist insurgency in Southern Thailand; and the numerous ethnic, often 'economized' conflicts in Myanmar and the crackdown on the Buddhist clergy following anti-regime protests in 2007.

All of these conflicts are 'cultural' in the sense that they focus on issues of collective identity, most often in the form of religion, language or historical experiences and narratives. At the same time, apart from Myanmar, all these conflicts have taken place in countries that can be characterized as democratic in contemporary times. This observation might be perplexing in light of expectations that democratic forms of government lead to peaceful societies (Hegre et al., 2001). The present analysis takes this puzzle as a starting point and focuses accordingly on the capabilities of the political systems in Southeast Asia to manage political conflict in general and cultural conflict in particular. In order to set these considerations in a wider context, not only democracies, but Southeast Asia as a whole will be examined.

Cultural conflicts have a reputation of being particularly hard to manage and of tending to be or to become intractable. In addition, there are indications that cultural conflicts tend to escalate faster. All of this can be attributed to the fact that conflicts about values and identities have a clear tendency to be absolute in character: Ontological or deontological 'truth' – the essential outlook on what is or what should be – is oftentimes not divisible and thus not open to negotiation. In contrast to 'causationist' definitions of cultural conflict (for example, Huntington, 1993), which regard a conflict as cultural if it is caused by cultural factors, our understanding of 'cultural' conflicts does not refer to the structural causes or the actors' motives leading to or sustaining a conflict, but to the *contested object*, the issue of the conflict. When defining a conflict as 'cultural', the *why* of the dispute is not relevant, but rather *what* is in dispute.

The object in dispute in a cultural conflict is collective identity. Thus, we regard the realm of culture as encompassing everything pertaining to the identity of a collective. This primarily includes language, religion, and historical experiences and narratives. In this conception, cultural conflict is a subtype of political conflict, the latter being a violent or non-violent communicative situation leading to the actual, potential or perceived reduction of physical security in a given territory.

We assume that the causes responsible for starting or sustaining a political conflict are different from the factors causing a conflict to escalate, or in other words, to become violent in its means. This distinction corresponds to two different ways of 'handling' a conflict: conflict resolution and conflict management. While conflict resolution attempts to eliminate the roots of the conflict or to address the aggravating experiences accumulated during its course, conflict management is preventive in nature: It is intended to keep a conflict from turning violent. Viewed from the other end, a conflict can only escalate if its management failed or was not even attempted. In this respect, conflict management failure can be seen as a necessary, albeit not sufficient, condition for conflict escalation.

Conflict management is 'political' if it is undertaken by a political system via authoritative decisions, that is, if the political system leads the parties to a political conflict to subject their conduct to a set of rules and regulations (Gromes, 2005, p.338). Political conflict management fails if these authoritative decisions are either not made or not implemented. We can say that political conflict management failure is likely if the capacity of a political system to prevent conflict escalation is low. Hence, what is of interest here is the factors that determine the conflict management capabilities of a political system.

The present chapter will proceed in six steps: As a first step, we develop the concept of cultural conflict. In the second step, we present core findings regarding the patterns and trends of cultural conflict in Southeast Asia. Next, we consider the theoretical foundations of political conflict management and provide an empirical overview regarding the relationship between regime type and conflict affectedness in Southeast Asia from 1945 to 2007. We will then develop a system–theoretical model of political conflict management capability. Based on this model, we will conduct as a fifth step a

Multi-Value Qualitative Comparative Analysis of contemporary Southeast Asia. In the final section, we present some tentative conclusions.

Conflict and culture

For the purposes of this chapter, we need a theoretically informed concept of cultural conflict that can be employed in empirical analysis. We have extensively outlined such a concept elsewhere (Croissant et al., 2009) and will therefore restrict ourselves to a few brief remarks here.

We start from the assumption that cultural conflicts are a specific type of political conflict. A political conflict is a communicative situation involving two or more actors ('parties to the conflict'; see Gurr, 1970, pp.223ff.). The parties involved are communicating; the measures adopted are the means of communication. The issue of the respective conflict – the contested object – can be regarded as the content of the communication. The means of communication may be not only verbal utterances, but can involve any form of social action.

The 'political' in political conflicts results from an interaction of the concepts of 'state', 'security' and 'highest-level social norms'. That is, political conflicts always refer to the state, either through the involvement of a nation-state or when the nation-state's most basic concern, ensuring security, is affected. This is the case when physical security is reduced within a given territory – regardless of whether this actually happens, is perceived to be happening, or might potentially happen. The threat of reduced security is always present if a party to a conflict claims that a highest-level social norm (for example, constitutional law, international law or human rights) has been violated and when this accusation is not addressed within the respective framework of the relevant norm (for example, before a national or international court of law recognized as legitimate by the affected party).

With regard to the substantive issue of the communication of the conflict, we can differentiate the phenomenon of political conflict in three ways:

- In *conflicts about political power*, the communication of the conflict hinges on access to authoritative positions in government, society or the international system ('distribution of power').
- In *socioeconomic conflicts*, the distribution of material goods and economic rights within a society or between societies, as well as the mechanisms underlying such a distribution, form the content of the dispute ('economic participation').
- In *cultural conflicts*, culture is the issue of the communication.

Empirically, these categories may overlap to a considerable extent (see Gromes, 2005, p.342), and many conflicts may be simultaneously assigned to more than one category. Yet the added value of the analytical differentiation of distinct conflict types lies in highlighting the specific, and perhaps new, characteristics of cultural conflicts vis-à-vis power–political or socio-economic conflicts.

Culture is understood here as a matrix of meaning that plays an essential role in generating and preserving a collective identity (Geertz, 1994, p.9). Everything a collective constructs in order to generate and preserve the collective identity, and which is then established by actors in a communicative situation as the structural context of this communication, can be assigned to the realm of culture. Political conflict as communication is always embedded in a structural context that forms the framework for the communicative process, not as a deterministic force, but as a means of standardizing the communication, as it makes certain issues and the use of certain means at certain times by certain actors more probable than conceivable alternatives (Krallmann and Ziemann, 2001, p.249; Hansen, 2000, p.39; Billington et al., 1991, p.5). First and foremost, it is the cultural dimension of this structural context – the 'cultural context' – that is important when dealing with cultural conflicts.

Cultural conflicts revolve around one or several not explicitly formulated identity-related themes: the 'conflict fields'. The concept of conflict field seeks to take into account not only the 'hard' claims (the 'conflict items'), usually stated clearly in a public controversy, but also 'softer' and more profound conflict issues. It must be emphasized that conflict fields represent issues, not motives: they express what the conflict is about, that is, the subject of communication, and not why the conflict is taking place, or in other words, what the causes of the conflict are. Addressing thematic conflict issues also leaves open whether actors authentically address these issues or, rather, instrumentalize them for purposes not (publicly) stated.

Three domains of culture come into play as conflict fields: religion, language and historicity. These domains arise from a consideration of the prerequisites of generating and maintaining a collective identity (Smelser, 1992, p.11; Hansen, 2000, p.47; Luhmann, 1984, p.224, 1985, pp.46ff.). First, the world's complexity and that of society must be reduced to make identity possible (symbolic complexity reduction through religion). Second, to be disseminated, identity must be communicated within the collective (symbolic communication by means of language). Third, to be preserved, identity must be reproduced on an ongoing basis (symbolic reproduction via tradition and historical narrative). Each of the cultural conflict fields can be operationalized by taking as indicators verbal or active references to a religious, linguistic and historical symbol (person or object) respectively. If at least one of these conflict fields has been activated by at least one of the relevant conflict actors, the respective conflict has been established as cultural.

Cultural conflicts in Southeast Asia

After conceptualizing political conflict in general and cultural conflict in particular, let us now turn to some lead-off findings with regard to the development and patterns of cultural conflict in Southeast Asia. We assign empirical conflicts to one or several of the outlined conflict fields on the basis of the Conflict Information System (CONIS) database at the University of Heidelberg (www.conis.org). CONIS evaluates information from public news sources and processes them for the purposes of event data analysis. In addition to examining actor-related structures – that is, which actors are present as well as their military, economic, institutional and sociocultural characteristics – the data shed light, first and foremost, on conflict measures, conflict issues and conflict intensities.

CONIS is distinguished from other databanks like the Correlates of War project (COW: Singer and Small, 1972; Small and Singer, 1982) and the Uppsala Conflict Database Program (UCDP: Gleditsch et al., 2002) by virtue of three quintessential features. First, CONIS covers all forms of political conflict worldwide since 1945 and is thus not restricted to individual regions of the world or solely to violent conflicts. Second, the databank covers conflict dynamics, that is, it provides data on the detailed phases of development in individual conflicts. Third, CONIS is a quantitative databank, and thus aiming at a large number of cases, on a qualitative basis. The measuring and categorizing of the conflicts is based not simply on the number of battle-related deaths as is the case in other research approaches but on 'content analysis' of the communications and actions between the conflict actors.

The dynamic conflict model developed for CONIS comprises, all in all, five intensity levels. The first level (dispute) is marked by the articulation of contradicting interests, the second (non-violent crisis) by the threat of using force. The third level (violent crisis) is characterized by the sporadic use of force. On the fourth level (limited war), force is used considerably and systematically. Finally, the fifth level (war) entails the massive and systematic use of force with the aim of reaching a final resolution of the conflict (see Schwank, forthcoming).

With regard to the relevance and patterns of cultural conflicts in Southeast Asia, our analysis produces five major findings. *First*, the general patterns of cultural conflict in Southeast Asia parallel the overall findings in Asia and throughout the world. Cultural conflicts in Southeast Asia as a proportion of non-violent conflicts total 33 per cent (worldwide, 38 per cent). They account for a total of 58 per cent of violent crises (worldwide, 59 per cent) and 59 per cent of limited wars and wars (worldwide, 64 per cent).

Second, there is no clear trend toward cultural conflicts in Southeast Asia. Unlike Asia as a whole, the gap in Southeast Asia between cultural and non-cultural conflicts is not widening. Only between the mid-1960s and the mid-1980s did cultural conflicts occur less frequently than non-cultural conflicts. During that time, regime conflicts dominated.

Admittedly, as Figure 12.1 shows, the number of cultural conflicts in Southeast Asia has grown more or less steadily and now clearly exceeds the number of non-cultural conflicts. Still, it cannot be said that specifically cultural conflicts have 'dramatically' increased. It is much rather the case that the overall number of conflicts has grown over the past six decades. Here, there is no pronounced growth in cultural conflicts.

Third, cultural conflicts in Southeast Asia tend to escalate faster than in the rest of Asia. When looking exclusively at the development of cultural conflicts over the course of time, we can clearly see a difference between Asia as a whole and Southeast Asia (see Figure 12.2). In Southeast Asia, there are considerably more warlike conflicts than violent crises – while in all other parts of Asia the relation between the two types of conflict is more balanced. Unlike in other regions of Asia, cultural conflicts generally take the form of warlike disputes, whereas there is no distinct trend toward 'small wars'.

Fourth, cultural conflicts in Southeast Asia are mostly domestic: 96 per cent of cultural conflicts in Southeast Asia take place within states (compared to 81 per cent worldwide). Moreover, two out of three domestic conflicts (67 per cent) in one or another way hinge on culture (worldwide, 56 per cent). By contrast, conflicts on cultural issues are rarely fought between states; the proportion of the non-cultural conflicts among interstate conflicts has reached 87 per cent in Southeast Asia. Evidently, regional governments have succeeded in developing mechanisms that prevent existing

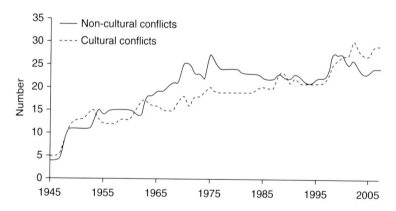

Figure 12.1   Cultural and non-cultural conflicts (domestic and international, 1945–2007)

Source: Author's calculations based on CONIS.

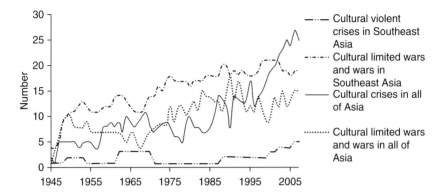

Figure 12.2 Cultural violent crises as well as limited wars and wars in Southeast Asia and Asia (domestic and international conflicts, 1945–2007)

Source: Author's calculations based on CONIS.

cultural tensions and conflicts within communities from 'spilling over' and thus turning into interstate conflicts.

Fifth, Indonesia, Myanmar and Thailand are particularly prone to cultural conflicts. Viewed from a historical and a more recent perspective, these three countries are the most affected by violent cultural conflict in Southeast Asia. Least affected are Singapore and Malaysia.

Political conflict management

The idea of *political conflict management* employed here rests on three basic assumptions. *First*, it differentiates between causes of political conflict *per se* and causes for conflict *escalation*:[1] The root causes leading to the formation of a political conflict are separated from the reasons why a given conflict escalates to a violent level. In the present context, we thus understand political conflict management as the mechanism by which a political system prevents a political conflict from turning violent. *Second*, in our view, one of the main functions of political systems is precisely this management of political conflicts, and thus, basically, the prevention of conflict escalation by means of authoritative decision-making (see Easton, 1953). Our *third* assumption is that the capabilities of a political system to make and to implement such a decision depend on the way in which those decisions are made and implemented. In other words, we assume that a political system's conflict management capabilities are essentially shaped by the structure of that system. The structure of governance in a given country is probably most concisely expressed in the level of democratization a society exhibits at a specific point of time.

Regime type and political conflict: Theoretical considerations

In empirical conflict research, the assumed relationship between the level of democratization and the risk of domestic political conflict – often termed 'domestic democratic peace' (Henderson and Singer, 2000) – primarily rests on the consideration that in democracies, social conflicts can be managed and solved peacefully (a) because democratic regimes are more responsive to the needs and demands of the people due to the re-occurrence of public elections, and (b) because democracy is in itself a procedure for non-violent conflict management that also institutionalizes its norms in the social sphere (Gromes, 2005).

Autocratic regimes, in contrast, are less responsive than democracies. They lack a 'ready-made' procedure for dealing with broad or deep antagonisms in society, which gives reason to expect that in autocracies, social conflicts are more likely to escalate. At the same time, however, autocracies are able to be more repressive than democracies, giving them the potential to suppress protest before it escalates (see, for instance, Fearon and Laitin, 2003; Henderson and Singer, 2000).

Due to these considerations, Gurr (1968, 1970) assumes that the relationship between democracy and domestic violence might be non-linear: Whereas democracies and autocracies, being situated on the far ends of the regime continuum, are able to manage social conflicts either through political participation or repression, 'hybrid regimes' (Zinecker, 2005) – also known as 'semi-democracies' or 'anocracies' – are supposed to be exposed to a greater risk of experiencing violent conflict, because their inconsistent institutional set-up, lacking both inclusionary legitimacy and control resources, precludes a peaceful as well as a repressive approach (Henderson and Singer, 2000; Gleditsch, 1995).

The majority of the empirical literature considers the aforementioned relationship between democratization and domestic violence to be well-founded, although criticism has been voiced as well. In the arguably most influential analysis in this context, Hegre et al. (2001), find evidence for an inverted-U relationship between the level of democratization and the risk of civil war (see also Muller and Weede, 1990; Henderson and Singer, 2000; Fearon and Laitin, 2003; Ellingsen, 2000).

Considering this, it seems reasonable to assume that democratic systems generally possess greater conflict management capabilities than either autocratic or anocratic systems. Due to their incoherent characteristics of governance, hybrid regimes appear to achieve only an inadequate outcome as far as the management of political conflicts is concerned. However, contrary to the inverted-U hypothesis, autocracies cannot particularly be said to fare better: even if an autocratic regime succeeds in quelling protest before it turns violent, the repression itself cannot be considered a non-violent measure. The risk of an autocratic system experiencing high-intensity violence like *civil war* might be reduced, but if *state repression* is itself considered low-intensity violence, autocracies are mostly not free from violent political conflicts, as the available conflict data show.

For Gromes (2005, pp.348–9, 352), the divisibility of conflict issues lies at the heart of democratic conflict management. *First*, the contested object itself must be divisible. Material objects like resources or territory can mostly be considered divisible. Absolute claims are therefore not accessible to peaceful conflict management. If a conflict is about political power, democracies have an advantage in that institutionalized power sharing has a temporal aspect. In this view, federal and consociational democracies (Lijphart, 1969, 1977) are even better equipped because they also practise vertical power sharing and horizontal power division respectively (see Reilly, 2006, pp.149, 169). The contested object – political power – becomes more divisible: there are simply more positions of political power to be distributed.

Second, ultimately every political conflict is concerned with the distribution of political power, for '[p]olitics is the authoritative allocation of values for a society' (Easton, 1953, p.129), which in this case is the power to decide who gets what from the contested object, that is, the power to manage the conflict. In addition to the aforementioned temporal, vertical and horizontal power-sharing arrangements, (liberal) democracies are characterized by constitutional limitations on the exertion of political power. In this way, democratic conflict management is endowed with a 'built-in safety device'. In contrast to autocratic conflict management, in a democracy the one who succumbs to a regulating mechanism does not have to fear for his or her life or freedom (Gromes, 2005, p.348), which enhances the fundamental trust in the arrangements made and thus the general performance of democratic conflict management.

Democratic conflict management's dependence on the divisibility of conflict issues may reduce this strategy's performance as far as cultural conflicts are concerned. Democratic conflict management has a lot of demanding prerequisites that are not easily fulfilled when identity-related antagonisms in the form of absolute claims to ontological or deontological 'truths' are at stake. For this reason, the conflict management advantages of the democratic approach, which focuses on power sharing, power dispersion and power limitation, may be cancelled out, so that democracies may fare no better than autocracies or anocracies in managing cultural conflict.

All of this leads us to two basic assumptions. *First*, democracies have better general conflict management capabilities than either autocracies or anocracies. Democratic regime phases are therefore expected to be less affected by political conflict than either autocratic or anocratic regime phases. *Second*, cultural conflicts are harder to manage than non-cultural conflicts, especially for democracies. Democratic regime phases are therefore expected to be as affected by cultural conflict as autocratic and anocratic regime phases.

Findings from Southeast Asia, 1945–2007

In order to examine these assumptions, we now turn to an analysis of the relationship between the level of democratization and the degree to which the Southeast Asian countries under consideration have been affected by violent domestic cultural and non-cultural conflict from 1945 to 2007.[2] Democracy came to Southeast Asia in two 'waves' which are known in political science as the second and the third waves (see Huntington, 1991). In this region, the second wave comprised the establishment of a number of democratic regimes after the end of the colonial era. It began in Myanmar in 1948 and ended in 1968 with the end of the democratic phase in Malaysia. No Southeast Asian democracy survived the subsiding of the second wave. With the end of the Cold War approaching, the third wave of democratization reached the Philippines in 1987 and witnessed the establishment of democracy in East Timor in 2002, but also the abandonment of democratic rule in Thailand in 2006. For present purposes, we determined the second-wave period to have lasted from 1945 until 1977, and the third-wave period from 1978 until 2007.

We can gather from Table 12.1 that the level to which autocracies were affected by cultural conflicts increased by 32.69 per cent from the second to the third wave period, while in anocracies the average cultural conflict affectedness decreased by 63.06 per cent, and in democracies by 29.01 per cent. Non-cultural conflict affectedness in autocracies fell by 29.24 per cent, and in anocracies and democracies by 66.91 and 70.33 per cent respectively. Thus, despite the general increase in the number of domestic and international violent and non-violent cultural and non-cultural conflicts in Southeast Asia (see Figure 12.1), the level to which countries where affected by domestic violent cultural and non-cultural conflicts decreased substantially – with one notable exception: the average cultural conflict affectedness increased in autocratic regimes. This effect can be chiefly attributed to Myanmar, which is characterized by a great number of 'ethnic' conflicts and a military government.

Table 12.1   Cultural and non-cultural domestic violent conflict affectedness of different regime types, 1945–1977 and 1978–2007

Regime phase	ACA	ANA	Regime phase	ACA	ANA	Regime phase	ACA	ANA
AUTO 1945–77	3.61	1.06	ANO 1945–77	1.57	1.39	DEMO 1945–77	4.55	3.00
AUTO 1978–2007	4.79	0.75	ANO 1978–2007	0.58	0.46	DEMO 1978–2007	3.23	0.89

Note: ACA = average cultural conflict affectedness per regime phase; ANA = average non-cultural conflict affectedness per regime phase; AUTO = autocratic regime phase; ANO = anocratic regime phase; DEMO = democratic regime phase.

If we compare the regime types during each period, we can see in Table 12.1 that anocratic phases almost consistently show the lowest conflict affectedness values – only the second wave period's average non-cultural conflict affectedness in anocracies is slightly higher than in autocracies. During the second wave, democracies in Southeast Asia were always more affected by domestic conflict than autocracies. This picture improved somewhat for democracies during the recent third wave: the average non-cultural conflict affectedness of democratic phases is not much higher than the corresponding value of autocratic phases, and with a value of 3.23, the average cultural conflict affectedness lies clearly below the autocratic level of 4.79.

Thus, contrary to what we expected from our theoretical considerations, we can discern a non-inverted U relationship between the level of democratization and the level of conflict affectedness. Unlike our assumption, there is no particular 'democratic advantage' detectable in Southeast Asia. On the contrary, democracies are, for the most part, affected even more than autocratic regimes.

If we focus exclusively on cultural conflicts, however, we can see our expectations largely confirmed: democracies do not perform better than non-democratic regimes. What is surprising, again, is the relatively low level of conflict affectedness of anocratic phases.

If we compare the cultural conflict affectedness of Southeast Asia's countries with the rest of Asia and Oceania,[3] Figure 12.3 reveals that the (non-inverted) U relationship between the level of democratization and the level of conflict affectedness seems to be a special characteristic of Southeast Asia,

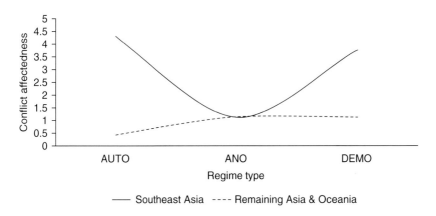

Figure 12.3 Relationship between regime type and cultural conflict affectedness in Southeast Asia and remaining Asia & Oceania (domestic violent conflicts, 1945–2007)

Note: AUTO = autocratic regime phase; ANO = anocratic regime phase; DEMO = democratic regime phase.

while the rest of Asia with Oceania region exhibits a relatively even distribution, which is more in line with our second assumption above.

These diachronic and cross-national findings are of a descriptive nature and can therefore only give indications as to the general relationship between regime type and degree of conflict affectedness. In order to investigate the causal mechanisms between these two variables, we will now turn to a closer analysis of the factors precipitating cultural and non-cultural conflict in present day Southeast Asia, and of the mechanisms of political conflict management.

The political conflict management model

With the present analysis focusing on violent domestic conflict, let us recall our assumptions above that, *first*, causes of political conflict *per se* and causes for conflict escalation are to be kept separate, and *second*, that political conflict management means political conflict escalation prevention. Thus, whatever the initial causes leading to the formation of a conflict situation, we assume that the reasons why a domestic conflict escalates to a violent level can be traced back to failures in conflict management by a political system. In this perspective, a political system's conflict management capability can be understood as the system's ability to prevent a non-violent political conflict from escalating, or to promote the de-escalation of violent political conflict, and can be measured via the respective country's level of conflict affectedness.

In order to identify the factors that lead either to positive conflict management capability or to conflict management failures, and applying our Political Conflict Management Model – devised as simply as possible – we turn to Easton's analytical approach to the political system (Easton, 1965, 1967). In essence, Easton sees the political system as transforming input into corresponding output. The output of a political system consists in decisions effectuating the 'authoritative allocation of values for a society' (Easton, 1953, p.129). As already noted, this allocation leads to decisions about who gets what from a contested object, that is, it leads to the management of a political conflict. Political conflict management failures can therefore be seen as output deficits of a political system.

According to Easton (1965, pp.112–13), influences from the societal environment form two distinct forms of input: demands and support. While demands refer to the output that a society expects a political system to provide, support indicates the factors provided by the society that enable the processing of a political system (Easton, 1967, pp.38–9 156–7). Easton further differentiates between two kinds of support: specific support, that is, concrete extractable resources, and diffuse support, or in other words, a society's general belief in the legitimacy of a political system (Easton, 1967, pp.278ff.).

Apart from circumstantial malfunctions within the 'black box' of the political system itself (see Easton, 1965, p.114), like 'wrong' or 'protracted' decisions due to 'bad governance', a political system's output deficit can be attributed to a corresponding input deficit, that is, to support that is insufficient or incompatible with respect to the demands. Thus, our model traces conflict escalation back to political conflict management failures – conceptualized as political output deficits – and further back to societal input deficits (see Figure 12.4).

We consider the input reaching a political system from the specific society in which it exists (thus disregarding input from the international society) to be of three kinds:

(1) *political input*, represented by the level of democratization and indicating the general legitimacy a political system is provided with in terms of political satisfaction and the specified legitimation of a government or a particular policy by means of political expression;
(2) *socioeconomic input*, represented by the level of economic development and indicating the degree of a society's economic satisfaction with a political system and the amount of revenues a political system can extract from a society, and thus by extension the state's coercion capabilities; and
(3) *cultural input*, represented by the linguistic and religious cohesion of a given society and indicating a coherent communicative framework and set of symbols and ideas that make communication less costly and misunderstanding less probable.

The following proxies have been employed: (1) the country-specific average for the years 2003 to 2007 of the 'polity2' regime type variable of the POLITY IV dataset; (2) the country-specific average for the years 2003 to 2007 of the infant mortality rate (the number of deaths of children of one year of age or younger per 1000 live births) from the United Nations World Population Prospects (2008 revision) dataset; (3) the degree of linguistic fragmentation from the SIL International Ethnologue 2005 dataset (Gordon, 2005), and the degree of religious fragmentation, computed on the basis of the Encyclopaedia Britannica Book of the Year 2007.

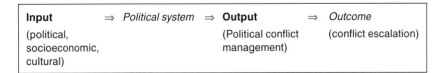

Input	⇒ *Political system*	⇒ **Output**	⇒ *Outcome*
(political, socioeconomic, cultural)		(Political conflict management)	(conflict escalation)

Figure 12.4   The political conflict management model

All three kinds of input account for the demands as well as the support, because demand and support are relative to each other: The more political or economic support there is in a society, the smaller the demand for political or economic improvement in this society; the more demanding a lack of cultural cohesion is, the less supporting the specific cultural structures in a given society can be for the political system.

As already noted, we conceptualize political conflict management failures as output deficits. These deficits are reflected in the ultimate outcome: the level of a society's affectedness by violent conflict, which can be considered as our dependent variable. We measure the value of this variable via the country-specific *average cultural and non-cultural conflict affectedness* for the years 2003 to 2007. Therefore, we are dealing with two different dependent variables.

A multi-value qualitative comparative analysis of Southeast Asia (2003–07)

In order to put our Political Conflict Management Model into action, we use the method of Qualitative Comparative Analysis (QCA), first developed by Ragin (1987). This method uses Boolean algebra to minimize the case-specific configuration, that is, the combination of the occurring values of the independent variables, in order to find the simplest possible solution for the dependent variable (Jahn, 2006, pp.419–20). QCA has three main advantages: (1) it is especially suited for a small or medium number of cases; (2) it is quantitative yet case-oriented, or in other words, it does not detach the variables from the analyzed cases; and (3) it gives special emphasis to determining necessary and sufficient conditions regarding a certain outcome (Cronqvist and Herrmann, 2006, p.16; Jahn, 2006, pp.420–21).

In order to solve certain methodological problems associated with conventional QCA – such as information loss due to data dichotomization, as well as the frequent occurrence of 'contradictions', that is, the appearance of identical configurations that result in contradicting outcomes – further variants of this method have been developed. One of these is Multi-Value Qualitative Comparative Analysis (MVQCA) by Cronqvist. MVQCA retains the idea of finding necessary and sufficient conditions by using Boolean logic, but unlike QCA, it does not require all of the data to be transformed into binary expressions (0, 1), opening up the possibility of assigning multiple values to each variable (for example, 0, 1, 2) (Cronqvist, 2003, p.2). The following analysis uses MVQCA.[4]

The truth tables (Tables 12.2 and 12.3) summarize the configurations which are empirically observable in our set of cases with regard to the two outcomes, average cultural conflict affectedness and average non-cultural conflict affectedness.[5] Table 12.4 represents the minimized MVQCA solutions for each set of conditioning factors for the specified outcomes.

Table 12.2 Truth table for outcome 'cultural conflict affectedness'

Infant mortality	Religious fragmentation	Linguistic fragmentation	Regime type	Outcome	Cases
2	0	0	1	1	Cambodia
1	1	2	2	1	Indonesia
2	1	2	0	1	Laos
0	1	2	1	0	Malaysia
2	1	1	0	1	Myanmar
1	0	2	2	1	Philippines
0	2	2	1	0	Singapore
0	0	2	1	1	Thailand
1	2	0	0	0	Vietnam

Table 12.3 Truth table for outcome 'non-cultural conflict affectedness'

Infant mortality	Religious fragmentation	Linguistic fragmentation	Regime type	Outcome	Cases
2	0	0	1	1	Cambodia
1	1	2	2	0	Indonesia
2	1	2	0	0	Laos
0	1	2	1	0	Malaysia
2	1	1	0	1	Myanmar
1	0	2	2	1	Philippines
0	2	2	1	0	Singapore
0	0	2	1	0	Thailand
1	2	0	0	0	Vietnam

Table 12.4 MVQCA results

Outcome	Results	Cases explained
Occurrence of cultural conflict	IM{2} + RF{0} + RT{2}	(Cambodia, Laos, Myanmar); (Cambodia, Philippines, Thailand); (Indonesia, Philippines)
Non-occurrence of cultural conflict	RF{2} + RF{1}*IM{0} + RF{1}*RT{1}	(Singapore, Vietnam); (Malaysia); (Malaysia)
Occurrence of non-cultural conflict	LF{1} + IM{1,2}*RF{0}	(Myanmar); (Cambodia, Philippines)
Non-occurrence of non-cultural conflict	IM{0} + RF{2} + RF{1}*LF{2}	(Malaysia, Singapore, Thailand); (Singapore, Vietnam); (Indonesia, Laos, Malaysia)

Note: IM = Infant Mortality; RF = Religious Fragmentation; LF = Linguistic Fragmentation; RT = Regime Type; '+' = logical 'OR', '*' = logical 'AND'.

The analysis shows that all three of the conditioning factors considered – the political, the socioeconomic, and the cultural – exert an influence on the occurrence of cultural as well as non-cultural conflicts in Southeast Asia.

A low level of socioeconomic development – indicated by a high infant mortality rate – is a crucial factor in explaining the occurrence of cultural conflicts in Cambodia, Laos and Myanmar. A low level of life satisfaction and of state revenues apparently impairs the conflict management capabilities of these countries. Conversely, the high level of socioeconomic development in Malaysia, Singapore, and Thailand seems to shield these countries, at least from non-cultural conflicts.

In contrast to our expectations, the results of our analysis clearly point to the fact that a low level of religious fragmentation conditions the occurrence of cultural conflict, while a high level of religious fragmentation may protect against cultural and non-cultural conflicts alike. A possible explanation for this 'religious homogeneity effect' is that a unitary framework of *Weltanschauungen* admittedly provides a political system with unfettered communication channels and a coherent climate of ideas and norms, but at the same time creates a 'closed sphere' in which the political system has to act, making it blind to 'deviant' communication channels and ideative and normative climates. This might be especially true for the cases of Thailand and the Philippines regarding the Muslim insurgencies in both countries. In contrast, a culturally highly diverse society forces the political system to actively communicate, precluding the possibility of 'autistic' communication strategies. Singapore provides an illustrative example for this case.

Arguably, the benign effects of religious heterogeneity might be reduced if we are dealing with only a medium level of religious fragmentation. However, as the cases of Indonesia, Laos and Malaysia show, this can apparently be counterbalanced by a high degree of linguistic fragmentation – albeit only as far as non-cultural conflicts are concerned.

Interestingly, however, in Myanmar the degree to which the country is affected by non-cultural conflict appears to be significantly influenced by its cultural structure, because the analysis finds that a medium level of linguistic fragmentation is a crucial factor here. Due to the territorial concentration of the languages in Myanmar, which gives rise to geographically defined 'ethnic groups', this finding points to the problems a political system experiences in managing political conflict within an ethnically highly diverse society dominated by one ethnic group.

A low or medium level of socioeconomic development in combination with a low level of religious fragmentation seems to 'merge the worst' from both dimensions; the occurrence of non-cultural conflicts in Cambodia and the Philippines can be attributed to the combined effects of these factors. In contrast, as is the case with Malaysia, the presence of several major religious groups can apparently be counterbalanced by advanced socioeconomic development, as far as cultural conflicts are concerned.

When we now turn to the third dimension considered, we can see that the regime type as a conditioning factor occurs solely in the realm of cultural conflicts, while non-cultural conflicts seem to be largely unaffected by it. In light of the specific parameter values for Indonesia and the Philippines, this can be understood as pointing to the particular shortcomings of *democratic* conflict management with respect to *cultural* conflicts: The democracies in Southeast Asia have particular problems in dealing with political conflicts focusing on cultural issues. A possible explanation for this is that while democratic conflict management relies on the effects of temporal, vertical and horizontal power-sharing arrangements and on constitutional limitations on the exertion of political power, the democratic regimes in Indonesia and the Philippines have had deficiencies in both power sharing and power limitation. First, both systems have observed the separation of powers (horizontal power sharing in a formal sense) and the alternation of government (temporal power sharing), but the inclusion of important (geographically and culturally defined) groups and their elites (horizontal power sharing in a sociological sense) and federal structures (vertical power sharing) have been inadequate – despite considerable efforts in this direction (see Bertrand, 2004, pp.210–3; see Reilly, 2006, pp.167–9;). This has a lot to do with an essentially *patrimonial,* 'top down' approach to democracy (Webber, 2006) in these countries. Second, and connected to this, limiting political power might be understood in these states, due to a considerable conflict history in both countries, as curtailing the government's power to counter insurgencies (see Bertrand, 2004, p.188). However, this attitude has also prevented the political system from accumulating trust from relevant parts of the population. Thus for a long time, the Philippine and Indonesian polities have cut themselves off from the essential resources needed for democratic conflict management.

In contrast, Malaysia has been free from violent cultural conflicts during the period under consideration. Because this country is characterized by a medium level of democratization combined with a medium level of religious fragmentation, it might be surprising that an anocratic regime could attribute its lack of cultural conflict to its 'anocraticity'. However, despite its democratic and liberal shortcomings, Malaysia (see Reilly, 2006), in relative contrast to Indonesia and the Philippines, has succeeded in integrating the relevant populations within its territory into the political system, in this regard comparable to Singapore.

Conclusions

Conflict management in Southeast Asia has been faced with a general increase in the number of cultural and non-cultural conflicts over the last six decades. Nevertheless, it would be an exaggeration to speak of a clear trend toward cultural conflicts in the region. The region's affectedness by domestic violent conflicts, in particular, decreased substantially – with the notable exception of the cultural conflict affectedness of autocratic regimes, a finding primarily attributable to the 'ethnic' conflicts in Myanmar. As elsewhere, cultural conflicts in Southeast Asia are an almost exclusively domestic phenomenon. Compared to the rest of Asia, however, cultural conflicts in Southeast Asia tend to escalate faster and at a high intensity. With regard to regime types, we can discern that democracies are for the most part more affected by political conflict than autocratic regimes. Anocratic regime phases, however, are generally least affected. This pattern is a special characteristic of Southeast Asia. The Multi-Value Qualitative Comparative Analysis of domestic violent conflicts from 2003 to 2007 yields the following three results.

(1) Low levels of socioeconomic development make a country prone to cultural as well as non-cultural conflict, while high levels of socioeconomic development make both types of conflict unlikely.
(2) A low degree of religious fragmentation is a 'favourable' condition for the formation of cultural and non-cultural conflicts, while a high degree appears to have benign effects, averting both types of conflicts.
(3) High levels of democracy do not automatically translate into effectual conflict management; if democracies do not strive for the highest ranks of substantial democratization, they might even be beaten by 'inclusive' anocracies.

These results lead to three corresponding suggestions regarding political conflict management in Southeast Asia.

(1) *Socioeconomic development* with a comprehensive distribution of wealth remains requisite to increasing both state strength and state legitimacy, two *sine qua non* conditions for successful political conflict management.
(2) Political systems dominated by one religious or 'ethnic' group act in culturally 'closed spheres' of communication, information, and perception, which make them 'blind' to divergent realities. In those societies, intercultural dialogue appears to be the only way to increase *politico-cultural awareness and sensitivity*, thus ensuring better conflict management capabilities.
(3) Democratic conflict management must rely on *substantial power sharing and power limitation*. These arrangements must be accountable for the inclusion of all relevant groups, also by establishing federal structures,[6] and for the accumulation of trust across the society through the observance of human rights.

Notes

1. The author would like to thank Thomas Wencker for his ideas on the difference between the causes of conflict and the causes of conflict escalation.
2. The country-year is the basic unit of our analysis. We use the 'polity2' variable of the POLITY IV dataset to determine each country-year's location on the regime continuum, ranging from –10 to +10 on the POLITY scale. Country-years with index values from –10 to –4 are considered autocratic, from –5 to +5 as anocratic, and from +6 to +10 as democratic. The conflict affectedness of each country-year has been calculated on the basis of the CONIS databank. We have included domestic cultural and non-cultural conflicts during their violent phases, but have excluded conflicts between states (international conflicts), as well as all non-violent conflict phases. For each country-year, we have determined the maximum intensity of each conflict extant in the respective country in a given year. These individual conflict intensity values have been weighted independently from each other. Violent crises have been weighted by the factor 1, limited wars by 3, and wars by 4. For each year, all of the weighted intensity values for a respective country have been summed up. The resulting value represents the specific conflict affectedness for the respective country-year. Summing up different country-year values – for example, for a country's democratic regime phase – yields the accumulated conflict affectedness for the sample. Dividing the accumulated affectedness value by the number of selected country-years yields the average conflict affectedness for the sample. As cultural and non-cultural conflicts have been treated separately, we distinguish between cultural conflict affectedness and non-cultural conflict affectedness. Brunei and East Timor had to be omitted from the sample due to a lack of data.
3. Asia & Oceania includes Pakistan, Central Asia and Mongolia, but excludes Afghanistan and the remaining Middle East, as well as Russia.
4. Our aim in applying MVQCA to our model is to obtain parsimonious results. One way to ensure this is to dichotomize the outcome variable values. Thus, if a country's value of average cultural or non-cultural conflict affectedness was 0 during the time under consideration, it received the value 0 in this category, and if it was > 0, it received the value 1. With regard to the condition variables, the religious and linguistic fragmentation indices range from 0.0 to 1.0, the POLITY index from –10 to +10. Here we applied two thresholds: regarding the fragmentation indices, the thresholds have been set at ≤ 0.33 and ≥ 0.66; regarding the POLITY index, at < –5 and > 5. This decision is based on finding non-linear effects of the said variables as far as conflict affectedness is concerned (cf. Croissant et al., 2009a). The infant mortality rate, however, is not expressed by index values with fixed minimum or maximum values. Here we performed an average linkage clustering on the empirical data (cf. Cronqvist, 2003, p.16), yielding two reasonable thresholds: < 15.00 and > 41.82. The computer programme 'Tool for Small-N Analysis (Tosmana)' by Cronqvist (2007) has been used for the MVQCA procedure.
5. The truth tables show no 'contradictions'. With regard to another methodological problem, the 'logical remainders', that is, configurations that are logically possible but that are not present among the empirically observable cases in the set (Jahn, 2006, p.424), there are two possible ways to minimize the configurations. For the remainders, no outcome can be assigned in an *a priori* way – they could therefore be excluded from the analysis entirely. This would lead to the most complex solution – in fact, every case would be assigned its own solution here. However,

228 *Christoph Trinn*

the remainders could also be excluded from the explanation but included in the minimization procedure – they would be used for the '0' and for the '1' outcome synthesis to formulate 'simplifying assumptions' (Rihoux and Ragin, 2004, pp.12ff.). This would lead to the most parsimonious solution, as applied here.

6. Bertrand argues that federalization or other forms of decentralization to create sub-national autonomy depend on four prerequisites: ethnically homogenous territorial units, a democratic regime, clear-cut, non-cooperative federalism, and fiscal decentralization as part of political devolution (Bertrand, 2004, p.187). See also Reilly (2006, p.171).

References

Bertrand, J. (2004) *Nationalism and Ethnic Conflict in Indonesia* (Cambridge: Cambridge University Press).

Billington, R., Strawbridge, S., Greensides, L. and Fitzsimons, A. (1991) *Culture and Society. A Sociology of Culture* (Houndmills: Macmillan Education).

Croissant, A., Wagschal, U., Schwank, N. and Trinn, C. (2009) *Kulturelle Konflikte seit 1945. Die kulturellen Dimensionen des globalen Konfliktgeschehens* (Baden-Baden: Nomos).

Cronqvist, L. (2003) *Using Multi-Value Logic Synthesis in Social Science*, http://www.tosmana.net/resources/ecpr_cronqvist.pdf [30 April 2009].

Cronqvist, L. (2007) 'Tool for Small-N Analysis (TOSMANA). Version 1.3', http://www.Tosmana.net/download.html [30 April 2009].

Cronqvist, L. and Herrmann, A. (2006) *Contradictions in Qualitative Comparative Analysis (QCA). Ways out of the Dilemma*, http://cadmus.iue.it/dspace/handle/1814/6305 [30 April 2009].

Easton, D. (1953) *The Political System. An Inquiry into the State of Political Science* (New York: Knopf).

Easton, D. (1965) *A Framework for Political Analysis* (Englewood Cliffs: Prentice-Hall).

Easton, D. (1967) *A Systems Analysis of Political Life* (New York,London,Sydney: Wiley).

Ellingsen, T. (2000) 'Colorful Community or Ethnic Witches Brew? Multiethnicity and Domestic Conflict during and after the Cold War', *Journal of Conflict Resolution*, 44 (2): 228–249.

Encyclopaedia Britannica (2007) *Book of the Year 2007* (Chicago: Encyclopaedia Britannica).

Fearon, J. and Laitin, D. (2003) 'Ethnicity, Insurgency, and Civil War', *American Political Science Review*, 97 (1): 75–90.

Geertz, C. (1994) *Dichte Beschreibung. Beiträge zum Verstehen kultureller Systeme* (Frankfurt am Main: Suhrkamp).

Gleditsch, N.P. (1995) 'Democracy and the Future of European Peace', *European Journal of International Relations*, 1 (4): 539–571.

Gleditsch, N.P., Wallensteen, P., Eriksson, M., Sollenberg, M. and Strand, H. (2002) 'Armed Conflict 1946–2001: A New Dataset', *Journal of Peace Research*, 39(5): 615–637.

Gordon, R.G., Jr. (ed.) (2005) *Ethnologue. Languages of the World,* Dallas, 15th edn, http://www.ethnologue.com/ethno_docs/distribution.asp?by=country [30 April 2009].

Gromes, T. (2005) 'Innerstaatliche Konflikte und die Wirkung von Demokratie' in Jahn E., Fischer, S. and Sahm A. (ed.), *Die Zukunft des Friedens. Bd2: Die Friedens- und*

Konfliktforschung aus der Perspektive der jüngeren Generationen (Wiesbaden: VS Verlag für Sozialwissenschaften).

Gurr, T.R. (1968) 'A Causal Model of Civil Strife. A Comparative Analysis using New Indices', *American Political Science Review*, 62 (4): 1104–1124.

Gurr, T. R. (1970) *Why Men Rebel* (Princeton: Princeton University Press).

Hansen, K. P. (2000) *Kultur und Kulturwissenschaft. Eine Einführung* (Tübingen, Basel: Francke).

Hegre, H., Ellingsen, T., Gates, S. and Gleditsch, N.P. (2001) 'Toward a Democratic Civil Peace? Democracy, Political Change, and Civil War, 1816–1992', *American Political Science Review*, 95 (1): 33–48.

Henderson, E. and Singer, D. (2000) 'Civil War in the Post-Colonial World, 1946–92', *Journal of peace research*, 37 (3): 257–299.

Huntington, S. (1991) *TheThird Wave. Democratization in theLate Twentieth Century* (Norman: University of Oklahoma Press).

Huntington, S. (1993) 'The Clash of Civilizations?', *Foreign Affairs*, 72 (3): 22–49.

Jahn, D. (2006) *Einführung in die Vergleichende Politikwissenschaft* (Wiesbaden: VS Verlag für Sozialwissenschaften).

Krallmann, D. and Ziemann, A. (2001) *Grundkurs Kommunikationswissenschaft* (München: Fink).

Lijphart, A. (1969) 'Consociational Democracy', *World Politics*, 21 (2): 207–225.

Lijphart, A. (1977) *Democracy in Plural Societies* (New Haven: Yale University Press).

Luhmann, N. (1984) *Soziale Systeme. Grundriß einer allgemeinen Theorie* (Frankfurt am Main:Suhrkamp).

Muller, E.N. and Weede, E. (1990) 'Cross-National Variation in Political Violence. A Rational Action Approach', *Journal of Conflict Resolution*, 34 (4): 624–651.

Ragin, C.C. (1987) *The Comparative Method. Moving Beyond Qualitative and Quantitative Strategies* (Berkeley,Los Angeles,London: University of California Press).

Reilly, B. (2006) *Democracy and Diversity. Political Engineering in the Asia-Pacific* (Oxford: Oxford University Press).

Rihoux, B. and Ragin, C.C. (2004) *Qualitative Comparative Analysis (QCA). State of the Art and Prospects*, http://www.asu.edu/clas/polisci/cqrm/APSA2004/RihouxRagin.pdf [30 April 2009].

Schwank, N. (forthcoming) *Konflikte, Krisen, Kriege. Eskalationsprozesse politischer Konflikte 1945-2008* (Baden-Baden: Nomos).

Singer, D.J. and Small, M. (1972) *The Wages of War 1816–1965. A Statistical Handbook* (New York, Sydney, Toronto: Wiley, John & Sons).

Small, M. and Singer, D.J. (1982) *Resort to Arms. International and Civil Wars, 1816–1980* (Beverly Hills: Sage).

Smelser, N.J. (1992) 'Culture. Coherent or Incoherent' in Münch, R. and Smelser, N.J. (eds), *Theory of Culture* (Berkeley, Los Angeles, Oxford: University of California Press).

United Nations Organization (2008) *World Population Prospects. The 2008 Revision Population Database*, http://esa.un.org/unpp/ [30 April 2009].

Webber, D. (2006) 'A Consolidated Patrimonial Democracy? Democratization in Post-Suharto Indonesia', *Democratization*, 13 (3): 396–420.

Zinecker, H. (2005) 'Regime-Hybride und innerstaatlicher demokratischer Frieden', in Jahn, E., Fischer S. and Sahm A. (eds), *Die Zukunft des Friedens. Bd2: Die Friedens- und Konfliktforschung aus der Perspektive der jüngeren Generationen* (Wiesbaden: VS Verlag für Sozialwissenschaften).

13

Does Regime Type Matter? Southeast Asia's New Democracies and the Democratic Peace Hypothesis Revisited

Jürgen Rüland and Paruedee Nguitragool

Introduction

Studies on Southeast Asia's political systems and democratization are abundant and have reached a high level of sophistication. No less numerous are studies on the foreign policy of Southeast Asian countries. Surprisingly, though, there is a conspicuous lack of studies connecting democratization and foreign policy. Those that exist tend to take an outward-in perspective, in which democracy is the dependent variable (Kuhonta, 2006; Dosch, 2008, 2009; Emmerson, 2009). They explore the extent to which external influences support or obstruct democratic change. Only very recently have a few studies reversed the research perspective and started to examine how democratization impacts on foreign policy (Dosch, 2007; Jones, 2009; Rüland, 2009). Some of these studies challenge the liberal proposition that democratization facilitates a more peaceful, more cooperative, and more predictable foreign policy. Yet empirical evidence for such counterintuitive findings is still limited. It rests on either single-country (Rüland, 2009) or single-issue studies (Jones, 2009). This chapter broadens the research agenda by comparing the foreign policies of Southeast Asia's new democracies on a longitudinal basis across a greater number of issues. It shows that the scepticism about the democratic peace hypothesis is justified. Southeast Asia's new democracies pursue a foreign policy that does not differ significantly from their autocratic predecessors. One explanation for this finding is that in Southeast Asia, democratic as well as non-democratic regimes operate under the same nationalistic cognitive frame.

There are two major steps to our exploration. First, we briefly review the theoretical arguments associated with the democratic peace hypothesis. In

the second part, we examine the peacefulness, predictability and cooperative performance of the foreign policy of Southeast Asia's three third-wave
democracies, that is, the Philippines, Thailand and Indonesia, thereby
concentrating on the last major period of democratization, although we
supplement our findings with insights gained from previous phases of democratization. Our arguments are summarized in the conclusion.

From the democratic peace hypothesis to nationalist populism

The foreign policy of democracies is more peaceful, more predictable, and
more cooperative than that of any other government system. This conventional wisdom seems to be supported by powerful theoretical arguments,[1]
such as the democratic peace hypothesis, which assumes that democracies
do not go to war with each other (Doyle, 1983). Variants of the democratic
peace hypothesis go even further, claiming that democracies are also less
frequently involved in wars with non-democracies (Rummel, 1979, 1983)
and that disputes in which democracies are involved are less likely to escalate into wars than conflicts between non-democracies (Maoz and Abdolali,
1989). In other words, the greater the number of democracies, the less likely
the chance of war. Studies following this line of thought hold that the normative underpinnings of democracy, such as respect for human rights,
the rule of law and good governance, facilitate a culture of compromise,
tolerance and peaceful dispute settlement. By externalizing a non-violent
domestic political culture to the international arena, democracies are seen
as contributing to more peaceful interstate relations.

The belief that democracies are more predictable rests on research findings that democracies are more committed to the agreements and treaties
they have entered than autocratic regimes (Gaubatz, 1996). Institutionalized
leadership change and a concern for the rule of law are important factors
preventing wild swings in the foreign policy of democracies. The same
applies to the domestic constraints governments face in foreign policy-
making, which has been conceptualized as a two-level game linking the
national and the international dimensions (Putnam 1988). In this process,
the same factors that make it difficult for democratic states to enter into
international commitments also make it harder to get out of them (Gaubatz,
1996, p.121).

The putative engagement of democracies in international institutions
also contributes to a more transparent, compliant, and ultimately, predictable foreign policy (Mansfield et al., 2002, p.477). Based on the neo-institutionalist assumption that institutions foster communication among actors,
facilitate the exchange of information, and hence build up trust, participation in international institutions should therefore lead to a more cooperative foreign policy.

More recent studies have challenged these assumptions. One objection maintains that the mere correlation of foreign policy with regime type leads to ambiguous results. Empirical studies have shown that there is considerable variation in the foreign policy behaviour of democracies. The categorization of a polity as 'democracy' alone is insufficient for making inferences about the nature and quality of its foreign policy. Disaggregating it into subtypes, such as parliamentarian and presidential democracies or majoritarian and consensus democracies, has also yielded no clear patterns of foreign policy behaviour. An investigation of the foreign policy-making process is thus needed. Some authors have argued that a foreign policy congruent with the democratic peace hypothesis can be expected only in political systems in which legislatures and civil society meaningfully participate in foreign policy-making (Peterson, 1995; Auerswald, 1999; Dieterich, 2007; Jones, 2009).

Finally, the work of Mansfield and Snyder (1995) and Snyder (2000) suggests that the democratic peace hypothesis only applies to established democracies. According to them, new democracies and countries in democratic transition are more frequently involved in wars than other types of political systems. Mansfield and Snyder attribute this to the observation that new democracies are highly susceptible to nationalist appeals. This is because in 'pacted transitions', the domestic power equation is in flux and is characterized by an intense competition between old and new elites. As a 'doctrine for the people, but not necessarily by the people' (Snyder, 2000, p.36), nationalism is attractive because it allows political elites to respond to the opening of the political space without fully granting civic rights (ibid.). In the absence of strong and mature democratic institutions, and as a result of strong historical legacies, even reformist forces must resort to nationalist populism to mobilize popular support. Competing elites, outbidding each other in nationalist rhetoric, thus also transform foreign policy-making into an issue area where safeguarding national self-interest becomes an enabling factor for political success.

The same nationalist populism that thrives under the conditions of 'weak central authority, unstable domestic coalitions, and high-energy mass politics' (ibid.) is also the source of the unpredictability of foreign policy. Nationalist populism, like any populism, is grounded in rhetoric and prestige strategies. It is relatively gains-oriented and, resting on the realization of short-term benefits, also open to opportunism and frequent policy *voltes-face*.

While Mansfield and Snyder's focus on nationalism rests on an essentially consequentialist logic, it tacitly opens up research to a cognitive dimension which has so far been neglected in studies on the democratic peace hypothesis. Nationalism is far more than merely an expedient political ideology instrumentalized by political elites in the power struggles after a regime change. Its profound impact, particularly in terms of mobilizing power, owes a great deal to the reinforcing effect of the mental representations of past historical experience. Nationalism has been entrenched deeply in the collective memory of Southeast Asians by the historical experiences of Western imperialism, colonial humiliation, and the nostalgic reminiscences on a great, pre-colonial imperial past. Nationalism in Thailand and Indonesia, for instance, is thus associated with frequent references to the economically prosperous and militarily powerful kingdoms of Ayudhaya and Majapahit. These references unwittingly retain and continually revive age-old enmities among neighbours, like those between Thais and Burmese, Thais and Khmer, and Khmer and Vietnamese. When a conflict between historical antagonists erupts, deeply sedimented images of enmity bubble to the surface. This is further reinforced where nationalist ideology is associated with ancient political doctrines, such as the Thai or Javanese variants of the Indian *Arthasastra,*[2] which when combined with an antagonistic nationalist ideology, effectively reproduces political realism, which underlines the importance of national interest, sovereignty, power, competition and strategic alliances (Jetschke and Rüland, 2009). Thus a more democratic polity that is driven by strong nationalist sentiments may not necessarily result in a more peaceful, more cooperative and more predictable foreign policy.

Democracies – more peaceful?

Are democracies more peaceful than autocracies? We approach this question by *first* scrutinizing the extent to which Southeast Asia's new democracies have been involved in armed interstate conflict, whether they initiated military clashes, and how they managed tensions. According to the democratic peace hypothesis, we would expect that democracies show more restraint in employing military force and that they prefer negotiation, mediation and diplomacy as the means for solving crises. This leads us to investigate the role of the military in foreign policy-making in the *second* part of this section. Military and defence policies are also reviewed to analyze whether there is an increasing tendency toward the peaceful settlement of conflicts.

Direct involvement in armed conflict and management of interstate tension

Empirical evidence regarding the conflict behaviour of Southeast Asian democracies is rather ambiguous. Statistical data from the Uppsala Conflict Data Program and newspaper reports on border clashes show that there is no significant variation between democratic and non-democratic phases of government in the three countries (see Table 13.1).

While Thailand has been most frequently involved in armed military encounters, there is an almost equal distribution of armed interstate conflicts across all regime types. Thailand's strong engagement in the Second

Table 13.1   Involvement of Southeast Asia's new democracies in violent interstate conflict, 1946–2009

Country	Year	Issue	Opponent
Indonesia	1962	West New Guinea	Netherlands
	1963–66	Konfrontasi	Malaysia
	1975	East Timor	Portugal, East Timor
	1999 (near military encounter)	East Timor	Australia
	2005 (near military encounter)	Ambalat	Malaysia
Thailand	1946	Cambodia	France
	1960, 1961	Laos	Neutralists, Pathet Lao
	1966, 1977, 1978	Border clashes	Cambodia
	1965–74	South Vietnam	North Vietnam, Vietcong
	1980, 1981, 1982, 1983, 1984, 1985, 1986, 1987	Clashes at Cambodian–Thai border	Vietnam
	1984, 1986, 1987, 1988, 2008	Border clashes, territorial claims	Laos
	1999, 2001, 2002, 2005, 2007, 2009	Border clashes	Myanmar
	2003	Cambodia, riots	Cambodia
	2003–04	Iraq, coalition of the willing	Iraqi terrorists
	2008, 2009	Cambodia, Preah Vihear	Cambodia
Philippines	1966–72	South Vietnam	North Vietnam, Vietcong
	1995, 1996, 1997, 1998	Maritime clashes; Spratly Islands	China
	2003–04	Iraq, coalition of the willing	Iraqi terrorists

Sources: Uppsala Conflict Data Program, The Jakarta Post, Bangkok Post, The Nation.

Indochina War fell exclusively under military rule. In 1960 and 1961, Thai troops fought in Laos against Neutralists and the pro-communist Pathet Lao forces. The kingdom had also stationed more than 11,500 soldiers in South Vietnam to support the American war effort between 1965 and 1971 (Wyatt, 1984). Frequent border clashes with Vietnamese forces were recorded during the Vietnamese occupation of Cambodia in the 1980s, a period in which an incremental democratization process began, but it came to an abrupt end with the military coup of February 1991. After the 1992 democratic transition, border skirmishes between Thai and Burmese government troops intensified. In October 2008, gun battles also raged across the Thai–Cambodian border over territory near the contested Preah Vihear

Temple, which was awarded to Cambodia by a 1962 International Court of Justice ruling (Wyatt, 1984; Meyer, 2009).

In the Philippines, deployment of an expedition corps to Vietnam coincided with the pre-1972 democratic period. However, in contrast to Thailand, the Philippines almost exclusively sent non-combat troops. With 1450 soldiers, the number of troops deployed was significantly lower than in the Thai case. Interestingly, there were no interstate military encounters involving the Philippines during the authoritarian phase (1972–86). After re-democratization, between 1995 and 1998, minor and near encounters with Chinese navy units occurred. In 1995, China occupied Mischief Reef and other small islands in parts of the Spratly Archipelago claimed by the Philippines and built military installations on them, provoking counter-measures by the Philippine navy. The Philippines, like Thailand, also participated in the US-led coalition of the willing in the Iraq war, but withdrew its 51-man contingent after the kidnapping of a Filipino civilian in July 2004.

The Indonesian case is somewhat more supportive of the democratic peace hypothesis. All of the wars in which Indonesia was a party took place under authoritarian rule: the New Guinea campaign against the vestiges of Dutch colonialism in 1962; the *Konfrontasi,* a low-intensity war against the newly formed Federation of Malaysia between 1963 and 1966; and the annexation of East Timor in 1975, when the former Portuguese colony was on the verge of independence. After democratization, Indonesia became entangled in two near encounters: the first with Australia during the East Timor crisis in 1999,[3] the second with Malaysia in 2005, when Malaysian warships allegedly hit an Indonesian navy vessel that was operating in disputed waters near the Ambalat Block in the Sulawesi Sea.[4]

Our examination so far suggests that regime type does not seem to have strong explanatory value for the foreign policy behaviour in Southeast Asia. Looking deeper, cognitive factors surface and seem to be of greater significance. As noted earlier, the revival of indigenous or localized political traditions based on a great historical past also resurrect ancient enmities. The frequent border clashes between the Thai military, on the one hand, and Burmese and Cambodian forces, on the other hand, cannot be dissociated from the centuries-long history of pre-colonial rivalries for hegemony and of wars, mutual conquest and the resultant images of enmity. The enmity and rivalry between Thailand and Cambodia, for instance, can be traced back more than 1,000 years. Khmer influence in peninsular Southeast Asia waned after the Ayudhya Kingdom conquered the ancient Khmer capital of Angkor and brought large parts of the Khmer empire under Thai suzerainty (Kasetsiri, 1976; Wyatt, 1984). Thai hegemony over the Khmer heartlands was only broken when Cambodia became a French protectorate at the end of the nineteenth century. More recently, during the Second World War, Thailand invaded and temporarily annexed parts of Western Cambodia, which it had ceded to the French half a century earlier (Wyatt, 1984). As noted Thai historian Charnvit Kasetsiri comments, Thais' 'anti-French feelings [...] were transferred to anti-Cambodian feelings after Cambodia got independence'.[5] Together with the historical legacies of war, conquest and conflict, they contributed to a relationship that is characterized by mutual antipathies, chauvinism, and nationalist grandstanding, which from time to time exploded into (border) violence.

During the latest round of hostilities, which followed the signing of a joint communiqué between Cambodia and the Samak Sundaravej government on the Preah Vihear Temple,[6] the royalists' nationalist rhetoric against the communiqué was powerful enough to mobilize popular support in many parts of the country. With the anti-Thai riots in Phnom Penh in January 2003 still fresh in the minds of the Thai public (caused by a Thai actress's alleged remarks about the Thai-ness of Angkor Wat) and media campaigns, provocations from ultranationalist Thai groups in the territory surrounding the temple, and elections in both countries, tension eventually boiled over and erupted in border shootings between Thai and Cambodian military units in October 2008 (Meyer, 2009). After the nationalist Democrat Party succeeded in securing a narrow majority in a special parliamentary voting session in December 2008, tensions continued throughout the following year.[7]

The Preah Vihear dispute is a good example of how nationalist fervour emotionalizes foreign policy issues; disputes over territory and culture, that is, issues strongly affecting national identity, are often accompanied by shrill nationalist rhetoric, which sometimes does not even shy away from thinly veiled threats against neighbouring countries. Another example of such an outburst is the Indonesian President Habibie's calling Singapore 'a red dot' on the map (Smith, 2000). The meaning of this less than subtle message was that Indonesia could swallow up Singapore at any time. Habibie's successor, Abdurrahman Wahid, also accused the island state of 'underestimating the Malays' and of profiting from its relations with Indonesia;[8] he also threatened to join forces with Malaysia to cut off water supplies to Singapore. In response to the dispute with Malaysia over Ambalat, alleged infringements on Indonesian cultural products, and the discriminatory treatment of Indonesian labour migrants, Indonesian nationalists formed the Gerakan Ganyang Malaysia (Movement to Crush Malaysia), a slogan reminiscent of the *Konfrontasi* period (Freistein, 2006, p.23). While only a few legislators joined this movement, there was nevertheless agreement across party lines that Indonesia should use force in case the Malaysian navy continued to enter maritime zones claimed by Indonesia.

The fact that the tensions between Indonesia and Malaysia thus echo the competition between the ancient Srivijaya and the Javanese Majapahit empires is important (Liow, 2005, p.50). It is not only staunchly nationalist parties such as the Partai Demokrasi Indonesia–Perjuangan (PDI-P) or Golkar that recommended military action against Malaysia; even representatives of

Islamic parties such as Partai Keadilan dan Sejahtera (PKS) or Partai Bulan Bintang (PBB) joined this chorus.[9] Yusron Ihza Mahendra, a PBB-member of the legislature's foreign affairs and defence commission, for instance, was quoted as follows: 'For a start, we can recall our ambassador in Malaysia to show a firm political stance. We can also give official warnings to Malaysia, and if all measures fail, then we'll have no choice but to "declare war".'[10] The nationalist orientation of Golkar and the PDI-P is well received by a substantial segment of Indonesian voters. Despite losses, the two parties came in second and third in the 2009 parliamentary elections, garnering a combined 28 per cent of the votes. Other parties, like Prabowo Subianto's Gerindra (literally, Movement for a Greater Indonesia), use their name to cash in on nationalist sentiment.

The execution of Filipina migrant worker Flor Contemplacion in Singapore in 1995 for murder aroused strong nationalist reactions in the Philippines. What enraged the Philippine public was the seemingly high-handed behaviour of the Singaporean authorities, who despite the doubts surrounding the case, ignored the appeals of Philippine President Fidel V. Ramos for clemency, or to at least delay the execution. In the process, the Philippines recalled their ambassador to Singapore, and Singaporean property in the Philippines was vandalized by angry mobs (Kessler, 2009).

This policy of rhetorical brinkmanship is often overlooked when the achievements of ASEAN and its norm of peaceful dispute settlement are highlighted (Kivimäki, 2008). While it is true that outright war could be prevented in these cases, the foreign policy behaviour of Southeast Asian democracies nevertheless does not coincide with the prescriptions of the democratic peace hypothesis. Nationalist rhetoric undermines mutual trust, reproduces the worldviews of political realism, reconstitutes historical legacies of enmity and forestalls change of identities.

The role of the military and defence policy

The influence of realist worldviews and nationalism on the foreign policy behaviour of Southeast Asian democracies can also be demonstrated by examining the influence of specific interest groups on foreign policymaking (Jones, 2009). The military, a functional group with a by tradition exceptionally strong nationalist outlook, is of particular interest to us. The Indonesian Defence University's motto, for instance, is 'Identity, Nationalism, Integrity', and a major military think tank, Lemhanas, is also known as National Resilience Institute. Nationalism in the military reflects the decisive role of the armed forces in the struggle for independence and in defending the nation against external and internal threats. Even if, as in Indonesia, the armed forces have increasingly come under civilian supremacy and democratic oversight (Sebastian, 2006; Mietzner, 2006, 2009; Beeson and Bellamy, 2008), they still tenaciously defend the remnants of the domains reserved to them under authoritarian rule. The military thus retains a major influence on national defence and the security-related dimensions of foreign policy. A recent case in point is the Thai military's hard-line policy in the Preah Vihear conflict with Cambodia, which thwarted the more conciliatory moves of the Thai government (Meyer, 2009, p.58).

Military influence on foreign policy-making also persists, even though a marked democratization of foreign policy-making has taken place. In Indonesia, the number of actors involved in foreign policy-making has substantially increased after regime change. A much more powerful legislature, a vibrant civil society, and independent think tanks, the media and academia have gradually eroded the erstwhile executive dominance in foreign affairs (Dosch, 2007, 2008; Rüland, 2009). Yet quite paradoxically, the legislature often joins the military in championing what is perceived as the national interest. The common denominator in this unlikely alliance is nationalism. This finding questions the democratic peace argument that a democratized foreign policy-making process with a strong parliament at the centre creates a more peaceful foreign policy (Dieterich, 2007).

This leads us to the question of whether the democracies initiated the hostilities with their non-democratic neighbours, or if their entanglements in violent conflicts were only acts of self-defence. Once more, the evidence is mixed. In the Thai–Burmese relationship, geography seems to matter as an intervening variable, exacerbating the cognitive factors discussed earlier. As most of Myanmar's ethnic insurgents and drug lords have their strongholds in regions close to the Thai border, fighting often spills over into Thailand when Burmese troops cross the border in hot pursuit of their opponents. Contributing to the volatile border situation is the location of refugee camps on Thai soil, suspected by the Burmese army to act as sanctuaries for rebels. Such perceptions reflect past experiences, when the Thai military had the reputation of using the ethnic rebels as buffers and as a device to weaken their Burmese archrival.

A more obvious case is the situation in the 1980s along the Thai–Cambodian border, where the Khmer resistance against the Vietnamese-supported Hun Sen regime operated from Thai soil. Border clashes with the Vietnamese or Cambodian government forces were thus indeed the result of Thai connivance with the rebels and tacit offers of sanctuary. In the conflict over Preah Vihear, hostilities seemed to have been provoked by the Thai military. Yet, Thais could claim that the anti-Thai riots of 2003 had severely eroded their trust in a peaceful dispute settlement and that the Cambodian declaration of Preah Vihear as a *Cambodian* World Heritage site in 2008 was a provocation. Similarly, Indonesians contend that their military alert in the Sulawesi Sea is the result of Malaysian military provocations. In the case of the disputed islands in the South China Sea, the Philippines can argue persuasively that they only responded to Chinese encroachments on Philippine territory.

Nationalist rhetoric and armed clashes seem to suggest that Southeast Asian democracies are not as peaceful as would be suggested by the democratic peace hypothesis. But to what extent do Southeast Asian democracies resort to mediation, adjudication, negotiation and diplomacy in interstate disputes? Again, the picture is ambiguous. Malaysia and Indonesia went to the International Court of Justice (ICJ) to settle their differences over the two disputed islands of Ligatan and Sipadan. Yet the question of why they did not refer the case to the ASEAN High Council, a dispute settlement mechanism established precisely for disputes of this kind, remains. Eventually, Malaysia won the case and Indonesia complied with the ruling, precisely as one would expect of a democracy committed to the rule of law. But the ruling pre-empted any legal recourse in the Ambalat conflict, where Indonesia – deterred by the adverse decision of the ICJ – refuses to agree to a judicial settlement.

In the Philippine–Chinese dispute over islands in the Spratly Archipelago and in the Malaysian–Indonesian dispute over Ambalat, there was or still is considerable diplomatic activity, but so far, only the Philippine–Chinese dispute could be pacified. The Spratly Declaration of Conduct signed between China and ASEAN in 2002 markedly reduced tensions in the contested area, even though it is not a binding treaty. By contrast, Indonesian–Malaysian talks on Ambalat have not been able to defuse the tensions so far. Government-to-government negotiations have also intermittently defused Thai–Burmese border tensions but likewise could not prevent the skirmishes flaring up again.

The record is somewhat less ambiguous when it comes to arms acquisition and military alliances. None of the three democracies pursued aggressive weapons acquisition programmes or entered threatening military alliances. A substantial increase in the military budget in Thailand[11] and Indonesia during the 2000s does not signify any major change in their defence policies. By reducing the military's extra-budgetary self-financing schemes, the budget increase is part of security sector reform in Indonesian (Human Rights Watch, 2006). With its *'bebas dan aktif'* (free and active) doctrine, Indonesia has always avoided becoming a member of multilateral military alliances. Instead, it prefers bilateral defence cooperation under legal treaties; military agreements with China, India, Australia and Singapore are good examples.[12] Thailand closed US military bases in 1976, and more recently, it rejected American requests to establish US weapons storehouses in Thailand (Wagener, 2009, pp.49–50).

In a landmark decision, the Philippine Senate ended the Philippine–American military bases agreement in 1991, and until 1992, the Philippines hosted the strategically important US Seventh Fleet in Subic Bay and a major air base near Angeles City. Six years later, in light of the Chinese advancement in the South China Sea, the Ramos administration partly reversed this decision by signing a Visiting Forces Agreement (VFA) with Washington, which allowed US warships to refuel and make repairs in the Philippines. After 11 September 2001, the Philippine government also agreed to station 660 Green Berets in the country under the auspices of the Balikatan exercise. Officially acting as advisers, the troops actively supported the Philippine military in its fight against Abu Sayyaf terrorists in the Sulu Archipelago. Thus, in general, the defence and security policies of Southeast Asia's democracies do not differ much from those of the non-democracies, except perhaps Myanmar. They are characterized by nominal, but not necessarily relative, increases in the defence budget, arms modernization programs, and low-intensity defence cooperation with major regional powers and neighbours – in fact, a policy of hedging and soft balancing against the major powers active in the region, in particular the US and China (He and Feng, 2008; Kuik, 2008).

Democracies – more cooperative?

Are democracies more cooperative than non-democracies? To answer this question, we examine the extent to which democratic governments join international organizations and international treaties. Are they party to more international cooperation agreements than non-democracies? Are they joining treaties that facilitate behaviour in line with the democratic peace hypothesis? Of particular interest for this line of questioning are treaties and organizations promoting key democratic norms such as human rights. To what extent have new democracies joined human rights treaties? And to what extent have democratic governments strengthened regional integration? Using information derived from databanks on international government organizations and qualitative research, we analyze how our three Southeast Asian democracies fared in this respect in the following sections.

A databank on international organizations compiled by Northwestern University[13] does not provide a clear picture on the membership of democracies in international organizations. Other available data, however, suggest that Southeast Asia's new democracies did not eagerly join international organizations. For Indonesia, only four new memberships were recorded for the period 1998–2009, ten for the Philippines for the period 1986–2009, and 12 for Thailand for the period 1992–2006.

An examination of the accession of Southeast Asian democracies to UN human rights conventions provides the expected picture. Table 13.2 indicates that democracies are more inclined than autocracies to make human rights commitments. This becomes particularly evident if we take a closer look at amendments to human rights conventions. Most of these amendments tightened existing rules, which may explain the fact that, in all of these cases, only democratic governments signed and ratified the amendments. The Philippines has signed and ratified the greatest number of

Table 13.2 Accession of Southeast Asian democracies to United Nations human rights conventions

Country	16 United Nations Human Rights Conventions, 1948–2008		10 Amendments of Human Rights Conventions, 1948–2008	
	Signed	Ratified	Signed	Ratified
Philippines	14 (11)	12 (9)	6 (6)	4 (4)
Indonesia	10 (6)	4 (2)	4 (4)	0 (0)
Thailand	7 (3)	1 (1)	4 (4)	1 (1)

In parentheses: Number of conventions signed or ratified by democratic governments.

Source: Amnesty International.

declarations, signing 14 out of 16 human rights conventions and ratifying 12 of them. Eleven of the 14 declarations were signed and 11 out of 12 ratified by democratic governments. The Philippines also signed six out of ten amendments to these conventions and ratified four. But like Indonesia and Thailand, it has so far failed to ratify the Rome Statute of the International Criminal Court.

With an impressive number of human rights agreements, the Philippines has assumed a leadership role in pressuring other, undemocratic states in Southeast Asia to adopt international principles and to soften their political stances. Ironically, this international status was pursued throughout the 1990s and 2000s, despite worsening domestic human rights records. Indonesia and Thailand signed and ratified many fewer declarations. What is remarkable is the strong discrepancy between signing and ratifying human rights conventions. Interestingly, in Thailand autocratic regimes have signed more human rights declarations than democratic governments. Commitments have also been circumscribed by addenda to rights conventions, which means that Indonesia and Thailand only cooperate as long as it does not affect their national sovereignty. Cooperation entailing a sacrifice of sovereignty is therefore eschewed.

Mansfield, Milner and Pevehouse recently argued that democracies are more inclined than autocracies to join regional integration schemes, but contrary to conventional wisdom, may be averse to deepening regional integration (Mansfield et al., 2008). In examining these propositions, we once more find ambiguous evidence. Table 13.3 correlates accession to regional or sub-regional organizations with regime type. The table suggests that, indeed, democracies have joined more regional organizations than autocracies. However, many of these regional organizations were either short-lived (ASA, Maphilindo, Asian Cooperation Dialogue, Southwest Pacific Forum) or are not very active (BIMSTEC, Mekong–Ganga Cooperation, GMS, IOR-ARC, East Asia Summit, ACM-ECS). In some cases they were formed for reasons

Table 13.3 Southeast Asian democracies' membership in and year of accession to regional organizations

Regional organization	Year of foundation	Accession under democratic rule	Accession under autocratic rule
Association of Southeast Asia (ASA)	1961	Philippines (1961)	Indonesia (1961)
Maphilindo	1963	Philippines (1963)	Indonesia (1963)
Association of Southeast Asian Nations (ASEAN)	1967	Philippines (1967)	Indonesia (1967) Thailand (1967)
Asia-Pacific Economic Cooperation (APEC)	1989	Philippines (1989) Thailand (1989) (semi-democratic)	Indonesia (1989)
Singapore–Johor–Riau (Sijori) Growth Triangle	1989		Indonesia (1989)
Northern Growth Triangle Indonesia–Malaysia–Thailand	1993	Thailand (1993)	Indonesia (1993)
ASEAN Regional Forum (ARF)	1994	Thailand (1994) Philippines (1994)	Indonesia (1994)
East ASEAN Growth Area (EAGA)	1995	Philippines (1995)	Indonesia (1995)
ASEAN Plus Three (APT)	1997	Philippines (1997) Thailand (1997)	Indonesia (1997)
Greater Mekong Subregional Economic Cooperation (GMS)	1992	Thailand (1992)	
Indian Ocean Rim Association for Regional Cooperation (IOR-ARC)	1997	Thailand (1997)	Indonesia (1997)
Bay of Bengal Initiative for Multi-Sectoral Technical and Economic Cooperation (BIMSTEC)	1997	Thailand (1997)	
Southwest Pacific Forum	2000	Indonesia (2000) Philippines (2000)	
Mekong–Ganga Cooperation	2000	Thailand (2000)	
Asian Cooperation Dialogue (ACD)	2001	Thailand (2001) Indonesia (2001) Philippines (2001)	
Ayeyawady–Chao Phraya–Mekong Economic Cooperation Strategy (ACM-ECS)	2002	Thailand (2002)	
East Asia Summit	2005	Indonesia (2005) Philippines (2005) Thailand (2005)	

Source: Authors' compilation.

other than regional cooperation; rather, their formation was a reflection of the founding nations' regional leadership ambitions, of political leaders' search for domestic legitimacy, and of distrust in the efficacy of existing regional organizations, and was part of institutional balancing strategies. The flurry of new regional organizations and forums being formed after 1997 is also reflective of the paralysis of ASEAN during the Asian financial crisis, which had raised severe doubts inside and outside Southeast Asia about the resilience and effectiveness of the grouping and spurred a search for alternatives (Rüland, 2000; Smith and Jones, 2007).

The record concerning the activities of democracies in deepening regional integration is also ambiguous. Although Thailand was calling for 'flexible engagement' in 1998, it was Anwar Ibrahim, then Deputy Prime Minister of Malaysia, who first openly criticized ASEAN's non-interference norm. Concerned about the contagion effect of the Asian financial crisis, which highlighted the increasing interdependence of ASEAN member countries and the ineffectiveness of national solutions, Ibrahim proposed 'constructive intervention'. The replacement of 'non-intervention' was, however, watered down by his ASEAN colleagues, who could only agree on 'enhanced interaction' and retained the principle of non-interference. The subsequent government of Prime Minister Thaksin Shinawatra, coming into office in 2001, quickly returned to the non-interference norm, especially after troubles started in Thailand's predominantly Muslim-populated south. Finally, the proposal to establish the ASEAN Free Trade Area (AFTA) as a vehicle to deepen economic integration was made by Anand Panyarachun's non-elected interim government, whereas the proposal to leapfrog from AFTA to an ASEAN Economic Community was spearheaded by the increasingly authoritarian Thaksin government and Singapore, a semi-democracy. Yet despite its integration rhetoric, Thailand has remained one of the most protectionist countries in the region (Ravenhill, 2001).

More recently, Indonesia has become a champion of democratizing and deepening ASEAN. In the debate on the ASEAN Charter, strong demands were aired in the media, in the legislature and in academia to discard non-interference, to enhance ASEAN's responsiveness by the introduction of majority decisions, to establish an effective ASEAN human rights mechanism, and to reform ASEAN from an essentially elitist, intergovernmental organization to a more people-centred one. In the end, however, the Indonesian government settled for a diluted form of the ASEAN Charter that retained the non-interference norm and created only a weak human rights mechanism.[14] Yet, it is possible to show that the calls for democratizing ASEAN were a thinly veiled rhetorical ploy for legitimizing Indonesian claims for regional leadership (Rüland, 2009). In the years following the Asian financial crisis and during the turbulent transition, Indonesia had lost its *primus inter pares* status in ASEAN. Economically recovered and politically more stable, it ended its inward-looking phase and returned to an active foreign policy to regain its former leadership status. That democratization is used to frame nationalist policies is reflected by the fact that Indonesia adamantly sticks to national sovereignty when it itself becomes the target of interference. Cases in point are the haze problem (Nguitragool, forthcoming) and separatist uprisings, such as in Papua. Although Indonesia has signed the ASEAN Transboundary Haze Pollution Treaty, it has not ratified it and is thus not obligated to uphold the provisions of the treaty. Moreover, frustrated by the opposition, some Indonesian think tanks and media have increasingly demanded that the country downsize its engagement in ASEAN and instead develop closer relations with major powers outside the region such as China and India.

In contrast to the Thai and Indonesian roles in ASEAN, the Philippines has never been a leading regional player. Their support of Surin's 'flexible engagement' initiative in 1998 and advocacy for an ASEAN parliament fizzled out inconclusively. The fact that the Philippines is a democracy did not at any point have a marked impact on the development of ASEAN.

Summing up, we may note that Southeast Asian democracies are slightly more cooperative than their non-democratic predecessor governments, but the difference is not significant. Democracies are driven by the same nationalist policy imperatives that drive non-democracies, which also limit their cooperative potential.

Democracies – more predictable?

Our survey of the cooperative tendencies and participation in international treaties and institutions leads us to the question of whether democracies' foreign policy is more predictable than that of non-democracies, and if yes, to what extent. In political science and international relations this is a contested question. Contrary to the assumption that information flows within international institutions facilitate cooperation and increase the predictability of foreign policy, critics point to democratically elected governments' dependence on public sentiment, which would expose democracies to populism and promote frequent policy shifts. In this section, we examine three indicators: 1) the frequency of abrupt changes in the security policy of Southeast Asian democracies; 2) changes in their foreign policy doctrines; and 3) major shifts in the regional cooperation agenda.

When we speak of abrupt changes in the area of security policy, we mean major strategic reorientations. Such realignments concern relations with the two major powers in Asia, the US and China. An incentive for shifts in the relationship to these two countries could be China's rise to global power status and the expectation that it may challenge US hegemony in the not so near future. Such a shift in the global power distribution would have major repercussions on security in Southeast Asia. Like during the Cold War era, the region would then become an arena for great power competition.

This realization, enhanced by the relatively fresh memories of colonization and pervasive nationalist ideology, has resulted in a power-sensitive policy orientation tilting toward pragmatic *realpolitik*.

Southeast Asian nations seek to accommodate lingering distrust of Chinese intentions by a policy of 'hedging' (Kuik, 2008). Hedging denotes a two-pronged, counteracting security strategy located on the continuum between bandwagoning and balancing. While bandwagoning stands for a generally accommodating, cooperative foreign policy approach toward the perceived threat, balancing is a security strategy by which smaller states seek alignments with stronger partners that may also include a military dimension (Kuik, 2008). The policies of Southeast Asian democracies vary in the mix of these two components and may be adjusted in response to new political configurations. Thailand's foreign policy behaviour tilts more toward the bandwagoning–balancing continuum than that of Indonesia. The Philippine security strategy is more based on balancing China than on bandwagoning. In the Thai case, there are bandwagoning elements evident in their support of controversial Chinese policies toward Tibet, Taiwan and the Falun Gong group (ibid., p.169) and in their military cooperation with China, which can be traced back to the Cambodian conflict in the 1980s. But it should be noted that Indonesia, too, has established cooperative relations with the Chinese military. All of these countries have engaged China in a dense network of diplomatic contacts, both on a regional and a bilateral level. Cooperative elements are further strengthened through economic ties with China under an ASEAN–China Free Trade Area (Dent, 2006). All three Southeast Asian democracies have markedly intensified economic transactions with China. Thailand increased its exports to China from 3.1 per cent in 1997 to 9.7 per cent in 2007, Indonesia from 4.2 per cent to 8.5 per cent, and the Philippines from 1 per cent to 11.4 per cent (Eckstein, 2009, p.67). By contrast, the balancing component includes the involvement of other powers in regional affairs and military cooperation (Kuik, 2008). All three states want to keep the US in the region as a balancer, and all three enjoy military relations with the US and other partners that include procurement of military equipment, training, and joint exercises.

Despite these variations, Southeast Asian democracies have been rather consistent in their hedging strategy. The probably most far-reaching policy shift was the termination of the US bases agreement by the Philippines in 1992, a decision that has been partly reversed, though, by the Visiting Forces Agreement of 1998. Another major policy change under a democratic government in the area of security dates back to the early 1970s; Thai Prime Minister Kukrit Pramoj made the decision to close US military installations in Thailand and to open diplomatic relations with China (Morell and Samudavanija, 1981). However, both decisions did not come as a big surprise at the time. After the Nixon doctrine was proclaimed and US forces were withdrawn from Indochina, stationing troops in Thailand was no longer in line with America's strategic interests in Southeast Asia. Thailand's diplomatic recognition of China was likewise a consequence of the US defeat in Vietnam and Washington's subsequent thaw in relations with Beijing; Prime Minister Chatichai Choonhavan's sudden announcement in 1989 of a new policy in the Cambodia conflict occurred during a period of progressive democratization but was hardly out of tune with developments in Indochina. Soon thereafter, the United States also ended their support of the Khmer resistance coalition, of which the genocidal Khmer Rouge was the most anachronistic party.

Nor did the three countries' earlier autocratic regimes experience major swings in their security policy. The exception was Indonesia's pro-Chinese policy in the mid-1960s, proclaiming a Jakarta–Hanoi–Bejing–Pyongyang axis under President Sukarno's 'guided democracy', and President Suharto's return to closer relations with the West after 1967. Attempts by the authoritarian regime under Thanin Kraivichien and the Thai military to reverse the rapprochement with China initiated by the democratic predecessor governments were short-lived. The Vietnamese invasion of Cambodia in 1979 forged closer ties between Thailand and China than ever before.

Insensitivity to regime type is not only a characteristic of the three democracies' security policy, it is also typical for foreign policy doctrines. The most illustrative case in this respect is Indonesia. Of all the democracies, Indonesia has developed the most articulate foreign policy doctrines. *Bebas-dan-aktif* (free and active) and *wawasan nusantara* (archipelagic principle) can be traced back to the 1940s and 1950s, while *ketahanan nasional* (national resilience) was conceptualized by the Suharto regime. However, in a political climate in which nationalist populism thrives, all three doctrines survived political transition.

Vibrant regional cooperation requires that member states have predictable policies. Southeast Asian democracies are predictable in one respect, although this has repeatedly thrown ASEAN into disarray: they are more critical of ASEAN's time-honoured non-interference norm than autocracies. Surin Pitsuwan's proposal of 'flexible intervention'; Indonesian demands for a more substantive ASEAN Charter; Indonesian, Philippine and Thai (under governments led by the Democrat Party) criticism of the reform-averse military junta in Myanmar; and Philippine President Estrada's call on Malaysian Prime Minister Mahathir to release his deputy Anwar Ibrahim after the latter's arrest for spurious, politically motivated charges – all of these initiatives caused serious irritations among ASEAN members. But again, such initiatives are not the exclusive prerogative of democracies. Anwar Ibrahim's call for 'constructive intervention' and Prime Minister Mahathir's outburst calling for an expulsion of Myanmar from ASEAN due to the embarrassment its human rights violations and harsh dictatorship had caused to the grouping demonstrate that non-democracies, too, may act at times in an unpredictable way.

We may thus once more conclude that the Southeast Asian examples do not provide persuasive evidence for claims that foreign policy is closely related to regime type. Neither democratic governments nor autocratic regimes underwent frequent or profound policy shifts. The bottom line for both was the desire to preserve a maximum of foreign policy autonomy and national sovereignty. This brings us back to the strong role of nationalism in foreign policy-making. As an ideational factor, nationalism had a strong impact on all regimes. While under authoritarian regimes the armed forces formed the vanguard of nationalism, the nationalist populism of political entrepreneurs and their political parties became a factor no democratic government could ignore.

Conclusion

The insights gained from only three cases are too limited for far-reaching conclusions, but they reinforce our scepticism against the democratic peace hypothesis. They suggest that regime type variables do not have strong explanatory value for the foreign policy behaviour in Southeast Asia. Indeed, the correlation between regime type and foreign policy is rather weak. Southeast Asia's democracies are not necessarily more peaceful than non-democracies. Nationalism, with its concomitant connotations of sovereignty, foreign policy autonomy and state survival, is deeply ingrained in the collective memory of elites and the broader public alike. Democracies and non-democracies are thus strongly influenced by the same cognitive dispositions that a more than 40-year history of cooperation under the auspices of ASEAN has so far not been able to erase. ASEAN regionalism and other forms of international cooperation may mitigate the effects of nationalist policies and reduce the unpredictability of *realpolitik*, but nationalist populism at home still retains old images of enmity and distrust. This explains why disputes occasionally turn violent and why they are often accompanied by aggressive nationalist rhetoric. Nationalism also reduces the cooperative performance of the three democracies which is not necessarily stronger than in the case of non-democracies and which has only in the case of the Philippines led to the full (formal) adoption of cosmopolitan human rights norms.

Notes

The authors would like to thank Philipp Eckstein, Nikolas Keßels, Julia Turchenko, and Jan-Simon Dörflinger for their capable research assistance. The study also benefited from fieldwork conducted in Indonesia in February and March 2008 by one of the authors as part of a study on 'Parliaments and Security Sector Governance in Indonesia and Nigeria' funded by the German Peace Research Foundation (DSF), Osnabrück, Germany.

1. For a thorough review of the literature on democratic peace, see Dieterich (2007). The following section draws on this review.
2. The *Arthasastra* is an ancient Indian political treatise that, similar to Machiavelli's *Prince*, preaches political realism and advises how a ruler may become a great conqueror. In addition to diplomacy and war, it covers other issues such as state, economy and administration. See, for instance, Boesche (2003).
3. See *The Jakarta Post*, 30 October 1999 and 1 November 1999.
4. See *The Jakarta Post*, 16 April 2005.
5. IPSNews, 7 November 2009. (http://ipsnews.net/newsasp?idnews=49180) (accessed 16 November 2009).
6. The Samak government was known as a surrogate political apparatus for ousted former Prime Minister Thaksin Shinawatra.
7. See channelnewsasia.com, 3 April 2009 (accessed 11 October 2009).
8. *The Jakarta Post*, 28 November 2000.
9. *Suara Pembaruan*, 3 March 2007 (accessed 13 July 2008) and 5 March 2007.(http://www.suarapembaruan.com/News/2007/03/05/Nasional/nas01.htm) (accessed 11 April 2008) and 'Indonesia Flexes its Diplomatic Muscle', Singapore Institute of International Affairs.
10. See *The Jakarta Post*, 9 June 2009.
11. The Thai government approved a defence budget of more than 10 billion baht (US $300 million) in 2009 in order to replace obsolete military vehicles.
12. However, the Defence Cooperation Agreement with Singapore signed in April 2007 has so far not been ratified by the Indonesian legislature.
13. See Northwestern University, Evanston and Chicago, Illinois http://www.library.northwestern.edu/govinfo/resource/internat/igo.html (accessed 29 September 2009).
14. See *The Jakarta Post*, 24 July 2009, pp. 9 and 11.

References

Auerswald, D. (1999) 'Inward Bound: Domestic Institutions and Military Conflicts', *International Organization*, 53 (3): 469–504.
Beeson, M. and Bellamy, J.A. (2008) *Securing Southeast Asia: The politics of Security Sector Reform* (London and New York: Routledge).
Boesche, R. (2003) 'Kautilya's Arthasastra on War and Diplomacy in Ancient India', *Journal of Military History*, 67 (1): 9–38.
Dent, C.M. (2006) *New Free Trade Agreements in the Asia-Pacific* (Basingstoke: Palgrave Macmillan).
Dieterich, S. (2007) *Demokratische Außenpolitik = Friedliche Außenpolitik? EinLiteraturbericht*, Düsseldorf: Parlamentarische Kontrolle von Sicherheitspolitik, paks_ working-paper 2.
Dosch, J. (2007) *The Changing Dynamics of Southeast Asian Politics* (London: Lynne Rienner).
Dosch, J. (2008) 'ASEAN's Reluctant Liberal Turn and the Thorny Road to Democracy Promotion', *The Pacific Review*, 21 (4): 527–545.
Dosch, J. (2009) 'Sovereignty Rules: Human Security, Civil Society, and the Limits of Liberal Reform', in Emmerson, D.K. (ed.), *Hard Choices* (Singapore: Institute of Southeast Asian Studies).
Doyle, M.W. (1983) 'Kant, Liberal Legacies and Foreign Affairs', *Philosophy and Public Affairs*, 12 (3): 205–235.

Eckstein, P. (2009) *Power, Trade, and the Asia-Pacific. A Review of Sino-American Balance of Power in the Region*, M.A. thesis, University of Freiburg.

Emmerson, D.K. (ed.) (2009) *Hard Choices* (Singapore: Institute of Southeast Asian Studies).

Freistein, K. (2006) *Die Praxis des 'ASEAN Way'. Über den Umgang mit zwischenstaatlichen Konflikten in Südostasien* (Frankfurt a.M.: Hessische Stiftung für Friedensforschung, HSFK-Report 4).

Gaubatz, K.T. (1996) 'Democratic States and Commitment in International Relations', *International Organization*, 50 (1): 109–139.

He, K. and Feng, H. (2008) 'If Not Soft Balancing, Then What? Reconsidering Soft Balancing and U.S. Policy Toward China', *Security Studies*, 17: 363–395.

Human Rights Watch (2006) *Too High a Price: The Human Rights Costs of the Indonesia Military's Economic Activities*, <http://www.hrw.org/en/reports/2006/06/20/too-highprice>, (accessed 23 November 2008).

IPSNews (2009), 16 November, <http://ipsnews.net/newsasp?idnews=49180>, (accessed 16 November 2009).

Jakarta Post (1999) 'Book Says Habibie Close to Declaring War', October 30, <http://thejakartapost.com>, (accessed 26 May 2006).

*Jakarta Post (*2005) 'RI, Malaysia Navies Make Peace Following Ambalat Incident', April 16, <http://thejakartapost.com>, (accessed 18 September 2008).

Jakarta Post (2009) 'Government Sticks to Diplomacy in Ambalat Issue', 9 June <http://www.thejakartapost.com>, (accessed 25 October 2009).

Jakarta Post (2009) 'A not-so-righteous body', 24 July, <http://www.thejakartapost.com>, (accessed on February 2010).

Jetschke, A. and Rüland, J. (2009) 'Decoupling Rhetoric and Practice: The Cultural Limits of ASEAN Cooperation', *The Pacific Review,* 22 (2): 179–203.

Jones, L. (2009) 'Democratization and Foreign Policy in Southeast Asia: The Case of the ASEAN Inter-Parliamentary Myanmar Caucus', *Cambridge Review of International Affairs,* 22 (3): 387–406.

Kasetsiri, C. (1976) *The Rise of Ayudhya. A History of Siam in the Fourteenth and Fifteenth Century* (Oxford: Oxford University Press).

Kessler, C. (2009) 'Democratic Citizenship and Labour Migration in East Asia', *Journal of East Asian Studies*, 8 (2): 181–204.

Kivimäki, T. (2008) 'Power, Interest or Culture – Is there a Paradigm that Explains ASEAN's Political Best?', *The Pacific Review*, 21 (4): 431–450.

Kuhonta, E.M. (2006) 'Walking Tightrope: Democracy Versus Sovereignty in ASEAN's Illiberal Peace', *The Pacific Review*, 19 (3): 337–358.

Kuik, C.C. (2008) 'The Essence of Hedging: Malaysia and Singapore's Response to a Rising China', *Contemporary Southeast Asia*, 30 (2): 159–185.

Liow, J.C. (2005) *The Politics of Indonesia-Malaysia Relations: One Kin, Two Nations* (Oxon and New York: Routledge).

Mansfield, E.D. and Snyder, J. (1995) 'Democratization and the Danger of War', *International Security*, 20 (1): 5–38.

Mansfield, E.D., Milner, H.V. and Pevehouse, J.C. (2008) 'Democracy, Veto Players and the Depth of Regional Integration', *The World Economy*, 31 (1): 67–96.

Mansfield, E.D., Milner, H.V. and Rosendorff, P.B. (2002) 'Why Democracies Cooperate More: Electoral Control and International Trade Agreements', *International Organization*, 56 (3): 477–513.

Maoz, Z. and Abdolali, N. (1989) 'Regime Types and International Conflict, 1817-1976', *Journal of Conflict Resolution*, 33 (1): 3–35.

Meyer; S. (2009) 'Preah Vihear Reloaded – Der Grenzkonflikt zwischen Thailand und Kambodscha', *Journal of Current Southeast Asian Affairs*, 28 (1): 47–68.

Mietzner, M. (2006) 'The Politics of Military Reform in Post-Soeharto Indonesia: Elite Conflict, Nationalism, and Institutional Resistance', *Policy Studies Series 23*, East-West Center Washington, Washington, DC.

Mietzner, M. (2009) *Military Politics, Islam, and the State in Indonesia. From Turbulent Transition to Democratic Consolidation* (Singapore: ISEAS).

Morell, D. and Samudavanija, C. (1981) *Political Conflict in Thailand: Reform, Reaction, and Revolution* (Cambridge: Oelgeschlager).

Nguitragool, P. (forthcoming) *An ASEAN Environmental Regime? Fighting Transboundary Haze Pollution in Southeast Asia* (London: Routledge).

Peterson, S. (1995) 'How Democracies Differ: Public Opinion, State Structure, and the Lessons of the Fashoda Crisis', *Security Studies*, 5 (1): 415–430.

Putnam, R.D. (1988) 'Diplomacy and Domestic Politics: The Logic of Two-Level Games', *International Organization*, 42 (3): 427–460.

Ravenhill, J. (2001) *APEC and the Construction of Pacific Rim Regionalism* (Cambridge: Cambridge University Press).

Rüland, J. (2000) 'ASEAN and the Asian Crisis: Theoretical and Practical Consequences for Southeast Asian Regionalism', *The Pacific Review*, 13 (3): 421–451.

Rüland, J. (2009) 'Deepening ASEAN Cooperation through Democratization? The Indonesian Legislature and Foreign Policymaking', *International Relations of the Asia-Pacific*, 9 (3): 373–402.

Rummel, R.J (1979) *Understanding Conflict and War* (Beverly Hills: Sage).

Rummel, R.J. (1983) 'Libertarianism and International Violence', *Journal of Conflict Resolution*, 27 (1): 27–71.

Sebastian, L. (2006) *Realpolitik Ideology. Indonesia's Use of Military Force* (Singapore: Institute of Southeast Asian Studies).

Smith, A. L. (2000) 'Indonesia's Foreign Policy under Abdurrahman Wahid: Radical or Status Quo State?', *Contemporary Southeast Asia*, 22 (3): 498–526.

Smith, M.L.R. and Jones, D.M. (2007) 'Making Process, Not Progress. ASEAN and the Evolving East Asian Regional Order', *International Security*, 32 (1): 148–184.

Snyder, J. (2000) *From Voting to Violence. Democratization and Nationalist Conflict* (New York and London: W.W. Norton & Company).

Suara Pembaruan (2007) *Pemerinthah Harus Tegas Soal Ambalat. DPR: Malaysia Anggap Remeh Indonesia,* 3 March, <http://www.suarapembaruan.com>, (accessed 13 July 2008).

Uppsala Conflict Data Progamme (2009) <http://www.pcr.uu.se/gpdatabase/search.php>.

Wagener, M. (2009) 'Zuverlässiges Königreich. Die USA, Thailand und die Logik des bandwagoning', *Journal of Current Southeast Asian Affairs*, 28 (3): 39–80.

Wyatt, D. K. (1984) *Thailand: A Short History* (London and Bangkok: Yale University Press).

14
Conclusion: The Challenges and Prospects of Democratic Governance in Southeast Asia

Aurel Croissant and Marco Bünte

Introduction

The purpose of this final chapter is to connect the insights derived from the previous chapters by focusing on three aspects of democratic governance in the region. We begin with the aspect of democratic consolidation. Second, we will provide a short comparative assessment of selected aspects of the political performance and governance of democratic and non-democratic regimes in the region. Finally, we will compare factors that are conducive or obstructive to democratic change and democratic stability.

Toward democratic consolidation – assessing progress and regress in democratization

The question of democratic endurance, deepening and consolidation forms a major link between the chapters in the first and second sections of this volume. There is no consensus among political scientists on a single concept of democratic consolidation. However, most scholars agree that while the transition to democracy entails the replacement of non-democratic by democratic institutions, the consolidation of democracy involves the legitimization of these institutions and the widespread internalization of the new democratic regime's basic behavioural norms (Gunther et al., 1995; Morlino, 1998; Merkel, 1998; Diamond, 1999).

A new democracy, however, cannot be consolidated without fulfilling the criteria for a liberal democracy, including an established and working rule of law; constitutionalism and, in particular, a clear separation of powers that functions in reality and allows for horizontal accountability; a vibrant and independent civil society; pluralism of political associations and institutions; freedom of media; and popularly elected political authorities who do not have to share the effective power to govern with non-elected or otherwise constitutionally legitimated 'veto powers'. Finally, a new democracy can be described as consolidated only when it enjoys 'broad and deep legitimation' such that a strong majority of the citizens and the relevant political actors support the democratic regime as the only game in town (Linz and Stepan, 1996, p.15; Diamond, 1999, p.65; Merkel, 1998, pp.59–62).

The contributions in this volume provide strong evidence, though, that none of the Southeast Asian democracies fulfill all of these criteria. With regard to what Juan Linz and Alfred Stepan describe as constitutional consolidation, only in Indonesia do 'all the actors in the polity become habituated to the fact that political conflict will be resolved according to the established norms and that violations of these norms are likely to be both ineffective and costly' (Linz and Stepan, 1996, p.5). Here, constitutional amendments passed between 1999 and 2002 have established the basic constituents of democracy, with a clear separation of powers between the executive, legislative and judicial branches and mechanisms of horizontal accountability, which in daily practice function relatively well. By contrast, semi-presidential democracy in East Timor has been facing intra-executive conflicts between president and prime minister, and subordination of the unicameral parliament to the political hegemony of the ruling Fretilin party. Presidentialism in the Philippines also experienced destabilizing crises in 2000–01 and again in 2005 (Kasuya, 2005). During the first crisis, a broad coalition of traditional politicians, disloyal military officers, social movements and religious leaders succeeded in deposing President Estrada by turning the president's misdemeanours into scandals, rekindling public outrage and mobilizing mass protests. President Gloria Arroyo, however, survived a similar challenge in 2005 because she was able to prevent the emergence of an inclusive protest coalition of political parties and social organizations or networks able to mobilize the mass public against her.

While the Philippines offers an interesting example of what Aníbal Pérez-Liñán (2009) describes as an emerging new pattern of political instability in presidential democracies, characterized by government instability without regime breakdown, Thailand is an extreme case of constitutional breakdown. Traditionally characterized by dispersion of political power, Thailand's parliamentary democracy was effectively transformed by the Thaksin government into an 'elective dictatorship' (see Croissant, Chapter 6 in this volume). This eventually led to the collapse of democracy in September 2006. Since then, and despite the free (but not fair) general elections in December 2007, Thailand has seen a tragic deepening of political polarization and instability.

Another shortcoming of democratic consolidation in Southeast Asia is the weakness of political parties and party systems. Political parties are particularly critical for the consolidation of new democracies because, on the one hand, the representation of the people cannot take place meaningfully unless parties organize that representation (Blondel et al., 1999, p.15). This requires a system of well-institutionalized political parties rooted in society. On the other hand, stable configurations of party systems that are well-institutionalized and both moderately polarized and fragmented can promote the effectiveness and efficiency of democratic institutions and thereby contribute to the functioning and legitimacy of the democratic system at large (Bosco and Morlino, 2006; Gunther and Diamond, 2003). However, the transience of political parties in countries such as Thailand and the Philippines makes it difficult for them to develop close links with voters. Furthermore, given that many parties arise and disappear like soap bubbles, it is difficult to imagine how parties can cooperate and accommodate competing demands from different electorates, because this requires some political certainty. Party inchoateness also creates an intermediary vacuum that can then be filled by populists such as Thaksin in Thailand or Joseph Estrada in the Philippines.

Third, and connected with problems of constitutional consolidation, at least three out of the four emerging democracies in the region are deficient in terms of 'behavioral consolidation' (Linz and Stepan, 1996, p.5). This refers to the political behaviour of powerful 'informal' political actors who are not legitimized by popular elections or constitutional mandate to exercise political authority, such as the military, key economic elites or powerful political movements (Merkel, 1998, p.57). Indonesia's democratic system has to deal with two potential antidemocratic veto actors: the military and radical Islamic forces. However, Croissant, Chambers and Völkel argue that the role of the military in politics has been constrained in recent years, whereas according to Ufen and to Thompson (this volume), political Islamic forces in Indonesia are much less radical and antidemocratic than in other Muslim countries in the region and are, in fact, a source for civil society groups. By contrast, in Thailand the question is not whether there are significant political groups that are seriously attempting to overthrow the democratic regime but rather whether there is any significant segment of the political elite that is actually able and willing to defend democracy against royalist elite entrepreneurs and 'Thaksinistas'.

East Timor and the Philippines have also experienced difficulties in managing antidemocratic actors. For instance, in the Philippines political elites and dynasties dominate the government because they wield considerable political and economic clout; control by the elites continues to be a barrier to reform (McCoy, 2009). Another problem is the insurgent groups that threaten the country's security. Military involvement in core areas of civilian government and the government's inaction in response to it also contravene democratic consolidation (Croissant, Chambers and Völkel, Chapter 11 in this volume). Finally, in East Timor the lack of both cooperation between elites and shared commitments to democracy contributes to the precariousness of democracy there. Lacking what Burton et al., (1992) call structural integration and value consensus, the political elites continue to harbour deep suspicions, 'encouraging their use of manipulations, subterfuge, and violence by proxy in their dealings with one another' (Guterres, 2006, p.*v*). While stopping short of outright warring, it is uncertain whether tensions among elites might be contained by the democratic institutions and procedures that have been put in place (ibid.).

The contributions in this volume also testify to the shortcomings of democratic consolidation in regard to the emergence of a democratized mass political culture and a vibrant 'civil society' in all of the four democracies. Shin and Cho's analysis (Chapter 2 in this volume) demonstrates the fragility and vagueness of the political cultures that underlie democracy in Southeast Asia. In addition, Park's analysis (Chapter 3) suggests that social associations do not perform as schools of democracy in this region. While they undoubtedly provide alternative means of political participation, and, through their actions, function as catalysts for the realization of public demands and interests, they contribute very little to the evolution of civic norms, beliefs and attitudes.

Moreover, recent events in Thailand and the Philippines testify to the potential dangers of deep divisions within a society, which are reflected in and shaped by polarized civil society organizations. In this regard, Mark Thompson's analysis demonstrates that 'the "dark side" of civil society may not be easily set apart from the "bright side"' (Armony, 2004, p.80). Increasingly violent street politics and extra-parliamentary protests in both countries remind us of Sheri Berman's warning about spasmodic and politicized civil society activism in weakly institutionalized political systems:

> If a country's political institutions are capable of channeling and redressing grievances, then associationism will probably buttress political stability and democracy by placing its resources and beneficial effects in the service of the status quo. [...] If, on the other hand, political institutions are weak and/or the existing political regime is perceived to be ineffectual and illegitimate, then civil society activity may become an alternative to politics for dissatisfied citizens [...]. In such situations, associationism will probably undermine political stability and have negative consequences for democracy by deepening cleavages, furthering dissatisfaction, and providing rich soil for oppositional movements to grow in. (Berman, 2001, p.40)

Social mobilization in the Philippines and in Thailand outpaced the development of political institutions able to process citizens' participation and demands. This resulted in disorder and political instability and 'pulled' the military into politics. Moreover, whether social associationism promotes or damages democratic culture or nurtures the deepening of nascent democracy also depends on the type of association and its aims (Barnes, 2005, p.9).

Altogether, the emerging picture is one of democracy in crisis in large parts of Southeast Asia, with slow progress in democratic deepening in Indonesia and serious setbacks in the Philippines, Thailand, and East Timor.

Toward better governance – comparing democracies and non-democracies

The contributions in this volume are also connected by their comparative analysis of political performance and the quality of governance in Southeast Asia. The four contributions in Part III all found that it is difficult to draw causal inferences about the impact of regime type on political performance. For example, the intraregional perspective reveals that regime type is not necessarily a good predictor for differences in the countries' human rights records. On the one hand, democracies are more inclined than autocracies to accept the global human rights system and to make commitments to human rights (Rich, Chapter 10 in this volume). On the other hand, Southeast Asian nations – even the most democratic regimes in the region – tend to do poorly on civil liberties and political rights relative to countries in other regions and at similar levels of human and economic development (Peerenboom, 2006). Although most countries in the region perform better under the categories of economic and social rights, relative both to civil and political rights and to other countries in their income group, there is little evidence to support the assumption that this is related to regime type. Rather, wealth appears to explain most of the variation in these categories (ibid., pp.29–31).

Likewise, other chapters suggest that in Southeast Asia, 'democracies are not necessarily more peaceful than non-democracies' (Rüland and Nguitragool, Chapter 13). With regard to the aspect of external peacefulness, Rüland and Nguitragool argue that 'insensitivity to regime type is a characteristic of the three democracies' security policy, and foreign policy doctrines'. In addition, Trinn's analysis demonstrates that higher levels of democratization in Southeast Asia do not translate into effectual conflict management. Regarding violent internal and, in particular, cultural conflicts in the region since 1945, Trinn further posits that 'democracies are for the most part *more* affected by political conflict than autocratic regimes' (Trinn, Chapter 12 in this volume; our emphasis), whereas anocracies or 'semi-democratic' regimes that are considered in the broader research literature as the most exposed to a greater risk of experiencing violent conflict are actually the least affected. His comparative analysis suggests that wealth and social demographics, again, explain the variation in conflict 'affectedness' better than levels of democratization.

These findings on specific aspects of political performance correlate to a large extent with the results of quantitative comparative research on governance in Southeast Asia. As mentioned in the introduction to this volume, the

World Bank's Governance Indicators Project (WGI) distinguishes six main dimensions of governance: (1) voice and accountability, (2) political stability and absence of violence/terrorism, (3) government effectiveness, (4) regulatory quality, (5) rule of law, and (6) control of corruption (World Bank 2008; see Chapter 1). As Hagopian (2005, pp.328–30) points out, the first two dimensions – voice and accountability along with political stability – capture the strength of democracy, the second two – government effectiveness and regulatory quality – its effectiveness, and the last two – rule of law and control of corruption – constitutionalism.

Table 14.1 shows the 2008 scores for the six dimensions of democratic governance for each Southeast Asian nation. It reveals that neither democratic nor non-democratic political regimes in the region received consistently positive or consistently negative average ratings. Not surprisingly, the 'electoral democracies' scored better in the dimension of voice and accountability than non-democratic regimes. However, the same is not necessarily true with regard to political stability. In fact, the authoritarian regimes in the region (except for Myanmar) seem to provide better stability than the 'young' democracies. With regard to the remaining indicators – government effectiveness, regulatory quality, rule of law, and control of corruption – there is no clear divide between democratic and autocratic political systems. Moreover, the democratic systems do not lead the region in any of the domains in terms of governance performance; rather, Singapore is the leader in five out of the six domains of governance.

Table 14.1 2008 WGI scores (from –2.5 to +2.5)

Country	Democracy		Effectiveness		Constitutionalism	
	Voice & accountability	Political stability	Government effectiveness	Regulatory quality	Rule of law	Control of corruption
Brunei	−1.00	+1.22	+0.89	+0.83	+0.51	+0.51
Cambodia	−0.94	−0.27	−0.81	−0.47	−1.08	−1.14
Indonesia	−0.14	−1.00	−0.29	−0.27	−0.66	−0.64
Laos	−1.71	−0.01	−0.84	−1.25	−0.90	−1.23
Malaysia	−0.58	+0.13	+1.13	+0.27	+0.49	+0.14
Myanmar	−2.24	−1.56	−1.68	−2.24	−1.48	−1.69
Philippines	−0.20	−1.41	0.00	−0.05	−0.49	−0.75
Singapore	−0.41	+1.33	+2.53	+1.92	+1.73	+2.34
Thailand	−0.56	−1.19	+0.11	+0.26	−0.03	−0.38
East Timor	+0.15	−1.13	−1.00	−1.40	−1.15	−0.89
Vietnam	−1.62	+0.32	−0.31	−0.53	−0.43	−0.76

The World Bank Governance Indicators' values for each country are weighted averages of the data available from a variety of sources for that country. With a mean of 0 and a standard deviation of 1, they could range from a low of −2.5 to a high of +2.5. Negative scores indicate sub-standard or relatively poor performance, while positive scores indicate relatively good performance.

Source: World Bank Governance Indicators, available at http://info.worldbank.org/governance/wgi/index.asp

Based on the findings of the World Bank Governance Indicators and other governance measurements such as the Bertelsmann Transformation Index (BTI) 2010, the political systems in the region can be divided into three broad governance categories that do not necessarily correspond to regime type; these are displayed in Table 14.2.

The first group consists of Singapore, Brunei and Malaysia. Viewed comparatively, they perform relatively well on most indicators of governance. Both the World Bank Governance Indicators and the management index of the BTI 2010 rank Singapore at the top of the countries in the region in terms of regulatory quality, government effectiveness, (formal) rule of law and corruption control, followed by the other two countries. They are also the top three Southeast Asian nations in Transparency International's Corruption Perception Index and perform very well on the most common measurements of state strength and state capacity such as BTI's 'State Weakness Index' (Bertelsmann Stiftung, 2009) and the 'Failed States Index' of the Fund for Peace (2007).

The second category combines the three 'emerging' democracies of Thailand, Indonesia and the Philippines, and the one-party regime of Vietnam. All four countries exhibit significant shortcomings in terms of rule of law, regulatory quality and corruption control. There is more close collusion between non-state and state elites, state capacity is much weaker, and governance quality is lower than in the countries in the first group. Furthermore, states in all four countries are less able to provide public goods such as welfare, health, predictable economic institutions and legal certainty.

The third category comprises Cambodia, Laos, Myanmar and East Timor. These countries perform weakly on most or all of the governance indicators. In Myanmar and East Timor, low governance quality correlates with extremely weak state capabilities and bureaucratic quality. Accordingly, the capability of governments and bureaucracies to effectually implement policy is extremely weak.

Table 14.2   Type of political regime and governance categories in South East Asia

		Levels of good governance (Dimension II and III)		
		High	Intermediate	Low
Regime Type (Dimension I)	Emerging democracies		Indonesia Thailand Philippines	East Timor
	Anocracies	Singapore Malaysia Brunei		Cambodia
	Autocracies		Vietnam	Laos Myanmar

A large number of Southeast Asian nations have failed to substantially improve their performance over the course of the past decade (see Table 14.3). Furthermore, there is not a single nation in the region in which there has been a positive change in all six domains of governance. On the positive side, there is Indonesia, which at least has improved its rating in four out of six dimensions; it has stabilized regulatory quality but has also experienced a decline in corruption control over the last ten years. Singapore's development has been mixed but generally positive. Of the remaining nations, in Brunei, Vietnam, Malaysia, Laos and Cambodia the quality of democratic governance has remained more or less stagnant (although Cambodia has significantly increased its level of political stability, arguably at the cost of the democratic quality of its political system). On the other hand, more performance dimensions changed significantly for the worse than for the better in Myanmar, the Philippines and Thailand.

If we compare the scores indicating changes in each dimension of governance in the countries of Southeast Asia, it becomes evident that in three of the six performance dimensions – voice and accountability, regulatory quality and corruption control – more countries experienced negative changes than positive ones. Only in the dimension of governmental effectiveness did significantly more countries experience positive changes than negative ones. In the domains of political stability and rule of law, there are (nearly) as many countries that experienced positive changes as there are cases of negative ones. The most dramatic declines occurred in voice and accountability and in controlling corruption, in which eight and nine of the ten countries, respectively, registered negative changes. It is in these findings that the crisis of democratic governance in Southeast Asia becomes most apparent. Stalled progress in governance and the decoupling of governance

Table 14.3   Changes in WGI scores over the period 1998–2008

Country	Voice & accountability	Political stability	Government effectiveness	Regulatory quality	Rule of law	Control of corruption
Brunei	−0.25	+0.02	−0.04	−0.05	−0.08	−0.08
Cambodia	+0.06	+0.88	+0.03	−0.26	0.00	−0.03
Indonesia	+0.90	+0.39	+0.56	0.00	+0.06	−0.52
Laos	−0.68	+0.31	−0.19	−0.22	+0.09	−0.54
Malaysia	−0.37	0.00	+0.60	−0.29	+0.02	−0.47
Myanmar	−0.29	−0.27	−0.49	−0.70	−0.14	−0.32
Philippines	−0.59	−1.24	+0.26	−0.25	−0.40	−0.38
Singapore	−0.68	+0.22	+0.40	−0.09	+0.26	+0.15
Thailand	−0.96	−1.59	+0.01	+0.10	−0.51	−0.40
East Timor	N/A	N/A	N/A	N/A	N/A	N/A
Vietnam	−0.26	−0.02	+0.29	+0.08	+0.03	−0.08

Source: World Bank Governance Indicators, available at http://info.worldbank.org/governance/wgi/index.asp

quality and democratization have become the major characteristics of political development over the last decade.

Prospects

Finally, the chapters in this volume are also connected by their interest in the implications of their observations for the future course of democratic development and governance in the region. Regarding the *global* future of democracy, it was some 25 years ago that Samuel Huntington wrote an article entitled 'Will More Countries Become Democratic?' Overall – outside Latin America – he concluded that the prospects for the (further) extension of democracy were 'not great' (Huntington, 1984, p.218). This conclusion, however, was qualified by his noting that it assumed no major changes in world developments (ibid.). Following the collapse of the Soviet Union eight years later, Francis Fukuyama argued that the liberal values of capitalism and democracy had finally won over the forces of communism, thereby leaving no alternative to democratic liberalism (Fukuyama 1992). Yet another two decades later, Fukuyama's democracy optimism has been replaced by a new pessimism in democratization studies (Merkel, 2010, p.17).

The pessimistic assessment of a global 'democratic rollback' (Diamond, 2008) is based on three main observations. First, over the past ten years or so, regime changes from dictatorship to democracy and endogenous democratizations, in particular, have become increasingly rare: apart from Indonesia's *reformasi* process, most major democratization processes since the late 1990s (for example, in Afghanistan, Iraq and Haiti) were military-enforced regime changes of uncertain outcome (Grimm and Merkel, 2009; Croissant and Thiery, 2010). Second, inasmuch as the latest wave of democratization has seen the collapse of non-democratic regimes around the globe, those that are left are probably the least viable for democracy, either because they lack the socioeconomic and institutional requisites for stable democracy or because they have proven to be highly resilient to the internal and external challenges of democratization (Siaroff, 2009, p.296; Merkel, 2010, p.28). Finally, the gap in democratic quality in new democracies is increasingly deepening. On the one hand, a group of about two dozen newly democratized polities have made significant progress toward consolidating as liberal democracies. On the other hand, several nations have made less progress, sometimes far less, as their transition toward liberal democracy appears to have stalled (Croissant and Thiery, 2010) or even failed when fragile democracy regressed into authoritarianism. The latter observation has also rekindled warnings against a 'democratic rollback' (Diamond, 2008).

Although the validity of these assessments is contested, the continuous shifts between sceptical and optimistic assessments of the global future of democratic governance suggest at the least that political science cannot predict the future of democracy any more precisely than it can other political events (see Siaroff, 2009, p.295). This is especially true for Southeast Asia, as the frequently noted heterogeneity of the region also means that, for all the symptoms of a crisis of democratic governance in the region, differences persist. The contributions in this volume testify to those differences.

Nevertheless, to provide a very general assessment of the prospects of democracy and democratic governance in the region, we can consider certain factors which are conducive or, in turn, obstructive to viable democratization and democratic survival. Against the backdrop of different theories of democratization, Alan Siaroff (2009) and Wolfgang Merkel (2010) have recently developed lists of selected indicators or factors that allow for tentative conclusions on the prospects for either viable democratization (Siaroff) or democratic breakdowns (Merkel). Both authors make prospective assessments by looking through a lens of modernization theory, structuralism and culturalist theory, therefore focusing their argument on macro- and domestic–structural variables rather than on agential factors.[1] Siaroff's list of 15 'threatening factors' seems to be the most appropriate one for our purposes. Table 14.4 includes 13 of these 15 factors. The remaining two – the type of economic system and geographic location – will be ignored here.[2] All indicators are dichotomous (yes = 1; no = 0), with yes indicating the presence of a factor which is (potentially) obstructive for viable democracy.

A first glance at Table 14.4 provides interesting, albeit limited, insights into the structural requisites for viable democratization in Southeast Asia. First of all, it suggests that all of the emerging democracies in the region display very few of the traits that scholars have identified as propitious for stable democracy.

A first issue results from the fact that they are all young and non-liberal ('electoral', 'defective') democracies. All other things being equal, new and less liberal democracies face a higher risk of authoritarian reversal than long-established liberal democratic polities, because in the latter, the established practices of tamed and consensually unified elite behaviour, strong and working institutions of checks and balances, effective mechanisms of representation and interest mediation, and strong mass support render them largely immune against endogenous threats of authoritarian reversal (Siaroff, 2009; Merkel, 2010).

This increased risk is clearly the case in Thailand, the Philippines and East Timor. Another set of 'threatening factors' relates to socioeconomic development and levels of modernization. Modernization theory posits that the odds that a country will sustain democracy are closely related to its level of socioeconomic development (Lipset, 1959). While the 'endogenous' variant of this theorem assumes that wealth and socioeconomic modernization *lead* to democracy, the 'exogenous' version of modernization theory argues that democracy is not a by-product of development (Boix and Stokes, 2003). However, '[o]nce a country has a democratic regime, its level of economic development has a very strong effect on the probability that democracy will survive' (Przeworski et al., 1996, pp.40–1). This is because wealth lowers the distributional conflicts within society 'through various sociological mechanisms' (Przeworski et al., 2000, p.101), which helps to stabilize democracy. Other scholars who are interested in the (socio)economic origins of democracy (and dictatorship) focus on the nature of economic institutions and the extent of income inequality (Acemoglu and Robinson, 2009), the distribution of power resources (Vanhanen, 1997), and the levels of education that help (or obstruct) the emergence of democratic values (Merkel, 2007).

However, in terms of per capita annual income adjusted for purchasing power parity in 2007, none of the four Southeast Asian democracies displays high income levels; ironically, Thailand ($8135) is the only country that exceeds Adam Przeworski's famous 'Argentina threshold' of US $6065, above which democracy seems impregnable and can be expected to survive, 'come hell or high water' (Przeworski et al., 1996, p.48).[3] At the same time, however, income distribution in Thailand (and the Philippines) is more unequal than in Indonesia and East Timor. Economic inequality in itself does not correlate in any simple way with democratic breakdown or antidemocratic populism either (Bermeo, 2009). However, the pervasive income inequality in Thailand and the Philippines, which reflects especially high urban–rural disparities, poses a sharp threat to the survival of democracy. The urban–rural and class divides provide opportunities for political entrepreneurs to mobilize support from subordinate groups by promising to redistribute resources to the poor; at the same time, democracy in Thailand and the Philippines lacks the self-defence mechanisms of established democracies that are necessary to survive the disruptive consequences of class divide.

While educational indicators are more favourable, all Southeast Asian democracies lack a strong, politically self-confident and well-organized industrial working class, which some scholars have identified as a key force in processes of democratization in Latin America, the Caribbean and Northwest and Southern Europe (Rueschemeyer et al., 1992). Furthermore, there is strong evidence that in most Southeast Asian nations, the bourgeoisie has not played the progressive role of a force for democratization that was envisaged by neo-Marxist authors (Rodan, 1996; Sidel, 2008; Thompson, Chapter 4 in this volume). Likewise, state-dependent, ethnically divided, or otherwise politically and economically vulnerable middle-class actors in Southeast Asia have been far less consistently in favour of democratization than modernization theorists (Lipset, 1959) have suggested. In general, the bourgeoisie and the middle classes have supported their own political inclusion, but at the same time have favoured political stability, economic development and secure property rights over the inclusion of subordinate groups and their demand for meaningful political participation, economic redistribution and social justice. Singapore's trajectory, as well as the ambiguity of the Thai and Philippine middle classes toward democracy,

Table 14.4 Prospects for democracy – conducive and obstructive factors

Indicators	Non-democracies							Emerging democracies			
	Brunei	Cambodia	Laos	Malaysia	Myanmar	Singapore	Vietnam	Indonesia	Philippines	Thailand	Timor Leste
Non-liberal democracy[a]	n.a.	n.a.	n.a.	n.a.	n.a.	n.a.	n.a.	1	1	1	1
Third-wave democracy[b]	n.a.	n.a.	n.a.	n.a.	n.a.	n.a.	n.a.	1	1	1	1
Weak state[c]	0	1	1	0	1	0	1	1	1	1	1
Lack of mass support for democracy[d]	n.d.	n.d.	n.d.	1	n.d.	1	1	1	1	1	n.d.
Lower than high income group[e]	0	1	1	1	1	0	1	1	1	1	1
Adult literacy rate below 70%[f]	0	0	0	0	0	0	0	0	0	0	1
Average yrs of schooling less than 7.0[g]	0	1	1	0	1	0	1	1	0	0	1
High income concentration[h]	1	1	0	0	0	1	0	0	1	1	0
Pop. more than 40 million[i]	0	0	0	0	1	0	1	1	1	1	0
Ethnically fragmented[j]	0	0	1	1	1	0	0	1	0	1	1

Military participation ratio 6.00 or above per 1000[k]	1	1	1	1	0	0	0	0	1	0
Military only conditionally subordinate or tutelary[l]	0	1	1	1	0	0	1	1	1	0
Party system not well institutionalized[m]	n.a.	n.a.	0	0	n.a.	0	1	1	1	1

[a] Based on information from the BTI 2010 and Freedom House 2009 (for East Timor); [b] Classification according to Shin and Tusalem (2009); [c] Total Failed States Index 2007 of 75.0 points or higher (Fund for Peace, Failed States Index, 2007, http://www.fundforpeace.org/web/index.php?option=com_content&task=view&id=229&Itemid=366; [d] See Shin and Cho, this volume; additional information from Chu et al., (2009); [e] According to World Bank classification, http://data.worldbank.org/about/country-classifications/country-and-lending-groups; [f] World Bank, World Development Indicators, 2005–08, earliest year. Adult literacy rate is the percentage of people ages 15 and above who can, with understanding, read and write a short, simple statement on their everyday life; [g] World Bank, Barro-Lee Data Set, http://databank.worldbank.org/ddp/home.do?Step=1&id=4 (2005); [h] Income share held by the wealthiest 20% of the population is 45% or more of the national income, 1998–2009, earliest available year; World Bank, World Development Indicators; [i] World Bank, World Development Indicators; [j] Ethnically fragmented defined as a value of 0.400 or higher in Fearon's data set (Fearon, 2003), plus data (East Timor; Brunei) from Croissant et al., (2009); [k] Calculated on basis of 'Armed forces personnel, total' and 'Population, total', World Development Indicators (2008); [l] Based on information from Croissant, Völkel, and Chambers, this volume; [m] Based on information from Hicken, this volume, and Croissant and Völkel (forthcoming).

illustrates this point (Rodan, 1996; Jones, 1998; Embong, 2001; Englehart, 2003; Thompson, 2007).

If we turn our attention to the nations in the region that are not yet democratized, it seems that the socioeconomic and structural conditioning factors for democratization to take place are also not very promising. Relative to other non-democracies in the region and compared with the already emerging democracies in Southeast Asia, the three nations of Singapore, Malaysia and Brunei are well-educated, high-income societies. Nevertheless, they also lack strong working classes or active middle classes that pressure for democratization. While there is little empirical (or for that matter, theoretical) reason to expect these countries to become democratic in the near future, one might hypothesize from the perspective of modernization theory that, once they have democratized, Singapore, Brunei and Malaysia might eventually become stable democracies (for Singapore, see Acemoglu and Robinson, 2009, p.353). This, however, does not apply to countries such as Cambodia, Vietnam, Laos and Myanmar. They are unlikely candidates for democratization, and are also top candidates for democratic fragility in the unlikely scenario of a major change in political institutions.

Then there are the threatening factors already discussed above such as the lack of broad and deep legitimation, the relatively low levels of institutionalization of party systems in the new democracies, and the fragile nature of civil–military relations.

In addition, problems of the state's insufficient institutional capacity in conjunction with the contested government monopoly on the use of force also pose threats to the sustainability of democracy in the region. While non-democratic regimes may be able to survive with low levels of state strength, a functioning and stable democracy is possible only in the presence of a set of effective and capable state institutions. Hence, a certain minimum of state effectiveness is a precondition for stable democracy (Linz and Stepan, 1996). However, processes of democratization in Southeast Asia have often undermined or weakened already fragile institutions of the patrimonial state (Hutchcroft, 1998; Marsh, 2006; Croissant, 2010). Compared to the four emerging democracies, some authoritarian regimes enjoy a significantly stronger state, such as in Brunei, Malaysia, Singapore and, albeit to a lower extent, in Vietnam. Again, theory suggests that the first three polities would enjoy considerably more favourable requisites for sustainable democracy (once democratized) than the rest of the region. Likewise, dictatorships in Myanmar, Laos and Cambodia exhibit a lack of institutional capacity and administrative capability that makes it highly unlikely that democracy could provide stability or sufficient governance quality.

Other analyses of the preconditions for democracy have posited a negative relationship between democracy and the level of linguistic, religious or general 'ethnic' fractionalization. Higher fractionalization increases the probability for politicized 'ethnic divisions', which in turn hinders democratic conflict management, consensus building and the process of compromise (Dahl, 1971, p.105). Hence, some scholars suggest that in the twentieth century, 'democracy has been significantly more successful in monoethnic societies than in ethnically divided and multiethnic societies' (Karatnicky, 2002, p.107). In this context, studies show that ethnicity and religion are a major cause of political conflict in Southeast Asia (see, for example, Trinn, Chapter 12 in this volume). At the same time, however, many observers agree that ethnic nationalism and communal violence in Southeast Asia are the outcome of both the political strategies of a country's elite and their constitutional engineering, rather than being a direct result of ethnic diversity itself.[4] Nevertheless, the frequently noted social and cultural heterogeneity of Southeast Asian nations provides at least non-conducive requisites for sustainable democracy that demand more capable conflict management, accommodative political strategies, and political institutions that can provide procedures and rules for the de-escalation of such conflicts.

Hence, we conclude that, despite successes in Indonesian democratization so far and variations between individual cases, all four Southeast Asian democracies have to cope with unfavourable structural conditions and largely missing requisites for sustainable democracy, and are therefore at medium to high risk of democratic failure. Of course, such an assessment has its limits, as it largely ignores agential factors that – as several chapters in this volume demonstrate – are also crucial for democratic survival, the deepening of democracy and improvements in democratic governance. Nevertheless, we need to acknowledge that with regard to the mid-to-long-term prospects for democratic endurance and democratic consolidation, much less the prospects for further democratization processes and better democratic governance, there seems to be little grounds for optimism. If one accepts the argument that economic prosperity, distribution of wealth and power resources, the institutional capacity and strength of states, ethnic fractionalization, the robustness of civil–military relations and the character of the party system all affect the prospects of liberal democratic development, then it may be naïve to expect too much progress in democratization and democratic governance in this part of the world. Rather, Southeast Asian nations probably have a long way to go before they will leave behind the current crisis of democratic governance.

Notes

1. This is not because agential factors are irrelevant. Human agency, to borrow from David Dressler's apt description of the 'agency–structure problem', is always the moving force behind events and the outcomes of political processes, but the choices and strategies of actors 'can be realized only in concrete historical circumstances that condition the possibilities for action and influence its course' (Dressler, 1989, p.443).

2. Siaroff argues that regional location influences the prospects for viable democracy, with Asia or the Middle East providing the most 'threatening' regional environments for democracy. We agree with both arguments, but obviously, the criterion has not much heuristic value for intraregional comparison. More or less the same is true of Siaroff's remaining criterion of the type of economic system. While Siaroff posits that, given the spillover from economic freedom to political freedom, a statist or even a mixed economy is less likely to be, or to remain, a democracy, in almost all of the Southeast Asian countries state intervention plays a highly significant role in economic development.
3. Przeworski et al. find that no democracy failed above a per capita GDP of $6055, Argentina's level in 1975. In 2007, GDP per capita (PPP US$) was 707 in East Timor, 3406 in the Philippines, 3712 in Indonesia and 8135 in Thailand. Interestingly, the 2006 coup in Thailand would seem to falsify Przeworski's observation. However, the income data used by Przeworski (Penn World Table) are not fully comparable to our data.
4. More recent research findings support this argument; see Fish and Brooks (2004), and Cederman et al.(2009).

References

Acemoglu, D. and Robinson, J.A. (2009) *Economic Origins of Dictatorship and Democracy* (Cambridge: Cambridge University Press).

Armony, A.C. (2004) *The Dubious Link: Civic Engagement and Democratization* (Stanford: Stanford University Press).

Barnes, C. (2005) 'Weaving the Web: Civil Society Roles in Working with Conflict and Building Peace', in Tongeren, P. (ed.), *People Building Peace II, Successful Stories of Civil Society* (London: Lynne Rienner).

Berman, S. (2001) 'Civil Society and Political Institutionalization', in Edwards, B., Foley, M. and Diani, M. (eds), *Beyond Tocqueville. Civil Society and the Social Capital Debate in Comparative Perspective* (Hanover: University Press of New England).

Bermeo, N. (2009) 'Does Electoral Democracy Boost Economic Equality?', *Journal of Democracy*, 20 (4): 21–35.

Bertelsmann Stiftung (2009) *Bertelsmann Transformation Index 2010* (Gütersloh: Verlag Bertelsmann Stiftung).

Blondel, J., Inoguchi, T. and Marsh, I. (1999) 'Economic Development v. Political Democracy', in J. Blondel, Inoguchi, T. and Marsh, I. (eds), *Democracy, Governance, and Economic Performance: East and Southeast Asia* (New York: United Nations University Press).

Boix, C. and Stokes, S.C. (2003) 'Endogenous Democratization', *World Politics*, 55 (4): 517–549.

Bosco, A., and Morlino, L. (2006) *Party Change in Southern Europe* (London: Routledge).

Burton, M., Gunther, R. and Higley, John (1992) 'Introduction: Elite Transformations and Democratic Regimes', in Higley, J. and Gunther, R. (eds), *Elites and Democratic Consolidation in Latin America and Southern Europe* (Cambridge: Cambridge University Press).

Cederman, L.E., Min, B. and Wimmer, A. (2009) 'Ethnic Politics and Armed Conflict. A Configurational Analysis of a New Global Dataset', *American Sociological Review*, 74 (2): 316–337.

Chu, Y., Diamond, L., Nathan, A.J. and Shin, D.C. (eds) (2009) *How East Asians View Democracy* (New York: Columbia University Press).

Croissant, A. (2010) 'Staatlichkeit und Demokratie in Südostasien', in Paul, A.T., Pelfini, A. and Rehbein, B. (eds), *Globalisierung Süd: Leviathan Sonderhefte* (Wiesbaden: VS Verlag).

Croissant, A., Wagschal, U., Schwank, N. and Trinn, C. (2009) *Kulturelle Konflikte. Die kulturellen Dimensionen des globalen Konfliktgeschehens seit 1945* (Baden-Baden: Nomos).

Croissant, A. and Völkel, P. (forthcoming) 'Party System Types and Party System Institutionalization. Comparing New Democracies in East and Southeast Asia', *Party Politics*.

Croissant, A. and Thiery, P. (2010) 'Eroding Democracy, or the Intransigence of Defective Democracy? Analyzing Democratic Transformations', in Bertelsmann Stiftung (ed.), *Bertelsmann Transformation Index 2010. Political Management in International Comparison* (Gütersloh: Verlag Bertelsmann Stiftung).

Dahl, R.A. (1971) *Polyarchy: Participation and Opposition* (New Haven: Yale University Press).

Diamond, L. (1999) *Developing Democracy Toward Consolidation* (Baltimore: The Johns Hopkins University Press).

Diamond, L. (2008) 'The Democratic Rollback. The Resurgence of the Predatory State', *Foreign Affairs*, 87 (2): 36–48.

Dressler, D. (1989) 'What's at Stake in the Agent-Structure Debate?', *International Organization*, 43 (3): 441–473.

Embong, A. R. (ed.) (2001) *Southeast Asian Middle Classes. Prospects for Social Change and Democratization* (Selangor: Benerbit).

Englehart, N.A. (2003) 'Democracy and the Thai Middle Class. Globalization, Modernization and Constitutional Change', *Asian Survey*, 43 (2): 253–279.

Fearon, J.D. (2003), 'Ethnic and Cultural Diversity by Country', *Journal of Economic Growth*, 8 (2): 195–222.

Fish, M.S. and Brooks, R.S. (2004) 'Does Diversity Hurts Democracy?', *Journal of Democracy*, 15 (1): 154–167.

Freedom House (2010) *Freedom in the World 2010*, <http://www.freedomhouse.org/template.cfm?page=505>, accessed 2 June 2010

Fukuyama, F. (1992) *The End of History and the Last Man* (New York: Harper Perennial).

Grimm, S. and Merkel, W. (2009) 'War and Democratization: Legality, Legitimacy and Effectiveness', in Merkel, W. and Grimm, S. (eds), *War and Democratization. Legality, Legitimacy and Effectiveness* (London/New York: Routledge).

Gunther, R. and Diamond, L. (2003) 'Types and Functions of Parties', in Gunther, R. and Diamond, L. (eds), *Political Parties and Democracy* (Baltimore: Johns Hopkins University Press).

Gunther, R., Diamandouros, N. and Puhle, H.J. (1995) 'Introduction', in Gunther, R., Diamandouros, N. and Puhle, H.J. (eds), *The Politics of Democratic Consolidation. Southern Europe in Comparative Perspective* (Baltimore/London: The John Hopkins University Press).

Guterres, F. (2006) *Elites and Prospects of Democracy in East Timor*, unpublished PhD thesis.

Hagopian, F. (2005) 'Conclusions: Government Performance, Political Representation, and Public Perceptions of Contemporary Democracy in Latin America', in Hagopian, F. and Mainwaring, S. (eds), *The Third Wave of Democratization in Latin America* (New York: Cambridge University Press).

Huntington, S. (1984) 'Will More Countries Become Democratic?', *Political Science Quarterly*, 99 (2): 193–218.

Hutchcroft, P. (1998) *Booty Capitalism: The Politics of Banking in the Philippines* (Ithaca: Cornell University Press).

Jones, D. M. (1998) 'Democratization, Civil Society, and the Illiberal Middle Class Culture in Pacific Asia', *Comparative Politics*, 30 (2): 147–169.

Karatnycky, A. (2002) 'Muslim Countries and the Democracy Gap', *Journal of Democracy*, 13 (2): 99–112.

Kasuya, Y. (2005) 'Patronage of the Past and Future: Legislators' Decisions to Impeach President Estrada of the Philippines', *The Pacific Review*, 18 (4): 521–540.

Linz, J.J., and Stepan, A.C. (1996) *Problems of Democratic Transition and Consolidation: Southern Europe, South America, and Post-Communist Europe* (Baltimore: Johns Hopkins University Press).

Lipset. S. M. (1959) 'Some Social Requisites of Democracy: Economic Development and Political Legitimacy', *American Political Science Review*, 53 (March): 69–105.

Marsh, I. (2006) 'Democratization and State Capacity in East and Southeast Asia', *Taiwan Journal of Democracy*, 2 (2): 69–92.

McCoy, A. W. (2009) *An Anarchy of Families. State and Families in the Philippines*, reprint edition with a new preface (Madison: The University of Wisconsin Press).

Merkel, W. (1998) 'The Consolidation of Past-Autocratic Democracies: A Multi-Level Model', *Democratization*, 5 (3): 33–67.

Merkel, W. (2007) 'Gegen alle Theorie? Die Konsolidierung der Demokratie in Ostmitteleuropa', *Politische Vierteljahresschrift*, 48 (3): 413–433.

Merkel, W. (2010) 'Are Dictatorships Returning? Revisiting the "democratic rollback" hypothesis', *Contemporary Politics*, 16 (1): 17–31.

Morlino, L. (1998) *Democracy between Consolidation and Crisis* (Oxford: Oxford University Press).

Peerenboom, R. (2006) 'An Empirical Overview of Rights Performance in Asia, France, and the USA: The Dominance of Wealth in the Interplay of Economics, Culture, Law, and Governance', in Peerenboom, R., Petersen, C.J. and Chen, A.H.Y. (eds), *Human Rights in Asia. A Comparative Legal Study of Twelve Asian Jurisdictions, France and the USA* (New York: Routledge).

Pérez-Liñán, A. (2009) *Presidential Impeachment and the New Political Instability in Latin America* (Cambridge: Cambridge University Press).

Przeworski, A., Alverez, M., Cheibub, J.A. and Limongi, F. (1996) 'What Makes Democracy Endure?', *Journal of Democracy*, 7 (1): 39–55.

Przeworski, A., Alverez, M., Cheibub, J.A. and Limongi, F. (2000) *Democracy and Development: Political Institutions and Well-Being in the World, 1950–1990* (Cambridge: Cambridge University Press).

Rodan, G. (ed.) (1996) *Political Oppositions in Industrializing Asia* (London, New York: Routledge).

Rueschemeyer, D., Huber-Stephens, E. and Stephens, J.D. (1992) *Capitalist Development and Democracy* (Chicago: University of Chicago Press).

Shin, D.C. and Tusalem, R. F. (2009) 'East Asia', in Haerpfer, C.W., Bernhagen, P., Inglehart, R.F. and Welzel, C. (eds), *Democratization* (Oxford: Oxford University Press).

Siaroff, A. (2009) *Comparing Political Regimes* (Toronto: Toronto University Press).

Sidel, J. (2008) 'Social Origins of Dictatorship and Democracy Revisited: Colonial State and Chinese Immigrant in the Making of Modern Southeast Asia', *Comparative Politics*, 40 (2): 127–147.

The Fund for Peace, Failed States Index Scores (2007) <http://www.fundforpeace.org/web '/index.php?option=com_content&task=view&id=229&Itemid=366>, accessed 3 March 2010.

Thompson, M.R. (1995) *The Anti-Marcos Struggle. Personalistic Rule and Democratic Transition in the Philippines* (New Haven: Yale University Press).

Thompson, M.R. (2007) 'The Dialectic of Good Governance and Democracy in Southeast Asia: Globalized Discourse and Local Response', *Globality Studies*, 10 (September): 1–21.

United Nations Statistics Department (2002–2008) <http://unstats.un.org/unsd/demographic /products/socind/education.htm#tech>.

Vanhanen, T. (1997) *Prospects of Democracy: A Study of 172 Countries* (New York: Routledge).

World Bank Governance Indicators (2008) *World Bank World Development Indicators (2005–2008)* <http://www.govindicators.org>.

Index